SILKS, SPICES
AND EMPIRE

Other books in

THE GREAT EXPLORERS SERIES

published by Tandem Books

conceived by
Vilhjalmur Stefansson

general editor
Evelyn Stefansson Nef

BEYOND THE PILLARS OF HERCULES
Rhys Carpenter

SOUTH FROM THE SPANISH MAIN
Earl Parker Hanson

WEST AND BY NORTH
Louis B. Wright and Elaine W. Fowler

THE MOVING FRONTIER
Louis B. Wright and Elaine W. Fowler

Silks, Spices and Empire

Asia seen through the eyes of its discoverers

OWEN and ELEANOR LATTIMORE

14 Gloucester Road, London SW7 4RD

Originally published in the United States by Delacorte Press, 1968

First published in Great Britain by
Universal-Tandem Publishing Co. Ltd, 1973

Copyright © 1968 by Owen and Eleanor Lattimore

All rights reserved

Maps by Andrew Mudryk

Printed in Great Britain by litho
by The Anchor Press Ltd and bound by
Wm. Brendon & Son Ltd, both of Tiptree, Essex

Grateful acknowledgement is made to the publishers listed below for permission to quote from their material:

CATHAY AND THE WAY THITHER, Volumes I and IV, edited by Sir Henry Yule: Published by The Hakluyt Society and used by permission of Cambridge University Press.

RECORDS OF THE GRAND HISTORIAN OF CHINA, translated from the *Shih Chi of Ssŭ-ma Ch'ien* by Burton Watson: Columbia University Press, New York, New York, 1961. Used by permission.

JOURNEY OF THE BUDDHIST PILGRIMS TO INDIA as published in THE TRAVELS OF FA-HSIEN or Record of the Buddhist Kingdoms, translated by H. A. Giles: Used by permission of Routledge & Kegan Paul Ltd.

THE TRAVELS OF AN ALCHEMIST, The Journey of the Taoist Ch'ang Ch'un from China to the Hindukush at the Summons of Chingiz Khan, translated and with an introduction by Arthur Waley: Used by permission of Routledge & Kegan Paul Ltd.

THE MONGOL MISSION, translated by a nun of Stanbrook Abbey, edited by Christopher Dawson: Copyright 1955 Sheed & Ward Inc. New York. Used by permission of Sheed & Ward Inc. and Sheed & Ward Ltd.

AKBAR AND THE JESUITS by Father P. Du Jarric: Used by permission of Routledge & Kegan Paul Ltd.

AN ACCOUNT OF TIBET, The Travels of Ippolito Desideri of Pistoia, S. J. edited by Filippo de Filippi: Used by permission of Routledge & Kegan Paul Ltd.

THE VOYAGE OF FRANÇOIS PYRARD, Volume I, edited by Albert Gray: Published by The Hakluyt Society and used by permission of Cambridge University Press.

HISTORY OF THE TWO TARTAR CONQUERORS OF CHINA by P. J. D'Orleans, S. J.: Published by The Hakluyt Society and used by permission of Cambridge University Press.

THE HEART OF A CONTINENT by Sir Francis E. Younghusband: Used by permission of John Murray, London.

SAND BURIED RUINS OF KHOTAN by M. Aurel Stein: (London, T. Fisher Unwin, 1903). Used by kind permission of Ernest Benn Limited.

A JOURNEY IN SOUTHERN SIBERIA by Jeremiah Curtin: Copyright 1909, 1937 by Alma M. Curtin. Reprinted by permission of Jeremiah Curtin Cardell.

BEYOND THE CASPIAN by Douglas Carruthers: Reprinted by permission of Oliver and Boyd, Edinburgh.

ON THE EAVES OF THE WORLD by Reginald Farrer: Used by permission of Edward Arnold (Publishers) Ltd.

CONTENTS

V. OCEAN DISCOVERERS AND EMPIRE BUILDERS

VI. WHEN THE WHITE MAN WAS A BURDEN

INTRODUCTION

❦ ❦

ANY RECORD of travel and discovery in eastern Asia must devote many or most of its pages to China, not only because China by sheer geographical bulk dominates much of Asia, but because the Chinese themselves, from very early times, kept records of their own discoveries and of their contacts with other peoples. Among those who devote their careers to the study of China, however, there are few who also qualify as specialists in knowledge of the regions that surround China. In this kind of diversified knowledge Owen and Eleanor Lattimore are almost unique. They have not only read the works of the great travelers, but have done some pretty impressive traveling themselves—in China, Mongolia, Chinese and Soviet Central Asia, and Siberia, beginning with their honeymoon journey from Peking through Central Asia to Kashmir and India. Ever since then they have been a working team—Owen the linguist and historian (his historical work has always emphasized the themes of geography and social and economic systems in their geographical setting) and Eleanor the organizer, editor, and assembler of research material. In this book, she selected the material, he wrote the first chapter and the introductions to other chapters.

Many fine names have been assembled and there are more to come in the Great Explorer Series, but I am most proud of having Owen Lattimore's name on the list. Vilhjalmur Stefansson, who first conceived the series, was a friend of Owen and Eleanor Lattimore when I first turned up to work in the Stefansson Polar Library in 1939. At our initial staff-lunch meeting I saw in action a happening that became familiar with the years, but never lost its charm. This was the special kind of dialogue that Owen and Stef engaged in when conditions were right. Quiet was required—it didn't matter how many other people were present if they were good listeners—and something to hold in the hand, a glass of wine or a cup of coffee. Then these two exceptional men, each expert in his chosen field and interested in everything that related to it directly or peripherally, would begin. In comparing Eskimo and Mongol ways, no detail was too small to be recited and followed by evaluation, comparison, and speculation. Both brought marvelous but different linguistic accomplishments to the discussion. Each could stir the other intellectually and bring out his best. Humor was not omitted, a satiric, tart sort in Stef's case and an earthier, more boisterous, punning kind in Owen's. Throughout 20 years we spent many evenings in this kind of exchange, for the Lattimores sometimes spent summers with us in the country. All four of us worked during the day writing or researching and looked forward to the happy hour in the evening when work ended and conversation began. A wise person once said that there are two things in the world that are no good unless they are shared—love and knowledge. During these evenings we shared what each had discovered during the day, knowing that the audience would be appreciative, critical, and discerning.

A few of the readers of this preface may be old enough to remember the McCarthy Era and its now difficult-to-believe emotional hysteria. That was a terrible time for the family and friends of those who were falsely accused of disloyalty to their country. Owen Lattimore was one such victim. His spirited defense, his refusal to be *used* as a cause afterward, and his ability to continue working at things like Mongolian studies, under the most harrowing conditions, earned the admiration of his good friends and of many persons he never met. He lost some of his so-called friends too, of course, but he gained some and those who remained had the useful quality of having been tested. The Stefansson-Lattimore friendship was close but became family-like during the terror. Owen's vindication was ours, and his success in founding the now flourishing University of Leeds Department of Chinese Studies (to which Mongolian Studies are now being added) was something we took as much pride in as he.

Owen started his career in Asia, not through the usual academic circles, but through the business world, and I cannot help thinking (since I share with him the lack of an earned academic degree) that this gave him invaluable experience and cultivated his ability to *reach* more people both during his studying and in the eventual dissemination of his vast store of knowledge. The University of Glasgow has conferred an honorary doctorate on him; the Royal Geographical Society long ago gave him their medal; he has more credentials and honors than he has need of.

The leitmotif of the Great Explorer Series—that a firsthand narrative of a discovery by the man who made it is more interesting than a later, rewritten account—is perfectly displayed in the pages that follow despite the great distances in time and geographical space that they span. A secondary theme developed as a result of my ignorance. Often I have been thrilled by the discovery of new and intellectually thrilling facts, only to find that they were well known to the scholars in the field, but *only* to them. It seemed unfair that they should have all the pleasure (like the rich in the old Cockney song), so the idea of emphasizing the sharing of scholarly goodies with the common reader was born. For example, new to me but old to the specialists was that what struck Marco Polo and so many of the travelers who followed him, was not only the luxury and Oriental magnificence they found in China, and its civil administration, which seemed superior to the European, but the *technical superiority* of the Chinese.

In *Silks, Spices and Empire* I hope the reader will share my pleasure in uncovering many "new" ideas. To insure that he misses a minimum, we have provided one of the foremost guides in the world, the distinguished Asian traveler, writer, geographer, and scholar, Dr. Owen Lattimore.

EVELYN STEFANSSON NEF

✥ I ✥

THE FIRST
EXPLORERS

NOT FAR from the headwaters of the Orkhon River lie the ruins of the great Mongolian capital of Karakorum, built by Ugedei, son of Chingis Khan. Here are also the ruins of the somewhat later Buddhist monastery of Erdeni Tso, destroyed by the Chinese after the fall of the Mongol Empire. Within sight of them, the Chinese of today, under a program of economic aid to Mongolia, have built a dam to supply electric power and also to divert water for irrigation, reviving the oasis of cultivation that once surrounded the medieval city in the vast land of herdsmen. The region is rich in history. Here the Orkhon Turks ruled in the eighth century, and everywhere can be found Neolithic burials, Bronze Age burials, and the Iron Age graves of the Hsiungnu, or early Huns.

But this land has also a much more ancient history. Not far below the water-power dam the river makes a loop around a little promontory topped by a natural, flat terrace. Here in the summer of 1961 my wife and I were talking with Ser-Ojav, an archaeologist and historian of the Mongolian Academy of Sciences, and A. P. Okladnikov, one of the greatest Soviet archaeologists, whose field experience ranges from China and Mongolia to the Arctic. The site here, said Okladnikov, was the richest palaeological find he had ever seen. No human bones had yet been found, but some of the tools could be matched with those of Peking Man, perhaps half a million years old. They could also be matched in another direction. "Here, look at these," Okladnikov said; "you could slip these onto a shelf in a museum in France, and the curator himself would not be able to swear they were not local finds."

I asked how they had come to discover the site. "It was easy," Okladnikov said. "During the last ice age in Europe, the earth was not covered with ice here in Mongolia or in eastern Siberia. There was, instead, a very heavy rainfall, and the rivers were much bigger than they are now. The palaeolithic men, the men of the Old Stone Age, were fishermen even more than they were hunters, and this terrace, with the river on three sides of it, was obviously a fishing platform and fishing camp. Then we found another indication. Come and look." He led us about 50 yards to where a small stream entered the Orkhon. On its banks were bushes on which fluttering white rags were tied—the remnants of shamanistic worship. "Right under those bushes," Okladnikov said, "there is a mineral spring. Until quite recently, the local Mongols regarded it as magical and used its water to cure sickness. Probably it has been revered continuously since the time of palaeolithic man, because we know from other sites that men in the Old Stone Age were as aware as we are of the difference between mineral springs and ordinary springs. So when we found a mineral spring and a natural fishing camp within 50 yards of each other, we knew we had only to dig."

These new discoveries in northern Mongolia are a reminder of the continuity between us and the past. Many of the links have been lost or have not yet been rediscovered, but there are enough to prove the complete chain. Davidson Black, the Canadian who started the search for Peking Man, was led onto the quest by finding a single tooth. After describing and analyzing its characteristics, he staked his scientific reputation on the statement that it was the tooth of a primitive human being, and not of some kind of ape, because it had a peculiarity (it was a "shovel-shaped incisor") that is rare in modern man, but more frequent in North China than elsewhere.

Because of conquests from north, south, east, and west the men of Peking today have many ancestors besides Peking Man, but the fact that Peking Man was one of their ancestors reminds us that there are two elements in history—continuity and change. "Europe," "Asia," "Old World," "New World" are comparatively new definitions, based on ideas. Long before these ideas existed, primitive man ranged the whole world. In the Old Stone Age he hunted, fished, and gathered edible plants. In the New Stone Age he made a revolutionary change from the gathering of the grainlike seeds of wild grasses—the forerunners of wheat, millet, and rice—to the planting and harvesting of grain.

A second revolutionary change was from the hunting of wild animals to domestication, making it possible to select some animals to butcher for food, others to provide milk, and still others to transport man himself and his goods. With these changes, "discovery and exploration" became more complicated. Once there had been chance encounters between bands in search of better hunting grounds or spots where fruit, berries, edible roots or seed grasses could be found. In the New Stone Age, the Bronze Age, and the early Iron Age larger bodies of people, with a more complicated social organization, moving in an orderly way, driving their herds and transporting their belongings on pack animals or in wagons, found the line of migration blocked here and there by settled farming communities whose villages and cities were strong points which could be defended, and also centers in which artisans produced pottery, textiles, and, later, metal wares, which could be used for trade as an alternative to war. Conversely, the settled peoples extended their territories as their population increased and developed them into kingdoms and states. The size, prosperity, and historical duration of a state were governed by an interplay of military, economic, political, and social factors.

What eventually emerges in history as the geographical concept of "Asia" developed out of discoveries both from within and from without its vague boundaries. From within, the Chinese of prehistory were among the earliest explorers of Asia, as they spread from their home in the great valley of the Yellow River to discover and occupy territories to the south and west and to discover others, to the west and north, through wars and trade.

From the archaeological record it is clear that other men of Asia also began to "discover Asia" very early. Products from the sub-Arctic and far Southeast Asia are found next to each other all along the coasts, from which they penetrated to great distances inland. There was a movement not only of trade goods

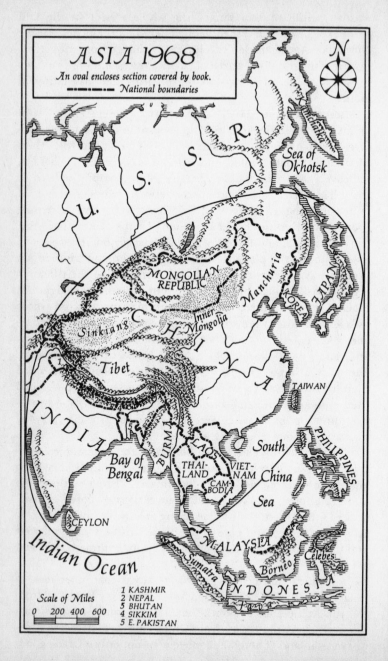

ASIA 1968

An oval encloses section covered by book.
---------- National boundaries

N

U. S. S. R.

Sea of
Okhotsk

Kamchatka

MONGOLIAN
REPUBLIC

Sinkiang   C   Inner Mongolia   Manchuria   H   I   N   A

Tibet

KOREA

JAPAN

TAIWAN

I   N   D   I   A

BURMA

LAOS

THAI-
LAND   VIET-
NAM

CAM-
BODIA

South

China

Sea

PHILIPPINES

Bay of
Bengal

CEYLON

Indian Ocean

MALAYSIA

Sumatra   I N D O N E S I A

Borneo

Celebes

Java

Scale of Miles

0   200 400 600

1 KASHMIR
2 NEPAL
3 BHUTAN
4 SIKKIM
5 E. PAKISTAN

but of the peoples themselves. Occasionally one finds along the coast of China individuals whose physical appearance—including kinky hair—suggests affinity with some of the people of Malaya and the Andaman Islands in the Indian Ocean.

When "discovery and exploration" began to become a record, it was first an unwritten record, the lore of traveler's tales, bits of useful knowledge passed on from one merchant to another, and the boasts, or tragic stories of defeat and disaster, of warriors who had been on distant expeditions; then a written record, preserving all these kinds of knowledge and adding chapters of new knowledge, new reports, new rumors. Both early and late, peculiarities can be noted in the record. Sometimes the "knowledge" transmitted is misinformation, and sometimes this is because it had been misunderstood or distorted in being passed from one speaker after another to one hearer after another, but sometimes it is misleading because it is deliberately cryptic, for there was much knowledge that people "in the know"—traders, warriors, priests, rulers—wanted to preserve and to pass on in a form which would be fully understood only by others "in the know."

Early Chinese records of their discoveries of new parts of Asia are of several kinds. The oldest surviving Chinese writing, on the "oracle bones" of about 1300 B.C., lists names of tribes whom the Chinese evidently considered "not Chinese." Sometimes there is a hint at what kind of people they were, as when a tribal name was written with the sign for "sheep," indicating that they were shepherds. This was the beginning of a long tradition: in the names of peoples whom they disliked or despised, the Chinese often included the sign for "dog" or that for "insect." By the fourth century B.C. there are descriptions of the nomadic peoples in Mongolia, and there are vague early legends, not easy to date, of mythical journeys to the northwest. Then, in the great imperial days of the first Han Dynasty there come the *Historical Memoirs* of Ssu-ma Ch'ien, who has been called the "Chinese Herodotus" and "the father of Chinese history." He recapitulates what was known to him of legend and recorded history; he himself traveled widely within China, visiting points of historic interest, and he collected and preserved the accounts of others who went farther than he did—like Chang Ch'ien, the pioneer of China's imperial expansion into Central Asia.

From the West, the earliest sparse references to Asia go back to Herodotus, who wrote of "the nomad Scythians who dwelt in Asia," and the records of the farthest conquests of Alexander, and many later, fuller accounts by Roman authors.

Chapters II and III deal with these two early streams of discovery—from China and from Rome. In later centuries, particularly after the twelfth, records become increasingly voluminous with the growth of trade and diplomacy and the zeal of Catholic missionaries, and our choice of excerpts from this wealth of literature becomes more and more difficult.

In choosing the records from which to quote we have tried to cover, chronologically, the whole sweep of recorded time from before the Christian era to the early decades of the twentieth century, and to cover, geographically, most of the areas of Asia. We have also tried to include a wide variety of subject matter and style of writing, so that, while some readers may not be interested in all of our selections, we feel sure that all readers will be interested in many of them and most readers in most of them.

We must make our own definition of "Asia." Such definitions have always been arbitrary. We still speak of "Asia Minor," but the term "Asia Major" has gone out of use—except as the title of a learned publication. "Near East," "Middle East," and "Far East" are, in the first place, terms which indicate zones of increasing distance from the eastern end of the Mediterranean. In the second place, they are variable terms. When some people speak of "Central Asia," they include some of the territory that other people include under the term "Middle East." "South Asia" and "Southeast Asia" are also imprecise terms. In the third place, all such terms are relative: the Near East, as seen from China, for example, could be called the beginning of the Far West.

Our definition, for the purposes of this book, is governed partly by the fact that it is one of a series. A part of Southeast Asia will be covered by Alexander Laing's book on the Pacific. Rhys Carpenter's volume includes an account of what Herodotus and, after him, the Greeks of classical times and the times of Alexander of Macedon knew about Mesopotamia, Persia, and the approaches to India. Our Asia in this book is principally China and India, including both Chinese and Russian Central

Asia, Tibet, and the mountainous regions between Central Asia and India. It includes also, to a lesser extent, Japan.

Although in this book we are going to be dealing only with written records, it is well to recall, as we start out, that even the earliest written records are only a continuation of a process that began thousands and thousands of years ago—as early as the first ability of men to communicate knowledge, emotion, and thought to each other in speech. The period of time with which we deal begins when China and Rome were already great empires. The great Silk Road had by then been in existence for centuries—but as a line along which tribes migrated and merchants exchanged their wares, the goods changing hands so often that the most distant buyers and sellers never knew each other. It was not yet dominated by the trade in silk, a commodity whose commercial value came to be expressed as much in diplomatic as in economic terms. This is where our collection of narratives begins.

☙ II ☙

ROME AND ASIA

HERODOTUS, in the fifth century B.C., visited South Russia and brought back stories of the Scythians he had found there and what they had told him of other tribes that frequently attacked and displaced each other. Concerning these peoples he also quotes an earlier Greek, Aristeas, as saying that, "possessed by Apollo, he reached the Issedonians. Above them dwelt the Arimaspi, men with one eye; still farther, the gold-guarding griffins, and beyond these, the Hyperboreans, whose country extended to the sea. Except the Hyperboreans, all these nations, beginning with the Arimaspi, continually encroached on their neighbors. Hence it came to pass that the Arimaspi gradually drove the Issedonians from their country, while the Issedonians dispossessed the Scyths; and the Scyths, pressing upon the Cimmerians, who dwelt on the shores of the southern sea [the Black Sea], forced them to leave their land." Although the name Hyperborean means "the most northern people," there is a theory that they were the Chinese.

All of Herodotus' geography and history is part of a great compilation setting the stage for the invasion of Greece by Xerxes. The doings of the Persians before Xerxes are therefore of importance to him, and it is thus that he happens to mention that Darius, who campaigned against the Scythians, also sent an expedition to discover where the Indus falls into the sea; the expedition reached the sea and then voyaged back along the coast to Persia. Acting on this information, Darius conquered part of northwest India and made regular use of the ocean route.

Half a millennium later Rome ruled all that any Greek city had ever controlled, and the western part of what had once been the Persian Empire; but the Roman legions never marched as far east as the armies of Alexander. East of the Mediterranean, and east and north of the Black Sea, the great problem of the Empire was to stabilize land frontiers far enough from the Mediterranean to provide security from invasion, but not so distant as to exhaust the manpower and wealth of the Empire in garrisoning them and supplying the garrisons. The strain of dealing with this problem led in the end to the establishment of the Eastern Roman Empire, ruled from Byzantium, while the Western Empire declined under the pressure of the barbarians of Northern and Central Europe.

For the Romans, Western and Eastern, of this whole period the question of very long-distance trade, travel and discovery beyond the *orbis terrarum* of the geographical world immediately known to them, was limited by several factors. There were no large surpluses of goods that the Romans had to export or else not sell at all. There were no more large territories adjacent to their existing frontiers that they felt they had to conquer and occupy for security reasons.

On the other hand, the East beyond Rome's empire still retained some of its ancient prestige as a region where civilization was even higher, and luxury more abundant and sophisticated, than in Rome itself. At the same time, there was enough wealth in Rome to pay for luxury goods. Moreover the Greeks, Syrians, and other peoples of Asia Minor and the Near East were great traders. To prohibit trade would have undermined their loyalty and made them look for patronage and protection to states not controlled by Rome.

So it comes about that those who frequented the Red Sea and Persian Gulf routes to India were mostly Syrians and others who, though Roman citizens, were not Italians, while Maës, whose agents penetrated far into Central Asia, was a Macedonian and it was from him that Ptolemy gained much of the information contained in the excerpts from his *Geography* included in this chapter. So also we have the complaint that the purchase of silk from China and pearls from the Persian Gulf was draining too much gold and silver out of Rome. And so it is, finally, that the Roman geographers collected no sensational information about powerful states that might threaten Rome with invasion from this direction.

Perhaps the most important factor making for "peaceful coexistence" was the Parthian state. After earlier wars that had shown that it was much too expensive for Rome to try to conquer Parthia, while the Parthians were not powerful enough to take over Rome's eastern provinces, a relationship was worked out that was satisfactory to Parthia partly because Parthia became a trade depot. The long-distance caravans from Central Asia halted there, instead of going through into Roman territory, and the Romans had to come there, buy the goods (with duties and fees added) and hire fresh transport to carry them on.

The *Periplus of the Erythrian Sea,* an anonymous book of directions for sailing the Indian Ocean, describes a city called Thinae, to which silk and other trade goods were brought overland through Bactria from eastern regions "which have never been explored." "Thinae," "Thin," "Tzinitza," and so on were names used for China, and were probably southern variants of the name of Ch'in, the state that had first unified China and made it an empire.

The Chinese were also called "Seres" or "Serices" by the Romans, probably from the Chinese word for "silk." Pliny and Pomponius Mela were the earliest authors to locate the Seres more or less accurately on the "Eastern Ocean." Pliny wrote of the Seres as people who, "though ready to engage in trade, wait for it to come to them instead of seeking it." On the other hand he summed up the geographical benefits of the stronger desire of the Romans for trade with Asia when he wrote "India is brought near by lust for gain."

As long as Roman traders could not themselves reach the territory where silk was grown, they were content with legends about it—that it was a fuzz collected from the leaves of plants, or, much later, that (getting a little nearer the truth) it was produced by large insects something like beetles and something like spiders. Even as late as 380 A.D. Ammianus Marcellinus accepted the statement in Pliny's *Natural History,* written about 70 A.D. and quoted in this chapter, that silk was a pale floss found growing on leaves, although Pausanius, writing 200 years before Ammianus, at least knew that it was spun by insects.

A change came in the sixth century, when the eggs of silk worms were at last brought to Byzantium. Once the Mediterranean world was able to produce its own silk, the economy of the states along the Silk Road was affected. They were less able to pay for peace and protection along the line of trade, and for this very reason the nomadic tribes began to look to them for plunder instead of subsidy. The long succession of Turkish incursions began to harass the eastern provinces of Byzantium and also South Russia. The Dark Ages began to close in and cut off the West from knowledge of the East, although at the same time the Arabs, the new masters of the Middle East, who even succeeded in converting some of the Turks to Islam, were able to multiply their wealth enormously and to acquire a knowledge of both West and East never rivaled by either China or Rome.

The excerpts from the meager records of the first centuries A.D., which follow, are interesting examples of the very limited knowledge that the West still had of the lands to the east of them. Of the authors not already identified, Cosmas was an Alexandrian Greek monk who had sailed as a merchant to India and Ceylon and had a fairly correct idea of where China was. His books were written between 535 and 550 A.D. Half a century later another Greek, named Simocatta, not quoted here, also wrote of China, and of wars and revolutions in Central Asia.

The translations of all of the excerpts which follow, in this chapter, are those used in *Cathay and the Way Thither*.[1]

From Pliny's *Natural History*

[Born A.D. 23, Died A.D. 79]

From the Caspian Sea and the Scythian Ocean the course [of the coast] makes a bend till the shore faces the east. The first part of that tract of country, beginning from the Scythian Promontory, is uninhabitable from eternal winter; the next portion is uncultivated and occupied by savage tribes, among whom are the Cannibal Scythians who feed on human flesh;

[1] *Cathay and the Way Thither,* ed. by Sir Henry Yule, Vol. I. [Full details of books mentioned in the text will be found in the Bibliography at the end of the book.]

and alongside of these are vast wildernesses tenanted by multitudes of wild beasts hemming in those human creatures almost as brutal as themselves. Then, we again find tribes of Scythians, and again desert tracts occupied only by wild animals, till we come to that mountain chain overhanging the sea, which is called Tabis. Not till nearly half the length of the coast which looks northeast has been passed, do you find inhabited country.

The first race then encountered are the SERES, so famous for the fleecy product of their forests. This pale floss, which they find growing on the leaves, they wet with water, and then comb out, furnishing thus a double task to our womenkind in first dressing the threads, and then again of weaving them into silk fabrics. So has toil to be multiplied; so have the ends of the earth to be traversed: and all that a Roman dame may exhibit her charms in transparent gauze.

The Seres are inoffensive in their manners indeed; but, like the beasts of the forest, they eschew the contact of mankind; and, though ready to engage in trade, wait for it to come to them instead of seeking it.

So far we have from the ancients. But we had an opportunity of more correct information in the reign of Claudius, when ambassadors came from the island. A freedman of Annius Plocamus, who had farmed the customs of the Red Sea from the Imperial Exchequer, after sailing round Arabia, was driven by storms past Carmania [the Kerman region of Iran], and on the fifteenth day made the port of Hippuri [on N. W. Ceylon]. Here he was entertained by the king with kindness and hospitality for six months; and, when he had learned to speak the language, in answer to the king's questions, told him all about Caesar and the Romans. Nothing that the king heard made such a wonderful impression on him as the opinion of the exactness of our dealings which he formed from seeing in some Roman money that had been taken that the coins were all of the same weight, though the heads upon them showed that they had been struck by different princes. And the stranger having particularly urged him to cultivate the friendship of the Romans, he sent these four ambassadors, the chief of whom was named Rachias. . . . These men also related that the side of their island which was opposite India, extended ten thousand stadia towards the southeast. The Seres, too, who dwell beyond the mountains of Emodus [Himalayas], and who are known to us by the commerce which is carried on with them, had been seen by these people; the father of Rachias had visited their country; and they themselves, on their travels, had met with people of the Seres. They described these as surpassing the ordinary stature of mankind, as having red hair, blue eyes, hoarse voices, and no common language to communicate by. The rest of what they told was just as we have it from our own traders. The goods carried thither are deposited on the further side of a certain river beside what the Seres have for sale, and the latter, if content with the bargain, carry them off; acting, in fact, as if in contempt of the luxury to which they ministered, and just as if they saw in the mind's eye the object and destination and result of this traffic.

Hence, one wonders more and more, how from beginnings so different, we have come now to see whole mountains cut down into marble slabs, journeys made to the Seres to get stuffs for clothing, the abysses of the Red Sea explored for pearls, and the depths of the earth in search of emeralds! Nay, more, they have taken up the notion also of piercing the ears, as if it were too small a matter to wear these gems in necklaces and tiaras, unless holes also were made in the body to insert them in!

But the sea of Arabia is still more fortunate; for 'tis thence it sends us pearls. And at the lowest computation, India and the Seres and that Peninsula put together drain our empire of one hundred million of sesterces every year. That is the price that our luxuries and our womankind cost us!

From the *Geography* of Ptolemy

[*Circa* A.D. *150*]

The inhabited part of our earth is bounded on the east by the Unknown Land which lies along the region occupied by the easternmost nations of Asia Major, the SINAE and the nations of SERICE; and on the south likewise by the Unknown Land which shuts round the Indian Sea, and encompasses that Ethiopia to the south of Libya which is called the land of Agisymba; to the west by the Unknown Land which embraces the Ethiopic Gulf of Libya, and then by the Western Ocean which lies along the most westerly parts of Libya and of Europe; and on the north by that continuation of the same ocean which encircles the Britannic Isles and the most northerly parts of Europe, and which goes by the names of Duecalydonian and Sarmatic, and by an Unknown Land which stretches along the most northerly parts of Asia Major, viz., Sarmatia, Scythia, and Serice. . . .

The Hyrcanian Sea, called also Caspian, is everywhere shut in by the land, so as to be just the converse of an island encompassed by the water. Such also is the case with that sea which embraces the Indian Sea with its gulfs, the Arabian Gulf, the Persian Gulf, the Gangetic Gulf, and the one which is called distinctively the Great Gulf, this sea being encompassed on all sides by the land. So we see that of the three Continents Asia is joined to Libya both by that Arabian Isthmus which separates Our Sea from the Arabian Gulf, and by the Unknown Land which encompasses the Indian Sea. . . .

The eastern extremity of the known earth is limited by the meridian drawn through the metropolis of the Sinae, at a distance from Alexandria of 119½°, reckoned upon the equator, or about eight equinoctial hours. . . . [Book vii, ch. 5.]

.   .   .   .

[*Speaking of persons who had made the voyage to India and spent much time in those parts, he proceeds:*]

From these persons also we have got more exact information about India and its kingdoms, as well as about the remoter parts of the region extending to the Golden Chersonese and thence to Cattigara [Hanoi or Canton?] For example they all agree in stating that in going thither your course is to the east, and in coming back again it is to the west, and they agree also in saying that no determinate time can be named for the accomplishment of the voyage, which varies with circumstances. They also agree that the land of the Seres with their metropolis lies to the north of the land of the Sinae, and that all that is further east than these is a Terra Incognita full of marshy lagoons in which great canes grow, and that so densely that people are able to cross the marshes by means of them. They tell also that there is not only a road from those countries to Bactriana by the Stone Tower, but also a road to India which goes through Palibothra [in the Ganges valley]. And the road from the metropolis of the Sinae to the port of Cattigara runs towards the southwest; so the former city would appear not to fall on the meridian of Sera and Cattigaras, as Marinus will have it, but to lie farther east.

Serice [2]

SERICE is bounded on the west by Scythia beyond Imaus, according to the line already defined [i.e., a line whose northern extremity is in *long.* 150°, *N. lat.* 63° and its southern extremity in *long.* 160°, *N. lat.* 35°]; on the north, by the Terra Incognita, in the latitude of the Island of Thule; on the east, by the Eastern Terra Incognita in the meridian of 180° from *lat.* 63° down to 3°0; on the south, by the remaining part of India beyond the Ganges along the parallel of 35° to the termination of that country in *long.* 173°, and then by the Sinae along the same line till you reach the frontier of the Terra Incognita, as it has just been defined.

Serice is girdled round by the mountains named Anniba, by the easternmost part of the Auxacian Mountains [possibly Aksu], by the mountains called Asmiraean, the easternmost part of the Kasian Mountains [perhaps Kashgar], by Mount Thagurus, by the most easterly part of the ranges called Hemodus and Sericus, and by the chain of Ottorocorrhas. Two rivers of especial note flow through the greater part of Serice; the river Oechardas is one of these, one source of which is that set forth as flowing from the Auxacian range, and the other from the Asmiraean range. . . . And the other is the river called Bautes, which has one source in the Kasian Mountains and another in the mountains of Ottorocorrhas [Utara Kuru of the Hindus].

The most northern parts of Serice are inhabited by tribes of cannibals. Below these the nation of the Annibi dwells to the north of the mountains bearing the same name. Between these last and the Auxacian Mountains is the nation of the Sizyges; next to them the Damnae; and then the Piaddae, extending to

[2] "Serice," here, apparently refers to the basin of Chinese Turkestan, although it was more often used as a name for China, the land of the "Seres."

the river Oechardus. Adjoining it are a people bearing the same name, the Oechardae.

And again, east of the Annibi are the Garenaei and the Nabannae. There is the Asmiraean country lying north of the mountains of the same name, and south of this extending to the Kasian Mountains the great nation Issedones; and beyond them to the east the Throani. Below them come the Ethaguri to the east of the mountains of the same name, and south of the Issedones the Aspacarae, and then the Batae, and farthest to the south, near the mountain chains Hemodus and Sericus, are the Ottorocorrhae.

The Land of the Sinae

The Sinae are bounded on the north by part of Serice, as has been defined already; on the east and the south, by the Terra Incognita; on the west, by India beyond the Ganges, according to the boundary already defined extending to the Great Gulf, and then by the Great Gulf itself, and those gulfs that follow it in succession, by the gulf called *Theriodes*, and by part of the gulf of the Sinae.

From the *History* of
Ammianus Marcellinus

[*Circa* A.D. *380*]

Beyond these regions of the two Scythias, towards the east, a circling and continuous barrrier of lofty mountains fences round the Seres, who dwell thus secure in their rich and spacious plains. On the west they come in contact with the Scythians; on the north and east they are bounded by solitary regions of snow: on the south, they reach as far as India and the Ganges. The mountains of which we have spoken are called Anniva and Nazavicium and Asmira and Emodon and Opurocarra. And these plains, thus compassed on all sides by precipitous steeps, are traversed by two famous rivers, Oechardes and Bautis, winding with gentle current through the spacious level; whilst the

Seres themselves pass through life still more tranquilly, ever keeping clear of arms and war. And being of that sedate and peaceful temper whose greatest delight is a quiet life, they give trouble to none of their neighbours. They have a charming climate, and air of healthy temper; the face of their sky is unclouded; their breezes blow with serviceable moderation; their forests are spacious, and shut out the glare of day.

The trees of these forests furnish a product of a fleecy kind, so to speak, which they ply with frequent waterings, and then card out in fine and slender threads, half woolly fibre, half viscid filament. Spinning these fibres they manufacture *silk*, the use of which once confined to our nobility has now spread to all classes without distinction, even to the lowest. Those Seres are frugal in their habits beyond other men, and study to pass their lives in peace, shunning association with the rest of mankind. So when foreigners pass the river on their frontier to buy their silk or other wares, the bargain is settled by the eyes alone with no exchange of words. And so free are they from wants that, though ready to dispose of their own products, they purchase none from abroad [xxiii, 6].

From *Christian Topography* by Cosmas Indicopleustes

.   .   .   .

For if Paradise were really on the surface of this world, is there not many a man among those who are so keen to learn and search out everything, that would not let himself be deterred from reaching it? When we see that there are men who will not be deterred from penetrating to the ends of the earth in search of silk, and all for the sake of filthy lucre, how can we believe that they would be deterred from going to get a sight of Paradise? The country of silk, I may mention, is in the remotest of all the Indies, lying towards the left when you enter the Indian Sea, but a vast distance farther off than the Persian Gulf or that island [Ceylon] which the Indians call SELEDIBA and the Greeks TAPROBANE. TZINITZA is the name of the country, and the Ocean compasses it round to the left, just as the same Ocean compasses Barbary round to the right. And the Indian philosophers, called Brachmans, tell you that if you were to stretch a straight cord from Tzinitza through Persia to the Roman territory, you would just divide the world in halves. And mayhap they are right.

For the country in question lies very much to the left, insomuch that loads of silk passing through the hands of different nations in succession *by land* reach Persia in a comparatively short time, whilst the distance from Persia *by sea* is vastly greater. For, in the first place, just as great a distance as the Persian Gulf runs up into Persia has the voyager to Tzinitza to run up from [the latitude of] Taprobane and the regions beyond it to reach his destination. And, in the second place, there is no small distance to be traversed in crossing the whole width of the Indian Sea from the Persian Gulf to Taprobane, and from Taprobane to the regions beyond [where you turn up to the left to reach Tzinitza]. Hence it is clear that one who comes by the overland route from Tzinitza to Persia makes a very short cut. And this accounts for the fact that such quantities of silk are always to be found in Persia [Book ii, p. 137–138].

The Introduction of the Silk-Worm
into the Roman Empire

1. From Procopius, *De Bello Gothico* [A.D. 500–565]

About the same time certain monks arrived from the [country of the] Indians, and learning that the Emperor Justinian had it much at heart that the Romans should no longer buy silk from the Persians, they came to the king and promised that they would so manage about silk that the Romans should not have to purchase the article either from the Persians or from any other nation; for they had lived, they said, a long time in a country where there were many nations of the Indians, and which goes by the name of SERINDA. And when there they had made themselves thoroughly acquainted with the way in which silk might be produced in the Roman territory. And when the emperor questioned them very closely, and asked how they could guarantee success in the business, the monks told him

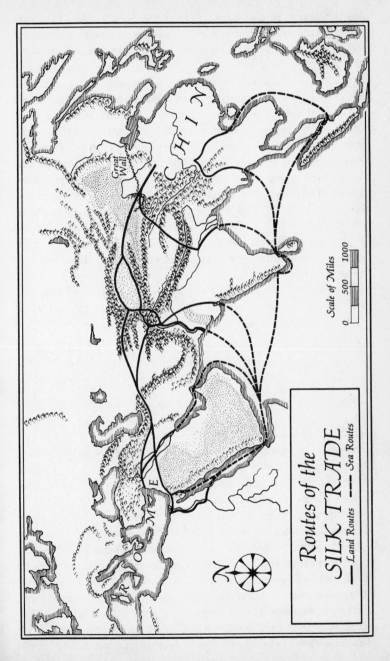

Routes of the
SILK TRADE

— Land Routes --- Sea Routes

Scale of Miles

0   500   1000

that the agents in the production of silk were certain caterpillars, working under the teaching of nature, which continually urged them to their task. To bring live caterpillars indeed from that country would be impracticable, but arrangements might be made for hatching them easily and expeditiously. For the eggs produced at a birth by one of those worms were innumerable; and it was possible to hatch these eggs long after they had been laid, by covering them with dung, which produced sufficient heat for the purpose. When they had given these explanations, the emperor made them large promises of reward if they would only verify their assertions by carrying the thing into execution. And so they went back again to India and brought a supply of the eggs to Byzantium. And having treated them just as they had said, they succeeded in developing the caterpillars, which they fed upon mulberry leaves. And from this beginning originated the establishment of silk-culture in the Roman territory [iv, 17].

[*Zonaras, in relating this story after Procopius, says that till this occurred the Romans did not know how silk was produced, nor even that it was spun by worms.*]

2. From Theophanes of Byzantium
[*End of sixth century*]

[*Finally, we have an account of how at last the mysterious silk worms were brought to Byzantium, concealed in the hollow sections of a bamboo cane.* O.L.]

Now in the reign of Justinian a certain Persian exhibited in Byzantium the mode in which [silk] worms were hatched, a thing which the Romans had never known before. This Persian on coming away from the country of the Seres had taken with him the eggs of these worms [concealed] in a walking-stick, and succeeded in bringing them safely to Byzantium. In the beginning of spring he put out the eggs upon the mulberry leaves which form their food; and the worms feeding upon those leaves developed into winged insects and performed their other operations. Afterwards when the Emperor Justinian showed the Turks the manner in which the worms were hatched, and the silk which they produced, he astonished them greatly. For at that time the Turks were in possession of the marts and ports

frequented by the Seres, which had been formerly in the possession of the Persians. For when Ephthalanus King of the
Ephthalites (from whom indeed the race derived that name)
conquered Perozes and the Persians, these latter were deprived
of their places, and the Ephthalites became possessed of them.
But somewhat later the Turks again conquered the Ephthalites
and took the places from them in turn. [Müller's *Fragmenta
Histor. Graec.*, IV, 270.]

❦ III ❧

ASIAN DISCOVERERS
OF ASIA

COMPARATIVELY little has been preserved of what the Chinese knew about lands and peoples beyond their own borders until the great Han dynasty, which ruled from about 200 B.C. to about 200 A.D. Under Wu Ti (the "Martial Emperor"), who came to the throne in 140 B.C., a number of missions were sent out into Central Asia.

These activities led to the opening of the Silk Road, along which Chinese goods, traded by the merchants of one country to those of the next, traveled all the way to Rome. It is notable, however, that the Chinese motive in developing this line of communications was not a search for export markets. China's Great Wall frontier was at this time chronically harried by the depredations of the Hsiung-nu or early Huns. The first great mission was sent into Central Asia for a diplomatic, not a commercial purpose. Its orders were to look for tribal allies and to encourage them to be hostile to the Hsiung-nu. The economic factor developed out of these political contacts. Not only did foreign merchants find it profitable to deal in Chinese silk (and porcelain and other goods) but the rulers of Central-Asian kingdoms and nomadic tribes found that control and protection of the trade brought them revenue, and that presents of Chinese luxuries were the most valuable gifts in negotiating alliances.

Chang Ch'ien, who headed the first great mission or embassy, made a report the substance of which was preserved by Ssŭ-ma

Ch'ien, the "father of Chinese history." This report was a state paper, concerned primarily with questions of policy and strategy. Trade and commodities are mentioned only when they are incidental to the interests of national policy. It is to such incidental mention that we owe some valuable historical information—as when Chang Ch'ien reported that in Central Asia he had seen Chinese products coming from the southwestern region of the modern provinces of Szechuan and Yunnan. He knew that these goods did not pass through northwest China and along the route of the desert caravans. Therefore they must go by some route through India, south of the huge Tibetan mass of mountains and plateaux. They must in fact have followed a route or routes along the general line of the famous wartime Burma Road, into Assam and India. This kind of information confirms the main written record of Chinese history: at that time most of China south of the Yangtze, and all of modern China that borders on Indochina and Burma, was still a pioneer zone of expansion and conquest for the Northern Chinese. They did not yet know, except in a hazy way, where their frontiers were, where China ceased to be China and alien territory began.

It is no wonder that the chronicles of China were at that time much less precise about the southern coast and the maritime routes than they were about the northern frontier and the routes into Central Asia. No danger of invasion threatened China from the south or from the coast. The dangerous tribes were in the north and northeast, and the Chinese *had* to know about them. Even three centuries later than Chang Ch'ien, in 166 A.D., when a foreign merchant was reported on the southern coast of China, claiming to be an envoy from An-tun, supposedly Marcus Aurelius Antoninus, it was recorded as a curious happening, not an important event.

It has been frequently suggested that on this occasion somebody who was really a merchant was pretending to be an envoy. The merchant, whoever he was, evidently knew the already well-established Chinese custom of "receiving tribute." If strangers appearing at the frontiers or on the coast of China "offered" their goods as "tribute," instead of demanding the right to trade, this was taken to mean that they were not a military threat and did not intend to make trouble politically. Their goods could be accepted graciously, and, if they were valuable, curious or strange enough, the merchants would be permitted to go all the way to the capital, and might even be received in audience by the emperor. In return, they would be presented with gifts —sometimes greater in value than the "tribute," as a mark of imperial favor. This procedure did not bind the emperor or his officials, like a trade agreement. It did not mean that the next comers would have a right of entry. Nor did the accepting of such "tribute" bind the emperor, or his officials, to accept sovereignty over such people, or any legal obligation to govern them or to protect them.

By the time of Fa Hsien, at the end of the fourth century A.D., and Hsüan Tsang, in the seventh century, a great deal had happened to make China a very different country from the slow-moving but invincible empire, the "Chinese Rome," that it had been under the Han. When the second Han dynasty fell, shaken by peasant rebellions, China fell apart into a number of kingdoms with changing frontiers and dynastic names, chronically at war with each other, and was not reunited under a long-lasting, powerful, stable dynasty until the founding of the T'ang dynasty (618–906). The first of the great Chinese Buddhist travelers from whom we quote in this book belongs to the age of disunity and violence; the second, to the brilliant opening period of the glorious T'ang dynasty.

Traditional Chinese accounts date the coming of Buddhism to China to the late Han period, but in fact Buddhism did not become an important religion, adopted by millions of Chinese and exerting an influence on emperors and the affairs of state, until the period of disunity. By this time most of North China was divided into kingdoms ruled either by barbarian conquerors from beyond the Great Wall or by the descendants of Chinese soldiers of fortune who employed barbarian troops and intermarried with the families of barbarian chiefs. This meant that, in striking contrast with the Han age of Chinese supremacy and self-assurance, what foreigners—barbarians—thought, and the way they did things, had become important.

It is not too fanciful to compare this age, when foreigners held power in much of China and when the Chinese were willing to listen to foreign teachers, and to go abroad to study and come back with Buddhist scriptures, with the late nineteenth century and the first half of the twentieth century, when again China felt the shock of foreign invasion and domination, when once more foreign ideas became important, and Chinese went abroad and came back with strange doctrines—Christianity, capitalism, the idea of a democratically governed republic, and finally Marxism—which is now being "made Chinese," as the Chinese made Indian Buddhism Chinese.

It was through the Central-Asian kingdoms along the Silk Road that the Chinese first came in contact with Buddhism. Its first teachers were men of Central Asia and of Bactria and then Gandhara—the region, that is to say, into which Buddhism had spread from Northwest India across North Afghanistan toward Iran and Central Asia. The first expounding of the doctrine must have been appallingly difficult. It seems to have been primarily the work of foreigners who had learned spoken Chinese, but not the written language, in Central Asia. These men had to flatten out the subtleties of philosophy and theology in, probably, a most unlearned spoken Chinese. Their converts had then to try to upgrade this teaching again into a reasonably learned, respectable literary Chinese. It is no wonder that in such a process a Chinese transformation of the Indian doctrine began almost immediately. It is also not surprising that the Chinese tradition of scholarship, which had survived the barbarian invasions of the north, soon insisted on a more learned investigation of Buddhism. Out of this there developed Chinese methods of translation and textual criticism that were truly scientific; but it is quite natural that there also survived a "popular" Chinese Buddhism, based on the spoken word and the telling of stories generation after generation, side by side with "learned" Buddhism.

Fa Hsien represents the conquest of Buddhism by scholarship. His is the earliest great name in a succession of pious scholars who were willing to face the truly fantastic chances and hardships of traveling thousands of miles to reach the holy places of the Buddhist tradition in India, and even Ceylon, in order to study the doctrine and come back with authoritative texts. Hsüan Tsang, two centuries later, carries on the same tradition of devotion to religion and to learning, but he represents a China by now once more militarily powerful, politically sophisticated, and culturally self-assured. There follow some interesting excerpts from the accounts of these three greatest of the early Chinese travelers—Chang Ch'ien, Fa Hsien, and Hsüan Tsang.

Chang Ch'ien and His
Account of Ferghana

[*Chang Ch'ien, the earliest known "official" Chinese traveler, was sent by the emperor Wu Ti in 138 B.C. on a mission to the Yueh-chih (an Iranian tribe then occupying Bactria who had once lived on the frontier of China) to persuade them to attack the Huns (Hsiungnu), his most dreaded enemies. On his way he was captured by the Huns and remained their prisoner for ten years, after which he escaped to Ferghana. He found the Yueh-chih in Tokharistan, which they had recently conquered, but he did not succeed in persuading them to attack the Huns.*

[*In 128 B.C. Chang Ch'ien attempted to return to China but was again captured. He finally reached China in 126 and was able to furnish the emperor with much valuable information.*

[*The following are excerpts from the annals of the Han dynasty historian Ssŭ-ma Ch'ien, describing Chang Ch'ien's mission and giving the substance of his report:*] [1]

After the Han had sent its envoy to open up communications with the state of Ta-hsia [Bactria], all the barbarians of the distant west craned their necks to the east and longed to catch a glimpse of China. Thus I made The Account of Ta-yüan. . . .

Chang Ch'ien was the first person to bring back a clear account of Ta-yüan [Ferghana]. He was a native of Han-chung and served as a palace attendant during the *chien-yüan* era [140–135 B.C.]. At this time the emperor questioned various Hsiung-nu who had surrendered to the Han and they all reported that the Hsiung-nu had defeated the king of the Yüeh-chih people [Indo-scythians] and made his skull into a drinking vessel. As a result the Yüeh-chih had fled and bore a con-

[1] From *Records of the Grand Historian of China*, translated from the Shih Chi of Ssŭ-ma Ch'ien by Burton Watson.

stant grudge against the Hsiung-nu, though as yet they had been unable to find anyone to join them in an attack on their enemy.

The Han at this time was engaged in a concerted effort to destroy the Hsiung-nu, and therefore, when the emperor heard this, he decided to try to send an envoy to establish relations with the Yüeh-chih. To reach them, however, an envoy would inevitably have to pass through Hsiung-nu territory. The emperor accordingly sent out a summons for men capable of undertaking such a mission. Chang Ch'ien, who was a palace attendant at the time, answered the summons and was appointed as envoy.

He set out from Lung-hsi, accompanied by Kan-fu, a Hsiung-nu slave who belonged to a family in T'ang-i. They traveled west through the territory of the Hsiung-nu and were captured by the Hsiung-nu and taken before the *Shan-yü*. The *Shan-yü* detained them and refused to let them proceed. "The Yüeh-chih people live north of me," he said. "What does the Han mean by trying to send an envoy to them! Do you suppose that if I tried to send an embassay to the kingdom of Yüeh in the southeast the Han would let my men pass through China?"

The Hsiung-nu detained Chang Ch'ien for over ten years and gave him a wife from their own people, by whom he had a son. Chang Ch'ien never once relinquished the imperial credentials that marked him as an envoy of the Han, however, and after he had lived in Hsiung-nu territory for some time and was less closely watched than at first, he and his party finally managed to escape and resume their journey toward the Yüeh-chih.

After hastening west for twenty or thirty days, they reached the kingdom of Ta-yüan. The king of Ta-yüan had heard of the wealth of the Han empire and wished to establish communication with it, though as yet he had been unable to do so. When he met Chang Ch'ien he was overjoyed and asked where Chang Ch'ien wished to go.

"I was dispatched as envoy of the Han to the Yüeh-chih, but the Hsiung-nu blocked my way and I have only just now managed to escape," he replied. "I beg Your Highness to give me some guides to show me the way. If I can reach my destination and return to the Han to make my report, the Han will reward you with countless gifts!"

The king of Ta-yüan trusted his words and sent him on his way, giving him guides and interpreters to take him to the state of K'ang-chü [Trans-Oxiana]. From there he was able to make his way to the land of the Great Yüeh-chih.

Since the king of the Great Yüeh-chih had been killed by the Hsiung-nu, his son had succeeded him as ruler and had forced the kingdom of Ta-hsia [Bactria] to recognize his sovereignty. The region he ruled was rich and fertile and seldom troubled by invaders, and the king thought only of his own enjoyment. He considered the Han too far away to bother with and had no particular intention of avenging his father's death by attacking the Hsiung-nu. From the court of the Yüeh-chih, Chang Ch'ien traveled on to the state of Ta-hsia, but in the end he was never able to interest the Yüeh-chih in his proposals.

After spending a year or so in the area, he began to journey back along the Nan-shan or Southern Mountains, intending to reenter China through the territory of the Ch'iang barbarians, but he was once more captured by the Hsiung-nu and detained for over a year.

Just at this time the *Shan-yü* died. . . . As a result of this the whole Hsiung-nu nation was in turmoil and Chang Ch'ien, along with his Hsiung-nu wife and the former slave Kan-fu, was able to escape and return to China. The emperor honored Chang Ch'ien with the post of palace counselor and awarded Kan-fu the title of "Lord Who Carries Out His Mission."

Chang Ch'ien was a man of great strength, determination, and generosity. He trusted others and in turn was liked by the barbarians. Kan-fu, who was a Hsiung-nu by birth, was good at archery, and whenever he and Chang Ch'ien were short of food he would shoot birds and beasts to keep them supplied. When Chang Ch'ien first set out on his mission, he was accompanied by over a hundred men, but after thirteen years abroad, only he and Kan-fu managed to make their way back to China. . . . The substance of his report was as follows:

Ta-yüan lies southwest of the territory of the Hsiung-nu, some ten thousand *li* [2] directly west of China. The people are settled on the land, plowing the fields and growing rice and wheat. They also make wine out of grapes. The region has many

[2] A *li* is about one third of a mile.

fine horses which sweat blood [3]; their forebears are supposed to have been foaled from heavenly horses. The people live in houses in fortified cities, there being some seventy or more cities of various sizes in the region. The population numbers several hundred thousand. The people fight with bows and spears and can shoot from horseback.

Ta-yüan is bordered on the north by K'ang-chü, on the west by the kingdom of the Great Yüeh-chih, on the southwest by Ta-hsia, on the northeast by the land of the Wu-sun, and on the east by Yü-mi and Yü-t'ien [Khotan].

West of Yü-t'ien, all the rivers flow west and empty into the Western Sea, but east of there they flow eastward into the Salt Swamp [Lob Nor]. The waters of the Salt Swamp flow underground and on the south form the source from which the Yellow River rises. There are many precious stones in the region and the rivers flow into China. The Lou-lan and Ku-shih peoples live in fortified cities along the Salt Swamp. The Salt Swamp is some five thousand *li* from Ch'ang-an. The western branch of the Hsiung-nu occupies the region from the Salt Swamp east to a point south of the Great Wall at Lung-hsi, where its territory adjoins that of the Ch'iang barbarians, thus cutting off the road from China to the west.

The Wu-sun live some two thousand *li* northeast of Ta-yüan, moving from place to place in the region with their herds of animals. Their customs are much like those of the Hsiung-nu. They have twenty or thirty thousand skilled archers and are very daring in battle. They were originally subjects of the Hsiung-nu, but later, becoming more powerful, they refused any longer to attend the gatherings of the Hsiung-nu court, though still acknowledging themselves part of the Hsiung-nu nation.

K'ang-chü is situated some two thousand *li* northwest of Ta-yüan. Its people likewise are nomads and resemble the Yüeh-chih in their customs. They have eighty or ninety thousand skilled archer fighters. The country is small, and borders Ta-yüan. It acknowledges nominal sovereignty to the Yüeh-chih people in the south and the Hsiung-nu in the east.

Yen-ts'ai lies some two thousand *li* northwest of K'ang-chü.

---

[3] The "bloody sweat" was apparently the result of parasites which caused small running sores in the hides of the horses.

The people are nomads and their customs are generally similar to those of the people of K'ang-chü. The country has over a hundred thousand archer warriors, and borders a great shoreless lake, perhaps what is known as the Northern Sea [Caspian Sea?].

The Great Yüeh-chih live some two or three thousand *li* west of Ta-yüan, north of the Kuei [Oxus] River. They are bordered on the south by Ta-hsia, on the west by An-hsi [Parthia], and on the north by K'ang-chü. They are a nation of nomads, moving from place to place with their herds, and their customs are like those of the Hsiung-nu. They have some one or two hundred thousand archer warriors. Formerly they were very powerful and despised the Hsiung-nu, but later, when Mo-tun became leader of the Hsiung-nu nation, he attacked and defeated the Yüeh-chih. Some time afterwards his son, the Old *Shan-yü*, killed the king of the Yüeh-chih and made his skull into a drinking cup.

The Yüeh-chih originally lived in the area between the Ch'i-lien or Heavenly Mountains and Tun-huang, but after they were defeated by the Hsiung-nu they moved far away to the west, beyond Ta-yüan, where they attacked and conquered the people of Ta-hsia and set up the court of their king on the northern bank of the Kuei River. A small number of their people who were unable to make the journey west sought refuge among the Ch'iang barbarians in the Southern Mountains, where they are known as the Lesser Yüeh-chih.

.   .   .   .

Ta-hsia is situated over two thousand *li* southwest of Ta-yüan, south of the Kuei River. Its people cultivate the land and have cities and houses. Their customs are like those of Ta-yüan. It has no great ruler but only a number of petty chiefs ruling the various cities. The people are poor in the use of arms and afraid of battle, but they are clever at commerce. After the Great Yüeh-chih moved west and attacked and conquered Ta-hsia, the entire country came under their sway. The population of the country is large, numbering some million or more persons. The capital is called the city of Lan-shih [Bactra] and has a market where all sorts of goods are bought and sold.

Southeast of Ta-hsia is the kingdom of Shen-tu [India]. "When I was in Ta-hsia," Chang Ch'ien reported, "I saw bamboo canes from Ch'iung and cloth made in the province of Shu [Ssuchuan]. When I asked the people how they had gotten such articles, they replied, 'Our merchants go to buy them in the markets of Shen-tu.' Shen-tu, they told me, lies several thousand *li* southeast of Ta-hsia. The people cultivate the land and live much like the people of Ta-hsia. The region is said to be hot and damp. The inhabitants ride elephants when they go into battle. The kingdom is situated on a great river.

"We know that Ta-hsia is located twelve thousand *li* southwest of China. Now if the kingdom of Shen-tu is situated several thousand *li* southeast of Ta-hsia and obtains goods which are produced in Shu, it seems to me that it must not be very far away from Shu. At present, if we try to send envoys to Ta-hsia by way of the mountain trails that lead through the territory of the Ch'iang people, they will be molested by the Ch'iang, while if we send them a little farther north, they will be captured by the Hsiung-nu. It would seem that the most direct route, as well as the safest, would be that out of Shu."

.   .   .   .

The emperor was therefore delighted. . . . He ordered Chang Ch'ien to start out from Chien-wei in Shu on a secret mission to search for Ta-hsia. The party broke up into four groups proceeding out of the regions of Mang, Jan, Hsi, and Ch'iung and P'o. All the groups managed to advance one or two thousand *li*, but they were blocked on the north by the Ti and Tso tribes and on the south by the Sui and K'un-ming tribes. The K'un-ming tribes have no rulers but devote themselves to plunder and robbery, and as soon as they seized any of the Han envoys they immediately murdered them. Thus none of the parties were ever able to get through to their destination. They did learn, however, that some one thousand or more *li* to the west there was a state called Tien-yüeh whose people rode elephants and that the merchants from Shu sometimes went there with their goods on unofficial trading missions. In this way the Han, while searching for a route to Ta-hsia, first came into contact with the kingdom of Tien [Burma].

Earlier the Han had tried to establish relations with the barbarians of the southwest, but the expense proved too great and no road could be found through the region and so the project was abandoned. After Chang Ch'ien reported that it was possible to reach Ta-hsia by traveling through the region of the southwestern barbarians, the Han once more began efforts to establish relations with the tribes in the area.

.   .   .   .

. . . The emperor occasionally questioned Chang Ch'ien about Ta-hsia and the other states of the west. Chang Ch'ien . . . replied, "When I was living among the Hsiung-nu I heard about the king of the Wu-sun people, who is named K'un-mo. K'un-mo's father was the ruler of a small state on the western border of the Hsiung-nu territory. The Hsiung-nu attacked and killed his father, and K'un-mo, then only a baby, was cast out in the wilderness to die. But the birds came and flew over the place where he was, bearing meat in their beaks, and the wolves suckled him, so that he was able to survive. When the *Shan-yü* heard of this, he was filled with wonder and, believing that K'un-mo was a god, he took him in and reared him. When K'un-mo had grown to manhood, the *Shan-yü* put him in command of a band of troops and he several times won merit in battle. The *Shan-yü* then made him the leader of the people whom his father had ruled in former times and ordered him to guard the western forts. K'un-mo gathered together his people, looked after them and led them in attacks on the small settlements in the neighborhood. Soon he had twenty or thirty thousand skilled archers who were trained in aggressive warfare. When the *Shan-yü* died, K'un-mo led his people far away, declared himself an independent ruler, and refused any longer to journey to the meetings of the Hsiung-nu court. The Hsiung-nu sent surprise parties of troops to attack him, but they were unable to win a victory. In the end the Hsiung-nu decided that he must be a god and left him alone, still claiming that he was a subject of theirs but no longer making any large-scale attacks on him.

". . . If we could make use of this opportunity to send rich gifts and bribes to the Wu-sun people and persuade them to move farther east and occupy the region which formerly belonged to the Hun-yeh king, then the Han could conclude an alliance of brotherhood with them and, under the circumstances, they would surely do as we say. If we could get them to obey us, it would be like cutting off the right arm of the Hsiung-nu! Then, once we had established an alliance with the Wu-sun, Ta-hsia and the other countries to the west could all be persuaded to come to court and acknowledge themselves our foreign vassals."

The emperor approved of this suggestion and, appointing Chang Ch'ien as a general of palace attendants, put him in charge of a party of three hundred men, each of which was provided with two horses. In addition the party took along tens of thousands of cattle and sheep and carried gold and silk goods worth a hundred billion cash. Many of the men in the party were given the imperial credentials making them assistant envoys so that they could be sent to neighboring states along the way.

When Chang Ch'ien reached the kingdom of the Wu-sun, the king of the Wu-sun, K'un-mo, tried to treat the Han envoys in the same way that the *Shan-yü* treated them. Chang Ch'ien was greatly outraged and, knowing that the barbarians were greedy, said, "The Son of Heaven has sent me with these gifts, but if you do not prostrate yourself to receive them, I shall have to take them back!"

With this K'un-mo jumped up from his seat and prostrated himself to receive the gifts. The other details of the envoys' reception Chang Ch'ien allowed to remain as before. Chang Ch'ien then delivered his message, saying, "If the Wu-sun will consent to move east and occupy the region of the Hun-yeh king, then the Han will send you a princess of the imperial family to be your wife."

But the Wu-sun people were split into several groups and the king was old. Living far away from China, he had no idea how large the Han empire was. Moreover, his people had for a long time in the past been subjects of the Hsiung-nu and still lived nearer to them than to China. The high ministers of the king were therefore all afraid of the Hsiung-nu and did not wish to move back east. The king alone could not force his will upon his subjects, and Chang Ch'ien was therefore unable to persuade him to listen to his proposal.

· · · · · · · · · ·

Chang Ch'ien dispatched his assistant envoys to Ta-yüan, K'ang-chü, the Great Yüeh-chih, Ta-hsia, An-hsi, Shen-tu, Yü-t'ien, Yü-mo, and the other neighboring states, the Wu-sun providing them with guides and interpreters. Then he returned to China, accompanied by twenty or thirty envoys from the Wu-sun and a similar number of horses which the Wu-sun sent in exchange for the Han gifts. The Wu-sun envoys thus had an opportunity to see with their own eyes the breadth and greatness of the Han empire.

On his return Chang Ch'ien was honored with the post of grand messenger, ranking him among the nine highest ministers of the government. A year or so later he died.

The Wu-sun envoys, having seen how rich and populous the Han was, returned and reported what they had learned to their own people, and after this the Wu-sun regarded the Han with greater respect. A year or so later the envoys whom Chang Ch'ien had sent to Ta-hsia and the other states of the west all returned, accompanied by envoys from those states, and for the first time relations were established between the lands of the northwest and the Han. It was Chang Ch'ien, however, who opened the way for this move, and all the envoys who journeyed to the lands in later times relied upon his reputation to gain them a hearing. As a result of his efforts, the foreign states trusted the Han envoys.

.   .   .   .

Sometime earlier the emperor had divined by the *Book of Changes* and been told that "divine horses are due to appear from the northwest." When the Wu-sun came with their horses, which were of an excellent breed, he named them "heavenly horses." Later, however, he obtained the blood-sweating horses from Ta-yüan, which were even hardier. He therefore changed the name of the Wu-sun horses, calling them "horses from the western extremity," and used the name "heavenly horses" for the horses of Ta-yüan.

. . . The emperor was very fond of the Ta-yüan horses and sent a constant stream of envoys to that region to acquire them.

The largest of these embassies to foreign states numbered several hundred persons, while even the smaller parties included over a hundred members, though later, as the envoys became more accustomed to the route, the number was gradually reduced. The credentials and gifts which the envoys bore with them were much like those supplied to the envoys in Chang Ch'ien's time. In the course of one year anywhere from five or six to over ten parties would be sent out. Those traveling to distant lands required eight or nine years to complete their journey, while those visiting nearer regions would return after a few years.

Journeys of the Buddhist Pilgrims to India

1. THE TRAVELS OF FA-HSIEN [4]

[Fa-Hsien was a Buddhist monk who, in the last year of the fourth century, set out to travel overland to India in order to bring back Buddhist texts which were not known in China. After an absence of fourteen years, he returned to Nanking, where he wrote the history of his travels.

[H. A. Giles, the translator of the excerpts which follow, described his journey as a "supremely dangerous mission. For Fa-Hsien, the hero of this adventure and the recorder of his own travels, practically walked from Central Asia across the desert of Gobi, over the Hindu Kush and through India down to the mouth of the Hoogly, where he took ship and returned by sea, after many hairbreadth escapes, to China, bringing with him what he went forth to secure—books of the Buddhist Canon and images of Buddhist deities."

[Fa-Hsien carried out his prodigious travels at a time corresponding to the Dark Ages of Europe, after the fall of the Roman Empire; but in Asia, in spite of the fall of the Han Empire, civilization still flourished. It is noteworthy that, although to Fa-Hsien as a Chinese the peoples of Central Asia must in one sense have been "barbarians," he treats with respect the high level of their cultural and especially their religious institutions. Sir Aurel Stein, some excerpts from whose travels we print later in this volume, took Fa-Hsien as a guide to the discovery of the sites of ancient cities and monasteries in what is now Sinkiang (the former Chinese Turkistan), the most north-

[4] From The Travels of Fa-Hsien (391–414 A.D.), translated by. H. A. Giles.

*western province of the Chinese People's Republic. We begin
here with Fa-Hsien at Kashgar and go on with parts of his
description of northern and southern India. Note that where the
translator uses the term "Shaman" he does not mean "a primitive magician" but "an Indian Buddhist initiate"* (sramana).]

After stopping [at Karghalik] for fifteen days, the party went
south for four days, and entering upon the Bolor-Tagh range,
arrived at the country of Tâsh-Kurghân, where they went into
retreat.

When this retreat was finished, they journeyed on for twenty-
five days and reached the country of Kâshgar, where they rejoined Hui-ching and his party. The king of this country was
holding the *pancha parishad,* which is called in Chinese "the
great quinquennial assembly." To this he invites Shamans from
all quarters, and these collect together like clouds. The place
where the priests are to sit is splendidly adorned beforehand
with streaming pennants and canopies of silk; silk, embroidered
with lotus flowers in gold and silver, is also laid over the backs
of the seats. When all is in order, the king and his ministers
make their offerings according to rite. The assembly may last
for one, two, or three months, and is generally held in the
spring. The king, when the assembly is over, further bids his
ministers to arrange their offerings for presentation, which ceremony may last for one, two, three, or even five days. When all
the offerings have been made, the king takes his own horse,
saddles and bridles it himself and causes a distinguished official
to ride it. Then, with some white felt and all kinds of jewels
such as Shamans require, he joins with the body of officials in a
vow to hand over those things as alms. As soon as this has been
done, the various items are redeemed from the priests with
money.

This country is mountainous and cold; and with the exception
of wheat, no grain will grow and ripen. When the priests have
received their annual (land) tithes, the mornings forthwith
become frosty; therefore the king is always urging the priests
to get the wheat ripe before pay-day.

This country has a spittoon which belonged to Buddha; it is
made of stone and of the same colour as his alms-bowl. There

is also one of Buddha's teeth, for which the people have raised a pagoda. There are over one thousand priests, all belonging to the Lesser Vehicle. From the hills eastward, the people wear coarse clothes like the Chinese, the only difference being that the former use felt and serge. The observances of the Faith by the Shamans are varied, and too numerous to be recorded here. This country is in the middle of the Bolor-Tagh range; and from this onwards all plants, trees, and fruits are different from those of China, with the exception of the bamboo, pomegranate, and sugar-cane.

From this point traveling westwards towards northern India, the pilgrims after a journey of one month succeeded in crossing the Bolor-Tagh range. On these mountains there is snow in winter and summer alike. There are also venomous dragons, which, if provoked, spit forth poisonous winds, rain, snow, sand, and stones. Of those who encounter these dangers not one in ten thousand escapes. The people of that part are called men of the Snow Mountains.

On passing this range the travelers were in northern India. Just at the frontier there is a small country, called Darêl, where also there are many priests, all of the Lesser Vehicle. In this country there was formerly a Lo-han who, using his divine power, carried a clever artisan up to the Tushita heavens to observe the height, complexion, and features of the Bodhisattva Maitreya, so that when he came down he might carve an image of him in wood. Altogether he made three journeys for observation and afterwards executed an image eighty feet in height, the folded legs of which measured eight feet across. On fast-days it always shines with a brilliant light. The kings of near countries vie with one another in their offerings to it. From of old until now, it has been on view in this place.

Keeping to the range, the party journeyed on in a south-westerly direction for fifteen days over a difficult, precipitous, and dangerous road, the side of the mountain being like a stone wall ten thousand feet in height. On nearing the edge, the eye becomes confused; and wishing to advance, the foot finds no resting place. Below there is a river, named Indus. . . .

From this point descending eastward for five days, the pilgrims arrived at the country of Gandhara, which was governed by Fa-i, the son of king Asoka.

Traveling from Gandhara southward for seven days, the pilgrims arrived at the country of Peshawar. Formerly, when Buddha was visiting this country in company with ten of his disciples, he said to Ananda, "When I have passed away, a king of this country, by name Kanishka, will raise a pagoda at this spot." Subsequently, when king Kanishka came into the world and was traveling about to see things, Indra, God of Heaven, wishing to originate in him the idea, caused the appearance of a little herd-boy building a pagoda in the middle of the road. "What are you making there?" said the king. "I am building a pagoda for Buddha," replied the boy. "Splendid!" cried the king; and he forthwith built a pagoda, over four hundred feet high and ornamented with all the preciosities combined, over the pagoda built by the little boy. Of all the pagodas and temples seen by the pilgrims, not one could compare with this in grandeur and dignity; and tradition says that of the various pagodas in the inhabited world this one takes the highest rank. . . .

[*It was customary to describe in general terms the deadly dangers of Tibet, the Karakoram plateau, and the Pamirs; Fa-Hsien relates, with simple pathos, the death of a companion. O. L.*]

In the second moon of winter, Fa-Hsien and his companions, three in all, went southward across the Little Snowy Mountains [Safed Koh], which retain the snow, summer and winter alike. On the northern side which is in the shade, it is frightfully cold; and when a gale gets up, it makes one shut the mouth and shiver. Hui-ching could go no farther; he foamed at the mouth, and said to Fa-Hsien, "I too cannot recover; you had better go on while you can; do not let us all pass away here";—and so he passed. Gently stroking the corpse, Fa-Hsien cried out in lamentation, "Our original design cannot be carried out; it is destiny; what is there to be done?"

Then the pilgrims once more struggled forward.

.   .   .   .

To the south of [the river Jumna], the country is called the Middle Kingdom [of the Brahmans]. It has a temperate climate, without frost or snow; and the people are prosperous and happy, without registration or official restrictions. Only those who till the king's land have to pay so much on the profit they make. Those who want to go away, may go; those who want to stop, may stop. The king in his administration uses no corporal punishments; criminals are merely fined according to the gravity of their offences. Even for a second attempt at rebellion the punishment is only the loss of the right hand. The men of the king's bodyguard have all fixed salaries. Throughout the country no one kills any living thing, nor drinks wine, nor eats onions or garlic; but chandalas are segregated. Chandala is their name for foul men [lepers]. These live away from other people; and when they approach a city or market, they beat a piece of wood, in order to distinguish themselves. Then people know who they are and avoid coming into contact with them.

In this country they do not keep pigs or fowls, there are no dealings in cattle, no butchers' shops or distilleries in their marketplaces. As a medium of exchange they use cowries. Only the chandalas go hunting and deal in flesh.

From the date of Buddha's disappearance from the world, the kings, elders, and gentry of the countries round about, built shrines for making offerings to the priests, and gave them land, houses, gardens, with men and bullocks for cultivation. Binding title-deeds were written out, and subsequent kings have handed these down one to another without daring to disregard them, in unbroken succession to this day. Rooms, with beds and mattresses, food, and clothes, are provided for resident and traveling priests, without fail; and this is the same in all places. The priests occupy themselves with benevolent ministrations, and with chanting liturgies; or they sit in meditation. When traveling priests arrive, the old resident priests go out to welcome them and carry for them their clothes and alms-bowls, giving them water for washing and oil for anointing their feet, as well as the liquid food allowed out of hours. By and by, when the travelers have rested, the priests ask them how long they have been priests and what is their standing; and then each traveler is provided with a room and bedroom requisites, in accordance with the rules of the Faith.

. . . .

At the end of this time he took passage on a large merchant vessel, and setting sail proceeded towards the southwest with the first of the favourable winter monsoon. After fourteen days and nights he reached the Land of the Lion [Ceylon], said by the inhabitants to lie at a distance of seven hundred yojanas from India. This country is on a great island, measuring fifty yojanas from east to west and thirty from north to south. The small islands round about are nearly one hundred in number, and are distant from one another ten, twenty, or even two hundred *li*. They are all subject to the mother island, and produce chiefly pearls and precious stones. There is one island where the Mani beads [fine pearls used for Buddhist rosaries] are found; it is about ten *li* square. The king sends men to guard it; and if any pearls are obtained, he takes three-tenths.

This country was not originally inhabited by human beings, but only by devils and dragons, with whom the merchants of the neighbouring countries traded by barter. At the time of the barter the devils did not appear, but set out their valuables with the prices attached. The merchants then gave goods according to the prices marked and took away the goods they wanted. And from the merchants going backwards and forwards and some stopping there, the attractions of the place became widely known, and people went thither in great numbers, so that it became a great nation.

The temperature of this country is very agreeable; there is no distinction between winter and summer. Plants and trees flourish all the year round, and cultivation of the soil is carried on as men please, without regard to the season.

When Buddha came to this country, he wished to convert the wicked dragons; and by his divine power he placed one foot to the north of the royal city and the other on the top of Adam's Peak, the two points being fifteen yojanas apart. Over the footprint to the north of the city a great pagoda has been built, four hundred feet in height and decorated with gold and silver and with all kinds of precious substances combined. By the side of the pagoda a monastery has also been built, called No-Fear Mountain, where there are now five thousand priests. There is a Hall of Buddha of gold and silver carved work with all kinds of precious substances, in which stands his image in green jade, over twenty feet in height, the whole of which glitters with the seven preciosities, the countenance being

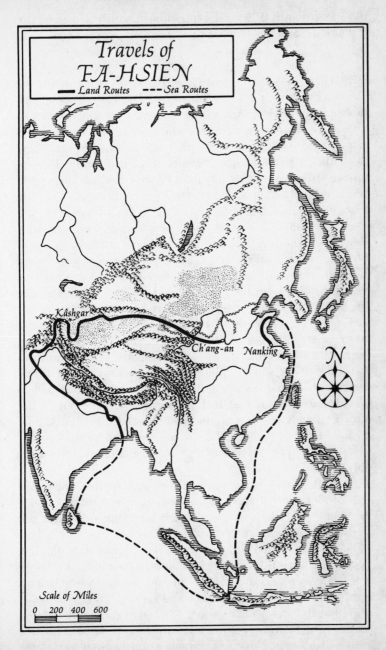

Travels of
FA-HSIEN
—— Land Routes --- Sea Routes

Kâshgar

Ch'ang-an   Nanking

N

Scale of Miles
0   200 400 600

grave and dignified beyond expression in words. On the palm of the right hand lies a priceless pearl.

.   .   .   .

Fa-Hsien . . . after repeated search obtained a copy of the Disciplines according to the school of "The Faith Prevailing"; also copies of the long Agamas on cosmogony, and of the miscellaneous Agamas on ecstatic contemplation, and subsequently of a collection of extracts from the Canon, all of which China was without. When he had obtained these in Sanskrit, he took passage on board a large merchant vessel, on which there were over two hundred souls, and astern of which there was a smaller vessel in tow, in case of accident at sea and destruction of the big vessel. Catching a fair wind, they sailed eastward for two days; then they encountered a heavy gale, and the vessel sprang a leak. The merchants wished to get aboard the smaller vessel; but the men on the latter, fearing that they would be swamped by numbers quickly cut the tow-rope in two. The merchants were terrified, for death was close at hand; and fearing that the vessel would fill, they promptly took what bulky goods there were and threw them into the sea. Fa-Hsien also took his pitcher and ewer, with whatever else he could spare, and threw them into the sea; but he was afraid that the merchants would throw over his books and his images, and accordingly fixed his whole thoughts upon Kuan Yin, the Hearer of Prayers, and put his life into the hands of the Catholic [Buddhist] Church in China, saying, "I have journeyed far on behalf of the Faith. Oh that by your awful power you would grant me a safe return from my wanderings."

The gale blew on for thirteen days and nights, when they arrived alongside of an island, and then, at ebb-tide, they saw the place where the vessel leaked and forthwith stopped it up, after which they again proceeded on their way.

This sea is infested with pirates, to meet whom is death. The expanse of ocean is boundless, east and west are not distinguishable; only by observation of the sun, moon, and constellations, is progress to be made. In cloudy and rainy weather, our vessel drifted at the mercy of the wind, without keeping any definite course. In the darkness of night nothing was to be seen but the great waves beating upon one another and flashing forth light like fire, huge turtles, sea-lizards, and such-like monsters of the deep. Then the merchants lost heart, not knowing whither they were going, and the sea being deep, without bottom, they had no place where they could cast their stone-anchor and stop. When the sky had cleared, they were able to tell east from west and again to proceed on their proper course; but had they struck a hidden rock, there would have been no way of escape.

And so they went on for more than ninety days until they reached a country named Java, where heresies and Brahmanism were flourishing, while the Faith of Buddha was in a very unsatisfactory condition.

After having remained in this country for five months or so, Fa-Hsien again shipped on board another large merchant vessel which also carried over two hundred persons. They took with them provisions for fifty days and set sail on the 16th of the 4th moon, and Fa-Hsien went into retreat on board the vessel.

A northeast course was set in order to reach Canton; and over a month had elapsed when one night in the second watch they encountered a violent gale with tempestuous rain, at which the traveling merchants and traders who were going to their homes were much frightened. However, Fa-Hsien once more invoked the Hearer of Prayers and the Catholic Church in China, and was accorded the protection of their awful power until day broke. As soon as it was light, the Brahmans took counsel together and said, "Having this Shaman on board has been our undoing, causing us to get into this trouble. We ought to land the religious mendicant on some island; it is not right to endanger all our lives for one man." A "religious protector" of Fa-Hsien's replied, saying, "If you put this religious mendicant ashore, you shall also land me with him; if not, you had better kill me, for supposing that you land him, when I reach China I will report you to the king who is a reverent believer in the Buddhist Faith and honours religious mendicants." At this the merchants wavered and did not dare to land him just then.

Meanwhile, the sky was constantly darkened and the captain lost his reckoning. So they went on for seventy days until the provisions and water were nearly exhausted, and they had to use sea-water for cooking, dividing the fresh water so that each man got about two pints. When all was nearly consumed, the merchants consulted together and said, "The ordinary time for the voyage to Canton is exactly fifty days. We have now exceeded that limit by many days; must we not have gone out of our course?"

Thereupon they proceeded in a northwesterly direction, seeking for land; and after twelve days and nights arrived south of the Lao mountain (on the Shantung promontory) at the boundary of the Prefecture of Ch'ang-kuang [the modern Kiaochou], where they obtained fresh water and vegetables. [*Thus they had, in fact, made their landfall far to the north of Canton. O. L.*]

And now, after having passed through much danger, difficulty, sorrow, and fear, suddenly reaching this shore and seeing the old familiar vegetables, they knew it was their fatherland; but not seeing any inhabitants or traces of such, they did not know what part it was. Some said that they had not got as far as Canton; others declared that they had passed it. Being in a state of uncertainty, some of them got into a small boat and went up a creek in search of any one whom they might ask about the place. These fell in with two hunters and brought them back to the vessel, telling Fa-Hsien to act as interpreter and interrogate them. Fa-Hsien began by reassuring them, and then quietly asked them, "What men are you?" They replied, "We are followers of Buddha." "And what is it you go among the mountains to seek?" continued Fa-Hsien. Then they began to lie, saying, "Tomorrow is the 15th day of the 7th moon; we wished to get something for a sacrifice (the lie!) to Buddha." Fa-Hsien then said, "What country is this?" They answered, "This is the boundary of the Ch'ang-kuang prefecture in Ch'ing-chou; all these parts belong to the Liu family." When they heard this the merchants were very glad, and at once requested that their effects might be landed, sending men off with them to Ch'ang-kuang.

The Prefect, Li I, was a devout believer in the Faith of Buddha; and when he heard that a Shaman had arrived who had brought Sacred Books and Images with him in a ship from beyond the sea, he immediately proceeded with his retinue to the seashore to receive these books and images and carry them back to his official residence. The merchants then returned to Yangchou [in Kiangsu], while Fa-Hsien received an invitation to remain at Ch'ing-chou a winter and a summer. When his summer retreat was over, Fa-Hsien, who had been far separated from his ecclesiastical authorities for many years, was desirous of reaching Ch'ang-an; but because of the great importance of his undertaking he accordingly proceeded south to the capital [Nanking] and handed over to the ecclesiastics there the Sutras and the Disciplines he had collected.

Fa-Hsien spent six years in traveling from Ch'ang-an to Central India; he stayed there six years, and it took him three more to reach Ch'ing-chou. The countries he passed through amounted to rather fewer than thirty. From the Sandy Desert westwards all the way to India, the dignified deportment of the priesthood and the good influence of the Faith were beyond all expression in detail. As, however, the ecclesiastics at home had had no means of hearing about these things, Fa-Hsien had given no thought to his own unimportant life, but came home across the sea, encountering still more difficulties and dangers. Happily, he was accorded protection by the divine majesty of the Precious Trinity, and was thus preserved in the hour of danger. Therefore he wrote down on bamboo tablets and silk an account of what he had been through, desiring that the gentle reader should share this information.

2. HSÜAN TSANG [5] (603–668)

[*Two hundred years after Fa-Hsien another monk, Hsüan Tsang, determined to "travel in the countries of the west in order to question the wise men on the points that were troubling his mind." He crossed the Gobi to Hami, was received with honor by the king of Turfan, and continued through Kucha to the camp of the Great Khan of the Western Turks, after crossing the ice-bound T'ien Shan. The Great Khan arranged for his onward journey to Gandhara (Peshawar), which he made by way of Tashkent and Samarkand and across the Oxus to Bactria, Balkh and Bamiyan and through the Khyber Pass.*

[*In Kashmir he found a learned monk with whom he studied for two years, after which he traveled widely in India, visited Assam, and finally returned home by way of the Pamirs, Kashgar, Khotan, Lop Nor and Tunhuang. Reaching court in 645 he*

[5] From *Buddhist Records of the Western World*, Vol. I.

*was granted a magnificent reception by the emperor. According
to Sir Percy Sykes, he was "undoubtedly the greatest known
traveler that the world had so far seen."*

[*While both Fa-Hsien and Hsüan Tsang made careful notes
of their routes, estimated distances and directions, the weather,
the names and sizes of towns and the customs, clothing and
character of the peoples they encountered, a very large part of
their records consisted of descriptions of religious beliefs and
observances, temples, holy places, miracles, myths and legends;
and often their observations of lay matters are larded with magic
and hearsay. Like most later explorers their records are full of
the hardships and dangers of travel. Happily they also occasionally noted, or retained, vivid memories of the beauty of a
landscape—such as Hsüan Tsang's description of the T'ien Shan:*

[*"The T'ien Shan mountain of ice forms the northern angle
of Pamir. It is most dangerous and its summit rises to the skies.
From the beginning of the world the snow has accumulated on
it and has turned into blocks of ice, which melt neither in
springtime nor in summer. They roll away in boundless sheets
of hard, gleaming white, losing themselves in the clouds."*]

Kingdom of K'iu-chi (Kuché)

The country of K'iu-chi is from east to west some thousand *li*
or so; from north to south about 600 *li*. The capital of the realm
is from 17 to 18 *li* in circuit. The soil is suitable for rice and
corn, also it produces grapes, pomegranates, and numerous
species of plums, pears, peaches, and almonds, also grow here.
The ground is rich in minerals—gold, copper, iron, and lead,
and tin. The air is soft, and the manners of the people honest.
The style of writing is Indian, with some differences. They excel
other countries in their skill in playing on the lute and pipe.
They clothe themselves with ornamental garments of silk and
embroidery. They cut their hair and wear a flowing covering [over their heads]. In commerce they use gold, silver, and
copper coins. The king is of the K'iu-chi race; his wisdom being
small, he is ruled by a powerful minister. The children born of
common parents have their heads flattened by the pressure of
a wooden board. . . .

To the north of a city on the eastern borders of the country,
in front of a Deva temple, there is a great dragon-lake. The

dragons, changing their form, couple with mares. The offspring is a wild species of horse, difficult to tame and of a fierce nature. The breed of these dragon-horses became docile. This country consequently became famous for its many excellent horses.

From very early time till now there have been no wells in the town, so that the inhabitants have been accustomed to get water from the dragon-lake. On these occasions the dragons, changing themselves into the likeness of men, had intercourse with the women. Their children, when born, were powerful and courageous, and swift of foot as the horse. Thus gradually corrupting themselves, the men all became of the dragon breed, and relying on their strength, they became rebellious and disobedient to the royal authority. Then the king, forming an alliance with the Tuh-kiueh [Turks], massacred the men of the city; young and old, all were destroyed, so that there was no remnant left; the city is now a waste and uninhabited.

.   .   .   .

On examination, we find that the names of India are various and perplexing as to their authority. It was anciently called Shin-tu, also Hien-tau; but now, according to the right pronunciation, it is called In-tu. The people of In-tu call their country by different names according to their district. Each country has diverse customs. Aiming at a general name which is the best sounding, we will call the country In-tu. In Chinese this name signifies the Moon. The moon has many names, of which this is one. For as it is said that all living things ceaselessly revolve in the wheel [of transmigration] through the long night of ignorance, without a guiding star, their case is like [the world], the sun gone down; as then the torch affords its connecting light, though there be the shining of the stars, how different from the bright moon; just so the bright connected light of holy men and sages, guiding the world as the shining of the moon, have made this country eminent, and so it is called In-tu.

The families of India are divided into castes, the Brahmans particularly [are noted] on account of their purity and nobility. Tradition has so hallowed the name of this tribe that there is no question as to difference of place, but the people generally speak of India as the country of the Brahmans.

The countries embraced under this term of India are generally spoken of as the five Indies. In circuit this country is about 90,000 *li;* on three sides it is bordered by the great sea; on the north it is backed by the Snowy Mountains. The north part is broad, the southern part is narrow. Its shape is like the half-moon. The entire land is divided into seventy countries or so. The seasons are particularly hot; the land is well watered and humid. The north is a continuation of mountains and hills, the ground being dry and salt. On the east there are valleys and plains, which being well watered and cultivated, are fruitful and productive. The southern district is wooded and herbaceous; the western parts are stony and barren. Such is the general account of this country.

.   .   .   .

The dress and ornaments . . . are varied and mixed. Some wear peacocks' feathers; some wear as ornaments necklaces made of skull bones; some have no clothing, but go naked; some wear leaf or bark garments; some pull out their hair and cut off their moustaches; others have bushy whiskers and their hair braided on the top of their heads. The costume is not uniform, and the colour, whether red or white, not constant.

The Shamans have only three kinds of robes. . . . The cut of the three robes is not the same, but depends on the school. Some have wide or narrow borders, others have small or large flaps. The *Sang-kio-ki* covers the left shoulder and conceals the two armpits. It is worn open on the left and closed on the right. It is cut longer than the waist. The *Ni-fo-se-na* has neither girdle nor tassels. When putting it on, it is plaited in folds and worn round the loins with a cord fastening. The schools differ as to the colour of this garment: both yellow and red are used.

The Kshattriyas [the warrior caste] and the Brahmans are cleanly and wholesome in their dress, and they live in a homely and frugal way. The king of the country and the great ministers wear garments and ornaments different in their character. They use flowers for decorating their hair, with gem-decked caps; they ornament themselves with bracelets and necklaces.

There are rich merchants who deal exclusively in gold trinkets, and so on. They mostly go barefooted; few wear sandals. They stain their teeth red or black; they bind up their hair and pierce their ears; they ornament their noses, and have large eyes. Such is their appearance.

They are very particular in their personal cleanliness, and allow no remissness in this particular. All wash themselves before eating; they never use that which has been left over [from a former meal]; they do not pass the dishes. Wooden and stone vessels, when used, must be destroyed; vessels of gold, silver, copper, or iron after each meal must be rubbed and polished. After eating they cleanse their teeth with a willow stick, and wash their hands and mouth.

Until these ablutions are finished they do not touch one another. Every time they perform the functions of nature they wash their bodies and use perfumes of sandalwood or turmeric.

When the king washes they strike the drums and sing hymns to the sound of musical instruments. Before offering their religious services and petitions, they wash and bathe themselves.

The letters of their alphabet were arranged by Brahmadeva, and their forms have been handed down from the first till now. They are forty-seven in number, and are combined so as to form words according to the object, and according to circumstances [of time or place]: there are other forms [inflexions] used. This alphabet has spread in different directions and formed diverse branches, according to circumstances; therefore there have been slight modifications in the sounds of the words; but in its great features there has been no change. Middle India preserves the original character of the language in its integrity. Here the pronunciation is soft and agreeable, and like the language of the Devas. The pronunciation of the words is clear and pure, and fit as a model for all men. The people of the frontiers have contracted several erroneous modes of pronunciation; for according to the licentious habits of the people, so also will be the corrupt nature of their language.

With respect to the records of events, each province has its own official for preserving them in writing. . . . In these records are mentioned good and evil events, with calamities and fortunate occurrences.

To educate and encourage the young, they are first taught to study the book of twelve chapters [Siddhavastu].

After arriving at the age of seven years and upwards, the young are instructed in the five Vidyas, Sastras of great importance. The first . . . explains and illustrates the agreement of words, and it provides an index for derivatives.

The second . . . treats of the arts, mechanics, explains the principles of the *Yin* and *Yang* and the calendar.

The third is called the medicinal treatise; it embraces formulae for protection, secret charms, medicinal stones, acupuncture, and mugwort.

The fourth . . . relates to the determination of the true and false, and reduces to their last terms the definition of right and wrong.

The fifth . . . relates to the five vehicles, their causes and consequences, and the subtle influences of these.

The teachers [of these works] must themselves have closely studied the deep and secret principles they contain, and penetrated to their remotest meaning. They then explain their general sense, and guide their pupils in understanding the words which are difficult. They urge them on and skilfully conduct them. They add lustre to their poor knowledge, and stimulate the desponding. If they find that their pupils are satisfied with their acquirements, and so wish to escape to attend to their worldly duties, then they use means to keep them in their power. When they have finished their education, and have attained thirty years of age, then their character is formed and their knowledge ripe. When they have secured an occupation they first of all thank their master for his attention. There are some, deeply versed in antiquity, who devote themselves to elegant studies, and live apart from the world, and retain the simplicity of their character. These rise above mundane presents, and are as insensible to renown as to the contempt of the world. . . .

After climbing precipices and crossing valleys, we go up the course of the Sin-tu [Indus] river; and then, by the help of flying bridges and footways made of wood across the chasms and precipices, after going 500 *li* or so, we arrive at the country of Po-lu-lo (Bolor or Baltistan).

.   .   .   .

Kia-shi-mi-lo [Kashmir]

The kingdom of Kashmir is about 7,000 *li* in circuit, and on all sides it is enclosed by mountains. These mountains are very high. Although the mountains have passes through them, these are narrow and contracted. The neighbouring states that have attacked it have never succeeded in subduing it. The capital of the country on the west side is bordered by a great river. It is from north to south 12 or 13 *li* and from east to west 4 or 5 *li*. The soil is fit for producing cereals, and abounds with fruits and flowers. Here also are dragon-horses and the fragrant turmeric, and medicinal plants.

The climate is cold and stern. There is much snow but little wind. The people wear leather doublets and clothes of white linen. They are light and frivolous, and of a weak, pusillanimous disposition. As the country is protected by a dragon, it has always assumed superiority among neighbouring people. The people are handsome in appearance, but they are given to cunning. They love learning and are well instructed. There are both heretics and believers among them. There are about . . . 5,000 priests. . . .

Hi-mo-ta-lo (Himatala) [6]

This country is an old territory of the country of Tu-ho-lo [i.e., inhabited by speakers of Tokharian, an Indo-European language then spoken also in Chinese Turkistan]. It is about 300 *li* in circuit. It is cut up by mountains and valleys. The soil is rich and fertile, and fit for cereals. It produces much winter wheat. Every kind of plant flourishes, and fruits of all sorts grow in abundance. The climate is cold; the disposition of the men violent and hasty. They do not distinguish between wrong and right. Their appearance is vulgar and ignoble. In respect of their modes of behaviour and forms of etiquette, their clothes of wool, and skin, and felt, they are like the Turks. Their wives wear upon their headdress a wooden horn about three feet or so in length. It has two branches in front, which signify father and mother of the husband. The upper horn denotes the father, the lower one the mother. Whichever of these two dies first, they remove one horn, but when both are dead, they give up this style of headdress.

The first king of this country was a Sakya, fearless and bold. To the west of the T'sung-ling mountains most of the people were subdued to his power. The frontiers were close to the

---

[6] Yule identifies Himatala with Darain.

Turks, and so they adopted their low customs, and suffering from their attacks they protected their frontier. And thus the people of this kingdom were dispersed into different districts, and had many tens of fortified cities, over each of which a separate chief was placed. The people live in tents made of felt, and lead the life of nomads.

. . . .

K'iu-sa-ta-na (Khotan)

Going east from the Taklamakan Desert [Khotan] we enter a great drifting sand desert. These sands extend like a drifting flood for a great distance, piled up or scattered according to the wind. There is no trace left behind by travelers, and oftentimes the way is lost, and so they wander hither and thither quite bewildered, without any guide or direction. So travelers pile up the bones of animals as beacons. There is neither water nor herbage to be found, and hot winds frequently blow. When these winds rise, then both men and beasts become confused and forgetful, and then they remain perfectly disabled. At times sad and plaintive notes are heard and piteous cries, so that between the sights and sounds of this desert men get confused and know not whither they go. Hence there are so many who perish in the journey. But it is all the work of demons and evil spirits.

Going on 400 *li* or so, we arrive at the old kingdom of Tu-ho-lo (Tukhara [Afghanistan]). This country has long been deserted and wild. All the towns are ruined and uninhabited.

From this going east 600 *li* or so, we come to the ancient kingdom of Che-mo-t'o-na, which is the same as the country called Ni-mo. The city walls still stand loftily, but the inhabitants are dispersed and scattered.

From this going northeast a thousand *li* or so, we come to the old country of Navapa [Navopura], which is the same as Leu-lan. We need not speak of the mountains and valleys and soil of this neighbouring country. The habits of the people are wild and unpolished, their manners not uniform; their preferences and dislikes are not always the same. There are some things difficult to verify to the utmost, and it is not always easy to recollect all that has occurred.

IV

MISSIONARIES AND
TRADERS BEFORE
1500

AT THE present time there is a controversy between Russian and Chinese communists about the historical significance of the great Mongol conquests begun by Chingis Khan and carried farther by his sons and grandsons. For the Russians they were an unmitigated disaster. Kiev, which was developing a high culture rivaling that of Western Europe, was ravaged. The Slavs were driven back to poorer, less productive lands, and cut off from the Black Sea trade and the civilizing influences that had flowed to them from Byzantium and the Mediterranean. Only slowly did the Grand Dukes of Moscow begin to build themselves up as a new power in the land—at first by the humiliating function of acting as tribute-collecting agents for the Mongols, until they were strong enough to attack their overlords, the Golden Horde.

The Chinese, on the other hand, believe that the Mongol conquest had some redeeming features. It enlarged the orbit of Chinese geography and history, and within China it brought unification on a grand scale. It was a forced unification, but it did not exhaust China's wealth or destroy its culture. On the contrary, the Mongols favored trade more than most Chinese dynasties (which usually discriminated against merchants in favor of landlords): and promotion of the exchange of goods promoted also the exchange of ideas. For Chinese nationalistic pride, the most important aspect of the traffic in ideas was the spread of Chinese influences westward, along trade routes pacified and policed by the Mongols.

The ideas that naturally occur to Westerners are somewhat different from both the Chinese and the Russian points of view. In Western European history the Mongol invasion, touching the European field of interest from the east, was a conjoint phenomenon with the Crusades, extending the fringes of European interest toward the east. Unlike Russia, Western Europe was not overrun and devastated by the Mongols. At first, when it seemed it might be, the advance of the Mongols was reported with horror and dread. Then, when the advance not only stopped but withdrew from Hungary and the Balkans into Russia, two hopeful ideas began to interest Europe. These ideas had very little general currency in Europe, it is true. They concerned almost exclusively a few statesmen of the time, and a few merchants.

The statesmen, notably the crusading St. Louis, King of France, were intrigued by the idea of persuading the Mongols to attack the Saracens from the rear while Europe attacked them from the front. The Mongols were known not to be Moslems, and this explains the lively European interest in two possibilities—that the legendary Christian king, Prester John, might be found somewhere in the Mongolian domains, and failing that, that the Mongol rulers might themselves be converted to Christianity. These hopes faded when the Westernmost Mongols adopted Islam instead of Christianity.

Among the merchants, especially those of Venice, who were already doing nicely out of the Crusades, the hope was that with the decline of Byzantium, which had been plundered and weakened by the Crusaders, who got there in a fleet chartered from the Venetians, trade could be extended into the lands conquered by the Mongols. Hence the great interest of Marco Polo in emphasizing the law and order that prevailed everywhere under Mongol rule. As this was an age of trade monopolies, he gives away nothing in actual know-how, the details of commodities and the handling of them, but he does engage in what today would be called "institutional" advertising—the promotion of the idea that the trade was there to be got.

Carpini and Rubruck, on the other hand, especially Rubruck, traveling in the mid-thirteenth century as emissaries to the Mongol rulers, were both diplomats and intelligence reporters, as diplomats ought to be, and so included much about trade and trade routes in their notes. Rubruck was an especially acute observer: he was the first European to give an intelligible account of Chinese writing—something not to be found in Marco Polo. John of Montecorvino, though a missionary, was much like the churchmen of the time who were diplomatic envoys—all were concerned with matters of state, and with the rivalries for power and influence that might affect the spread of the religion they represented. John of Monte Corvino was concerned about his predecessors, the Nestorian Christians whom he found holding a position of advantage when he arrived in the Cathay of the Mongols. It is ironic that we owe information about the Nestorians, some of which is obtainable nowhere else, to the dislike and distrust with which they were regarded by their co-religionists of the Roman persuasion.

While the Mongol conquests made it possible for Europeans to travel to Cathay, they also made it possible for Chinese to travel westward. One of these was Ch'ang Ch'un, a Taoist monk who, because of the general reputation of the Taoists for studying the secrets of longevity, and his own personal reputation as a seer versed in the mysteries of nature, was summoned to visit Chingis Khan, then campaigning in Central Asia. Two things are important about this journey. In the first place, the Mongols had not yet conquered more than the fringes of North China. For China as a whole, they were still a menace on the horizon. In the second place, most of North China had by this time been ruled for some three centuries by two barbarian dynasties in succession—the Kitan of the Liao Dynasty, who came from the borderland of Manchuria and Mongolia, and the Jurchid of the Chin Dynasty, who came from the heart of Manchuria. Northwest China was under the rule of still other barbarians, the Tanggud of the Hsi Hsia Dynasty, the founders of which came from Tibet. All during this period, however, Central and South China had continued under the rule of a Chinese dynasty, the Sung. Chinese culture, philosophy, art and poetry not only survived but flourished, and Chinese in the north, like Ch'ang Ch'un, who lived under barbarian rule were oriented culturally not toward their barbarian rulers but toward their southern kinsmen. For reasons like these the report of a traveler like Ch'ang Ch'un was of poignant interest to his countrymen; it was likely to influence the judgment of educated and influential men when they contemplated the likelihood of being conquered by the Mongols. And Ch'ang Ch'un's report gave such an impression of Chingis Khan as a true, all-conquering "Son of Heaven" that it can only have favored appeasement and submission.

The Travels of an Alchemist [1]:
CH'ANG CH'UN

[*When Ch'ang Ch'un, the learned Chinese Taoist priest, was invited by Chingis Khan to visit the Mongol court "10,000 li to the west, the Emperor sent an escort of twenty Mongol warriors to guide and protect the travelers. Ch'ang Ch'un took nineteen of his own followers along, including his pupil Li Chih-ch'ang, the historian of the expedition from whose narrative we quote. In 1219 the party started the long journey which took them north from Peking to Mongolia, southwest through Tashkent and Samarkand and thence south to Perwan (just north of Kabul) in Afghanistan.*]

On the first day of the fourth month (April 24) we reached Prince Tämügä's encampment. By now the ice was beginning to melt and there was a faint touch of colour in the grass. When we arrived a marriage was being celebrated in the camp. From five hundred *li* [2] round the headmen of the tribes had come, with presents of mares' milk, to join in the feast. The black wagons and felt tents stood in rows; there must have been several thousand of them.

On the seventh day the Master interviewed the Great Prince, who questioned him concerning the possibility of extending one's span of life. The Master said that only those who had fasted and observed certain rules could be told of these things.

---

[1] From *Travels of an Alchemist*, translated by Arthur Waley.
[2] A *li* is about one third of a mile.

It was agreed that he should receive instruction on the day of the full moon. But by then heavy snow was falling and the matter was overlooked. Or rather, His Highness seemed to have changed his mind, for he now said that it would be improper for him to anticipate his father in receiving instruction from one whom the Great Khan had been at pains to summon from so great a distance. But he ordered A-li-hsien to bring the Master back to him after the interview with the Emperor was over.

.   .   .   .

In this country it is cold in the morning and hot in the evening; there are many plants with yellow flowers. The river flows to the north-east. On both banks grow many tall willows. The Mongols use them to make the frame-work of their tents. After sixteen days traveling we came to a point where the Keru-len makes a loop to the north-west, skirting some mountains. We therefore could not follow it to its source, but turned south-west, into the Yü-ērh-li post-road. Here the Mongols we met were delighted to see the Master, saying they had been expecting him since the year before. . . .

The peaks of the great mountains were now gradually becoming visible. From this point onwards, as we traveled west, the country remained hilly and well-inhabited. The people live in black wagons and white tents; they are all herdsmen and hunters. Their clothes are made of hides and fur; they live on meat and curdled milk. The men wear their hair in two plaits that hang behind the ears. The married women wear a head-dress of birch-bark, some two feet high. This they generally cover with a black woollen stuff; but some of the richer women use red silk. The end (of this head-dress) is like a duck; they call it *ku-ku*. They are in constant fear of people knocking against it, and are obliged to go backwards and crouching through the doorways of their tents.

On the 27th day of the eighth month (September 15th) we reached the foot of the Yin Shan. Here some Uighurs came out to meet us, and presently we reached a small town. The ruler of the place brought us grape-wine, choice fruits, large cakes, huge onions, and strips of Persian linen, a foot for each person. . . .

Further west is the large town of Beshbalig. The king's officers, with many of the nobles and people, and some hundred

Buddhist and Taoist (? Manichean) priests came in great state
a long way out of the town to meet us. The Buddhist priests
were all dressed in brown. The head-dresses and robes of the
Taoists were quite different from those worn in China.

. . . .

On the eighteenth day of the eleventh month (December 3rd,
1221) after crossing a great river, we reached the northern out-
skirts of the mighty city of Samarkand. The Civil Governor his
Highness I-la, together with the Mongol and local authorities,
came to meet us outside the town. They brought wine and set
up a great number of tents. Here we brought our wagons to a
stop. . . .

The town is built along canals. As no rain falls during the
summer and autumn, two rivers have been diverted so as to run
along every street, thus giving a supply of water to all the inhabitants. Before the defeat of the Khwārizm Shah there was a
fixed population here of more than 100,000 households; but
now there is only about a quarter this number, of whom a very
large proportion are native Hui-ho. But these people are quite
unable to manage their fields and orchards for themselves, and
are obliged to call in Chinese, Kitai and Tanguts. The administration of the town is also conducted by people of very various
nationality. Chinese craftsmen are found everywhere. Within
the city is a mound about a hundred feet high on which stands
the Khwārizm Shah's new palace. . . .

The Governor gave a banquet in his honour, and sent ten
pieces of gold brocade, but the Master would not receive them.
After that he sent a monthly allowance of rice, corn-flour, salt,
oil, fruits, vegetables and so on; he became every day more attentive and respectful. Noticing that the Master drank very
little he begged to be allowed to press a hundred pounds of
grapes and make him some new wine. But the Master answered:
"I do not need wine. But let me have the hundred pounds of
grapes; they will enable me to entertain my visitors."

These grapes keep for a whole winter. We also saw peacocks
and large elephants which come from India, several thousand *li*
to the south-east.

. . . .

At the end of the intercalary month (February 12th, 1222) the envoy and his horsemen returned from their reconnoitring. Liu Wēn reported to the Master that the Khan's second son (Chagatai) had advanced with his troops and repaired the damaged boats and bridges. The local bandits were dispersed, Ho-la, Pa-hai and others had been to the Prince's camp and informed him that the Master desired an audience with the Emperor. The prince replied that his father had proceeded to the southeast of the Great Snow Mountains (Hindukush), but that the snow in the mountain pass at present lay very deep for more than a hundred *li,* and it would be impossible to get through. The prince, however, pointed out that his own encampment lay directly on the route to the Emperor's, and invited the Master to stay with him, till a journey across the mountains was practicable.

.   .   .   .

Hence we traveled south-east, and towards evening halted near an ancient canal. On its banks grew reeds of a peculiar kind not found in China. The larger ones keep green all through the winter. Some of these we took and made into walking-sticks. Some we used that night to hold up the wagon-shafts, and so strong were they that they did not break. On the small reeds the leaves fall off in winter and grow afresh in the spring. A little to the south, in the hills, there is a large bamboo with pith inside. This is used by the soldiers to make lances and spears. We also saw lizards about three feet long, blue-black in colour.

It was now the twenty-ninth of the third month (May 11th) and the Master made a poem. After four more days of traveling we reached the Khan's camp. He sent his high officer, Ho-la-po-tē to meet us. . . . When arrangements had been made for the Master's lodging, he at once presented himself to the Emperor, who expressed his gratitude, saying: "Other rulers summoned you, but you would not go to them. And now you have come ten thousand *li* to see me. I take this as a high compliment."

The Master replied: "That I, a hermit of the mountains, should come at your Majesty's bidding was the will of Heaven." Chingiz was delighted, begged him to be seated and ordered food to be served. Then he asked him: "Adept, what Medicine of Long Life have you brought me from afar?" The Master replied: "I have means of protecting life, but no elixir that will prolong it." The Emperor was pleased with his candour, and had two tents for the Master and his disciples set up to the east of his own. . . .

The weather was becoming very hot and the Emperor now moved to a high point on the Snow Mountains to escape the heat, and the Master accompanied him. The Emperor appointed the fourteenth of the fourth month (June 24th) as the day on which he would question the Master about the Way. This engagement was recorded by his state officers, Chinkai, Liu Wēn and A-li-hsien, as well as by three of his personal attendants. But just as the time was arriving, news came that the native mountain bandits were in insurrection. The Emperor was determined to deal with them himself, and put off the meeting till the first of the tenth month (November 5th). The Master begged that he might be allowed to return to his former quarters in the city. "Then," said the Khan, "you will have the fatigue of traveling all the way back here again." The Master said it was only a matter of twenty days journey, and when the Khan objected that he had no one whom he could give him as an escort the Master suggested the envoy Yang A-kou. . . .

We crossed a great mountain where there is a "stone gate," the pillars of which look like tapering candles. Lying across them at the top is a huge slab of rock, which forms a sort of bridge. The stream below is very swift, and our horsemen in goading the pack-asses across lost many of them by drowning. On the banks of the stream were the carcases of other animals that had perished in the same way. The place is a frontier pass, which the troops had quite recently stormed. When we got out of the defile, the Master wrote two poems.

Now when he reached the Khan's camp, at the end of the third month the grass was green and trees everywhere in bloom, and the sheep and horses were well grown. But when with the Khan's permission he left, at the end of the fourth month, there was no longer a blade of grass or any vegetation. On this subject the Master wrote a set of verses.

John of Plano Carpini

[*John of Plano Carpini and William of Rubruck give us the first authentic accounts of the meeting of western Christendom and the Far East at a dramatic time in history—the thirteenth century when the entire oriental world was being torn apart and then linked together again in a new way, with the Middle East and Russia by Chingis Khan and his followers.*

[*By 1245 Russia had become a province of the Mongol Empire, and the new pope, Innocent IV, fearing further onslaught on western Europe, sent two Franciscans, Lawrence of Portugal and John of Plano Carpini (1245–1247), to attempt to avert the threat. John was a prominent member of his order in western Europe, but was sixty-five years old, fat, and had no foreign language. He was more a political ambassador than a missionary, and his book is the most widely known of all the early European accounts of the Mongols.*

[*The following excerpts* [3] *describe how he traveled to the Mongol capital, Karakoram, where he witnessed the enthronement of Guyuk as Great Khan. He concluded that a great new campaign against the West was being planned, to which the West must submit. He brought back a letter to the Pope from the Khan.*

[*Important additional information gathered by Carpini and his companions has now been published in the* Tartar Relation *bound up with the* Vinland Map *(Yale University Press, 1965).*]

We entered the land of the Mongols, whom we call Tartars. We were, I think, journeying through this country for three weeks riding hard, and on the feast of St. Mary Magdalene [July 22nd] we reached Cuyuc, who is now Emperor. We made the whole of this journey at great speed, for our Tartars had been ordered to take us quickly so that we could arrive in time for the solemn court which had been convened several years back for the election. And so we started at dawn and journeyed until night without a meal, and many a time we arrived so late that we did not eat that night but were given in the

[3] From *The Mongol Mission*, by Christopher Dawson.

morning the food we should have eaten the previous evening. We went as fast as the horses could trot, for the horses were in no way spared since we had fresh ones several times a day, and those which fell out returned, as has already been described, and so we rode swiftly without a break.

On our arrival Cuyuc had us given a tent and provisions, such as it is the custom for the Tartars to give, but they treated us better than other envoys. Nevertheless we were not invited to visit him for he had not yet been elected, nor did he yet concern himself with the government. The translation of the Lord Pope's letter, however, and the things I had said had been sent to him by Bati. After we had stayed there for five or six days he sent us to his mother where the solemn court was assembling. By the time we got there a large pavilion had already been put up made of white velvet, and in my opinion it was so big that more than two thousand men could have got into it. Around it had been erected a wooden palisade, on which various designs were painted. On the second or third day we went with the Tartars who had been appointed to look after us and there all the chiefs were assembled and each one was riding with his followers among the hills and over the plains round about.

On the first day they were all clothed in white velvet, on the second in red—that day Cuyuc came to the tent—on the third day they were all in blue velvet and on the fourth in the finest brocade. In the palisade round the pavilion were two large gates, through one of which the Emperor alone had the right to enter and there were no guards placed at it although it was open, for no one dare enter or leave by it; through the other gate all those who were granted admittance entered and there were guards there with swords and bows and arrows. If anyone approached the tent beyond the fixed limits, he was beaten if caught; if he ran away he was shot at, but with arrows however which had no heads. The horses were, I suppose, two arrow-flights away. The chiefs went about everywhere armed and accompanied by a number of their men, but none, unless their group of ten was complete, could go as far as the horses; indeed those who attempted to do so were severely beaten. There were many of them who had, as far as I could judge, about twenty marks' worth of gold on their bits, breastplates, saddles and cruppers. The chiefs held their conference inside the tent and, so I believe, conducted the election. All the other people however were a long way away outside the afore-mentioned palisade. There they remained until almost mid-day and then they began to drink mare's milk and they drank until the evening, so much that it was amazing to see. We were invited inside and they gave us mead as we would not take mare's milk. They did this to show us great honour, but they kept on plying us with drinks to such an extent that we could not possibly stand it, not being used to it, so we gave them to understand that it was disagreeable to us and they left off pressing us. . . .

There were more than four thousand envoys there, counting those who were carrying tribute, those who were bringing gifts, the Sultans and other chiefs who were coming to submit to them, those summoned by the Tartars and the governors of territories. All these were put together outside the palisade and they were given drinks at the same time, but when we were outside with them we and Duke Jerozlaus were always given the best places. I think, if I remember rightly, that we had been there a good four weeks when, as I believe, the election took place; the result however was not made public at that time; the chief ground for my supposition was that whenever Cuyuc left the tent they sang before him and as long as he remained outside they dipped to him beautiful rods on the top of which was scarlet wool, which they did not do for any of the other chiefs. They call this court the Sira Orda.

Leaving there we rode all together for three or four leagues to another place, where on a pleasant plain near a river among the mountains another tent had been set up, which is called by them the Golden Orda; it was here that Cuyuc was to be enthroned on the feast of the Assumption of Our Lady, but owing to the hail which fell, the ceremony was put off. This tent was supported by columns covered with gold plates and fastened to other wooden beams with nails of gold, and the roof above and the sides on the interior were of brocade, but outside they were of other materials. We were there until the feast of St. Bartholomew, on which day a vast crowd assembled. They stood facing south, so arranged that some of them were a stone's throw away from the others, and they kept moving forward, going further and further away, saying prayers and genuflecting towards the south. We however, not knowing whether they were uttering incantations or bending the knee to God or another, were unwilling to genuflect. After they had done this for a considerable time, they returned to the tent and placed Cuyuc on the imperial throne, and the chiefs knelt before him and after them all the people, with the exception of us who were not subject to them. Then they started drinking and, as is their custom, they drank without stopping until the evening. After that cooked meat was brought in carts without any salt and they gave one joint between four or five men. Inside however they gave meat with salted broth as sauce and they did this on all the days that they held a feast.

At that place we were summoned into the presence of the Emperor, and Chingay the protonotary wrote down our names and the names of those who had sent us, also the names of the chief of the Solangi and of others, and then calling out in a loud voice he recited them before the Emperor and all the chiefs. When this was finished each one of us genuflected four times on the left knee and they warned us not to touch the lower part of the threshold. After we had been most thoroughly searched for knives and they had found nothing at all, we entered by a door on the east side, for no one dare enter from the west with the sole exception of the Emperor or, if it is a chief's tent, the chief; those of lower rank do not pay much attention to such things. This was the first time since Cuyuc had been made Emperor that we had entered his tent in his presence. He also received all the envoys in that place, but very few entered his tent.

.   .   .   .

. . . A lofty platform of boards had been erected, on which the Emperor's throne was placed. The throne, which was of ivory, was wonderfully carved and there was also gold on it, and precious stones, if I remember rightly, and pearls. Steps led up to it and it was rounded behind. Benches were also placed round the throne, and here the ladies sat in their seats on the left; nobody, however, sat on the right, but the chiefs were on benches in the middle and the rest of the people sat beyond them. Every day a great crowd of ladies came.

The three tents of which I have spoken were very large. The

Emperor's wives however had other tents of white felt, which were quite big and beautiful. At that place they separated, the Emperor's mother going in one direction and the Emperor in another to administer justice. The mistress of the Emperor had been arrested; she had murdered his father with poison at the time when their army was in Hungary and as a result the army in these parts retreated. Judgment was passed on her along with a number of others and they were put to death.

At the same time the death occurred of Jerozlaus, Grand Duke in a part of Russia called Susdal. He was invited by the Emperor's mother, who gave him to eat and drink with her own hand as if to show him honour. On his return to his lodging he was immediately taken ill and died seven days later and his whole body turned bluish-grey in a strange fashion. This made everybody think that he had been poisoned there, so that the Tartars could obtain free and full possession of his lands. An additional proof of this is the fact that straightway, without the knowledge of Jerozlaus's suite there, the Emperor sent a messenger post haste to Russia to his son Alexander telling him to come as he wished to give him his father's lands. Alexander was willing to go but waited, in the meantime sending a letter saying that he would come and receive his father's lands. Everybody, however, believed that if he did come he would be put to death or at least imprisoned for life.

After the death of Jerozlaus, if I remember the time correctly, our Tartars took us to the Emperor. When he heard from them that we had come to him he ordered us to go back to his mother, the reason being that he wished on the following day to raise his banner against the whole of the Western world—we were told this definitely by men who knew, as I have mentioned above—and he wanted us to be kept in ignorance of this. On our return we stayed for a few days, then we went back to him again and remained with him for a good month, enduring such hunger and thirst that we could scarcely keep alive, for the food provided for four was barely sufficient for one, moreover, we were unable to find anything to buy, for the market was a very long way off. If the Lord had not sent us a certain Russian, by name Cosmas, a goldsmith and a great favourite of the Emperor, who supported us to some extent, we would, I believe, have died, unless the Lord had helped us in some other way.

Before the enthronement Cosmas showed us the Emperor's throne which he himself had made and his seal which he had fashioned, and he also told us what the inscription was on the seal. We picked up many other bits of private information about the Emperor from men who had come with other chiefs, a number of Russians and Hungarians knowing Latin and French, and Russian clerics and others, who had been among the Tartars, some for thirty years, through wars and other happenings, and who knew all about them, for they knew the language and had lived with them continually some twenty years, others ten, some more, some less. With the help of these men we were able to gain a thorough knowledge of everything. They told us about everything willingly and sometimes without being asked, for they knew what we wanted.

.   .   .   .

The present Emperor may be forty or forty-five years old or more; he is of medium height, very intelligent and extremely shrewd, and most serious and grave in his manner. He is never seen to laugh for a slight cause nor to indulge in any frivolity, so we were told by the Christians who are constantly with him. The Christians of his household also told us that they firmly believed he was about to become a Christian, and they have clear evidence of this, for he maintains Christian clerics and provides them with supplies of Christian things; in addition he always has a chapel before his chief tent and they sing openly and in public and beat the board for services after the Greek fashion like other Christians, however big a crowd of Tartars or other men be there. The other chiefs do not behave like this.

Two days later, that is to say on the feast of St. Brice [November 13th], they gave us a permit to depart and a letter sealed with the Emperor's seal, and sent us to the Emperor's mother. She gave each of us a fox-skin cloak, which had the fur outside and was lined inside, and a length of velvet; our Tartars stole a good yard from each of the pieces of velvet and from the piece given to our servant they stole more than half. This did not escape our notice, but we preferred not to make a fuss about it.

We then set out on the return journey. We traveled throughout the winter, often sleeping in the desert on the snow except when we were able to clear a place with our feet. When there were no trees but only open country we found ourselves many a time completely covered with snow driven by the wind. . . .

The Journey of William of Rubruck [4]

[*William of Rubruck was probably a native of Flanders and his birth and death dates are unknown. His emphasis is on the western and Mongolian parts of the Mongol Empire; he did not enter China. After his Mongolian journey he was detained in Palestine by his order until he obtained the King's permission to return to Paris. Here he met Roger Bacon, whom he seems to have fascinated, for Bacon refers to him at length in his* Opus Majus, *the only contemporary account of him which we have. Thanks to Bacon, interest in William of Rubruck grew in England, where the only manuscripts of this great medieval traveler survive. Where Marco Polo gives us the traveler's tale of a merchant interested in wealth and luxury, the agents of the Pope and King Louis the Crusader compiled what were essentially intelligence reports. In fact they represented the CIA (Christian Intelligence Agency) of their time.*

[*William's mission for the French king to the court of the great Khan consisted of two Franciscans, himself and Bartholomew of Cremona, a clerk named Gosset who was in charge of the presents for the Khan, and an* inefficient *dragoman named Abdullah, Latinized as "Homo Dei."* Leaving *the French court at Acre they entered the Mongol* world *through eastern Europe and Russia via the old highway to Central Asia, through Constantinople and the Crimea.*]

Friar William of Rubruck, least in the Order of Friars Minor, to the most excellent Lord and most Christian Louis, by the grace of God illustrious King of the French, health and continual triumph in Christ.

.   .   .   .

And so on the third day after leaving Soldaia we came across the Tartars; when I came among them it seemed indeed to me

[4] From *The Mongol Mission*, edited by Christopher Dawson.

as if I were stepping into some other world, the life and customs of which I will describe for you as well as I can.

The Tartars and Their Dwellings

The Tartars have no abiding city nor do they know of the one that is to come. They have divided among themselves Scythia, which stretches from the Danube as far as the rising of the sun. Each captain, according to whether he has more or fewer men under him, knows the limits of his pasturage and where to feed his flocks in winter, summer, spring and autumn, for in winter they come down to the warmer districts in the south, in summer they go up to the cooler ones in the north. They drive their cattle to graze on the pasture lands without water in winter when there is snow there, for the snow provides them with water.

The dwelling in which they sleep has as its base a circle of interlaced sticks, and it is made of the same material; these sticks converge into a little circle at the top and from this a neck juts up like a chimney; they cover it with white felt and quite often they also coat the felt with lime or white clay and powdered bone to make it a more gleaming white, and sometimes they make it black. The felt round the neck at the top they decorate with lovely and varied paintings. Before the doorway they also hang felt worked in multicoloured designs; they sew coloured felt on to the other, making vines and trees, birds and animals. They make these houses so large that sometimes they are thirty feet across; for I myself once measured the width between the wheel tracks of a cart, and it was twenty feet, and when the house was on the cart it stuck out at least five feet beyond the wheels on each side. I have counted to one cart twenty-two oxen drawing one house, eleven in a row across the width of the cart, and the other eleven in front of them. The axle of the cart was as big as the mast of a ship, and a man stood at the door of the house on the cart, driving the oxen.

In addition they make squares to the size of a large coffer out of slender split twigs; then over it, from one end to the other, they build up a rounded roof out of similar twigs and they make a little entrance at the front end; after that they cover this box or little house with black felt soaked in tallow or ewes' milk so that it is rain-proof, and this they decorate in the same way with multicoloured handwork. Into these chests they put all their bedding and valuables; they bind them onto high carts which are drawn by camels so that they can cross rivers. These chests are never removed from the carts. When they take down their dwelling houses, they always put the door facing the south; then afterwards they draw up the carts with the chests on each side, half a stone's throw from the house, so that it stands between two rows of carts, as it were between two walls.

The married women make for themselves really beautiful carts which I would not know how to describe for you except by a picture; in fact I would have done you paintings of everything if I only knew how to paint. A wealthy Mongol or Tartar may well have a hundred or two hundred such carts with chests. Baatu has twenty-six wives and each of these has a large house, not counting the other small ones which are placed behind the large one and which are, as it were, chambers in which their attendants live; belonging to each of these houses are a good two hundred carts. When they pitch their houses the chief wife places her dwelling at the extreme west end and after her the others according to their rank, so that the last wife will be at the far east end, and there will be the space of a stone's throw between the establishment of one wife and that of another. And so the *orda* [camp, headquarters] of a rich Mongol will look like a large town and yet there will be very few men in it.

One woman will drive twenty or thirty carts, for the country is flat. They tie together the carts, which are drawn by oxen or camels, one after the other, and the woman will sit on the front one driving the ox while all the others follow in step. If they happen to come on a bad bit of track they loose them and lead them across it one by one. They go at a very slow pace, as a sheep or an ox might walk.

When they have pitched their houses with the door facing south, they arrange the master's couch at the northern end. The women's place is always on the east side, that is, on the left of the master of the house when he is sitting on his couch looking towards the south; the men's place is on the west side, that is, to his right.

On entering a house the men would by no means hang up their quiver in the women's section. Over the head of the master there is always an idol like a doll or little image of felt which they call the master's brother, and a similar one over the head of the mistress, and this they call the mistress's brother; they are fastened on to the wall. Higher up between these two is a thin little one which is, as it were, the guardian of the whole house. The mistress of the house places on her right side, at the foot of the couch, in a prominent position, a goat-skin stuffed with wool or other material, and next to it a tiny image turned towards her attendants and the women. By the entrance on the women's side is still another idol with a cow's udder for the women who milk the cows, for this is the women's job. On the other side of the door towards the men is another image with a mare's udder for the men who milk the mares.

When they have foregathered for a drink they first sprinkle with the drink the idol over the master's head, then all the other idols in turn; after this an attendant goes out of the house with a cup and some drinks; he sprinkles thrice towards the south, genuflecting each time; this is in honour of fire; next towards the east in honour of the air, and after that to the west in honour of water; they cast it to the north for the dead. When the master is holding his cup in his hand and is about to drink, before he does so he first pours some out on the earth as its share. If he drinks while seated on a horse, before he drinks he pours some over the neck or mane of the horse. And so when the attendant has sprinkled towards the four quarters of the earth he returns into the house; two servants with two cups and as many plates are ready to carry the drink to the master and the wife sitting beside him upon his couch. If he has several wives, she with whom he sleeps at night sits next to him during the day, and on that day all the others have to come to her dwelling to drink, and the court is held there, and the gifts which are presented to the master are placed in the treasury of that wife. Standing in the entrance is a bench with a skin of milk or some other drink and some cups.

In the winter they make an excellent drink from rice, millet, wheat and honey, which is clear like wine. Wine, too, is conveyed to them from distant regions. In the summer they do not bother about anything except cosmos. Cosmos [koumiss, kumys] is always to be found inside the house before the entrance door, and near it stands a musician with his instrument. Our lutes and viols I did not see there but many other instruments such as are not known among us. When the master begins to drink, then one of the attendants cries out in a loud voice. "Ha!" and the musician strikes his instrument. And when it is a big feast they are holding, they all clap their hands and also dance to the sound of the instrument, the men before the master and the women before the mistress. . . .

As for their food and victuals I must tell you they eat all dead animals indiscriminately and with so many flocks and herds you can be sure a great many animals do die. However, in the summer as long as they have any cosmos, that is mare's milk, they do not care about any other food. If during that time an ox or a horse happens to die, they dry the flesh by cutting it into thin strips and hanging it in the sun and the wind, and it dries immediately without salt and without any unpleasant smell. Out of the intestines of horses they make sausages which are better than pork sausages and they eat these fresh; the rest of the meat they keep for the winter. From the hide of oxen they make large jars which they dry in a wonderful way in the smoke. From the hind part of horses' hide they make very nice shoes.

They feed fifty or a hundred men with the flesh of a single sheep, for they cut it up in little bits in a dish with salt and water, making no other sauce; then with the point of a knife or a fork especially made for this purpose—like those with which we are accustomed to eat pears and apples cooked in wine—they offer to each of those standing round one or two mouthfuls, according to the number of guests. Before the flesh of the sheep is served, the master first takes what pleases him; and also if he gives anyone a special portion then the one receiving it has to eat it himself and may give it to no one else. But if he cannot eat it all he may take it away with him or give it to his servant, if he is there, to keep for him; otherwise he may put it away in his *captargac,* that is, a square bag which they carry to put all such things in: in this they also keep bones when they have not the time to give them a good gnaw, so that later they may gnaw them and no food be wasted.

How They Make Cosmos [Kumys]

Cosmos, that is mare's milk, is made in this way: they stretch along the ground a long rope attached to two stakes stuck into the earth, and at about nine o'clock they tie to this rope the foals of the mares they want to milk. Then the mothers stand near their foals and let themselves be peacefully milked; if any one of them is too restless, then a man takes the foal and, placing it under her, lets it suck a little, and he takes it away again and the milker takes it place.

And so, when they have collected a great quantity of milk, which is as sweet as cow's milk when it is fresh, they pour it into a large skin or bag and they begin churning it with a specially made stick which is as big as a man's head at its lower end, and hollowed out; and when they beat it quickly it begins to bubble like new wine and to turn sour and ferment, and they churn it until they can extract the butter. Then they taste it and when it is fairly pungent they drink it. As long as one is drinking, it bites the tongue like vinegar; when one stops, it leaves on the tongue the taste of milk of almonds and greatly delights the inner man; it even intoxicates those who have not a very good head. It also greatly provokes urine.

For use of the great lords they also make caracosmos, that is black cosmos, in this wise. Mare's milk does not curdle. Now it is a general rule that the milk of any animal, in the stomach of whose young rennet is not found, does not curdle; it is not found in the stomach of a young horse, hence the milk of a mare does not curdle. And so they churn the milk until everything that is solid in it sinks right to the bottom like the lees of wine, and what is pure remains on top and is like whey or white must. The dregs are very white and are given to the slaves and have a most soporific effect. The clear liquid the masters drink and it is certainly a very pleasant drink and really potent.

. . . .

I will tell you about their garments and their clothing. From Cathay and other countries to the east, and also from Persia and other districts of the south, come cloths of silk and gold and cotton materials which they wear in the summer. From Russia, Moxel, Great Bulgaria and Pascatu, which is Greater Hungary, and Kerkis, which are all districts towards the north, and full of forests, and from many other regions in the north which are subject to them, valuable furs of many kinds are brought for them, such as I have never seen in our part of the world; and these they wear in winter. In the winter they always make at least two fur garments, one with the fur against the body, the other with the fur outside to the wind and snow, and these are usually of the skins of wolves or foxes or monkeys, and when they are sitting in their dwelling they have another softer one. The poor make their outer ones of dog and goat.

They also make trousers out of skins. Moreover, the rich line their garments with silk stuffing which is extraordinarily soft and light and warm. The poor line their clothes with cotton material and with the softer wool which they are able to pick out from the coarser. With the coarse they make felt to cover their dwellings and coffers and also for making bedding. Also with wool mixed with a third part horse-hair they make their ropes. From felt they make saddle pads, saddle cloths and rain cloaks, which means they use a great deal of wool. . . .

.   .   .   .

As for their marriages, you must know that no one there has a wife unless he buys her, which means that sometimes girls are quite grown up before they marry, for their parents always keep them until they sell them. They observe the first and second degrees of consanguinity, but observe no degrees of affinity; they have two sisters at the same time or one after the other. No widow among them marries, the reason being that they believe that all those who serve them in this life will serve them in the next, and so of a widow they believe that she will always return after death to her first husband. This gives rise to a shameful custom among them whereby a son sometimes takes to wife all his father's wives, except his own mother; for the orda of a father and mother always falls to the youngest son and so he himself has to provide for all his father's wives who come to him with his father's effects; and then, if he so wishes, he uses them as wives, for he does not consider an injury has been done to him if they return to his father after death.

.   .   .   .

Mangu's Court

The Chan was sitting on a couch wearing a speckled and shiny fur like seal-skin. He is a flat-nosed man of medium height, about forty-five years old; a young wife was sitting next to him and a grown-up daughter, who was very ugly, Cirina by name, was sitting on a couch behind them with some little children. For that dwelling had belonged to one of his wives, a Christian, whom he had loved deeply and by whom he had had the said daughter. Although he had introduced in addition the young wife, nevertheless the daughter was mistress of all that court which had belonged to her mother.

Then the Chan had them ask us whether we would like to drink wine or *terracina,* that is rice wine, or caracosmos, that is clear mares' milk, or *bal,* that is mead made from honey, for these are the four drinks they use in winter. I replied: "Sir, we are not men seeking our desire in drink; whatever pleases you satisfies us." Then he had some of the rice drink brought for us, it is clear and tastes like white wine; out of respect to him we sipped it for a short time. To our misfortune our interpreter was standing near the cup-bearers, who gave him a great deal to drink and he got drunk immediately. . . .

Then I spoke:

"First of all we render thanks and praise to God Who has brought us from such far distant regions to see Mangu Chan to whom He has given great power on earth. And we pray Christ, under Whose dominion we all live and die, that He will grant him a good and long life."

For they always wish a blessing to be asked on their life. Then I told him:

"Sir, we heard that Sartach was a Christian and the Christians who heard this were delighted, especially my Lord the French King. And so we went to him and my Lord the King sent him a letter by us containing words of peace, and among other things he testified as to what kind of men we are and requested him to allow us to remain in his territory; for our office is to teach men to live according to the law of God. Sartach, however, sent us to his father, Baatu; Baatu sent us here to you. You are a man to whom God has given great dominion on earth, we therefore beg Your Puissance to grant us leave to stay in your country to carry out the service of God on behalf of you, your wives and your children. We have neither gold nor silver nor precious stones which we could present to you; we have but ourselves and we offer ourselves to serve God and pray to Him for you. At least give us permission to stay here until the cold has passed, for my companion is so weak that he can in no wise, without endangering his life, bear to ride any further.". . .

Then the Chan began to reply: "Just as the sun spreads its rays in all directions, so my power and the power of Baatu is spread everywhere. Therefore we have no need of your gold or silver." Up to this point I understood my interpreter but beyond this I could not grasp a single complete sentence, which showed me clearly that he was drunk. And Mangu Chan himself appeared to me intoxicated. He ended however by saying, so it seemed to me, that he was not pleased that we had gone to Sartach first rather than to him. Then I, seeing my interpreter's incapacity, kept quiet, except that I begged him not to be offended at what I had said about gold and silver, for I had said it not because he had need of or desired such things, but rather because we would gladly have honoured him with both temporal and spiritual gifts.

He then told us to get up from our knees and sit down again and after a short time we took leave of him and went out, and his secretaries and his interpreter, who is bringing up one of his daughters, went with us. . . .

. . . They assigned a man to us to look after us and we went to the monk. When we were coming away from him in order to return to our lodging, the aforementioned interpreter came to meet us and said: "Mangu Chan has pity on you and grants you permission to stay here for the space of two months, by which time the intense cold will be over, and he informs you that ten days' journey from here there is a fine city called Caracorum; if you wish to go there he will have you provided with all that you need; if however you wish to remain here you may and you will have what is needful; it will however be wearisome for you to ride with the *orda*." I replied: "May the Lord keep Mangu Chan and grant him a long and good life! We have found here this monk and we believe that he is a holy man and has come to these parts by the will of God, and so we would like to stay with him seeing that we too are monks and we could say our prayers together for the Chan's good estate." He then left us in silence.

The day of the Epiphany [January 6th] was approaching and the Armenian monk, Sergius by name, told me that he was going to baptize Mangu Chan on the day of the feast. I begged him to do all in his power to enable me to be present so that I could bear witness of what I had actually seen, and he promised he would.

The day of the feast arrived and the monk did not send for me, but at midday I was summoned to the court, and I saw the monk coming away from there with some priests, and he had his cross and the priests a thurible and a Gospel-book. On that day Mangu Chan had made a great feast; and it is his custom to hold court on such days as his soothsayers tell him are feast days or the Nestorian priests say are for some reason sacred. On these days the Christian priests come first with their paraphernalia, and they pray for him and bless his cup; when they retire the Saracen priests come and do likewise; they are followed by the pagan priests who do the same. The monk told me that the Chan only believes in the Christians; however, he wishes them all to come and pray for him. But he was lying, for he does not believe in any of them as you will hear later; yet they all follow his court like flies honey, and he gives to them all and they all think they enjoy his special favour and they all prophesy good fortune for him.

.   .   .   .

After our arrival at Mangu's orda, he only moved camp in a southerly direction twice; after that he began to return northwards, that is towards Caracorum. . . .

From the place where I found Mangu Chan as far as Cathay, it was twenty days' journey in a southeasterly direction; as far as Onankerule which is the Mongols' own territory where Chingis' orda is, it was ten days' journey due east; and as far as this eastern district there was not a town to be found. There was, however, a tribe called Su-Mongol, that is Mongols of the water, for "su" is the same as water. These men live on fish and by hunting, for they have neither flocks of sheep nor herds of cattle. Similarly towards the north there is no town, but a poor tribe who keep cattle and are called Kerkis. There are also the Orengai there who bind polished bones under their feet and propel themselves over the frozen snow and ice at such a speed that they can catch birds and animals.

.   .   .   .

Mangu's Palace at Caracorum, and
the Feast of Easter

At Caracorum Mangu has a large orda close by the city walls; it is surrounded by a brick wall as are our priories of monks. There is a large palace there in which he holds his drinking festival twice in the year, once round about Easter when he passes by that way and once in the summer on his return. The second is the more important for on that occasion there assemble at his court all the nobles anywhere within a two months' journey; and then he bestows on them garments and presents and displays his great glory. There are many other buildings there, long like barns, and in these are stored his provisions and treasures.

At the entrance to this palace, seeing it would have been unseemly to put skins of milk and other drinks there, Master William of Paris has made for him a large silver tree, at the foot of which are four silver lions each having a pipe and all belching forth white mares' milk. Inside the trunk four pipes lead up to the top of the tree and the ends of the pipes are bent downwards and over each of them is a gilded serpent, the tail of which twines round the trunk of the tree. One of these pipes pours out wine, another caracosmos, that is the refined milk of mares, another *boal*, which is a honey drink, and another rice mead, which is called *terracina*. Each of these has its silver basin ready to receive it at the foot of the tree between the other four pipes. At the very top he fashioned an angel holding a trumpet; underneath the tree he made a crypt in which a man can be secreted, and a pipe goes up to the angel through the middle of the heart of the tree. At first he had made bellows but they did not give enough wind. Outside the palace there is a chamber in which the drinks are stored, and servants stand there ready to pour them out when they hear the angel sounding the trumpet. The tree has branches, leaves and fruit of silver.

And so when the drinks are getting low the chief butler calls out to the angel to sound his trumpet. Then, hearing this, the man who is hidden in the crypt blows the pipe going up to the angel with all his strength, and the angel, placing the trumpet to his mouth, sounds it very loudly. When the servants in the chamber hear this each one of them pours out his drink into its proper pipe, and the pipes pour them out from above and below into the basins prepared for this, and then the cup-bearers draw the drinks and carry them round the palace to the men and women.

The palace is like a church with a middle nave and two side aisles beyond two rows of pillars and there are three doors on the south side; inside before the middle door stands the tree, and the Chan himself sits at the northern end high up so that he can be seen by everyone; and there are two stairways leading up to him, and the man bringing him his cup goes up by the one and comes down by the other. The space in the middle between the tree and the steps up to him is empty, and there the cup-bearer stands and also envoys who are bringing gifts. The Chan sits up there like a god. On his right-hand side, that is to the west, are the men, on the left the women, for the palace extends from the north southwards. To the south, next to the pillars on the right, are rows of seats raised up like a balcony, on which sit his son and brothers. It is the same on the left where his wives and daughters sit. Only one wife sits up there beside him; she however is not as high up as he is.

When the Chan heard that the work was finished he gave orders to the master to place it in position and get it in working order, and he himself about Passion Sunday went ahead with the small dwellings leaving the large ones behind. The monk and we followed him and he sent us another bottle of wine. He journeyed through mountainous districts and there was a strong wind and severe cold and a heavy fall of snow. Consequently about midnight the Chan sent to the monk and us asking us to pray to God to lessen the cold and the wind, for all the animals accompanying them were in danger, especially because at that season they were with young and bringing forth. Thereupon the monk sent him some incense, bidding him put it on the coals as an offering to God. I do not know if he did this, but the storm, which had lasted for two days and was already entering on its third, did abate.

On Palm Sunday we were near Caracorum. At dawn we blessed branches of willow, which as yet bore no sign of buds, and about three o'clock we entered the city, the cross raised on high with the banner, and passing the Saracen quarters, where the bazaar and market are, we went to the church. The Nestorians came to meet us in procession. On entering the church we found them ready to celebrate Mass; when this had been celebrated they all received Holy Communion and asked me if I wished to communicate. I replied that I had had a drink and it is not lawful to receive the Sacrament except fasting.

Mass having been said, it was now evening and Master William took us with great joy to his lodging to have supper with him. His wife, who was born in Hungary, was the daughter of a man from Lorraine and she knew French and Coman well. We also came across another man there, Basil by name, the son of an Englishman, who had been born in Hungary and knew the same languages. After supper they accompanied us with great rejoicing to our hut, which the Tartars had set up for us in a square near the church along with the monk's oratory.

The following day the Chan entered his palace and the monk and I and the priests went to him.

And so we made our entrance into that orda, which is very well laid out and in summer they convey streams of water in all directions to irrigate it. We next entered the palace, which was full of men and women, and we stood before the Chan having at our backs the tree I have mentioned which together with its basins occupied a large part of the palace; the priests brought two little blessed cakes of bread and fruit on a dish which they presented to the Chan after they had pronounced a blessing, and a butler took them to him as he sat there in a place very high and lifted up. He immediately began to eat one of the cakes and sent the other to his son and his younger brother, who is being brought up by a Nestorian and knows the Gospel, and he also sent for my Bible so that he could look at it. After the priests the monk said his prayer, and I after the monk. Then the Chan promised that the following day he would come to the church, which is quite large and beautiful, and the roof above is all covered with silk interwoven with gold. The following day he went on his way, sending a message of excuse to the priests saying he dared not come to the church for he had learned that the dead were carried there.

We however stayed behind at Caracorum with the monk and the other priests of the court to celebrate Easter. . . . At that time there was a large crowd of Christians there—Hungarians, Alans, Ruthenians, Georgians, Armenians—all of whom had not set eyes on the Sacrament from the time they had been taken prisoner, for the Nestorians were unwilling to admit them into their church unless they were re-baptised by them, so they said. However, to us they made no mention of this, on the contrary they acknowledged to us that the Roman Church was the head of all the Churches and that they would receive a Patriarch from the Pope if only the way were open. They freely offered us their Sacrament and made me stand at the door of the choir so that I could see how they celebrated, and also on Easter Eve I stood near the font so that I could see their way of baptising. . . .

There are two districts there: the Saracens' quarter where the markets are, and many merchants flock thither on account of the court which is always near it and on account of the number of envoys. The other district is that of the Cathayans who are all craftsmen. Apart from these districts there are the large palaces of the court scribes. There are twelve pagan temples belonging to the different nations, two mosques in which the law of Mahomet is proclaimed, and one church for the Christians at the far end of the town. The town is surrounded by a mud wall and has four gates. At the east gate are sold millet and other grain, which is however seldom brought there; at the west sheep and goats are sold; at the south oxen and carts; at the north horses.

. . . .

As mentioned above Mangu Chan has eight brothers, three by the same mother and five of the same father. One of the former he sent into the country of the Assassins, whom they call Mulibet, and commanded him to kill them all; another went to attack Persia and has already entered it and is about to invade the country of Turkey, so it is believed, and from there he will send out armies against Baghdad and Vastacius; one of the others he sent into Cathay against some who are not yet subject to him; the youngest uterine brother, by name Arabuccha [Arik Buka], he has kept with him and he has the orda of their mother who was a Christian and Master William is his slave.

One of his brothers on his father's side captured Master William in Hungary in a city called Belgrade, in which there was a Norman bishop from Belleville near Rouen. At the same time he captured a nephew of the bishop and I saw him there at Caracorum. He gave Master William to Mangu's mother for she begged hard to have him; after her death Master William passed into the possession of Arabuccha along with all the other appurtenances of his mother's orda and through him he was brought to the notice of Mangu Chan, who, after the completion of the work I have described, gave this master a hundred *iascot,* that is a thousand marks.

.   .   .   .

The letter [Mangu] is sending to you being at length finished, I was summoned and they translated it. I have written down the gist of it as well as I could grasp it by means of an interpreter and it is as follows:

"This is the decree of the eternal God. In heaven there is but one eternal God, on earth there is but one lord Chingis Chan, the son of God, Demugin Cingei, that is the sound of iron." (They call Chingis the sound of iron because he was a smith; and puffed up with pride they now call him the son of God.)

"This is the message which is spoken to you: whosoever there be Mongol, or Naiman, or Merkit, or Mussulman, wherever ears can hear and whithersoever a horse can go, there make it heard and understood: from the time they hear my decree and understand, and will not to believe, but wish to make war against us, you will hear and will see that they will have eyes, but will not see, and when they wish to hold anything they will be without hands, and when they wish to walk they will be without feet. This is the decree of the eternal God. By the power of the eternal God throughout the great realm of the Mongols, let the decree of Mangu Chan be known to the lord of the Franks, King Louis and to all the other lords and priests and to all the world of the Franks so that they may understand our message. The decree of the eternal God was made by Chingis Chan, but this decree has not reached you from Chingis Chan or from others after him.

"A certain man, David by name, came to you as if he were an

envoy of the Mongols but he was a liar, and you sent your
envoys with him to Keu Chan. It was after the death of Keu
Chan that your envoys arrived at his orda. Chamus his wife
sent you cloths of *nasic* and a letter. But how could that wicked
woman, more vile than a dog, know about matters of war and
affairs of peace, and how to pacify a great race and see how to
act for good?"

(Mangu told me with his own lips that Chamus was the worst
kind of witch and that by her sorcery she had destroyed her
whole family.)

"The two monks, who came from you to Sartach, Sartach sent
to Baatu; Baatu however, seeing that Mangu Chan is chief over
the Mongol people, sent them to us.

"Now, in order that the great world and the priests and the
monks might all live in peace and rejoice in the good things of
life and in order that the decree of God might be heard among
them, we wished to appoint Mongol envoys to accompany your
aforementioned priests. The priests however gave answer that
between us and you there was a land of war and many evil
men and difficult going, and therefore they were afraid they
would be unable to bring our envoys to you safe and sound, but
they said that if we gave them our letter containing our decree
they would take it to King Louis. This is the reason why we
have not sent our envoys with them, but by the hands of these
your priests we have sent to you the decree of the eternal God
in writing.

"It is the decree of the eternal God which we have made known
to you. When you have heard and believed it, if you wish to
obey us, send your envoys to us; in this way we shall know
for sure whether you wish to be at peace or war with us. When
by the power of the eternal God the whole world from the rising
of the sun to the going down thereof shall be at one in joy and
peace, then it will be made clear what we are going to do; if,
when you hear and understand the decree of the eternal God,
you are unwilling to pay attention and believe it, saying 'Our
country is far away, our mountains are mighty, our sea is vast,
and in this confidence you bring an army against us—we know
what we can do: He who made what was difficult easy and what
was far away near, the eternal God, He knows.' "

The Travels of Marco Polo[5]

[*Even while he was still alive, two traditions about Marco Polo (1254–1323?) began to take form. The first was that he was a romantic teller of tall tales, the second was that he had brought back a great many important facts, until then unknown. In modern times the first tradition has been embellished, or rather decked out, with a good deal of sentimentality and dreadful, fake-antique whimsy. The second has been solidly confirmed by his great scholarly editors, such as Yule and Cordier, Pelliot and Moule. Even what he reported by hearsay was rather less distorted by his own credulity than was common in the Middle Ages. The two traditions can be linked together if we remember to recall that Marco Polo the trader was a "businessman" of the mediaeval kind: You got the kind of business you were after by being adroit, by ingratiating yourself with the great and mighty, who then rewarded you by granting you, not on the basis of haggling about costs, but by favor, and as a gesture of munificence, the opportunity to amass jewels and other articles of luxury. To have won the favor of a potentate like Kublai Khan was, in the eyes of Marco Polo's contemporaries, a first-class business coup, and he was entitled to boast.*]

Emperors and Kings, dukes and marquesses, counts, knights and burgesses, and all ye, whoever ye be, who wish to know of the various races of men, and of the diversities of the different regions of the world, take this book and have it read to you. You shall find in it all the mighty wonders, all the great singularities of the vast regions of the East—of the Greater Armenia, of Persia, of Tartary, and of India, and of many a country besides—set down by us clearly and in due order, as they were recounted by Messer Marco Polo, called *Milione*, a wise and noble citizen of Venice, who saw them with his own eyes. Some things there will, in truth, be that he did not see, but only

[5] From *The Travels of Marco Polo*, translated into English from the text of L. F. Benedetto by Professor Aldo Ricci.

heard tell of by men worthy of credit. And we will set down the things seen as seen, and those heard as heard, that our book may be correct and truthful, without any falsehood.

．　．　．　．　．　．　．　．　．　．　．　．

Here Is Told of the Personal Appearance and Conduct of the Great Kaan

The personal appearance of the great King of Kings whose name is Cublai, is as follows. He has a fine figure, neither tall nor short, but of middle height. He has the proper amount of flesh, and is exceedingly well shaped in all his limbs. His countenance is white and red, like a rose, his eyes black and beautiful, his nose shapely and well placed.

He has four wives, all of whom he considers legitimate. (The eldest of the sons he has by his four wives must by law be the Lord of the Empire when the Great Kaan dies.) They are all called Empresses, the proper name of each being added. Each of them has a court of her own. None has less than three hundred most beautiful and handsome maidens. They also have many eunuchs as pages, and many other servants, both male and female. Hence each lady has 10,000 persons in her court. And every time the Great Kaan wishes to lie with one of these four wives of his, he summons her to his chamber, and sometimes he himself goes to her chamber.

He also has many concubines, and I will tell you how he obtains them and uses them. You must know that there is a province where lives a race of Tartars called Ungrat. The city is likewise called Ungrat. The people there are most beautiful and white. When he pleases, for the most part every two years, the Great Kaan sends envoys to that Province to find him the most beautiful damsels, according to a certain scale of beauty that he gives them—four hundred or five hundred of them, or more or less, as he pleases. And the beauty of these damsels is appraised in this way. When the envoys arrive, they summon all the damsels in the province; and there are appraisers, especially deputed for this task, who look at and examine one by one the members of each of them, their hair, their face, their eyebrows, their mouth, their lips, and their limbs, and see that they are all in due proportion to the rest of their body. Then they appraise some at 16 carats, others at 17, 18, 20, or more or less, according as they are more or less beautiful. And if the Great Kaan has ordered that those to be brought to him should be of 20 or 21 carats, the required number of that value is taken to him. When they come to his presence, he has them appraised once more by other appraisers, and out of the whole number he chooses for his own chamber some 30 or 40 of those that are valued highest. Then he has one given to each of the wives of his barons, to have them sleep in the same bed with them, and see carefully whether they are virgins, and perfectly healthy under every point of view, whether they have a quiet sleep or else snore, whether their breath is good and sweet, or else evil, and whether they in any way have an unpleasant odour. When they have been thus diligently examined, those that are found to be beautiful and good and sound under every aspect, are appointed to wait on the Lord. . . .

. . . .

Here Is Told of the Palace of the Great Kaan

Know, then, in truth that for three months in the year, namely December, January, and February, the Great Kaan lives in the capital of Cathay, called Cambaluc [Peking]. In this city he has his great palace, and I will tell you how it is built.

All round the city there is a first row of walls, square in shape, each side being eight miles long. All along the wall there is a deep ditch, and in the middle of each side a gate through which pass all the people who come to this city. Then there is a space of a mile, where the troops live. Then you come to another square wall, twenty-four miles long. [This is the real city wall, and we will speak of it later. The Great Kaan's palace is within this wall, but, to reach it, two more rows of walls have to be passed.]

First of all there is a great square wall, with sides a mile long, that is to say, it is four miles all round. It is exceedingly thick, quite ten paces high, and all white and embattled. In each corner stands a most beautiful and rich palace, where the Great Kaan's warlike equipment is kept, such as bows, quivers, saddles, bridles, bow-strings, and all else that is necessary for an army. Further, in the middle of each side is another palace similar to those in the corners; hence, all round there are eight palaces in all. And all eight of them are full of the Great Lord's war-equipment. And you must know that in each palace there is only one kind of thing. Thus, in one there are bridles, saddles, stirrups and all other kinds of harness for horses; in another, bows, bow-strings, quivers, arrows, and other things belonging to archery; in another again, there are breastplates, corslets, and other such objects of boiled leather; and so on, in the others.

Within this wall is another wall, the enclosure being rather greater in length than in breadth. Round it, also, are placed eight palaces, built like the others, in which likewise the Great Kaan's war-harness is kept. . . .

In the middle of these circuits of walls rises the Great Kaan's palace, which is built as I shall tell you. It is the largest that was ever seen.

Towards the north, it touches the last of the walls we have spoken of, but, on the south side, there is an empty space before it, where the barons and soldiers walk. It has no upper floor, but the basement is ten palms higher than the ground surrounding it, and the roof is surpassingly high. Flush with the floor of the palace, there is a marble wall, running all round, two paces wide. . . . On each side of the palace is a great marble staircase, which leads from the ground to the top of the marble wall, and by which one reaches the palace. The inside walls of the halls and rooms are all covered with gold and silver, and on them are painted beautiful pictures of ladies and knights and dragons and beasts and birds and divers other things. The ceiling is also made in such a way that one sees nothing else on it, but pictures and gold. The great hall is so vast and large that quite six thousand men could banquet there. There are so many rooms as to surpass all belief. The beauty and size of this palace are so great that no one on earth, who had the necessary skill, could have planned or built it better. The roof is varnished in vermilion, green, blue, yellow, and all other colours; and so well and cunningly is this done, that it glitters like crystal, and can be seen shining from a great way off all round. And you must know that the roof is so strongly and firmly built that it lasts for years without number.

. . . .

Between the two walls of which I have spoken, there stretch meadows with fine trees, full of animals of different kinds, such as white stags, and the animals that make musk, and roe-bucks, and fallow-deer, and vair and many other kinds of beautiful animals. The space between the two walls is all full of these fine beasts, with the sole exception of the roads along which the people pass. . . .

And I assure you that the streets of the city are so straight and broad that one can see from one end to the other of them, and they are so arranged that from each gate one can see the opposite one. There are many beautiful palaces, many beautiful hostelries, and many beautiful houses. And everywhere along the main streets there are rooms and shops of every kind. All the plots of ground on which the houses are built, are square, and laid out with straight lines, and in each plot there are large and spacious palaces, with their proper courtyards and gardens. These plots are given to the heads of families, so that so-and-so of such a family has received such a plot, and so-and-so of such another family has received such another plot; and so on. And round each of these square plots, there are beautiful streets, along which one walks. In this way the whole of the inner city is arranged in squares, just like a chess-board; and it is so beautiful, and so skilfully arranged, that it is not possible to describe it.

In the middle of the city, there is an immense palace, with a large clock, that is to say, a bell, which is struck three times at night, to warn the people that from that moment no one may go out into the streets. Once that bell has struck three times, no one dares go about the city, except it be for some urgent reason, as for a woman in labour or for a sick person; and those who do thus go about, must carry a light with them. . . .

Outside the city, beyond each gate, are large suburbs, so built that the suburb of each gate borders on those of the next two. They stretch to a distance of three or four miles, so that the inhabitants of the suburbs are more numerous than those of the city. In each suburb, to a distance of perhaps a mile from the city, there are many beautiful fondacos in which the merchants lodge, who come from different lands; to each nation a given fondaco is assigned, that is, as we should say, one to the Lombards, another to the Germans, another again to the French.

There are, too, twenty-five thousand harlots, counting those of the suburbs of the new city together with those in the old city, who serve men with their bodies for money. They have a general overseer; there is an overseer, too, for each hundred and for each thousand, but they are all responsible to the general. The reason why these women have an overseer is that, every time envoys arrive at the Great Kaan's court on business of his, and stop in Taidu at his expense—and indeed they are provided for in the most honourable manner—this overseer's duty is to give every night one of these harlots to the said envoys and to every man in his train. And every night they are changed, receiving no wages, for this is the tribute they pay to the Great Kaan.

Further, guards ride all night about the city, in groups of thirty or forty, seeing whether anyone is abroad in forbidden hours, namely, after the third stroke of the bell; and if they find anyone, they take him, and straightway put him in prison. Next morning, the proper officers question him, and if they find him guilty of some misdeed, they give him a certain number of blows with a stick, according to the seriousness of the offence; and at times people die of those blows. For this is how they inflict punishments for crimes, nor will they shed blood, since the *Bacsi*, that is, their wise astrologers, have told them that it is wicked to shed human blood.

How the Great Kaan Keeps Table at High Feasts

When the Great Kaan holds his court and receives at his table, the manner of it is as follows.

The Great Lord's table is much higher than the others. He sits on the north side, so as to look towards the south. Near him, on his left, sits his first wife; on his right, but rather lower, so that their heads are on a level with the Great Lord's feet, sit his sons, his grandsons, and all his kinsfolk who belong to the Imperial line.

. . . .

In the middle of the hall where the Great Kaan holds the banquet, stands a beautiful contrivance, very large and richly decorated, made like a square coffer, three paces wide along each side, and cunningly wrought with beautiful gilt sculptures of animals. In the middle, it is hollow, and in it stands a great vessel of pure gold, holding as much as a large cask: it is full of wine. All round this vessel, namely at each corner, there are smaller ones, of the size of a firkin; in these there are excellent drinks; in one there is mare's milk, in another camel's milk, and so on. On the coffer stand the Great Kaan's cups, in which he is offered drink.

. . . .

You must also know that many great barons are also appointed to take charge of the Great Kaan's food and drink; and their mouths and noses are muffled up with beautiful silk and gold cloths, in order that no breath or odour of their bodies may come near the Great Kaan's food and drink.

When the Great Kaan is about to drink, all the numberless instruments of every kind that are in the hall begin to play. A page offers him the cup, and then straightway steps back three paces, and kneels. At the very moment the Great Kaan takes the cup, all the barons and other people present, fall on their knees, and make signs of great obeisance. Then the Great Kaan drinks. And every time he drinks they do as you have heard.

. . . .

Here Is Told of the High Feast That the Great Kaan Holds on His Birthday

. . . .

On his birthday, the Great Kaan dresses in wondrous robes of beaten gold, and twelve thousand barons and knights also dress in the same colour and after the same fashion. But though their robes are of the same colour and fashion, yet they are not so costly; but all the same they are of silk and gold. And all of them have great golden belts. This raiment is given them by the Great Kaan. And I assure you that some of these robes are adorned with precious stones and pearls to the value of 10,000 gold bezants. Robes of this value are not rare. And you must know that thirteen times a year does the Great Kaan give rich robes to these twelve thousand barons and knights; and all these robes are similar to his own, and of great value. It is truly a wonderful thing, as you may see, and such as no other Lord in the world, but he, could possibly do or keep up.

Here Is Told of the Splendid Feast Held by the Great Kaan on Their New Year's Day

You must know that their New Year's Day comes in February. The Great Kaan and all his subjects celebrate it as I shall tell you.

It is the custom that the Great Kaan and all his subjects, both men and women, old and young, should on that day dress in white robes, if they have but the means to do so. This they do because white clothes seem to them an excellent thing and of good omen. So they dress in white on New Year's Day, that they may be lucky and happy all the year. And on that day, all peoples, and provinces, and lands, and kingdoms, subject to the Great Kaan, send him great gifts of gold, and silver, and pearls, and precious stones, and many splendid white cloths. This they do in order that their Lord may during the whole year, have treasure in abundance, and be happy and joyful. And I tell you, too, that the barons and knights, and all the people, exchange presents of white things, and they embrace and greet one another with joy and mirth. And they say to one another, as we also do: "May all that you do this year be lucky and fortunate." And this they do in order to enjoy prosperity and good fortune all the year.

And you must also know that on that day more than a hundred thousand splendid white horses are given to the Great Kaan; and if they are not absolutely white all over, they are at least almost completely white. Of white horses there is great abundance in those parts. When they make gifts to the Great Kaan, it is their custom that the giver should, if he can, follow this observance, namely give nine times nine units of the thing given. Thus, if the present is one of horses, nine times nine horses are given, namely eighty-one; if it is gold, then nine times nine pieces of gold; if it is cloth, nine times nine pieces of cloth; and so on for all things.

On that day, too, his elephants are taken out, which amount

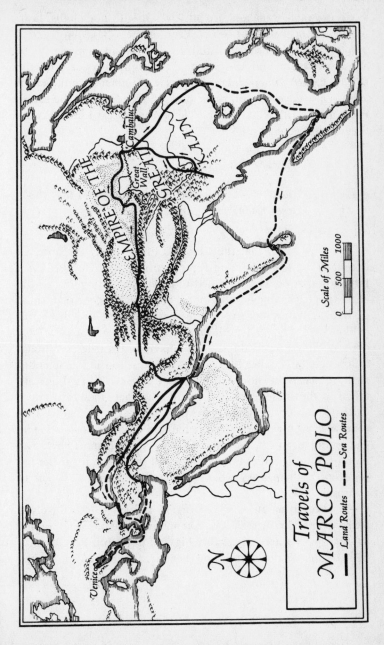

Travels of
MARCO POLO
—— Land Routes ---- Sea Routes

Scale of Miles
0   500   1000

EMPIRE OF THE
GREAT KHAN

Great
Wall

Cambaluc

Venice

to no less than 5000, and are all covered with fine cloths, bearing figures of birds and beasts. Each of them bears on its back two surpassingly beautiful and richly-wrought coffers, full of the Lord's plate, and of other precious things necessary for the White Court. Then there follows an immense number of camels, also covered with rich cloths, and loaded with the things necessary for this feast. And all file past the Great Lord; it is the finest sight that ever was seen.

.   .   .   .

Here Is Told of the Lions, Leopards, and Lynxes that the Great Kaan has Trained for the Chase; and Here Is Also Told of the Eagles

You must know that the Great Kaan has many leopards, all excellent for the chase and for catching game. He also has a large number of lynxes trained to hunt, and very good for the chase. He has many very big lions, too, much bigger than those of Babylon; they have very fine coats, and are of a beautiful colour, being striped lengthways in black, red, and white. They are trained to take wild boars, wild oxen, bears, wild asses, stags, fallow-deer, and other beasts. And I assure you it is a splendid sight to see those lions catch their quarries. When lions are taken to the chase, each lion is put in a cage on a cart, and a little dog with him. The reason they are placed in cages is that otherwise they would be too fierce and anxious to fall on the game, and it would be impossible to hold them. They have, moreover, to be led to the windward of the game, for if the latter scented them, they would flee, and not wait for them to approach.

He also has a multitude of eagles, trained to catch wolves, foxes, deer and roes; and they take many of them. Those trained to catch wolves are remarkably big and powerful. For you may be sure there is not a wolf, however big, that can escape them.

.   .   .   .

*Here Is Told How the Great Kaan Goes Hunting
in Order to Take Beasts and Birds*

.   .   .   .

All the Great Kaan's birds, as well as those of the barons, have a little silver tablet attached to their legs, bearing the name of the owner and of the keeper. In this way the birds are recognised as soon as they are taken, and returned to their owners. And if one does not know whose the bird is, it is brought to a baron called *Bularguchi,* a word signifying "the keeper of things without an owner." For you must know that if a horse or a sword or a bird or anything else is found, without its owner being known, it must at once be brought to that baron, and he has it taken and put away. If he who finds it does not straightway give it up, he is held to be a thief. And those who have lost something go to that baron; if he has the object, he at once has it handed over. . . .

And when the Great Kaan goes on this expedition I have told you of, in the neighbourhood of the Ocean Sea, there is no lack of fine sights in the way of the hunting of birds and beasts. There is no amusement in the world equal to it. And the Great Kaan always goes on four elephants, in a beautiful wooden chamber, all lined inside with cloths of beaten gold, and covered outside with lions' skins. He always remains inside it when fowling, as he is troubled with the gout. The Great Lord always keeps in it twelve of his best gerfalcons. There are also many barons and ladies to amuse him and keep him company. And when he goes journeying in that chamber placed on the elephants, you must know that if the barons who ride round him, cry out: "Sire, cranes are passing!" then he has the chamber uncovered above, and, on seeing the cranes, he has the gerfalcons he wants, brought to him, and casts them. The gerfalcons fight at length with the cranes, and generally take them. The Great Lord watches the sight, remaining in his bed, and finds great pleasure and amusement in it. And all the barons and knights ride round their Lord. And truly there never was, nor do I believe there is now, any man on earth able to have so much pleasure and delight as the Kaan, and to procure it with such ease.

So the Great Lord travels on until he reaches a place called Cachar Modun. Here he finds his tents pitched, and those of his sons, barons, and concubines. . . .

. . . Around these tents stand all the other tents, excellently constructed and arranged. The Lord's concubines also have splendid tents. And the gerfalcons and hawks and other birds and beasts have many immense tents. What more shall I tell you? Know in very truth that there are so many people in that camp that verily it is a marvel. One would think the Kaan was in his finest city. For people flock from all sides. And, further, he brings all his servants with him, and with him are also his leeches, and astrologers, and falconers, and other officers in great number. And everything is as orderly as in his capital.

How the Great Kaan Makes People Use Paper for Money

You must know that in this city of Cambaluc is the Great Lord's mint, and it is so arranged that one may well say that the Great Kaan is a perfect alchemist! And I will straightway prove it to you.

Know, then, that he has money made as follows. He has the bark taken of a certain kind of tree, that is to say of the mulberry-tree, the leaves of which are eaten by silkworms; then he has the thin layer of skin that lies between the bark and the trunk, removed; and he has this shredded and pounded into a kind of paste, together with glue; this he then has rolled out into sheets, something like paper, which are completely black. When the sheets are ready, he has them cut up into pieces of different sizes, but all of a rectangular shape, of greater length than breadth. The smallest piece is worth half a small tornesel; then there is one worth a whole tornesel (a small one, of course); then there is one worth half a silver *grosso;* then one worth a whole silver *grosso* (equivalent to a Venetian silver *grosso*); then there are some worth two, five, and ten *grossi,* and others worth one, two, three, or more bezants, up to ten. And all these sheets bear the Great Lord's seal. For you must know that all that money is issued with as much authority and solemnity as if it were of pure gold or silver. To each piece, certain officers, duly deputed for this task, write their names, and set their seals.

When the money is all ready, the chief of these officers, especially deputed by the Kaan, smears the seal entrusted to his keeping with vermilion, and presses it on the paper, so that the impress of the seal smeared with vermilion remains upon it. Then that particular piece of money becomes authentic. And if anyone were to forge it, he would suffer capital punishment. . . .

When this paper-money has been prepared in the way I have told you, he has all payments made with it, and he has the money spent in all the provinces and kingdoms and lands that he rules over. And no one dares refuse it on pain of death. . . .

Further, many times a year merchants arrive in Cambaluc in groups, bringing pearls, precious stones, gold, silver, and other things, such as gold and silver cloths, and they offer all these things to the Great Kaan. The latter sends for twelve wise men, who see to these things and have much experience, and he bids them examine what the merchants bring, and have it paid what they consider the proper price. Then these twelve wise men look at the things and, appraising them according to their consciences, straightway have the value paid, to the advantage of the merchants, in the paper-money I have told you of. The merchants accept it very willingly, having to use it for all the purchases they make throughout all the lands of the Great Lord. And you may well believe that the things the merchants thus bring in the course of a year amount to quite 400,000 bezants in value. The Great Lord has everything paid for in that paper.

. . . .

How from the City of Cambaluc Many Roads Lead Out into Sundry Provinces

You must know that from this city of Cambaluc many roads lead out into sundry provinces; I mean one road leads to one province, and another road to another province. Each road bears the name of the province to which it leads. . . . For the way the Great Kaan's messenger-service works, is truly admirable; it is indeed arranged in a most excellent manner.

You must, in fact, know that along those roads the envoy of the Great Kaan who leaves Cambaluc and rides twenty-five miles, reaches at the end of that stage . . . a horse-post station. There the envoy finds a very large and fine palace, where the Great Kaan's envoys lodge, with splendid beds, furnished with rich silk sheets, and with everything else that an important envoy may need. And if a king should go there, he would be splendidly lodged. Here the envoys also find no less than four hundred horses, always kept there by the Great Kaan's orders, in readiness for any envoys of his that he may send somewhere.

And even when the envoys have to traverse roadless and mountainous regions, without houses or hostels, the Great Kaan has had post-stations built there, with the palace and all the other things, such as horses and harness, that the other stations have. Only the distances are larger, for they are placed at thirty-five, and even more than forty miles, from one another. The Great Kaan also sends people to live there and till the soil, performing the necessary services for the posts. Thus large villages are formed.

. . . .

Someone might wonder how there are people enough to perform all these duties, and how they live. The answer is that all the Idolaters, and the Saracens likewise, each take six, eight, or ten wives, according to the number they can keep, and beget an infinite number of children. Thus you come across many of them who have more than thirty sons, all armed, following them. This is on account of the many wives. We, instead, have only one wife, and if she is barren, a man will end his days with her without begetting a single son; so we have not so many people as they. As for food, they have enough, since, for the most part, they make use of rice, panic, and millet, especially the Tartars, the Cathayans, and those of the province of Manji; and in their countries these plants yield a hundred measures for every one of seed sown. These people have no bread, but merely cook those three kinds of grain with milk, or else meat, and so eat them. In those parts wheat does not yield so much, but they eat what they have of it in the form of pan-cakes or other kind of pastry. In their countries no arable land is left barren. Their cattle increase and multiply immensely, and so, when they go campaigning, there is none of them but takes six, eight, or more horses for his personal use. Hence one may easily understand how it is that in those parts there is such a multitude of people, and how they can live in such plenty. . . .

How the Great Kaan Has Help Given to His Subjects in Case of Diseases of Crops or Cattle

Know, then, further, in very truth, that the Great Lord sends messengers throughout all his dominions—lands, kingdoms, and provinces—to see whether his subjects' crops have suffered from the weather, or from locusts or other plagues. And if they find that in some place the people have suffered damages, and lack corn, he not only exempts them from that year's tribute, but also himself has them furnished with corn, in order that they may have enough to eat and sow. And this is truly a great bounty on the part of the Great Lord.

This he has done in summer. In winter he has the same done for the cattle. Thus, if his messengers find that a man has lost his cattle on account of a murrain, he has some of his own given to the man, taking them from those he receives as tithes from the provinces; so he has him helped, and also exempts him for that year from all tribute.

.   .   .   .

How the Great Kaan Has Trees Planted along the Highroads

Now you must know the Great Kaan has bidden that on the highroads along which his messengers, as well as merchants and other people, travel, trees should be planted on both sides, at a distance of two paces from one another. And truly they are so high and big, that they can be seen from afar. The Great Kaan has had this done so that people should be able to see the roads and not miss their way, for you will find these trees even along desert roads; and then they are of great comfort to traders and wayfarers.

Along the roads, then, in every province and kingdom, the Great Kaan has trees planted so long as the soil makes it possible. In sandy and desert tracts, and on rocky mountains, where it would be impossible, he has stone cairns and pillars set up to

show the way. And he has certain barons to whom he has committed the task of seeing to it that those roads are constantly
kept in good condition. Further, as regards what we have said
about the trees, the Great Kaan has them planted all the more
willingly as his soothsayers and astrologers have told him that
he who plants trees lives long. . . .

Here Is Told of a Kind of Stone
That Burns like Wood

You must know that all over the province of Cathay there is
a kind of black stone, which is dug out of the mountains like
any other kind of stone, and burns like wood. These stones
make no flame, except a little at the beginning when they are
lit, like charcoal, and by merely remaining red-hot they give
out great heat. They keep alight better than wood. If you put
them into the fire at night and kindle them well, I assure you
that they remain alight all night, so that you will still find the
fire burning in the morning. And you must know that these
stones are burnt all over the province of Cathay. True it is that
there is no lack of firewood, namely, logs, but there is such a
multitude of people, and so many stoves, that is to say baths, are
constantly being heated, that the wood would not suffice; for
there is no one but, if he can, goes at least thrice a week, and
every day in winter, to the stoves to have a bath; every noble-
man and rich man, further, has a bath in his own house to wash
in. Thus the supply of wood would never be enough for so
many fires. Hence they make great use of those stones not only
because they are cheaper, but also because in this way they can
save much wood. . . .

How the Great Kaan Gives Many Alms to the Poor

Now that I have told you how the Great Lord ensures abundance of corn for his people, I will next tell you how he gives
many alms to the poor of the city of Cambaluc. You must know
that he has a list drawn up of honourable and worthy families
of Cambaluc who have fallen through some misfortune into
indigence, and who, being unable to work, lack food. To these
families, that may be of six, eight, ten, or more, or less persons,

the Great Lord has wheat and other kinds of corn given, so that they may have sustenance for the whole year. And the number of these families is very considerable. When the proper time comes round, these families apply to the officials entrusted with all the Great Kaan's expenses, who live in a palace set apart for this purpose. They then show a paper stating how much they have received for their sustenance in the previous year, and so are provided for, to that extent, for the coming year. The Great Kaan also provides them with clothes, as he receives tithes on all wool, silk, hemp, and other materials of which clothes are made; these materials he has woven and made into cloth, in a building set aside for the purpose, where they are stored; and as all craftsmen are obliged to give him a day's work every week, the Great Kaan has clothes made out of the pieces of cloth, distributing to the aforesaid poor families such as are suitable for winter or summer, as the case may be. He also provides his army with clothes, and in every city has woollen cloth woven, paying for it with the city's tithes. And you must know that, according to their ancient customs, before they knew the Law of the Idolaters, the Tartars never gave alms; indeed, if a poor man went up to them, they drove him away rudely, saying, "Go with the curse of God, for if He loved you as He loves me, He would have done some good to you." But since the wise men of the Idolaters, and especially the *Bacsi* we mentioned before, told the Great Kaan that it was virtuous to provide for the poor, and that his idols would be greatly pleased thereby, he provided for the poor in the way we have said. And I assure you that if anyone goes to the Kaan's court to ask for bread, he is not denied it, alms being given to all those who go there; not a day passes but the proper officials dispense more than thirty thousand dishes of rice, or panic, or millet. This is done all the year round. Truly this is great bounty on the part of the Lord, who is merciful towards the poor among his subjects. And his subjects are so grateful to him for this, that they adore him like a god. . . .

The Second Letter
of John of Monte Corvino [6]

[*A fascinating fragment of the history of Christian missionary expansion during the Middle Ages, far less known than accounts of the Crusades, for instance, is found in the letters of three Franciscan friars. They lack the literary and historical importance of Rubruck and Carpini, but the accounts of John of Monte Corvino, Peregrine, and Andrew of Perugia, form a link between the earliest travelers and the later Jesuit missionary accounts. They tell the heroic, lonely tale of the first Roman Catholic missionary efforts in China.*

[*John of Monte Corvino was born in southern Italy in 1247 and was first sent by the Franciscans to Armenia and Persia before Pope Nicholas IV despatched him to the court of the great Khan. He left Rome in 1289 and visited Argun at his capital of Tabriz (Taurus, Persia). From there he left two years later on what was to be the longest and most successful of the Franciscan journeys. At the court of the Mongol Emperor of China he spent twelve solitary years before Rome recognized his efforts and appointed him Archbishop of Khanbalik (Peking). Under his guidance the mission flourished for twenty years and for another forty under his successors, down into the second half of the fourteenth century, when Tamerlane the conqueror put an end to all Christian missionary efforts for more than a century.*

[*In contrast to the Franciscans who traveled to Mongolia by land, John of Monte Corvino reached China by the sea route around India. He thus anticipated the great European age of maritime discovery, and his name may be linked with that of Marco Polo, who went to China by land and returned (most of the way) by sea.*]

I, Brother John of the Order of Friars Minor, departed from Tauris [Tabriz] a city of Persia, in the year of Our Lord 1291 and entered India and I was in the country of India and in the

[6] From *The Mongol Mission,* edited by Christopher Dawson.

Church of St. Thomas the Apostle for 13 months. . . . And going on further, I reached Cathay, the kingdom of the Emperor of the Tartars, who is called the Great Chan. Indeed I summoned the Emperor himself to receive the Catholic faith of Our Lord Jesus Christ with the letters of the Lord Pope, but he was too far gone in idolatry. Nevertheless he behaves very generously to the Christians and it is now the twelfth year that I have been with him. However the Nestorians, who call themselves Christians, but behave in a very unchristian manner, have grown so strong in these parts that they did not allow any Christian of another rite to have any place of worship, however small, nor to preach any doctrine but their own. For these lands have never been reached by any apostle or disciple of the apostles and so the aforesaid Nestorians both directly and by the bribery of others have brought most grievous persecutions upon me, declaring that I was not sent by the Lord Pope, but that I was a spy, a magician and a deceiver of men. And after some time they produced more false witnesses, saying that another messenger had been sent with a great treasure to the Emperor and that I had murdered him in India and made away with his gifts. And this intrigue lasted above five years, so that I was often brought to judgment, and in danger of a shameful death. But at last, by God's ordering, the Emperor came to know my innocence and the nature of my accusers, by the confession of some of them, and he sent them into exile with their wives and children.

.   .   .   .

Also I have purchased by degrees forty boys of the sons of the pagans, between seven and eleven years old, who as yet knew no religion. Here I baptized them and taught them Latin and our rite, and I wrote for them about thirty psalters and hymnaries and two breviaries by which eleven boys now know the office. And they keep choir and say office as in a convent whether I am there or not. And several of them write psalters and other suitable things. And the Lord Emperor takes much delight in their singing. And I ring the bells for all the Hours and sing the divine office with a choir of "sucklings and infants." But we sing by rote because we have no books with the notes.

Of Good King George

A certain king of these parts, of the sect of the Nestorian Christians, who was of the family of that great king who was called Prester John of India, attached himself to me in the first year that I came here. And was converted by me to the truth of the true Catholic faith. And he took minor orders and served my Mass wearing the sacred vestments, so that the other Nestorians accused him of apostasy. Nevertheless he brought a great part of his people to the true Catholic faith, and he built a fine church with royal generosity in honour of God, the Holy Trinity and the Lord Pope, and called it according to my name "the Roman church." This King George departed to the Lord a true Christian, leaving a son and heir in the cradle, who is now nine years old. But his brothers who were perverse in the errors of Nestorius perverted all those whom King George had converted and brought them back to their former state of schism. And because I was alone and unable to leave the Emperor the Chan, I could not visit that church, which is distant twenty days' journey. Nevertheless if a few helpers and fellow workers were to come, I hope in God that all could be restored for I still hold the grant of the late King George.

.   .   .   .

Finis

Given in the city of Cambaliech of the kingdom of Cathay, in the Year of Our Lord 1305, the 8th day of January.

The Letter of
Andrew of Perugia

[*Brother Andrew wrote the letter which follows in 1318, before he became bishop of Zayton (Ch'uan-chou-fu) in 1323. He probably died in 1332. By this time communication between these missionaries and Europe was by sea rather than by land,*

*and when the Mongol (Yuan) dynasty in China was overthrown
in 1368, even this link was broken until the coming of the Jesuits
more than two centuries later.*]

Brother Andrew of Perugia of the Order of Friars Minor,
called by divine permission to be a bishop, to the reverend
father Brother Guardian of the Convent of Perugia: greeting
and everlasting peace in the Lord.

You should know that I with Brother Peregrine of good memory, my fellow bishop and the inseparable companion of my
pilgrimage, with much labour and weariness, fasting and hardship and danger by land and by sea, in which we were robbed
of everything, even our tunics and habits, came at last with the
help of God to the city of Cambaliech, the imperial residence
of the Great Chan, in the year of Our Lord's Incarnation 1318,
as I suppose. Here we consecrated the Archbishop according to
the mandate given us by the Apostolic See, and stayed there
almost five years. Throughout this time we received *alafa* from
the noble Emperor for the food and dress of eight persons. For
alafa is a grant which the Emperor makes to the envoys of great
men, to ambassadors, solders, artificers in different crafts, min-
strels, poor men and persons of every sort and kind; and the
sum of these grants exceeds the income and expenditure of
many Western kings.

.   .   .   .

There is a certain large city by the ocean called Zayton in the
Persian tongue. In this city a rich Armenian lady has built a
church, fair and large enough, which she has given and bequeathed with suitable endowment to Brother Gerard the
Bishop and our brethren that were with him, after it had by
her will been made a cathedral by the Archbishop.

.   .   .   .

Here then I have taken up my abode, and I live on the
bounty of the Emperor which I have already referred to and
which, according to the estimate of the Genoese merchants, may
amount to the value of a hundred gold florins or thereabouts.
And a great part of this alms I have spent in this house and I

think there is not a heritage among all those in our province to be compared with it for beauty and convenience.

.   .   .   .

In this vast empire there are verily men of every nation under heaven and of every sect; and each and all are allowed to live according to their own sect. For this is their opinion, or I should say their error, that every man is saved in his own sect. And we can preach freely and securely, but of the Jews and the Saracens none is converted. Of the idolaters, exceedingly many are baptized: but when they are baptized they do not adhere strictly to Christian ways.

. . . The great city of Zayton, where we are, is on the sea and is distant about three months' journey from Cambaliech the great.

Given at Zayton the 3rd of the Kalends of January in the Year of Our Lord 1318.

Ibn Batuta's Travels in
Bengal and China [7]

[*Ibn Batuta was born in Tangier in 1304, and started on his travels at the age of twenty-one. His first journey was to Egypt, where he married two wives. Besides his travels in Africa, he visited Mecca, the Caucasus and India. From Delhi the King sent him on an embassy to China bearing fabulous gifts to the emperor, who was the last Mongol ruler of China. In 1353 he returned to Fez, where he was ordered by the Sultan to write the history of his travels.*

[*In his day ibn-Batuta was considered "a bit of a Munchausen," and Yule and Cordier, from whose version the extracts in this chapter are taken, conceded that the historical events that he relates as taking place while he was in China are "positive fiction." Nevertheless, in his travels as a whole he gathered a great deal of information. It was characteristic of the Arab trav-*

---

[7] From *Cathay and the Way Thither,* edited by Sir Henry Yule and Henri Cordier. Vol. IV.

*elers that, in an age that accepted tall tales as readily as it did
facts, they gathered and reported more facts than most.]*

. . . They now arrived at the country of TAWÁLISI, which
Yule calls a "questionable kingdom."

It is very extensive, and the sovereign is the equal of the King
of China. He possesses numerous junks with which he makes
war upon the Chinese until they sue for peace, and consent to
grant him certain concessions. The people are idolaters; their
countenances are good, and they bear a strong resemblance to
the Turks. They are usually of a copper complexion, and are
very valiant and warlike. The women ride, shoot, and throw
the javelin well, and fight in fact just like the men. We cast
anchor in one of their ports which is called KAILÚKARI. It is
also one of their greatest and finest cities, and the king's son
used to reside there. When we had entered the harbour soldiers
came down to the beach, and the skipper landed to speak with
them. He took a present with him for the king's son; but he was
told that the king had assigned him the government of another
province, and had set over this city his daughter, called Urdujá.

The second day after our arrival in the port of Kailúkari, this
princess invited the *Nákhodah* or skipper, the *Karáni* or purser,
the merchants and persons of note, the *Tindail* or chief of the
sailors, the *Sipahsalár* or chief of the archers, to partake of a
banquet which Urdujá had provided for them according to her
hospitable custom. The skipper asked me to accompany them,
but I declined, for these people are infidels and it is unlawful to
partake of their food. So when the guests arrived at the Princess's
she said to them: "Is there anyone of your party missing?" The
captain replied: "There is but one man absent, the *Bakshi* (or
Divine), who does not eat of your dishes." Urdujá rejoined:
"Let him be sent for." So a party of her guards came for me,
and with them some of the captain's people, who said to me:
"Do as the Princess desires."

So I went, and found her seated on her great chair or throne,
whilst some of her women were in front of her with papers
which they were laying before her. Round about were elderly
ladies, or duennas, who acted as her counsellors, seated below
the throne on chairs of sandalwood. The men also were in front

of the Princess. The throne was covered with silk, and canopied with silk curtains, being itself made of sandalwood and plated with gold. In the audience hall there were buffets of carved wood, on which were set forth many vessels of gold of all sizes, vases, pitchers, and flagons. The skipper told me that these vessels were filled with a drink compounded with sugar and spice, which these people use after dinner; he said it had an aromatic odour and delicious flavour; that it produced hilarity, sweetened the breath, promoted digestion, etc., etc.

As soon as I had saluted the princess she said to me in the Turkish tongue *Husn misen yakhshi misen (Khúsh misan? Yakhshi misan?)* which is as much as to say, Are you well? How do you do? and made me sit down beside her. This princess could write the Arabic character well. She said to one of her servants *Dawát wa batak katur,* that is to say, "Bring inkstand and paper." He brought these, and then the princess wrote *Bismillah Arrahmán Arrahím (*In the name of God the merciful and compassionate!) saying to me "What's this?" I replied *"Tanzari nám"* (Tangri nam), which is as much as to say "the name of God"; whereupon she rejoined *"Khush,"* or "It is well." She then asked from what country I had come, and I told her that I came from India. The princess asked again, "From the Pepper country?" I said "Yes." She proceeded to put many questions to me about India and its vicissitudes, and these I answered. She then went on, "I must positively go to war with that country and get possession of it, for its great wealth and great forces attract me." Quoth I, "You had better do so." Then the princess made me a present consisting of dresses, two elephant-loads of rice, two she buffaloes, ten sheep, four rothls of cordial syrup, and four *Martabans,* or stout jars, filled with ginger, pepper, citron and mango, all prepared with salt as for a sea voyage.

The skipper told me that Urdujá had in her army free women, slave girls, and female captives, who fought just like men; that she was in the habit of making incursions into the territories of her enemies, taking part in battle, and engaging in combat with warriors of repute. He also told me that on one occasion an obstinate battle took place between this princess and one of her enemies; a great number of her soldiers had been slain, and her whole force was on the point of running away, when Urdujá rushed to the front, and forcing her way through the ranks of the combatants till she got at the king himself with whom she was at war, she dealt him a mortal wound, so that he died, and his troops fled. The princess returned with his head carried on a spear, and the king's family paid a vast sum to redeem it. And when the princess rejoined her father he gave her this city of Kailúkari, which her brother had previously governed. I heard likewise from the same skipper that various sons of kings had sought Urdujá's hand, but she always answered, "I will marry no one but him who shall fight and conquer me!" so they all avoided the trial, for fear of the shame of being beaten by her.

We quitted the country of Tawálisi, and after a voyage of seventeen days, during which the wind was always favourable, we arrived in CHINA.

This is a vast country; and it abounds in all sorts of good things, fruit, corn, gold and silver; no other country in the world can rival China in that respect. It is traversed by the river which is called *Ab-i-Haiyah,* signifying the Water of Life. It is also called the river SÁRÚ, just like the Indian river. Its source is among the mountains near the city of KHÁNBÁLIQ, which are known by the name of *Kuh-i-Búznah* or Monkey Mountains. This river runs through the heart of China, for a distance of six months' journey, reaching at last Sín-ul-Sín. It is bordered throughout with villages, cultivated plains, orchards, and markets, just like the Nile in Egypt; but this country is still more flourishing, and there are on the banks a great number of hydraulic wheels. You find in China a great deal of sugar as good as that of Egypt, better in fact.

The cocks and hens of China are very big, bigger in fact than our geese. The hen's egg also there is bigger than our goose eggs; whilst their goose on the other hand is a very small one. I one day bought a hen which I wanted to boil, but one pot would not hold it, and I was obliged to take two! As for the cocks in China they are as big as ostriches! Sometimes one sheds his feathers and then the great red object is a sight to see! The first time in my life that I saw a China cock was in the city of Kaulam. I had at first taken it for an ostrich, and I was looking at it with great wonder, when the owner said to me: "Pooh! there are cocks in China much bigger than that!" and when I got there I found he had said no more than the truth. . . .The flesh of swine and dogs is eaten by the Chinese pagans, and it is sold publicly in their markets. They are generally well-to-do opulent people, but they are not sufficiently particular either in dress or diet. You will see one of their great merchants, the owner of uncountable treasure, going about in a dirty cotton frock. The Chinese taste is entirely for the accumulation of gold and silver plate. They all carry a stick with an iron ferule, on which they lean in walking, and this they call their third leg.

Silk is very plentiful in China, for the worms which produce it attach themselves to certain fruits on which they feed, and require little attention. This is how they come to have silk in such abundance that it is used for clothing even by poor monks and beggars. Indeed, but for the demand among merchants, silk would there have no value at all. Among the Chinese one cotton dress is worth two or three of silk.

The people of China of all mankind have the greatest skill and taste in the arts. This is a fact generally admitted; it has been remarked in books by many authors, and has been much dwelt upon. As regards painting, indeed, no nation, whether of Christians or others, can come up to the Chinese; their talent for this art is something quite extraordinary. I may mention among astonishing illustrations of this talent of theirs, what I have witnessed myself, viz., that whenever I have happened to visit one of their cities, and to return to it after a while, I have always found my own likeness and those of my companions painted on the walls, or exhibited in the bazaars. On one occasion that I visited the Emperor's own city, in going to the imperial palace with my comrades I passed through the bazaar of the painters; we were all dressed after the fashion of Irák. In the evening on leaving the palace I passed again through the same bazaar, and there I saw my own portrait and the portraits of my companions painted on sheets of paper and exposed on the walls. We all stopped to examine the likenesses, and everybody found that of his neighbour to be excellent!

China is the safest as well as the pleasantest of all the regions on the earth for a traveler. You may travel the whole nine months' journey to which the empire extends without the slightest cause for fear, even if you have treasure in your charge. For at every halting place there is a hostelry superintended by an officer who is posted there with a detachment of horse and foot.

Every evening after sunset, or rather at nightfall, this officer visits the inn accompanied by his clerk; he takes down the name of every stranger who is going to pass the night there, seals the list, and then closes the inn door upon them. In the morning he comes again with his clerk, calls everybody by name, and marks them off one by one. He then despatches along with the travelers a person whose duty it is to escort them to the next station, and to bring back from the officer in charge there a written acknowledgment of the arrival of all; otherwise this person is held answerable. This is the practice at all the stations in China from Sín-ul-Sín to Khánbáliq. In the inns the traveler finds all needful supplies, especially fowls and geese. But mutton is rare.

To return, however, to the particulars of my voyage, I must tell you that the first Chinese city that I reached after crossing the sea was ZAITÚN. Although *Zaitún* signifies *olives* in Arabic, there are no olives here any more than elsewhere in India and China; only that is the name of the place. It is a great city, superb indeed, and in it they make damasks of velvet as well as those of satin which are called from the name of the city *Zaituniah;* they are superior to the stuffs of Khansá and Khánbáliq. The harbour of Zaitún is one of the greatest in the world—I am wrong: it is *the* greatest! I have seen there about one hundred first-class junks together; as for small ones they were past counting. The harbour is formed by a great estuary which runs inland from the sea until it joins the Great River.

In this, as in every other city of China, every inhabitant has a garden, a field, and his house in the middle of it, exactly as we have it in the city of Segelmessa. It is for this reason that the cities of the Chinese are so extensive. The Mahomedans have a city by themselves.

When the chief of the council had learned all particulars about me, he wrote to the Kán, i.e. the Emperor, to inform him that I had arrived from the King of India. And I begged the chief that whilst we were awaiting the answer he would send some one to conduct me to Sín-ul-Sín, which these people call Sin-Kalán, which is also under the Kán, as I was desirous to visit that part of the country. He consented, and sent one of his people to accompany me. I traveled on the river in a vessel which was much like the war galleys in our country, excepting that the sailors rowed standing and all together amidships, whilst the passengers kept forward and aft. For shade they spread an awning made of a plant of the country resembling flax, but not flax; it was, however, finer than hemp.

We traveled on the river for twenty-seven days. Every day a little before noon we used to moor at some village, where we bought what was needful, and performed our midday prayers. In the evening we stopped at another village, and so on until we arrived at Sin-Kalán, which is the city of Sín-ul-Sín. Porcelain is made there, just as at Zaitún, and it is there also that the river called *Ab-i-Haiyáh* (or water-of-life) discharges itself into the sea, at a place which they call the confluence of the seas. Sín-ul-Sín is one of the greatest of cities, and one of those that has the finest of bazaars. One of the largest of these is the porcelain bazaar, and from it china-ware is exported to the other cities of China, to India, and to Yemen.

In the middle of the city you see a superb temple with nine gates; inside of each there is a portico with terraces where the inmates of the building seat themselves. Between the second and third gates there is a place with rooms for occupation by the blind, the infirm or the crippled. These receive food and clothing from pious foundations attached to the temple. Between the other gates there are similar establishments; there is to be seen (for instance) a hospital for the sick, a kitchen for dressing their food, quarters for the physicians, and others for the servants. I was assured that old folks who had not strength to work for a livelihood were maintained and clothed there; and that a like provision was made for destitute widows and orphans. This temple was built by a King of China, who bequeathed this city and the villages and gardens attached, as a pious endowment for this establishment. His portrait is to be seen in the temple, and the Chinese go and worship it.

In one of the quarters of this great city is the city of the Mahomedans, where they have their cathedral mosque, convent, and bazaar; they have also a judge and a Shaikh, for in each of the cities of China you find always a Shaikh of Islam, who decides finally every matter concerning Mahomedans, as well as a Kâzi to administer justice. I took up my quarters with Auhad-uddín of Sinjár, one of the worthiest, as he is one of the richest, of men. My stay with him lasted fourteen days, during which presents from the kâzi and the other Mahomedans flowed in upon me incessantly. Every day they used to have a fresh entertainment, to which they went in pretty little boats of some ten cubits in length, with people on board to sing. . . .

The day after my visit to the shaikh I set out on my return to the city of Zaitún, and some days after my arrival there an order was received from the Kán that I was to proceed to the capital, with arrangements for my honourable treatment and for defraying my expenses. He left me free to go by land or by water as I chose; so I preferred going by the river.

They fitted up a very nice boat for me, such as is used for the transport of generals; the Amír sent some of his suite to accompany me, and furnished provisions in abundance; quantities also were sent by the kâzi and the Mahomedan merchants. We traveled as the guests of the sultan, dining at one village, and supping at another; and after a passage of ten days we arrived at KANJANFÚ. This is a large and beautiful city surrounded by gardens, in an immense plain. One would say it was the plain of Damascus! . . .

When we arrived at the capital Khánbáliq, we found that the Kán was absent, for he had gone forth to fight Firuz, the son of his uncle, who had raised a revolt against him in the territory of KARAKORÚM and BISHBÁLIQ, in Cathay. To reach those places from the capital there is a distance to be passed of three months' march from the capital through a cultivated country. I was informed by the Sadr-ul-Jihán, Burhán-uddín of Ságharj, that when the Kán assembled his troops, and called the array of his forces together, there were with him one hundred divisions of horse, each composed of 10,000 men, the chief of whom was called *Amír Túmán* or lord of ten thousand. Besides these the immediate followers of the sultan and his household furnished 50,000 more cavalry. The infantry consisted of 500,000 men. When the emperor had marched, most of the amírs revolted, and agreed to depose him, for he had violated the laws of the *Yasák*, that is to say, of the code established by their ancestor Tankíz Khán, who ravaged the lands of Islam. They deserted to the camp of the emperor's cousin who was in rebellion, and wrote to the Kán to abdicate and be content to retain the city of Khansá for his apanage. The Kán refused, engaged them in battle, and was defeated and slain.

This news was received a few days after our arrival at the capital. The city upon this was decked out, and the people went about beating drums and blowing trumpets and horns, and gave themselves over to games and amusements for a whole month. The Kán's body was then brought in with those of about a hundred more of his cousins, kinsfolk, and favourites who had fallen. After digging for the Kán a great *Náwús* or crypt, they spread it with splendid carpets, and laid therein the Kán with his arms. They put in also the whole of the gold and silver plate belonging to the palace, with four of the Kán's young slave girls, and six of his chief pages holding in their hands vessels full of drink. They then built up the door of the crypt and piled earth on the top of it till it was like a high hill. After this they brought four horses and made them run races round the emperor's sepulchre until they could not stir a foot; they next set up close to it a great mast, to which they suspended those horses after driving a wooden stake right through their bodies from tail to mouth. The Kán's kinsfolk also, mentioned above, were placed in subterranean cells, each with his arms and the plate belonging to his house. Adjoining the tombs of the principal men among them to the number of ten they set up empaled horses, three to each, and beside the remaining tombs they impaled one horse a-piece.

It was a great day! Every soul was there, man and woman, Musulman and infidel. All were dressed in mourning, that is, the Pagans wore short white dresses, and the Musulmans long white dresses. The Kán's ladies and favourites remained in tents near the tomb for forty days; some remained longer; some a full year. A bazaar had been established in the neighbourhood, where all necessary provisions, etc., were for sale. I know no other nation in our time that keeps up such practices. The pagans of India and China burn their dead; other nations bury them, but none of them thus bury the living with the dead. However honest people in Súdán have told me that the pagans of that country, when their king dies, dig a great pit, into which they put with him several of his favourites and servants together with thirty persons of both sexes, selected from the families of the great men of the state. They take care first to break the arms and legs of these victims, and they also put vessels full of drink into the pit.

An eminent person of the tribe of Masúfah, living among the Negroes in the country of Kúber, who was much held in honour by their king, told me that when the king died they wished to put a son of his own into the tomb with some other children belonging to the country. "But I said to them," continued this eminent person, "how can you do this, seeing the boy is neither of your religion nor of your country? And so I was allowed to ransom him with a large sum of money."

When the Kán was dead, as I have related, and Firuz, the son of his uncle, had usurped the supreme power, the latter chose for his capital the city of KARAKORÚM, because it was nearer to the territories of his cousins, the kings of Turkestan and Má-wará-n-Nahr. Then several of the amírs who had taken no part in the slaughter of the late Kán revolted against the new prince; they began to cut off the communications, and there was great disorder.

Revolt having thus broken out, and civil war having been kindled, the Shaikh Burhán-uddín and others advised me to return to (Southern) China before the disturbances should have arisen to a greater pitch. They went with me to the lieutenant of the Emperor Firuz, who sent three of his followers to escort me, and wrote orders that I should be everywhere received as a guest. So we descended the river to Khansá, Kanjánfu and Zai-tún. When we reached the latter place, I found junks on the point of sailing for India, and among these was one belonging to Malik-ul-Záhir, Sultan of Java (Sumatra), which had a Mahomedan crew. The agent of the ship recognised me, and was pleased to see me again. We had a fair wind for ten days, but as we got near the land of Tawálisi it changed, the sky became black, and heavy rain fell. For ten days we never saw the sun, and then we entered on an unknown sea. The sailors were in great alarm, and wanted to return to China, but this was not possible. In this way we passed forty-two days, without knowing in what waters we were. . . .

Ambassador to the Court of Timur (1403–6)[8]:
RUY GONZALEZ DE CLAVIJO

[*Ruy Gonzales de Clavijo was a Spanish traveler of the fifteenth century. In 1403 Henry III of Costello sent him as ambassador to the court of Timur in Samarkand, to which he traveled by way of Rhodes, Constantinople and Teheran. In 1406 he returned to Madrid, where he served as chamberlain at the court until the king's death in 1407.*]

"The city [of Samarcand] is also very rich in merchandize which comes from other parts. Russia and Tartary send linen and skins; China sends silks, which are the best in the world, (more especially the satins), and musk, which is found in no other part of the world, rubies and diamonds, pearls and rhubarb, and many other things. The merchandize which comes from China is the best and most precious which comes to this city, and they say that the people of China are the most skilful workmen in the world. They say themselves that they have two eyes, the Franks one, and that the Moors are blind, so that they have the advantage of every other nation in the world. From India come spices, such as nutmegs, cloves, mace, cinnamon, ginger, and many others which do not reach Alexandria.

"When the lord returned to the city [from the war against the Turk], the ambassadors from Cathay arrived, with others to say that the lord held that land, subject to the emperor of Cathay, and to demand the payment of tribute every year, as it was seven years since any had been paid. The lord answered that this was true, but that he would not pay it. This tribute had not been paid for nearly eight years, nor had the emperor of Cathay sent for it, and the reason why he did not send for it, was this.

"The emperor of Cathay died, leaving three sons, to whom he bequeathed his territories. The eldest son wished to take the shares of the other two. He killed the youngest, but the middle one fought with the eldest, and defeated him, and he, from despair at the consequences which he dreaded would follow his treatment of his youngest brother, set fire to his palace, and perished with many of his followers. The middle brother, therefore, reigned alone. As soon as he was quietly established in his own empire, he sent these ambassadors to Timour Beg, to demand the tribute which was formerly paid to his father, but we did not hear whether he resented the answer which was given by Timour.

"From Samarcand to the chief city of the empire of Cathay, called Cambalu, is a journey of six months, two of which are passed in crossing an uninhabited land, never visited by anyone but shepherds, who wander with their flocks, in search of pasture. In this year as many as eight hundred camels, laden with merchandize, came from Cambalu to this city of Samarcand, in the month of June. When Timour Beg heard what the ambassadors from Cathay had demanded, he ordered these camels to be detained, and we saw the men who came with the camels. They related wonderful things, concerning the great power of the lord of Cathay: we especially spoke to one of these men, who had been six months in the city of Cambalu, which he said was near the sea, and twenty times as large as Tabreez. The city of Cambalu is the largest in the world, because Tabreez is a good league in length, so that Cambalu must be twenty leagues in extent. He also said that the lord of Cathay had so vast an army that, when he collected troops to march beyond his own territory, not counting those who thus departed with him, four hundred thousand cavalry and more were left to guard the land; he added that it was the custom of this lord of Cathay not to allow any man to mount a horse, unless he had a thousand followers; and he told many other wonders concerning this city of Cambalu, and the land of Cathay.

"This emperor of Cathay used to be a gentile, but he was converted to the faith of the Christians.

.   .   .   .

"Fifteen days journey from the city of Samarcand, in the direction of China, there is a land inhabited by Amazons, and to this day they continue the custom of having no men with them, except at one time of the year; when they are permitted, by their leaders, to go with their daughters to the nearest settlements, and have communication with men, each taking the one who pleases her most, with whom they live, and eat, and drink, after which they return to their own land. If they bring forth daughters afterwards, they keep them; but they send the sons to their fathers. These women are subject to Timour Beg; they used to be under the emperor of Cathay, and they are Christians of the Greek Church. They are of the lineage of the Amazons who were at Troy, when it was destroyed by the Greeks."

V

OCEAN DISCOVERERS AND EMPIRE BUILDERS

AFTER the rounding of the Cape of Good Hope by Bartholomew Diaz in 1488, the discovery of America by Columbus in 1492, the reaching of India by the route around Africa by Vasco Da Gama in 1498, and the crowning achievement of the circumnavigation of the world by Ferdinand Magellan's expedition of 1519–21 (though Magellan himself was killed in the Philippines), the histories of the Old World and the New World began to draw together in a true World History. The greatest acceleration in this new chapter of discovery came in a period of little more than fifty years, a truly miraculous half-century, from say 1588, the date of England's defeat of the Spanish Armada, to 1644, the "formal" date of the Manchu conquest of China (which had in fact begun a full generation earlier).

In these few decades we have, after 1588, the founding of the East India Company on the last day of the year 1600, followed quickly by the founding of Dutch, Swedish, and French East India Companies; the opening of French Canada by Champlain in the same decade, and the voyage of the *Mayflower* in 1620. During the same period occurred the rapid penetration of Siberia by the Cossacks up to the borders of Mongolia and Manchuria and the Pacific coast, and the career of Nurhachu, the founder of Manchu rule in China, though he did not live to enter Peking; he was born in 1559 and called himself Emperor from 1616.

During this half-century of transformation, the center of

gravity of world power shifted, and the motives of geographical discovery changed. The two processes interacted on each other. First for the Greek city-states and then for Byzantium, the Black Sea had meant access—a trade route—to Russia, but not a land empire in Russia. For the Egyptians, and later the Persian Empire, the Red Sea, the Persian Gulf, and even the monsoon route to India, had also meant trade, but not the imperial control of an overseas empire. For the Romans the Mediterranean, an enclosed sea, which they called *mare nostrum* ("our sea") was the focal area that enabled them to combine control of Southern Europe, North Africa, and Asia Minor; but though they were thus a maritime power, they never became an oceanic power. They halted at the North Sea and did not venture into the Atlantic. They traded with India, but never even dreamed of conquest there.

In a somewhat similar way China, at the other end of the Old World, was a great and solid continental power. The Chinese had very early and very distant maritime contacts. In the Middle Ages, through their own merchants and through Arab and other merchants, they were in contact with Indonesia and even the Indian Ocean; but never in their history did the Chinese attempt to create an overseas "colonial" empire—not even in the islands of Japan, so near to them. The only attempt to conquer Japan—and it was unsuccessful—was by the Mongols, when they ruled China.

The great change came at the turn from the sixteenth to the seventeenth century. Power began to shift from countries with armies to countries with navies. Although the change was rapid, it was not completed everywhere at the same time. Russia, by its conquest of Siberia, became a more and more gigantic continental power at the same time that England and Holland, rather insignificant countries at the edge of Europe, were transforming themselves into empires based on naval power.

Perhaps the best symbol of change was the rapid decay of the Mogul empire, which had conquered most of India from Central Asia, at the very time when England and France, in seaborne rivalry, were appearing on India's coasts. The Mogul empire in its glory, under Akbar, is described by the Jesuit Father Pierre du Jarric. The change went on more slowly farther to the east, with the Manchus first conquering China from the landward side and then having to give way, step by step, to the importunate seaborne adventurers, led by the English, from the coast. William Hickey, in his accounts of India, Indonesia, the Malay Straits, and Canton, not to mention his early adventures in the West Indies, preserves for us the buoyant, confident mood that by the end of the eighteenth century, characterized the English. With great regret we have not been able to include anything from his long autobiography in this volume—he is the kind of writer who can be recommended to those who have an appetite for following up footnotes and references.

In between, we have the accounts of Tibet by the Jesuit father Desideri and the Jesuit lay brother Benedict Goës—the one who at last, in a fitting and rather symbolic way, identified the Cathay of the Middle Ages with the land of the "Seres" of classical times. From this time on we have the rivalry of the European nations to control Asia from the sea, a struggle no longer simply to get rich by trading with Asia, but to get rich in Asia and to use these riches to create power in Europe. From this time on, therefore, we have travelers who bring back not merely tales of wonder, and not merely tips on profitable trade, but information useful to policy-makers and to governments.

Akbar and the Jesuits [1]:

PIERRE DU JARRIC

[Father Pierre Du Jarric (1566–1677), born in Toulouse, entered the Society of Jesus in order to become a missionary. Instead, he spent most of his life teaching philosophy and moral theology at Bordeaux. Unable to get into the field himself he did the next best thing, gathering up the accounts of those luckier than himself into a three-volume, 2,500-quarto-page compilation, much of it from rare manuscript sources and from at least four different languages. The lack of contemporary accounts of the Emperor Akbar's courts makes Jarric's Histoire *important because it contains the "earliest impressions of the Mogul Empire ever recorded by European writers." Except for the Englishman Ralph Fitch, who visited the court in 1585, the*

[1] From *Akbar and the Jesuits,* by Father P. Du Jarric.

Jesuit Fathers were the only Europeans to visit northern India in the sixteenth century. (From the Preface of Akbar and the Jesuits.)]

Akbar, the Great Mogul

This beautiful, rich, and spacious province, which the Romans called *India citerior,* or *India intra Gangem* (India on this side of the Ganges), and which we call Indostan, is to-day in the possession (at least, for the most part) of a powerful monarch who is generally known as the Great Mogor, his ancestors having been termed Mogores by the inhabitants of that part of India which first came under their sway.

This monarch is of the lineage of the great Tamerlan, or Tamberlan, the Tartar king whom men have called the scourge of God; the same who, having made war upon Bajazet, the emperor of the Turcs, and first of that name, defeated him in a pitched battle, and having taken him prisoner, kept him, like some wild bird, in an iron cage, and fed him as though he had been a dog with the remnants from his own table. Similarly, when he wished to mount his horse, he compelled his captive to offer his back as a mounting-step, and for this purpose led him whithersoever he went by a chain of iron, or, as some say, of gold.

From this man was descended, in a direct male line, he of whom we are about to speak. He was the seventh descendant of Tamerlan, or, as others say, the eighth king after him, which means the same thing. He was born in the province of Chaquata, [Chaghatai], which extends on the south to Indostan, on the west to Persia, and on the north to the country of the Tartars. Howbeit, the inhabitants resemble Turcs rather than Tartars or Persians, and, for the most part, they speak the language of the former, though not with the elegance and purity of the Turcs themselves. The gentlefolk, and others who follow the court, speak Persian, but their pronunciation differs from that of the Persians, and they use many foreign words. This king had a brother who was prince, or king of Cabul, a kingdom lying to the north of Cambaya [Cambay, Guzarate], between Persia and India, and which is believed by many to be the Arachosia of the ancients. This is the sole kingdom which the successors of Tamberlan have retained in their possession, having been driven from all the other kingdoms, provinces, and principalities which their ancestors had conquered, though they afterwards regained some of these which they now hold, with the addition, as we shall presently see, of other newly acquired territories.

The immediate successors of the great Tamberlan, lacking the spirit and prowess of their ancestor, were unable to resist the repeated onslaughts of the Patanes [Pathans] (who are the same as the Parthes), and, in the end, were expelled from all their inherited possessions except the province or kingdom of Cabul. But the great-grandchildren and successors of the same, finding themselves driven to bay in a small corner of their ancestral domains, turned so fiercely on their enemies that they not only drove them from the countries of which they themselves had been dispossessed, but made themselves masters of all that now comprises the kingdom of the Great Mogor.

It was the king Baburxa [Babur Shah], grandfather of him of whom we are speaking, who invaded this part of Indostan, and driving the Parthes before him, confined them to the islands of Bengala. But on the death of Baburxa, the Parthes regained their courage, and made fierce war upon his son Emmaupaxda [Humayun Padshah], attacking him with such vigour that he was driven back with dishonour to Cabul.

Seeing that he had no force capable of resisting such powerful enemies, Emmaupaxda appealed to the king of Persia to aid him in the recovery of his estates and seignories. The Persian promised him assistance, provided that he was willing to embrace the law of Mahomet as taught by Hali, which the Persians follow. Emmaupaxda having accepted this condition, the Persian king sent him many thousands of soldiers, with whose aid he recaptured all his father's possessions, driving the Parthes from every part of the Mogor kingdom. He was succeeded by him who is the subject of our present inquiry. The name of this king was Echebar, or, as some call it, Achebar, but, as we shall see, he styled himself in his royal letters, Mahumet Zelabdin Echebar [Muhammad Jalalu-d din Akbar].

Echebar continued the war which his predecessor had waged against the Parthes (or Patanes, as they are now called in India). He invaded the kingdom of Bengala, of which they had taken possession, expelling them from all but a few islands; though, as we shall see, they subsequently gave him much trouble. He next captured Cambaya, and after that many other of the kingdoms of Indostan. He continued his conquests as long as he lived, so that his sway extended almost to the territories of the kings of Narsinga, Calecut, and other countries bordering the sea, even to the island of Goa, so that he was greatly dreaded in all these lands. His court was attended by many kings, some of whom he had reduced by force of arms, while others had tendered their submission voluntarily, that they might not be deprived of their kingdoms. Sometimes as many as twenty kings were to be seen at his court, each having the right to wear a crown, and the least of whom was as powerful as the king of Calecut. Besides these, there are many others who stay in their kingdoms, and who, in order that they may be exempt from personal service, pay a larger tribute than those who attend at court. Some of these kings are Pagans, and other Mahometans; but Echebar, although he professed, at least outwardly the Mahometan faith, placed more trust in the former than the latter.

As to the limits of his empire, these cannot yet be stated with accuracy; for until the time of his death, which took place on the 27th of October, 1605, he was constantly making new conquests. We are told that in the year 1582 his territories stretched westward to the Indus, and further north to the confines of Persia. The eastern boundaries were the same as those of the kingdom of Bengala, of which he was master. On the north was Tartarie, and on the south the sea which washes the shores of Cambaya. Nowhere else, except in Bengala, did his empire extend to the sea; for the kings of the Malabars, the Portuguese, the king of Narsinga, and certain others, hold, in addition to their other possessions, all the maritime ports. The rest belongs to the great Mogor, whose territories, all included, are estimated to have been, at that time, six hundred leagues in length, and four hundred in breadth; but since then he has annexed the kingdom of Caximir [Kashmir], and several others.

The country is, for the most part, fruitful, producing the needs of life in abundance; for between the two famous rivers, the Indus and the Ganges, which wind over the greater portion of it, watering it like a garden, there are nine others which empty themselves into these two; namely, the Taphy [Tapti], the

Heruada [Narbada], the Chambel, and the Tamona [Jumna], flowing into the Ganges, and the Catamel [Sutlej], the Cebcha [Beas], the Ray [Ravi], the Chenao [Chenab], and the Rebeth [Jhilam], flowing into the Indus, which the people call the Schind. From this we can judge of the fertility of this region, and of the wealth of the great Mogor. For all the kingdoms and provinces which he conquers he holds as his own, appointing his captains, or the kings whom he has dispossessed, as his lieutenants over them. From these he takes a third portion of the revenues, the remainder being for their personal needs, and the maintenance of the soldiers, horses, and elephants which each of them is bound to keep in readiness for any emergency that may arise. The wealth of these provinces is increased by the extensive trade which is carried on in drugs, spices, pearls, and other precious things, and also in civet, cotton cloth, cloth of gold, woollen stuffs, carpets, velvet and other silken fabrics, as well as in every kind of metal. Horses also are brought in large numbers from Persia and Tartary.

But his military strength is even more formidable. For in the various provinces throughout his empire he has in his pay captains dependent on him, each of whom commands twelve or fourteen thousand horse. These they are compelled to maintain, as has already been stated, out of the revenues of the provinces which the king has assigned to them. Besides these, there are others of inferior rank who maintain seven or eight thousand horse, as well as a number of elephants trained for warfare. The king has in his stables five thousand of these elephants, all ready to march at his will. As to the number of elephants in the whole of the kingdom, it has been estimated that he can put into the field fifty thousand, all well armed, in the manner about to be described. In a war with his brother, the Prince of Cabul, who marched in great force against him, Echebar took the field with fifty thousand cavalry, all chosen men, and five thousand fighting elephants, besides innumerable infantry; and this is leaving out of account the thousands of followers, mounted and on foot, whom he left in garrisons, or in other places, requiring protection. In time of war, he recruited his army from all classes of the people, Mogores, Coronans [Khurasanis], Parthes, Torquimaches, Boloches, Guzarates, and other Industans, whether Pagans or Mahometans.

He goes into battle with many pieces of artillery, which are placed in the front line. The elephants are kept in the rear, and are armed in the following fashion. To protect the head from blows, it is covered with a plate of iron, or tough hide. A sword is attached to the trunk, and a dagger to each of the long tusks which protrude from the mouth. Each animal bears on his back four small wooden turrets, from which as many soldiers discharge their bows, arquebusses, or muskets. The driver is protected by a cuirass, or by plates of metal overlapping like scales. Elephants thus equipped are not placed in the front line, as they would shut out the enemy from the view of the soldiers, and would, when wounded, break the ranks of the soldiers, and throw the army into disorder. They are kept in the rear of the force; and should the enemy penetrate so far, this formidable troupe is brought suddenly into action, to bar his further progress. These beasts, even when unarmed, can do great damage. They seize with their trunks those whom they find in their path, and raising them in the air as high as they are able, dash them to the ground and trample them under their feet. At other times they attack with their iron-sheathed heads, butting after the manner of rams.

The city of Delhi had formerly been the residence of the kings of Mogor. Echebar, however, first took up his abode at another city called Agra; and when two of his children died there, he caused another city of great beauty to be built, which was named Pateful, or Fatefur. But after his conquest of the kingdom of Lahor, he made its capital city, Lahor, his usual residence.

It was in the year 1582 that his court was first visited by Fathers of the Company. He was then about forty years of age, of medium stature, and strongly built. He wore a turban on his head, and the fabric of his costume was interwoven with gold thread. His outer garment reached to his knees, and his breeches to his heels. His stockings were much like ours; but his shoes were of a peculiar pattern invented by himself. On his brow he wore several rows of pearls or precious stones. He had a great liking for European clothes; and sometimes it was his pleasure to dress himself in a costume of black velvet made after the Portuguese fashion; but this was only on private, not on public occasions. He had always a sword at his side, or at any rate so near by that he could lay his hand upon it in a moment. Those who guarded his person, and whom he kept constantly near him, were changed each day of the week, as were his other officers and attendants, but in such a manner that the same persons came on duty every eighth day.

Echebar possessed an alert and discerning mind; he was a man of sound judgment, prudent in affairs, and, above all, kind, affable, and generous. With these qualities he combined the courage of those who undertake and carry out great enterprises. He could be friendly and genial in his intercourse with others, without losing the dignity befitting the person of a king. He seemed to appreciate virtue, and to be well disposed towards foreigners, particularly Christians, some of whom he always liked to have about him. He was interested in, and curious to learn about many things, and possessed an intimate knowledge not only of military and political matters, but of many of the mechanical arts. He took delight in watching the casting of pieces of artillery, and in his own palace kept workmen constantly employed in the manufacture of guns and arms of various descriptions. In short, he was well informed on a great variety of matters, and could discourse on the laws of many sects, for this was a subject of which he made a special study. Although he could neither read nor write, he enjoyed entering into debate with learned doctors. He always entertained at his court a dozen or so of such men, who propounded many questions in his presence. To their discussions, now on one subject, now on another, and particularly to the stories which they narrated, he was a willing listener, believing that by this means he could overcome the disadvantage of his illiteracy.

Echebar was by temperament melancholy, and he suffered from the falling-sickness [epilepsy]; so that to divert his mind, he had recourse to various forms of amusement, such as watching elephants fight together, or camels, or buffaloes, or rams that butt and gore each other with their horns, or even two cocks. He was also fond of watching fencing bouts; and on certain occasions, after the manner of the ancient Romans, he made gladiators fight before him; or fencers were made to contend until one had killed the other. At other times, he amused himself with elephants and camels that had been trained to dance to the tune of certain musical instruments, and to perform

other strange feats. But in the midst of all these diversions—
and this is a very remarkable thing—he continued to give his
attention to affairs of state, even to matters of grave importance.

Often he used to hunt the wild animals that abound in these
regions. For this purpose he employed panthers instead of hunting-dogs; for in this country panthers are trained to the chase
as we train dogs. He did not care much for hawking, though he
had many well-trained falcons and other birds of prey; and
there were some expert falconers amongst his retainers. Some
of these were so skilful with the bow that they very rarely missed
a bird at which they shot, even though it was on the wing, and
though their arrows were unfeathered.

To catch wild deer he used other deer which had been trained
for this purpose. These carried nets on their horns in which the
wild deer that came to attack them became entangled, upon
which they were seized by the hunters who had been lying in
concealment near by. When on a military campaign, he used to
hunt in the following manner. Four or five thousand men were
made to join hands and form a ring round a piece of jungle.
Others were then sent inside to drive the animals to the edge
of the enclosure, where they were captured by those forming
the ring. A fine was levied on those who allowed an animal to
break through and escape.

So much for the king's recreations. We will now turn to more
serious matters. That any person might be able to speak to him
on business of importance, Echebar appeared twice daily in public, and gave audience to all classes of his subjects. For this purpose he made use of two large halls of his palace, in each of
which was placed on a raised dais a splendid and costly throne.
To the first of these halls all his subjects had access, and there
he listened to all who sought speech with him. But to the second
none was admitted but the captains and great nobles of his
kingdom, and the ambassadors who came from foreign kings to
confer with him on affairs of importance. Eight officers, men of
experience and good judgment, were in constant attendance on
him. Amongst these he apportioned the days of the week, so
that each had his special day for introducing those who desired
an audience. It was their duty to examine the credentials of all
such persons, and to act as masters of ceremony, instructing
them, more especially if they were foreigners, how to make rev-

erence to the king, and how to comport themselves in his presence; for on these occasions much ceremony is observed, it being the custom, amongst other things, to kiss the feet of the king on saluting him. When giving audience, the king is also attended by a number of secretaries, whose duty is to record in writing every word that he speaks. This is a custom much practised by the princes of Persia, and other eastern countries.

For the administration of justice, there are magistrates whose judgement is final, and others from whom there is an appeal. In every case the proceedings are verbal, and are never committed to writing.

The king of whom we are speaking made it his particular care that in every case justice should be strictly enforced. He was, nevertheless, cautious in the infliction of punishment, especially the punishment of death. In no city where he resided could any person be put to death until the execution warrant had been submitted to him, some say, as many as three times. His punishments were not, ordinarily, cruel; though it is true that he caused some who had conspired against his life to be slain by elephants, and that he sometimes punished criminals by impalement after the Turkish fashion. A robber or sea-pirate, if he had killed no one, suffered the loss of a hand; but murderers, highwaymen, and adulterers were either strangled or crucified [attachez en croix], or their throats were cut, according to the gravity of their crimes. Lesser offenders were whipped and set free. In brief, the light of clemency and mildness shone forth from this prince, even upon those who offended against his own person. He twice pardoned an officer high in his service, who had been convicted of treason and conspiracy, graciously restoring him to favour and office. But when the same officer so far forgot himself as to repeat his offence a third time, he sentenced him to death by crucifixion.

Echebar seldom lost his temper. If he did so, he fell into a violent passion; but his wrath was never of long duration. Before engaging in any important undertaking, he used to consult the members of his council; but he made up his own mind, adopting whatever course seemed to him the best. Sometimes he communicated his intentions to his councillors, to ascertain their views. If they approved, they would answer with the words "Peace be to our lord the King." If anyone expressed an adverse opinion, he would listen patiently, answer his objections, and point out the reasons for his own decision. Sometimes, in view of the objections pointed out to him, he changed the plans he had made.

. . . .

In consequence of this disaster [an attack by a band of robbers], the King at once left Lahor, though it was said that he had decided to do so before it happened, and went to spend the summer in the kingdom of Caximir [Kashmir], or as others call it, Cascimir, which he had recently conquered. Thither he was accompanied, at his own request, by Father Hierosme Xauier and Benoist de Gois, Father Emmanuel Pignero being left at Lahor to complete the building of the church and the house, which had already been commenced. The kingdom of Caximir is one of the pleasantest and most beautiful countries to be found in the whole of India, we may even say in the East. It is completely surrounded by very high mountains, which for the greater part of the year are covered with snow, and all the rest of the kingdom is a beautiful plain clothed in verdure, diversified with groves, orchards, gardens, and well watered by springs and rivers: a very pleasant land for those who dwell therein. Owing to the mountains, the climate of the country is somewhat cold, though it is more temperate than that of the kingdom of Rebat, which joins Caximir on the east. In the month of May, great numbers of wild-duck come from the mountains of Rebat and settle in huge flocks on the streams which flow near to the town of Caximir, the capital of the kingdom, because of the warmer climate. About three leagues from the town there is a lake of sweet water which, though not more than two leagues in circuit and half a league broad, is so deep that large vessels can float upon it. In the middle there is an artificial island on which the King has a palace, where he refreshes himself when he goes to shoot the duck which abound on this lake. On the banks of a river, the waters of which flow through the lake, there is a species of very large tree, the trunk and leaves of which resemble those of the chestnut. . . . The wood is very dry, and has a grain like rippling water; it is much used for making small caskets and similar articles. The country abounds in wheat, rice, and other food grains. They plant vines at the roots of the mulberry trees, so that grapes and mulberries are seen hanging from the same branches. People say that this kingdom was one of the most formidable in these parts, and that the Great Mogor would never have been able to subdue it but for the factions which existed amongst the inhabitants. Knowing that it was a kingdom divided against itself, he invaded it with a large army, and easily made himself master of it. Formerly all the people of this country were Gentiles; but about three hundred years ago they joined the sect of Mahomet, and the majority of them are now Saracens.

When the Great Mogor retired to this kingdom of Caximir, with all his household and family, Father Hierosme Xauier, observing that he had now more leisure, resolved to speak to him on the subject of his conversion, intending, when the opportunity offered, to remind him, on the one hand, of the great blessings he had received from God, and on the other hand, of the chastisements which the same Seigneur had sent for his admonition, hoping that thereby he might induce him to hear with attention, and not at odd moments as hitherto, the things relating to the salvation of his soul, and that in the end he would find himself able to accept and follow the holy law. But when they reached Caximir, the Father was attacked by a severe illness, which lasted for the space of two months. During this time, the King showed him much kindness, giving orders for the liberal supply of all his wants, and sending his own physician to attend him; he even went in person to see him, which was a very special favour; for it is his custom never to visit anyone. Towards the end of the summer, when the Father began to recover, the King himself fell sick. On several occasions during his illness, he sent for the Father, and had him brought to the chamber where he lay, which even the greatest lords of his court were seldom permitted to enter. Owing to these illnesses, the Father had no opportunity, before the return to Lahor, of speaking to the King as he had intended on the subject of his conversion.

Whilst they were in the kingdom of Caximir there was so grievous a famine that many mothers were rendered destitute, and having no means of nourishing their children, exposed them for sale in the public places of the city. Moved to compassion by this pitiable sight, the Father bought many of these little ones, who, soon after receiving baptism, yielded up their spirits to their Creator. A certain Saracen, seeing the charity of the Father towards these children, brought him one of his own; but the Father gave it back to the mother, together with a certain sum of money for its support; for he was unwilling to baptise it, seeing that, if it survived, there was little prospect of its being able to live a Christian life in that country. At daybreak the next morning, however, the mother knocked at the door of his lodging, and begged him to come to her house and baptise the child, as it was about to die. Accompanied by some Portuguese, he went with her to the house and baptised the child, having first obtained the consent of its father. The latter, after it was dead, wished to circumcise it; but this the Father would not permit, but buried it with Christian rites. There was another mother, a Mahometan woman, who brought to him, under similar circumstances, her infant son to be baptised; and in this case, too, as soon as the rite had been performed, the spirit of the little sufferer ascended to heaven.

An Account of Tibet [2]:
IPPOLITO DESIDERI

[*A persistent, romantic legend turned up periodically in the past that told of the existence beyond the Himalayas of isolated Christian communities dating from the earliest days of the church. It was in response to a fresh flowering of this rumor that Ippolito Desideri (1684–1733), while still studying for the priesthood in Rome, determined to reach Tibet and test it.*

[*Desideri was the first European to follow the southern foot of almost the whole trans-Himalaya mountain range. He was a sharp and conscientious observer and his geography of Tibet is still considered classic.*

[*He arrived in Lhasa in 1716 and at his first audience with the king obtained permission to preach and to buy a house. (The latter was a special mark of favor since foreigners could ordinarily not buy but only rent houses.) Desideri studied the Tibetan language with great devotion, eventually writing a*

[2] From *An Account of Tibet*, edited by Felippo de Felippi.

book in the language. Not surprisingly, it was a critique of the Tibetan religion and a defense of his own. When, at the end of five years, he was recalled it marked the end of the Jesuit mission in that part of the world.]

On the twentieth of June, 1715, we arrived at the city of Lhe [Leh], otherwise Lhata, capital of Second Thibet [Ladak]. The journey from Kascimir [Kashmir] to Lhata, which takes forty days, can only be accomplished on foot. The path, so narrow that we were obliged to go in single file, leads up the sides of very high and terrible mountains; in places it had been destroyed by avalanches or heavy rains and there was no foothold. Then the guide would go in front and cut a step the size of a man's foot with his axe, and giving me his left hand helped me to put my foot into the step while he excavated another, until we again struck the narrow path. In other places the mountain was still so covered with ice and snow that the risk on the narrow pathway was great; if your foot slipped nothing could save you from falling headlong down into the torrent below. Many of the men who, as I have said, go from Kascimir to fetch loads of wool, lose their lives or are crippled for ever. One of our servants slipped on the ice, fell, and rolled down the mountain side. We feared he was lost, but the load strapped on his shoulders fortunately buried itself in the snow and checked his fall. Thus the other men were able to go down carefully and save their comrade and his load. The reflected rays of the sun from the snow, in which we marched all day, caused my eyes to inflame, and I was in some fear for my sight. While in a part of the valley between two high and steep mountains, I was moved by a curiosity to go and examine a big rock shaped roughly like an elephant, not artificially, but by nature. Suddenly my companion and the servants shouted aloud to me, and I had hardly gone twenty paces when, with a noise like loud thunder, a huge mass of congealed snow fell from the mountain above on the very spot I had just left. In some places there was really no road at all, only large boulders and rocks covered the ground, over which we had to climb like goats with great trouble and difficulty. As no animal can travel over such bad roads, the whole journey from Kascimir to Lhata . . . must be done on foot and, as the land produces nothing and is sparsely inhabited, all provisions—that is, rice, vegetables, and butter, as well as luggage—must be carried by men. To conclude, I may say that from Kascimir to the end of the Great Desert, which I shall describe later, is a journey of five months, during which there is no shelter; in rain, snow, or hard frost one has to pass the night in the open country.

Second Thibet, or Lhata-yul [Ladak], is two months' journey in length. . . . It is mountainous, sterile, and altogether horrible. Barley is the chief product; a little wheat is grown, and in some places apricots. Trees are scarce, so wood is hard to procure. There are many sheep, especially very large geldings; their flesh is most excellent, and their wool extraordinarily fine. Musk deer also exist. In valleys at the foot of mountains, and also near streams, the natives find a good deal of gold, not in large nuggets, but as gold dust. They eat meat, and the flour of roasted barley, and drink Ciang [Chang], a sort of beer made from barley, which I shall mention hereafter. Their clothes, made of wool, are of suitable shape and make. They are not at all arrogant, but rather submissive, kindly, cheerful, and courteous. The language of this country does not differ much from that of Third Thibet [Tibet proper], and the Religion and books relating to religion are similar. There are numerous monasteries and a great many monks; their superior is a chief Lama, who, to qualify for the post, must have studied for some years in a University in Third Thibet, as must any monk who aspires to be promoted to a higher grade. A number of merchants from Kascimir engaged in the wool trade live in this Kingdom, and they are allowed to have mosques and openly to hold their religion. Occasionally merchants come from the kingdom of Kotan [Khotan] with well-bred horses, cotton goods, and other merchandise. Some come from Third Thibet by way of the great desert and bring tea and tobacco, bales of silk, and other things from China. There are villages but only one city in this kingdom, Lhe or Lhata, which is the capital where the Grand Lama and the absolute Sovereign live. It is situated in a large plain surrounded by mountains, and dotted with villages. The city at the foot of the hill gradually extends upwards until you reach the Residence of the Grand Lama and the Royal Palace, both large, fine buildings. Above, nearly on the summit of the hill, is a fortress, while the city is defended by walls on either side and below. The houses, strongly built, are roomy and well adapted to the country.

. . . .

*Journey across the Great Desert of Ngnari Giongar,
and Assistance rendered by a Tartar Princess and her Followers*

Trescij-Khang lies on the edge of a vast, sterile and terrible desert, to cross which takes about three months. We could find no guide, and for us to attempt such a journey alone meant certain death. The Lama, the Governor, and the Castellan took much trouble to find someone who knew the desert or who was returning to Third Thibet. Some time passed and then God, who never abandons those who put their trust in Him, provided us with the best escort that can be imagined. Two days' journey from Trescij-Khang is a large district called Cartoa [Gartok], garrisoned by a strong body of Tartar and Thibetan troops subject to the King of Third Thibet, not only to defend Trescij-Khang and divers villages, but to prevent armed bandits from approaching by little known paths and invading the country. At the head of these troops was a Tartar Prince, and since his death two years before, his wife had been in command. She had now obtained permission to return with her soldiers to Lhasa, the garrison being replaced by new troops under another commander, and early in October she came to Trescij-Khang to make the last arrangements. We were presented and begged her to allow us to travel under her protection to Lhasa. With most kind words the Princess replied that she would do all in her power not only to help us, but to make the long and difficult journey as pleasant as possible; adding that she esteemed it a great honour to be able to assist two Lamas from a distant land. During the short time she was at Trescij-Khang she insisted on our dining with her every day.

On October the ninth, having made all necessary preparations, we left Trescij-Khang, and on the eleventh arrived at Cartoa, where we waited until the Princess was ready to depart.

At the head of our caravan rode a number of the Princess's servants and some squadrons of Tartar cavalry, followed by the Princess and her Tartar ladies, all on horseback, her ministers and the officers of her army; then came more Tartar cavalry with whom we generally rode; the rear guard was composed of cavalry, partly Tartar, partly Thibetan, the baggage train, provisions, and a crowd of men on foot and led horses. We left Cartoa in the second half of October, and arrived at the highest point reached during the whole journey in this desert called Ngnari Giongar on the ninth of November. . . . Close by is a mountain of excessive height and great circumference, always enveloped in cloud, covered with snow and ice, and most horrible, barren, steep, and bitterly cold [Mount Kailas]. . . .

Owing to the snow on this mountain my eyes became so inflamed that I well nigh lost my sight. I had no spectacles, and the only remedy, as I learnt from our escort was to rub the eyes with snow.

Winter is the best time for traveling in these countries, because the snow gives water for drinking and in summer the roads are impracticable for three months owing to the rain. . . .

On December the first we reached more level country almost free of snow, called Toscioá, where we halted two days to rest men and horses. There we found several tents of the herdsmen who roam all over the desert pasturing the herds of horses, mules, and especially mountain cows belonging to the Grand Lama and the King. Farther on we came to a plain called Retoa, where there is a lake so large that it takes people several days to walk round. It is believed to be the source of the Ganges. But from my own observation and from what I heard from various people who knew this country and the whole of Mogol, it seemed that the above mentioned mountain Ngnari Giongar must be regarded as the fountainhead not only of the river Ganges, but also of the Indus. Mount Ngnari Giongar being the highest point of this region the water drains off on two sides. To the west it flows through Second Thibet to Lesser Thibet until it reaches the Mountains of Kascimir, and finally, near Lesser Guzarat forms the wide, navigable river Indus. On the eastern side, another large body of water flows into lake Retoa and eventually forms the river Ganges. This agrees with the detailed accounts in old writers about the gold sand found in the Ganges. They must have lied if the source of the great river is elsewhere, for it is only on the banks and in the sand of Lake Retoa that any large quantity of gold is collected, being washed down from the Mountain Ngnari Giongar by heavy rains and melting snow. If it is admitted that the fountainhead of the river Ganges is on this mountain then the old writers speak the truth, and my observations confirm their words. Thibetans and merchants come there from time to time to search for and collect the gold sand, to their great profit; and as I have already said, this superstitious people make pilgrimages to the lake, devoutly walk round it and think thereby to gain great indulgences.

On the twenty-second of December we reached another large plain and found more tents belonging to men tending herds of cattle, the property of the King or the Grand Lama. I must not forget to add that, although this great Desert is so barren and uninhabited, it yields a considerable revenue to the King and the Grand Lama by reason not only of the quantity of gold, but of the innumerable loads of most exquisite butter made from the milk of these mountain cows, the duties paid by merchants passing through Cartoa, and divers other things.

On the fourth of January, 1716, we at last quitted the great Desert and arrived at a big place called Ser-kia [Saka dzong] well fortified as beseems a frontier town, where dwelt a great Governor, head of the province of Zang-to [Upper Tsang].

Having given you but a brief description of our journey across the Desert I must add a few details for the better understanding of the difficulties. To begin with, for three whole months the traveler finds no village, nor any living creature; he must therefore take with him all provisions, such as tea, butter, flour or parched barley and meat, which becomes so frozen that, like our ham, it will keep for a long time. Not only must one carry provisions for the men, but barley and flour for the horses, the ground being generally so covered with snow that they can find no food. Water is frozen hard and for cooking you have to thaw snow or ice over a fire. Now wood is not to be found in the desert, save here and there a few prickly bushes, and to make a fire one has to search for the dry dung of horse and cattle. Your bed at night is the earth, off which you often have to scrape the snow, and your roof is the sky, from which falls snow and sleet. You can, it is true, have camp tents of Tartar fashion, like a round house and portable, but animals are needed to carry them and servants to pitch them. The com-

mon linen tents afford some comfort, but are extremely incon-
venient, because of the difficulty of driving the big iron pegs
into sandy or frozen ground to keep them steady against the
prevailing violent winds. Snow and frost also render them stiff
and very heavy. Clothes are another great difficulty. Should you
desire to be clean and decently dressed, you are exposed to the
bitter cold and run the risk of losing nose, fingers, toes and even
your life. If you look to utility instead of cleanliness, you must
bear the great weight of sheepskins and put up with the dirt
and the insects which accumulate after long wear. Before leaving
Trescij-Khang we, our three Christian servants, and the infidel
interpreter bought . . . Tartar coats, much used also by the Thibetans and by priests when on a journey. They are made of
sheepskin and reach to the knees, the wool is inside, and the
outside skin is covered with fine woollen cloth or coloured
cotton which comes from China. As they do not protect the legs
or the head, I had made in Trescij-Khang for ourselves and for
our people some long boots of sheepskin, and caps which not
only cover the head, but the ears and the neck. I afterwards
found that my invention, suggested partly by self-love and
partly to protect our servants against frostbite or even death,
were in common use among our escort. Tartars and Thibetans
also cover their faces with a kind of half-mask made of fine
lambskin, and these I bought. To save the eyes from the reflection of the sun's rays off the snow, they wear a concave shield
woven of black horse- or ox-hair. Although this journey is made
on horseback and not on foot, yet it is most irksome on account
of starting every morning before sunrise and not dismounting
till the sun sets; and what with the mountains, ice, dearth of
pasture and continual snow, many horses die on the road. We
left Lhata with seven horses; only two reached Lhasa, one worn
out and with many sores, the other in such bad condition that
it died a few days after our arrival. Add to this the dangerous
roads in such a horrible country, always going up and down
those terrible mountains in the midst of snow and ice, exposed
to most inclement weather and biting cold winds.

I will briefly describe to you our life. At daybreak we two
Fathers got up, took down the frozen camp tent and loaded it
on a horse, with our money and a few necessary things, then we
saddled our horses and those of our servants and of our inter-

preter, drank our tea . . . and collected the kitchen utensils. We then rode till sunset. When we reached the camping ground and selected a place as free from snow as possible, we set up our tent, searched for big stones to keep it steady, unsaddled the horses, unpacked our bundles, and then went to find dry horse and cattle dung for the fire. While our servants prepared the dinner we Fathers said matins and lauds for the following day and other prayers. Then having seen our horses well covered, watered and fed, we retired to rest. The night was rather a cessation of fatigue than real repose, for the intense cold and the intolerable annoyance of the insects harboured in our clothes prevented any real sleep.

But in all this discomfort and suffering we were much comforted by the loving kindness and paternal assistance of God, in whose service alone we had undertaken this journey and exposed ourselves willingly to whatever might happen. Thus we hardly felt the hardships, but with courage, good health and contented minds we conversed together, and with others, as though we were traveling for amusement and pleasure. A great help to us also was the kindly, almost maternal, interest the Princess took in our welfare. For instance, the difficulty, as I have already said, of finding materials for a fire, or fodder for our tired horses was great, and almost every evening she would send us a little from her own store; again, she occasionally sent us a live sheep or some game, rice and suchlike things. As I had learnt a little of the language from our interpreter, she would call me to her side along the road, and when we arrived at the camping place she would order my horse to be cared for and invite me to her tent, which had been already prepared, until the other Father and our people came up; give me some refreshment and ask me about our country, Europe, our customs, our Holy Law, the images of Saints in my Breviary, my manner of praying and the meaning of my prayers, my journeys in other countries and the customs I had noticed there.

On the twenty-second of November, when it was already getting dark, thinking the other Father had arrived with our people, I took leave of the Princess; but could find no one. Much troubled, I waited till about the third hour of the night, when at last our three Christian servants arrived with the baggage horse. I anxiously asked about the Father and the interpreter;

they said that by his orders they had left them behind; the Father's horse having fallen exhausted in the snow, he decided to wait until the poor beast recovered a little. Still more alarmed I went to find the Gubra or Prime Minister of the Princess, and heard he was in her tent. So I sent in a message begging him to grant me a moment's interview. The Princess at once ordered me to come in and tell her what I wanted, and commanded some Tartar horsemen to go at once with a led horse to find the Father, and made me sit down to supper with her. The night was quite dark and the Tartars went back on our steps shouting aloud, and after a long time found the Father buried in snow and the interpreter half frozen. They had been unable to make the horse get up and as all the rearguard had passed they did not dare to move lest they should entirely lose their way. The Tartars lifted the Father on to the led horse and the interpreter on to his, which was in pretty good condition, and conducted them to our tent, where by orders of the Princess a good fire had been lit and supper prepared. In addition to all this the Princess sent next morning to ask how the Father was, and one of her own horses for his use until we could in some way buy another. A few days later, owing to constant ascending and descending mountains in deep snow, my horse refused to move; dismounting I found a big sore on his back. So I led him, hurrying as fast as I could after the others. The Princess who happened to pass by told me to mount and ride near her until we reached the camping ground. I showed her what a state my horse was in, when she at once ordered one of her officers to give me his and that evening she arranged that two of her horses were to be at our service until the end of the journey. . . .

Arrival at the first inhabited Place in Third and Greatest Thibet. Continuation of the Journey to the Capital. Visits to the King and the Ministers. Commencement of my Mission in that Kingdom.

. . . Finally, two years and four months after I left Goa, and one year and a half since our departure from Delly [Delhi], and ten whole months since leaving Kascimir, we arrived, by the grace of God, on the eighteenth day of March, 1716, at the city

of Lhasa, capital of this Thibet, which once before had been
selected as a seat of our Missions. My companion had always
lived in hot climates and feared the intense cold and the thin
air, so after staying a few days at Lhasa to recuperate, he left
[on April sixteenth] by the more frequented road through
Nepal and returned to Hindustan. Thus I remained for some
time alone, the only Missionary, indeed the only European in
this immense country of the three Thibets. . . .

Lhasa is densely populated, not only by natives, but by a large
numbers of foreigners of divers nations, such as Tartars,
Chinese, Muscovites, Armenians, people from Cascimir, Hindustan and Nepal, all established there as merchants, and who have
made large fortunes. The houses are generally large and spacious, built of stone and three storeys high. Many families
inhabit the ground and first floors, while the owner lives in the
upper part. The rooms are well planned, many are large and
there are spacious halls with balconies. In most of these houses
the floors of the principal rooms are very fine, made of tiny
stones of various colours, well arranged and cemented with
resin of pine-trees and other ingredients; these are beaten for
many days until the floor becomes one homogeneous mass like
porphyry, quite smooth and shining, so that when washed it is
like a looking-glass. There is usually a chapel in every house, . . .
with carved and gilt cupboards in which are kept statuettes
of their idols and some religious books. In front of these cupboards are shelves on which burn small lamps, and brass vases
stand containing offerings of water, barley, flour, fruits, and such
like things. Incense is also burnt. Thibetan houses are the same
all over the Kingdom, only some are built of earth. It is true
the earth is very adhesive and is mixed with small pebbles. It is
kneaded in moulds or boxes into a solid mass and then pressed
until quite hard. Of these bricks (so to speak) the houses are
built and they are so solid that I have seen repeated blows given
by a pickaxe before they could be demolished.

In the centre of the City is a large square where from early
morning until sundown a fair is held; indeed from three o'clock
after midday until evening one can find everything, and the
crowd is so great that it is difficult to get across the square. On
the Northern side is a splendid palace called Trussi-Khang, the
King's residence. It was built at great cost by the late Grand

Lama. He built it in order to go there from time to time and amuse himself by seeing the ladies of Lhasa dance: hence its name of Trussi-Khang, which means the House of Dancing. The architecture of the King's palace is fine, strong and with symmetrically distributed windows and balconies. There are three floors surmounted by handsome cornices which resemble those on our houses or by a terrace. It is built of brick; in the centre the surface is not smooth, but spotted and granulated in grotesque style, and red in colour. Inside are two large and very long courtyards ornamented with a series of porticos. The palace is wide, long, and very big. In length it is nearly half the size of the great square; that is to say about the length of the palace of St. Mark in Rome, but the height is less.

On the Western side of the square is an ancient large Temple called Lha-brang or Palace of the Gods. Inside are many chapels dedicated to the various idols of this people, in which large lamps burn night and day, fed with melted butter instead of oil. There are some fine pictures in the entrance portico. This Temple (like others in Thibet) has a great pagoda-roof, covered with metal and other work, and bas-reliefs, all richly gilt. Round the edge, especially at the four corners, hang bells which ring with every gust of wind. This roof is not square and flat, but raised in the middle, and on the ridge are various figures. It is supported by some tall and strong columns and a great balustrade, through the openings of which light comes into the temple. All round the outside of the balustrade is a frieze of beautiful bas-reliefs in gilt metal. Services are held here every day by the monks of the adjoining monastery and are attended by a devout crowd of laymen and monks. A very broad street surrounds it, with some fine houses, and all day long troops of Thibetans walk round and round the Temple, always keeping it on their right; they think thus to gain great indulgences. Some of the more devout even lie down flat and, marking where their head touches the ground, get up, and again lie down, putting their feet where their head has been, and thus go round and round the temple. No one, not even the King, is allowed to ride in this street, but is obliged to dismount and lead his horse or go some other way. . . .

Just inside the gate, on the left, is the famous Potala, residence of the Grand Lama of Thibet. I shall describe this Grand

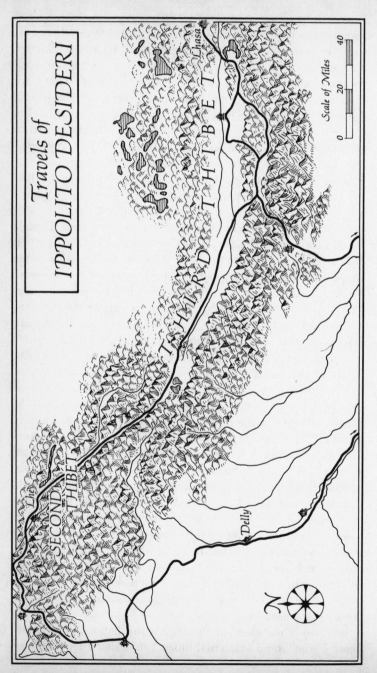

Lama later, now I shall only speak of his fine Palace of Potala. Potala is a huge rock of considerable circumference and somewhat high. Below this rock to the South is a handsome square surrounded by high walls with great gates and bulwarks like a fortress, on the inside are fine colonnades. From here a wide, well-conceived and easy staircase leads up to the summit of the rock where stands a sumptuous palace five storeys high. The centre of the façade of this palace corresponding to the principal apartments is most perfect and well proportioned, the two wings do not quite correspond; still it is a fine building. . . .

Concerning the Grand Lama, Head of the Thibetan Religion

. . . The hierarchy existing in Thibet is not secular but superior to all temporal and regular government. Head of all is the Grand Lama of Thibet, who is like the Pontiff of this blind and superstitious people, and the chief of all other Lamas. To explain the devotion of the Thibetans to their Grand Lama and why they not only respect him, but invoke his aid and offer sacrifices to him and adore him, you must know that one of their most sacred and worshipped idols . . . is called Cen-ree-zij. They say that for ages this Cen-ree-zij has been reincarnated as a human being uninterruptedly in Thibet or in one of the adjoining countries, not so much from a desire to receive the homage of his beloved Thibetans, as to be ready to help them when in need, to guide them in their religion so that it may never waver in the Kingdom, and to lead them in the path of virtue and thereby insure their eternal and perfect felicity. To achieve this, they say that in all his successive incarnations he is always born as the Grand Lama, that is to say, absolutely alien to things of this life and head Master and Director of Thibet in all matters pertaining to religion. In short the Thibetans believe that their Grand Lama Cen-ree-zij voluntarily becomes a man for the good of the Kingdom and the salvation of their souls. . . . Not only does he show himself to his beloved Thibetans, but to foreigners, not only does he receive visits in his palace, but on some festivals he goes abroad, and is seen by all in public and solemn state. I must add that when the Grand Lama grows old, or is ill, or dies, this people show the

greatest veneration and love for him, believing that it is out of
love for them and for their salvation that he has, not once but an
infinite number of times, become a man, and taken upon
himself the hardships and misery which afflict fragile, decrepit,
and mortal humanity. . . .

The Thibetans affirm that the Grand Lama ere he dies pre-
dicts the place where in a few months he is to be born anew
and bids them go there and search for him. After the lapse of
a few years a child whose birth, reckoning from his conception,
coincides with the times predicted by the late Grand Lama and
the years passed since his death, says he is the Grand Lama
who died in such a year, such a month, and on such a day.
He declares that he has been born anew in order to continue
helping his devoted Thibetans, and demands to be reinstated
in the palace of Potala. The news soon spreads to the Court,
whereupon the King and the government order that several
Lamas, doctors and monks of high standing, authority and
prudence, should go and carefully examine, discuss, and judge,
whether the boy really be the new-born Grand Lama or not.
When they arrive at the place, together and singly they question
the boy several times in order to discover whether he really be
the new-born Grand Lama. During this examination the boy
relates that in his former state such and such a thing had
happened to him; so and so were his friends; that he often used
certain books, describing what they were like; that in such a
box, shut in a particular way, were certain things; and gives
other and various details. The envoys after conferring together
come to the conclusion that the boy having remembered clearly
and minutely so many things concerning the late Grand Lama
of Thibet, there could be no doubt that he is the Grand Lama
born again for the good of his country. Then they prostrate
themselves at the boy's feet, worship him with great affection
and many tears, and return to the Court to render a full account
of their mission, demanding that the boy shall be brought to
Lhasa, installed in his residence of Potala and enthroned, which
is done with great solemnity. This is what the Thibetans say and
believe. When I spoke about this to several persons they said
they were convinced that it was a fraud arranged between the
child's relations and some Lamas and monks to deceive the
credulous Thibetans; that they secretly instructed him and
only let him speak when he knew his lesson well. These were

all discreet and learned persons in authority, and highly respected, and they have constantly said this is the only explanation, refusing to believe that it is an artifice of the devil as I have asserted. They deny that the devil could have so much power. Another reason they give is that this thing happens not once but very frequently, and finally they say it is unbelievable that God can permit that so numerous a people should be repeatedly confirmed in their false belief. Perchance the reader may be inclined to believe the people who attribute all this to the boy's relations and the Lamas and others who teach him what to say, and not to the machinations of the devil. . . .

About the Thibetan Monks and Nuns, their Monasteries, Convents, Dress, Organization, and Habits

Monks and nuns, who are very numerous, are also much respected by the Thibetans. The monasteries are very large and there are many of them; each is ruled by at least one Lama and another monk who holds the office of Ker-Koo [Gé-kö, provost], which means that he attends to all correspondence, sees that the rules are absolutely obeyed, and superintends punishments. There are four grades of Thibetan monks. The first are Lamas; the second are Rangiamba, or doctors and teachers who, after studying for twelve years in some monastery, which is also a university, and holding many public disputations, are at last promoted to be doctors. . . . The third grade are the Ke-long, who have not only taken monastic vows, but far more severe ones. They swear to their Lama to preserve absolute chastity, to obey him implicitly, and take so strict a vow of poverty that they may possess nothing, and must beg their food day by day. They are only permitted to have one garment, which must be a gift, and one dish for food and drink, and may only accept enough for one day. It is true this is not strictly observed. They also swear not to touch any intoxicating liquor, or smoke tobacco or eat garlic, and various other things. They are only allowed one meal a day, so the Ke-long eat no supper but only drink a little *cia* or some other liquid. They must pray several times a day and make sacrifices. They wear a yellow cap shaped like a mitre and a yellow robe under the red cloak worn by all the priesthood. . . .

In Thibet there is no definite age for taking the habit, but generally small children of four or five years of age are put into the monasteries, partly to accustom them to the life from early years and to induce them to study, partly because their avaricious parents are glad to be quit of the son or daughter destined for a religious life, and partly from superstition. . . . They think the child is born with the instinctive desire to become a religious, and so make him or her take the habit at the age of four or five and live in a monastery or a nunnery.

The children who are to become monks or nuns are presented to the Lama of the monastery or convent which is to be their home by their parents and a few monks. The Lama cuts off their hair, bestows upon them a new name and consigns them to the care of a Rangiamba, or to an old monk who is master of the novices, to be instructed in religious matters, reprimanded and even punished. After some years the novice goes to a monastery-university to perfect himself in different sciences.

Lamas, Ranjambas, Ke-longs, Traba, and nuns all wear the same habit. Their hair must be quite shaved, and indoor and out they wear a woollen yellow cap with long fringes of wool, shaped like the crown of our hats, but with lappets behind and on the sides reaching to the shoulders; those on the sides are generally turned up. . . . Their habit consists of a tunic of red cloth which reaches to the hips; it has no buttons, but is wide and overlaps and is held in its place by a girdle of yellow wool, generally netted. It has no sleeves but may be trimmed with red or yellow damask, and for the Lamas with brocade.

Monasteries and nunneries are absolutely separated, though ruled by the same Lama. Women may not enter a monastery and men may not enter a nunnery, save the Lama or the King and their attendants. Monks cannot leave their monasteries without the permission of the Lama or of the Ker-Koo, but the nuns enjoy more liberty. They can either live in the convent or in the house of their family, only going to attend solemn functions in the convent. Many of them prefer this, as at home they get better food and can work for their parents, but they are obliged to wear the habit. Those who live in the convent must attend prayers every day in the temple and are given food, but often in quite insufficient quantities; they cannot go out unless the Mother Superior or the mistress gives permission, but they are allowed to work and earn money for their own use.

Of the Thibetan Religion with regard to Morality, Virtue and Vice, and Rules of Conduct

. . . Ten sins to be avoided are specified in the Thibetan religion. Three are of the body; four of the tongue; three of the heart. The corporeal sins are murder, lust and theft. Those of the tongue are lying, grumbling, reviling and using idle and lewd words. Those of the heart are coveting the goods of, or desiring to do evil to others, and secret dissent from the truths and maxims of their Law and Faith. . . .

As to the sin of murder, killing an animal is as heinous an offence as murdering a man. The mere thought or the intention of committing a murder is regarded as a sin, even if the crime is not accomplished. Thus they specify as sins, taking weapons, preparing poisons, using spells, and such-like things, attempting to kill a person or inducing others to do so. If the person or the animal attacked is not mortally wounded, but dies later, provided his or its death is a result of the attempt to murder, the sin is the same. Finally in this, as in all other sins, the pleasure felt in committing a crime is an additional and distinct sin.

The sins of lust are divided as follows: Sexual intercourse with an improper person, improper intercourse, intercourse in an improper place, and at an unseemly time. The improper persons specified are the mother, married or religious women, relatives, and finally self-abuse and intercourse between persons of the same sex. In all this they agree with our moral laws. As to the place, a temple, or the neighbourhood of a Ccióten, the presence of a Lama, a Master, a Cian-giulb-sem-baa, a Superior, a father or a mother or a relation. As to the time, when the woman is in her menstrual period, is about to give birth to or is suckling a child, is ill, or when it is a day of fasting.

They distinguish simple theft from theft with violence; theft done by a person, or by others at his instigation. In theft is included the non-payment of debts, making fraudulent contracts, damaging the property of other people and similar acts.

They specify virtues, as they do sins, into three of the body, four of the tongue, and three of the heart; but these are more negative than positive, as they consist in abstaining from committing any of the above-mentioned sins. Advising others and inducing them to practise virtue is a virtue by itself. There are also positive virtues such as faith, hope, and charity, in addition to alms, prayers, compassion, diligence and fervour, contemplation, and others about which there exist many admirable treatises.

[*Father Du Jarric, in his account of Akbar, mentions his fellow Jesuit Benedict Goës, who, as we have noted in our introduction to this chapter, succeeded in reaching China by the high mountain route from India, and correctly identified Cathay and China with the land of the Seres of the classical authors. He is another of the pioneers who, for lack of space, cannot be included here; instead, in recognition of the growing importance of the sea routes, we turn to the stormy voyage of François Pyrard.*]

The Voyage of François Pyrard (1602)[3]

[*Inspired by Dutch and English successes, the French also took part in searching for a new way to the East Indies. At the beginning of the seventeenth century enterprising citizens of St. Malo, Laval and Vitré formed a company and purchased two vessels, the* Croissant *and the* Corbin, *hoping to lead the way for their countrymen. St. Malo, a bustling commercial town second only to Dieppe in importance, was more famous at the time for its piracy than its legitimate trade. François Pyrard (ca. 1570–1620), our author, was born in Laval. His birth and death dates are unknown but on May 18, 1601, when his voyage on the* Corbin *began, he was somewhere between twenty and thirty years old. Pyrard and his shipmates had a series of almost incredible adventures against romantic and colorful backgrounds. His gifts as a linguist brought him to the notice of emperors and sultans and permitted him to obtain special treatment for himself and his shipmates on several occasions.*]

[3] From *The Voyage of François Pyrard*, translated and edited by Albert Gray, Vol. I.

Pitiable wreck of the ship "Corbin," wherein the
author was, on the reefs of the Maldives.—How
the men were saved at an island with much trouble,
and the miseries endured by them.

What I have said of the discomforts and troubles of our voyage up to this point is as nothing compared with what happened after. I shall now describe misery, the greatest that can be imagined, and I am assured there are none in reading it but will deplore an event so sad and lamentable, which ruined and completely overpowered us. This is how it happened.

The first day of July 1602, being 5° N. of the line, with fine weather, neither too calm nor too much wind, we perceived at break of day that the *Croissant* had lost her big boat, which she had towed from St. Laurence, where it had been made use of as a pinnace. It had been arranged at St. Malo, between our commander and the Merchant Company, that we should build a pinnace at the first land we touched on the other side of the Cape of Good Hope, and for this purpose we had brought all suitable timber, a mast and ropes, ready prepared, and requiring only to be put together. It is very necessary on long voyages to have a pinnace to reconnoitre with in unknown places, to land with on occasion, and to enter rivers where a big ship cannot or dare not venture. I mention particularly the loss of the boat used as a pinnace, and our want of the latter, for with it the *Croissant* might have saved our men. Soon after, we sighted at a distance great reefs, which surrounded a number of small islands, amid which we perceived a little sail. We approached our General, and let him know that we no longer saw the boat. But we were told that in the past night it had been filled by a heavy sea, and had broken the tow-rope and had gone to the bottom. After this our mate, who alone spoke on these occasions (the captain and lieutenant being both ill, and our English pilot speaking no French), asked what islands they were we saw. The General and his pilot replied that they were called the islands *de Diego de Roys*. In truth, we had left the *de Roys* Islands four and twenty leagues behind us in the west. There was great dispute between those of the *Croissant* and ourselves as to these islands and reefs; for our captain, pilot, mate, and second mate

held that they were the Maldives, and that we must take care:
the General and his pilot thought otherwise. We saw little
boats, which seemed willing to approach and pilot us—as, indeed, I afterwards learnt from the natives was the case; but our
General would not wait, and imprudently took no notice of
them. All day passed in this discussion; we continued our
course, keeping near each other till the evening, when our ship
went down the wind to bid the General good-night, and to get
his orders for the night. Then our mate asked if the passage was
open, and the General said it was, and that he was certain they
were the de Roys Islands, and no other; nevertheless, as these
were unknown parts, and for fear lest there should be other rocks
or reefs before us, the best thing was to put about after dark in the
opposite course, and sail towards the west until midnight, and
after midnight to tack about and get the ship to her previous
position, running east to arrive by daybreak where we then
were, or a little further on, so that we should not make any
more way in the night, and get lost before we knew where we
were. At nightfall we obeyed the orders of the General. The
captain, who was very ill, charged me to warn the mate and second mate to keep a good look-out . . . for in his opinion we
were in a dangerous part of the Maldives, notwithstanding the
opinion of the pilot of the *Croissant*.

Our General intended to pass by the north of these islands,
between the head of them and the coast of India; but, on the
contrary, we were running right into the midst of them, to our
peril. The pilots said they would be careful; for all who have
the duty of navigation in those parts must cautiously avoid the
dangerous banks and reefs from a hundred leagues off, if he can,
otherwise there is great risk in passing through these islands
without losing your ship. But misfortune was pressing close
upon us, and notwithstanding the foresight of our captain, who
could not set right the others' ignorance, that which had not
happened once during the voyage now came to pass, viz., everyone was fast asleep that night, even those on watch. The mate
and second mate had been carousing, and were drunk. The
light usually kept on the poop for reading the compass was out,
because the man at the wheel, who had charge of the light and
the hour-glass, had fallen asleep, as had also the ship's boy that
attended him; for it is customary for the man at the helm always

to have a ship's boy by him. What was worse, the ship was
steered to the east half an hour, or three-quarters at most, too
soon. So, while we were thus all asleep, the ship struck heavily
twice, and as we started with the shock, she suddenly struck a
third time, and heeled over. I leave you to imagine the condition of all on board,—what a pitiful spectacle we presented,—
the cries and lamentations of men who find themselves wrecked
at night on a rock in mid-ocean, and await a certain death.
Some wept and cried with all their might; others took to
prayers; others confessed to each other; and far from having a
captain to command and encourage us, we had one that aggra-
vated our sorrows. For it was a month and more since he had
left his bed; but the fear of death caused him incontinently to
rise in his shirt, and, feeble as he was, fall a-crying among us.
The ship having half-heeled over, we cut the masts to prevent
her going quite over, and then fired a cannon-shot to warn the
Croissant to keep back. But she was in no danger, as she was
well behind us, and was keeping a good look-out. We all thought
that the ship must go to the bottom, as we could see nothing
but heavy waves going over us; and that, in fact, must have
happened if we had struck upon a rock. About three-quarters
of an hour after, dawn appeared, and we sighted some islands
at not more than five or six leagues distance beyond the reefs,
and the *Croissant* quite close to us, but unable to succour us.
Our ship remained firm on her side, and being on a reef, could
still hold together for a while; for had it been on sand, she
must have heeled over altogether, and we should have been
drowned to a man. This gave us some consolation, and the
courage to endeavour to save our lives and to get to land, although in our present plight there was but little hope of that,
seeing what a distance the land was off: and even then we ran
the risk of being denied a landing, or of being killed by the
natives. We then bethought us to prepare some craft to carry
us, as we could no longer expect to get out the galion or the
boat. We took spars, rods, and those stout beams called *aniennes,*
which are at each side of ships, and are useful for spars and rods
when occasion demands. . . . These we bound together in the
manner of a large hurdle, and on to that we nailed a number of
planks and boards brought up from below. . . . This was sufficient to carry us all easily, and to save a large quantity of bag-

gage and merchandise to boot. We were working at this raft or *panguaye* all hands, and with all our power, from daybreak until two or three hours after noon; but our labour was all in vain, as it was impossible to get it over the reef and afloat. This made us lose all courage and hope; besides, as I have said, there seemed no chance of getting the galion, which was well forward in the ship below the second deck, and all the masts were cut, and there was no means of fixing a pulley to raise it withal; moreover, the sea was so heavy and stormy that the waves and swell [*louesme*] were going right over the ship to the depth of a pike and more, and we were every moment in danger of having them over us. In addition to this, the sea was so tempestuous (for we saw the waves break for more than two miles distance, with a horrible noise, over the reefs and rocks) that the galion could not have resisted its violence.

Such being our condition, we perceived a boat approaching us from the island, as if to reconnoitre, but it did not come within half a league of us. When we saw it, the best swimmer among us threw himself into the water and made for her, begging the men in her by all manner of signs and cries to come to our aid; but they would do nothing for all his efforts, so that he was constrained at his peril to return. We could not imagine the reason for this inhumanity and barbarism. But I afterwards found that all persons were strictly prohibited from boarding or approaching a wrecked ship, except by command of the king or by leave of the nearest king's officers, who in such case are allowed to save the men, giving information at once to the king. For the rest, I could not sufficiently wonder that, in the midst of our misery, many of the sailors and mariners ceased not to drink and eat, and to consume the ship's victuals even beyond the necessities of nature, saying to the others of us who remonstrated, that we were all as good as lost, and that they preferred to die in that fashion. Then they swore and fought, and some broke open the chests of others whom they saw at their prayers (having ceased to think more of the things of this world), and no longer acknowledged their captain, making no more account of him than of their comrades, and saying that, as the voyage was at an end, they were no longer bound to obey him. I was horrified at this; and I make bold to say that seamen of this temper, of whom I have seen but too many, leave their souls

and conscience on land, so irreligious, demoralised, and insolent have I seen them to be.

To return to my story. Though we despaired of our lives, we
made an attempt to get out the galion, at which we worked our
best, as we had done at the raft in the morning. Having got it
out with vast trouble, we all did our best to equip it and put it
to rights, all broken as it was by the waves; but darkness came
on before it was quite ready, and we remained the following
night on board in our evil plight, and amid great distress and
danger, the ship being very full of water, while the waves frequently passed over our heads and drenched us again and again.

Next day, the 3rd July 1602, in the morning, we got the
galion over the reefs with great trouble and risk, ourselves swim-
ming the while. This done, we all got on board, taking with us
swords, arquebuses, and small pikes, and pulled towards the
islands. Our galion, being heavily laden, made much water,
and almost capsized several times by the violence of the winds
and waves. At last, after much fatigue, we got ashore at one of
the islands called *Pouladou*.

As soon as we reached the shore, the natives who were waiting
for us would not permit us to land till we were first disarmed by
them. So we having surrendered at discretion to the islanders,
they permitted us to land and then pulled up our galion, and
took out of it the rudder, masts, and other things necessary for
its equipment, and sent them all to the neighbouring islands,
whither also they pulled all the boats of their own island, leaving not a single one behind. I perceived from this first view that
they were a spirited and quick-witted race. As their island was
small (not a league in circumference), and its inhabitants numbered only twenty or twenty-five, they had to fear the arrival
with arms of a greater number than themselves, lest we should
make ourselves masters of their island and escape by aid of their
boats, which would have been easy enough had we known their
weakness; but, as I have said, they took the right measures.

On our disembarking we were all led to a building in the
middle of the island, where they gave us some fruit, coconuts,
and limes. Thither, too, came the lord of the island, called
Ybrahim and *Pouladouquilague*, who appeared to be of great
age. He knew some words of Portuguese, by means of which he
put many questions to us; after which his people searched us

and took away everything we carried, saying that all that appertained to the king, after a ship was wrecked. This lord of the island was a great lord, and, as I afterwards learnt, nearly related to the Christian king of the Maldives, who is at Goa. Seeing that we had a piece of scarlet, he asked us what that was. We replied that we had brought it to present to the king; and although all that was in the ship was his, yet was that brought to be presented to him whole and unspoiled by the sea water. As soon as they heard that it was for the king, not a man of them dared to take it or touch it, or even to look at it. We were, nevertheless, minded to cut off a piece, about two or three ells, for a present to the lord of the island, in hopes that we should be the better treated. He took it, and thanked us with effusive gratitude, but made us promise not to tell anyone, otherwise he would rather have died than taken it. Soon after, hearing that some officers of the king were coming, he changed his mind, and brought it back, begging us not to tell that he had so much as handled it. For all that, the king heard of it at least six months later, and was wroth against him, and would have sent for him, had he not been then in the last stage of a disease, whereof he died at the age of seventy-five years. . . .

The king soon sent his brother-in-law with a goodly number of soldiers in barques to go to our wreck and get from it all he could. This was the brother of the chief queen, and was entitled *Ranabandery Tacourou,* his own name being Mouhamede. When he came to the island *Pouladou,* where we were, we were treated better on the occasion of his arrival, and were taken often to the ship to help in getting out the merchandise, baggage, and all the wearing apparel. But they laughed at the advice we gave them, for they knew better than we. As it was impossible for the boats to go over the reef, they fastened a cable to the ship, while the other end was lashed to a big rock of the reef; and so, by holding on to this rope with one hand, we could go and come over the reef to the ship in safety; while so doing, the waves only passed over our heads, and could not overthrow us nor carry us off. For the rest, they had a very pretty contrivance for getting off the cannon and other heavy things, although these were all in the hold, as I shall tell in the proper place.

So for several days they got out our merchandise and took it away to the king; but before that, the king's brother-in-law, by virtue of his commission, separated us one from another, and distributed some of us among the surrounding islands (the greater number remaining at *Pouladou*), and on his return took with him our captain, ill as he was, and five or six others. He was presented to the king, and was well received. The king promised to get a ship ready to carry him to Achen, in the island of Sumatra, whither our General had gone; and I know not but he might have kept his word. Our captain, however, died at Malé, the residence of the king, about six or seven weeks after. In all expeditions to the ship they took some one of us in the same way. As for me, the king's brother-in-law, in separating us, took me away from those at *Pouladou,* and put me with two others on a little island called *Paindoüe* (distant from *Pouladou* a league only), where there were no more people than in the other. Here my two companions and I were well received from the very first, and, thanks to the lord who brought us, we had a sufficiency of food.

Divers judgments passed for adultery, lewdness, and other crimes.—Amorous humour of the Indian women. —Of the Grand Pandiare; and the strange resolution of a Mulatto.

I shall now relate divers occurrences that happened during my time to particular inhabitants of the island; among others, to a Gentile Canarin of Cochin, a man of great means and position. For eight whole years he had come and gone about the islands, having everywhere houses, factors, and domestics, speaking the language quite well, and being, in fact, naturalised. One day this man was surprised lying with a woman of the islands. He had kept her for six months, and she was but a poor servant girl. He was presently haled with her before the Grand Pandiare, to whom he protested that he had done her no manner of harm; that he desired to become of their faith, and would marry the woman. This was done, and he became a Mahometan; and it appeared that he had for a long time desired this end, for that he owed much money at Cochin, as to which he became bankrupt. He espoused this woman and made a great lady of her: for there, strangers, both men and women, can wear whatever they please. When he made the promise he was set free, but upon her judgment was passed according to the law: all her hair was shaved, then she was bathed in old and stinking oil, her head put in an old sack of sail-cloth, and then she was beaten at all the cross-roads and round the island. This is their manner of punishing all men and women taken in adultery or fornication. But there, as here, money does everything and saves from everything. As for the conversion of the man, he was borne in triumph through the streets and round the island, accompanied by the greatest lords, and by the people of all sorts and conditions; he was presented with much money and raiment and a new name: for there, names are given at pleasure and by whomsoever, be it father, mother, kindred, or even the first comer; and also at any time, and not only at birth or circumcision, insomuch that it seemed to me they give names as we do here to dogs and horses: for the name first given by whomsoever is the one that sticks to a man.

The Pandiare that passed the said judgment was a Cherife of Arabia, that is, one of a family the most respected and noble among these people, as being of the race of Mahomet. He was a very good man, and was greatly beloved of the king. . . .

While this Pandiare was in office I saw him one day do exemplary justice on a large number of women. They were about twenty-five or thirty in number, some of the greatest ladies in the land, who were accused of a crime whereof I never heard tell before; it is practised only at the Maldives, and is called *Pouy tallan*. In truth, the women of all India are naturally much addicted to every kind of ordinary lewdness; but those of the Maldives in particular are so tainted with this vice that they have no other talk or occupation, and hold it a boast and a virtue one with another to have some bravo or gallant, upon whom they lavish all such favours and tokens of love as a man could wish of a woman. Among other things, they never let them want for betel, prepared and served in some elaborate and extraordinary style, with some cloves put inside, or else a little black seed, the most tasty, odoriferous, and pleasant to the mouth that can be conceived. As for the men, they cull flowers and arrange them neatly in the manner of bouquets, and send them to the ladies out of gallantry. There are certain white flowers of a full scent on which they can write and grave what

they will with the point of a knife, and thereon they write three
of four verses on the subject of their passion. . . .

Many reasons may be assigned for the fact that the women are
of a disposition so hot and amorous; but the principal seem to
me to be that they are exceedingly lazy, and do nothing but ever
lie rocked in daintiness. Next, that they are continually eating
betel, a very heating herb; and in their ordinary fare use so
many spices that sometimes I could hardly put the food to my
mouth; also garlic, onions, and other such heating things. Add
to this, that the climate is directly under the line, a condition
which renders the men more sluggish and less capable; yet for
all that, most have two or three wives apiece,—I mean such as
can afford to keep them. They are also lazy, idle fellows, more
like women, their chiefest exercise being to lie abed with t..em,
and then more often with desire than effect.

But to return to the justice done upon those women: two at
first were taken in the act, one of whom was married to one of
the king's chief officers, and he loved her dearly. Now, their law
and custom obtains that when a king's officer or any of his
family is a delinquent, before proceeding to justice the Grand
Pandiare sends word to the king, asking if it be his pleasure
that the process be according to the ordinary forms. This the
king never refuses. So the Grand Pandiare, having informed the
king of the conduct of the two women, the king replied that he
willed justice to be done, not only upon these two, but upon
many others, who, as he had heard, had for a long while been
engaged in this business, and that a strict inquisition should be
made. Forthwith, too, he sent the husband of one of the women,
with two of his most intimate advisers, to assist at the inquiry
and trial, and bade them expressly tell the Pandiare to omit no
part of his orders, for that if any remained unpunished, he
would take the law into his own hands; insomuch that all the
people incontinently assembled from all parts of the island, and
even the highest grandees came, many of whom to prosecute
their own wives. During this procedure the king had all the
doors of his palace closed, so that none should enter to beg the
royal favour towards his wife: thus was equal justice done. The
poor wretches all accused one another, and even the men who
had personal or hearsay knowledge of it, brought them forward,

and named aloud whose wives they were. About thirty of these women were publicly punished; first they had their hair cut,—a mark of great infamy with them; then they were beaten with thick thonged whips of leather, in such wise that two or three died. Thereafter all were absolved, with a warning that if they returned to these practices they should be drowned. Subsequently, however, I saw certain of the same party who were again arrested, and were not drowned, but only beaten with those whips which are called *gleau*. The sin of man and man is very common, and though the book of their law prescribes the penalty of death, yet they heed not that; and nowhere in the world are these enormities more common and less punished; wherein may be seen the curse and wrath of God upon these wretches, who are led by the falsity and unrighteousness of their law to fall into the abyss of these horrible vices.

About the same time I saw justice done upon a youth of seventeen years of age. He was the son of an Ethiopian Cafre and of a woman of the islands, such a one being called Mulastre. He had the greatest resolution and courage that I was ever witness of, for alone he had the assurance to attack six or seven other men. He became so mischievous, that with a single companion he went about the islands in a boat, thieving and harrying whatever he could, and assaulting the poor folk in cruel fashion. But at length he was caught, and had his right hand cut off. While he was being punished, I saw no change upon his countenance, nor did he utter the slightest cry, no more than if he was feeling nothing. This punishment in no way changed his humour, for he was no sooner healed than he returned to his former courses, insomuch that when he was caught again they were constrained to cut off his left foot, whereof he made no more account than of his fist: for his resolution was such that he himself taught the man that was cutting him how he ought to do it, without ever showing any trace of pain. He had by him a vessel full of boiling coconut oil, into which he himself thrust his leg, all as though it had been cold water. I think that such determined courage has never been seen in a boy. . . .

A Voyage to Cochinchina, 1792–93 [4] :
SIR JOHN BARROW

[*Born in Ulverston of humble beginnings, John Barrow (1764–1848) through his ability and intellectual gifts eventually moved among lords and dukes and was himself knighted for his services to Great Britain in 1804. Lord Melville, first Lord of the Admiralty, appointed Barrow second secretary in 1804, a position he held almost without interruption for forty years.*

[*Barrow went everywhere and is said to have written on every subject except politics. One hundred ninety-five articles of his appeared in the* Quarterly Review *alone, and he published many books. He is famous in Arctic as well as China circles for publishing a plan for the discovery of the Northwest Passage in 1817, a "proposal notable in the history of Arctic exploration and the origin of some of the noblest exploits of seamanship" in the nineteenth century. He was one of the founders of the Royal Geographical Society of London and Point Barrow, the northernmost part of Alaska, was named after him. He enjoyed wonderful health and "his singularly fortunate life was ended by as fortunate a death," suddenly, with no illness, in his eighty-fifth year.*]

Batavia

If a stranger should happen to make his first entrance into the city of Batavia about the middle of the day, he would be apt to conclude it deserted by the inhabitants. At this time the doors and windows are all shut, and not a creature, except perhaps a few slaves, is stirring in the streets. But if he should enter the city in the morning or the evening, his eye will not be less attracted by the vast crowds of people moving about in the principal streets, than by the very great variety of dress and complexion which these crowds exhibit. Here he will at once behold every tint of colour, except that of rosy health, from the pallid hue of the sickly European, through the endless shades of brown and yellow, to the jetty black of the Malabar; and the dresses of the several nations, both as to fashion and materials, are as various as their colour and cast of countenance. That class of men which bears a complete sway over the island is by much the least numerous; it is even rare to see a single *wel edele hoog gebooren Hollander, a right honourable high-born Dutchman,* condescending to walk the streets. "Nothing from Europe," he observes, "but Englishmen and dogs walk in Batavia." Whenever he has occasion to take this kind of exercise, he puts on his full dress suit of velvet, and is attended by a suitable retinue of slaves: sensible how very necessary it is, where power is but ideal, to put on an imposing appearance. But the Armenians, the Persians, and the Arabs, always grave and intent on business; the half-cast merchants from the different ports of Hindostan; and, above all, the Chinese, some in long sattin gowns and plaited tails reaching almost to their heels, and others crying their wares to sell, or seeking employment in their several professions, dressed in large umbrella hats, short jackets, and long wide trowsers; the Javanese loitering carelessly along, as if indifferent to every thing around them; the free Malays, with half-averted eye, looking with suspicion on all who come across them; and slaves, from every nation and country of the East, condemned to trudge in the same path with the carriages:—all these, in the early and latter parts of the day, may be seen bustling in crowds in the streets of Batavia.

It would far exceed the limits I have prescribed, were I to enter at full length into the manners and peculiar customs of all or any of these people; but I shall endeavour to give such a general sketch or outline of the character and situation of the Dutch, the Chinese, the Javanese, the Malays, and the Slaves, as may serve to throw some light upon their respective conditions in this great and once wealthy city, which, from a miserable village of thatched hovels, rose into splendour and opulence, by the adventurous and successful commerce of the Dutch, in the happy days of their freedom and independence.

On our first visit to Batavia, we were received with great ceremony at the gates of the castle by the old Governor *Van Alting,* accompanied with the *wel edele heeren,* composing the Council of India. . . .

It happened to be about the middle of the day, when the sun was vertical, and not a breath of wind stirring; the mercury in Fahrenheit's thermometer at 89° in the shade; when, after abundant ceremony in the open air, we were introduced into a close narrow room, with a couple of windows at one end, nearly filled with fat "sleek-headed men," dressed in suits of velvet stiffened with buckram. In this narrow room, and mixed among these warmly clad gentlemen, we were seated round a table covered with crimson velvet, on chairs whose corresponding cushions were stuffed with feathers. And though the very appearance of the furniture alone was enough to induce a fever, two or three little chafing-dishes with live coals were set on the table, for the accommodation of those who were inclined to smoke a pipe of tobacco, which, with wine, spirits, and cakes, were handed round to the company.

The ceremony of our introduction being ended, we proceeded from the castle to the country-house of *Van Weegerman,* the second in council, to which we were conveyed in small carriages, each drawn by a pair of ponies, and driven by a black coachman, who, mounted on a high box, with a large three-cornered hat and an enormously long whip, formed no unimportant part of the equipage. . . . We entered his villa by a draw-bridge thrown across a moat, with which it was surrounded, and which was intended as well for ornament as defence. Behind the house was a considerable piece of ground laid out with much formality into a sort of pleasure garden intersected, rather injudiciously it would seem in such a climate, with fish ponds and canals or, more correctly speaking, with puddles and ditches of dirty water. The ground was well stocked with all kinds of tropical fruits, and many rare plants peculiar to the island. Orange trees of a large size, shaddocks and mangoes were loaded with fruit; and every individual of the vegetable world seemed to flourish with a vigorous luxuriance, except a few sickly European plants, which were here and there seen drooping in pots. On observing to our host how very bountiful nature had been to this island in the distribution of some of her choicest stores, he replied, *"Ya mynheer het is wel waär."* "You are very right, Sir, we have abundance of every thing; and yet," continued he, *"het is een vervloekt land,"* "it is an accursed country, to say the best of it, where *we eat poison and drink pestilence at every meal."* In what this poison and pestilence consisted will best appear by a short description of *Van Weegerman's* dinner.

We had scarcely set foot in the house when a procession of slaves made its appearance, with wine and gin, cordials, cakes and sweetmeats; a ceremony that was repeated to every new guest who arrived. After waiting a couple of hours the signal for dinner was given by the entrance of three female slaves, one with a large silver bason, the second with a jar of the same metal filled with rose water for washing the hands, and the third with towels for wiping them. The company was very numerous and, the weather being remarkably close, the velvet coats and powdered wigs were now thrown aside, and their places supplied with short dimity jackets and muslin night-caps. I certainly do not remember ever to have seen an European table so completely loaded with what Van Weegerman was pleased to call *poison* and *pestilence.* Fish boiled and broiled, fowls in *curries* and *pillaws,* turkies and large capons, joints of beef boiled and roasted and stewed, soups, puddings, custards, and all kinds of pastry, were so crowded and jumbled together that there was scarcely any room for plates. Of the several kinds of dishes there was generally a pair: a turkey on one side had its brother turkey on the other, and capon stared at capon. A slave was placed behind the chair of each guest, besides those who handed round wine, gin, cordials, and Dutch or Danish beer, all of which are used profusely by the Dutch under an idea that, by promoting perspiration, they carry off in some degree the effects of the poison and pestilence. After dinner an elegant desert was served up of Chinese pastry, fruits in great variety, and sweetmeats.

There were not any ladies in company. Van Weegerman being a bachelor had no females in his house, except his haram of slaves amounting to about fifty in number, assorted from the different nations of the East, and combining every tinge of complexion from the sickly faded hue of a dried tobacco leaf to the shining polish of black marble. . . . The Governor's daughter, who by the mother's side was of a dingy breed, was so bespangled with jewels that, according to the Dutchmen's valuation, she was whispered to be worth twenty thousand rixdollars, or about four thousand pounds, as she then stood.

These ladies, thus splendidly adorned to appear in company,

are dressed, when at home, just like their slaves, in long loose printed or chequered cotton gowns, bare headed, bare necked, bare legged, and bare footed. Their only object at home is to keep themselves cool, and at their perfect ease; and by so doing, and living a more temperate life, the mortality is by no means so great among the women as in the other sex.

A little after midnight a magnificent supper was served up in the great hall which, it is almost unnecessary to add, consisted of every luxury and delicacy that the united stores of Asia and Europe could supply. The company amounted at least to one hundred and fifty persons. The old Governor who, with the rest of the Dutchmen, had hitherto kept on his full dressed suit of velvet, now threw off his coat and wig, and took his seat at table in a light muslin jacket and a night-cap. Many of the ladies, following his example, laid aside their spangled gowns, and appeared in their dimity jackets. These jolly dames took especial care that the strangers should be well plied with wine, to which, at the same time, they were by no means backward in helping themselves. Some of the elder sort sat at table to a late hour, while the younger part returned to the ball-room, where reels and jigs and hornpipes now took place of country dances. A *Scoto-Batavian* officer displayed his raw-boned activity in a saraband, to the great amusement of the native dames, who had seldom witnessed such nimble capering. So fascinating was the entertainment that it was near four in the morning before the company dispersed.

It is almost superfluous to remark how very ill suited is the mode of life I have here described to an equinoxial climate. But the Dutchman, whose predominant vice in Europe is avarice, rising into affluence in an unhealthy foreign settlement, almost invariably changes this part of his character and, with a thorough contempt of the frugal maxim of *Moliere's L'Avare,* lives to eat rather than eats to live. His motto is, "Let us eat and drink, for to morrow we die." He observes, it is true, the old maxim of rising at an early hour in the morning, not however for the sake of enjoying the cool breeze, and of taking moderate exercise, but rather to begin the day's career of eating and drinking. His first essay is usually a *sopie* or glass of gin, to which succeed a cup of coffee and a pipe. His stomach thus fortified, he lounges about the great hall of the house, or the viranda if in the country, with a loose night-gown carelessly thrown over his shoulders, a night-cap and slippers, till about eight o'clock, which is the usual hour of breakfast. This is generally a solid meal of dried meat, fish and poultry made into curries, eggs, rice, strong beer and spirits. *Currie* and rice is a standing dish at all meals and at all seasons of the year, being considered as an excellent stimulus to the stomach. The business of the day occupies little more than a couple of hours, from ten to twelve, when he again sits down to dinner, a meal that is somewhat more solid than the breakfast. From table he retires to sleep and remains invisible till about five in the evening, when he rises and prepares for taking a ride or a walk, but generally the former. In the open doors of the little covered carriages male or female slaves, or both, sit on the steps, according as they may happen to be occupied by gentlemen or ladies.

From seven to nine are the usual hours for receiving and returning visits, when they play cards, drink wine, and smoke tobacco. In the dry season these evening parties generally meet in the little summer-houses which . . . are built on the margin of the canals, snuffing the nauseous effluvia which abundantly evaporate from the nearly stagnant water, and tormented by myriads of mosquitoes and other insects, for the propagation of which the climate, the dirty water, and the evergreen trees, are so remarkably favourable. The inhabitants, however, are so passionately attached to their canals and their trees, that a proposal in the Council to fill up the one and cut down the other had almost produced an insurrection in the city. But neither these insects, troublesome as they are, nor the stench of the water, can be considered as the most offensive nuisances to which those evening parties are liable to be exposed. The lower class of the inhabitants, the Javanese, the Malays, the Chinese, and the slaves of every nation, descend the steps of wooden ladders placed down the sides of the canals, and there, without any ceremony, perform the rites of the goddess who, in our country at least, is usually worshipped in retirement. Both men and women are constantly meeting on the same step, without being in the least disconcerted with themselves, or molested by the presence of the parties in the summer-houses or bye-standers in the street. The man turns his back to the water, and the woman faces it. At this time of the day the canals are all alive with the numbers of men, women, and children, that promiscuously plunge into the water. The women are considered as the best swimmers, paddling with their hands in the same manner as quadrupeds do, and not striking out as is the common practice among Europeans.

But these conveniencies and amusements which the canals afford, and which are carried on under the eyes of the parties of pleasure assembled on their banks, gross as they are, may be considered as still less disgusting than a general usage in the city, by which they are immediately succeeded. I have somewhere met with an observation, that an Englishman in building a house first plans out the kitchen, and a Dutchman the necessary. But the Dutch in Batavia, like the good people of Edinburgh, have contrived to dispense with conveniencies of this kind, for which I have heard two different reasons assigned: one is, that the heat of the climate would operate so as to create a putrid fever in the city; and the other, that the great bandicoot rat, of which I have spoken in the last chapter, would infest the temple in such a manner as to render the resort to it unsafe, especially for the male sex: the first is absurd, the last ridiculous. Instead, however, of such places of retirement they substitute large jars, manufactured for the occasion in China, narrow at top, low, and bulging out in the middle to a great width. These jars remain undisturbed, in a certain corner of the house, for twenty-four hours; at the end of which time, that is to say at nine in the evening, the hour when all the parties usually break up and return to their respective homes, the Chinese *sampans* or dirt boats begin to traverse the canals of the city. At the well known cry of these industrious collectors of dirt, the slaves from the opposite houses dart out with their loaded jars, and empty their contents in bulk into the boats. In this manner the Chinese scavengers, paddling in their sampans along the several canals, collect from house to house, for the use of their countrymen who are the only gardeners, "the golden store." Such a custom, in such a climate, can be no less injurious to health than it is indecent and disgusting. But the Dutch appear to be as insensible of the one as they are reconciled to the other. If they happen to catch a passing breeze charged with the perfume of these jars, they coolly observe, *"Daar bloeit de foola nonas horas"*—the nine o'clock flower is just in blossom."

The blooming of the *nine o'clock flower* is the signal for all parties to disperse and betake themselves to their respective homes, where, after a smoking hot supper, which is always ready to receive them, they immediately retire to rest. The ill effects that must necessarily result from such an intemperate life as I have here described are, indeed, not less pernicious than "poison and pestilence." The natives are destroyed at an early period of life, and the new comers rarely get over what is called "the seasoning." Those few that escape grow unwieldy and corpulent, but are soft, lax, and weak, affording no bad illustration of an ancient doctrine recorded by Pliny, *"Somno concoquere corpulentiae quàm firmitati utilius."*—"Digestion in sleep is more conducive to corpulency than strength." In fact, such habits of life, in such a climate, could not fail to exhaust the strength and enfeeble the constitution. The functions of life are fatigued, the powers of the body are worn out by luxury, indolence, and voluptuousness; and when disease attacks them, the feeble victim, without nerves or stamina to resist it, falls a speedy sacrifice, and sinks into the grave. Deaths of this kind are so frequent at Batavia, that they scarcely make any impression upon the minds of the inhabitants. The frequency of the event has rendered it familiar; and they shew no signs of emotion or surprize, beyond the shrug of the shoulder, when they hear in the morning of the death of the person with whom they supped in seemingly good health the evening before.

Unexpected promotions and extraordinary removes to situations, different from what the successful candidates were originally designed, are not unfrequently the consequences of the great and rapid mortality of Batavia. Our friend Weegerman left his native country in the humble capacity of sailmaker to one of the Company's ships. The barber has more than once quitted the shaving profession for the pulpit. The physicians have almost invariably emerged out of that class of men whose original occupation was the handling of a razor, and who, in their native country,

"—shav'd, drew teeth, and breath'd a vein."

The next description of the inhabitants of Batavia, who in numbers and in opulence exceed the former, is the Chinese. These people, as appears from their records, first obtained a settlement on Java about the year 1412. As intruders, but not conquerors, it is probable they have at all times been subject to harsh and oppressive treatment; but the restrictions and extortions under which they at present labour seem to be as unnecessary and impolitic as they are unjust. That they should consent to the Mahomedan Malays and Javanese exercising their devotions in the same temple which they built at their own expence, and consecrated to the god of their own worship, is by no means an unfavourable feature in their character; but on the part of the Dutch, who enforce the measure, it is one of the greatest insults that could well be offered. The Chinese hospital or infirmary, which was erected by voluntary contributions from their own community, and is supported by legacies, by profits arising from theatrical exhibitions and fire-works, and by a small tax on marriages, funerals, and celebrations of public festivals, is equally open for the benefit and reception of those who have not contributed towards the establishment, and who do not belong to their society. Into this admirable institution are indiscriminately admitted the infirm and the aged, the friendless and the indigent, of all nations. Towards the support of those institutions, the temple and the infirmary, their contributions are voluntary; but, exclusive of these, their industry is severely taxed by the Dutch government. Every religious festival and public ceremony, every popular amusement, as well as every branch of individual industry, are subject to taxation. They are even obliged to pay for a licence to wear their hair in a long plaited tail, according to the custom of their country; for permission to bring their greens to market, and to sell their produce and manufactures in the streets. Yet to the industry and the exertions of these people are the Dutch wholly indebted for the means of existing with any tolerable degree of comfort in Batavia. Every species of vegetable for the table is raised by them in all seasons of the year, and at times when the most indefatigable attention and labour are required. They are masons, carpenters, blacksmiths, painters, upholsterers, tailors, and shoemakers; they are employed in the arts of distilling, sugar-refining, pottery, lime-burning, and every other trade and profession that are indispensably necessary for making the state of civilized society tolerably comfortable. They are, moreover, the contractors for supplying the various demands of the civil, military, and marine establishments in the settlement; they are the collectors of the rents, the customs, and the taxes; and, in short, are the monopolizers of the interior commerce of the island, and, with the Malays, carry on the principal part of the coasting trade.

That influence which would naturally follow from the management of concerns so very important and extensive, could not long be regarded by a weak and luxurious government without jealousy. Those arts which Europeans have usually employed with success in establishing themselves in foreign countries, and which the Dutch have not been backward in carefully studying and effectually carrying into practice, with regard to the natives of Java, could not be applied with the least hope of success to the Chinese settlers. These people had no sovereign to dethrone, by opposing to him the claims of an usurper; nor did the separate interests of any petty chiefs allow them, by exciting jealousy, to put in execution the old adage of *divide et impera,* divide and command. With as little hope of success could the masters of the island venture to seduce an industrious and abstemious people from their temperate habits, by the temptation of foreign luxuries; and their general disposition to sobriety held out no encouragement for the importation of spirituous liquors and intoxicating drugs. For though the Chinese, who are in circumstances to afford it, make use of opium to excess, yet this is a luxury in which the common people of this nation rarely think of indulging. The Dutch, therefore, who were weak in point of numbers, had recourse to a more decisive and speedy measure of getting rid of a redundancy of population, which had begun to create suspicion and alarm. They put them to the sword.

The horrible scenes that were exhibited in this abominable transaction, which took place in the year 1740, have frequently been mentioned, but the subject was never fairly investigated. The cause has been ascribed solely to the Dutch Governor *Valkanier,* who, disappointed in not being able to extort a large sum of money from the Chinese chiefs for permission to celebrate some particular feast, accused them of a plot against the government. Many others, however, are supposed to have been implicated in this affair; and it is strongly suspected that, in order to get rid of farther inquiry, the coadjutors found it expedient to put an end to the Governor by poison. The causes assigned on the public records of Batavia are too absurd to deserve the least degree of credit. By these it would appear that a man, assuming the character of a descendant of the Emperor of China, formed a conspiracy with some of the Princes of Java, the object of which was to exterminate the Dutch; that, with this view, they had provided themselves with a quantity of *wooden cannon* to batter down the walls of the city; that their plan was to seize the persons of the Governor General and the Council, whose destiny was to be that of umbrella-bearers to the Chinese chief; but the wives of these noble personages were to be cut into minced meat, in order to be eaten by the Chinese at one of their solemn feasts; that a general *auto da fe* was to be held in the early part of the day for all Dutchmen that should be taken, and in the evening that all the women were to suffer the same death. Their children were to be slaves to the imperial family.

On such ridiculous surmises was the Chinese chief dragged to the stadt-house, where the most horrid tortures were employed for the purpose of extorting from him the confession of a crime which it had never entered into his mind to commit; and, at the same time, about five hundred of this' nation were thrown into prison. The Dutch guards were doubled; and, while the work of torture was going on, a fire, unluckily for the Chinese, broke out in that quarter of the suburbs which was particularly inhabited by them. This accident, occurring at the distance of half a mile without the walls, was nevertheless construed into a malicious intention to set fire to the whole city. The gates were doubly guarded, the half-cast burghers were armed, the soldiers drawn out, and the sailors landed from the ships in the road. The Chinese were ordered, by proclamation, to confine themselves to their houses; but terror overcoming their discretion, and fearful of being murdered within doors, they rushed forth to meet their fate in the streets. The horrid tragedy now began, and neither age nor sex could avail in preserving the victims from assassination. About four hundred who had fled to their hospital, and five hundred who had been imprisoned, were speedily put to death. Numbers without the city, who had hastened to the gates to learn what was doing within, were set upon by the soldiers and put to death. Within, the streets ran with blood.

No sooner had the work of destruction ended than that of plunder began. The soldiers and sailors were seen scrambling among the dead bodies, their hats and pockets loaded with dollars, quarrelling for the spoil, fighting, maiming, and murdering one another. This extraordinary affair took place on the 9th of October; the whole of the 10th was a day of plunder; and on the 11th they began to remove out of the streets the dead bodies, the interment of which employed them eight days. The number said to have perished, according to the Dutch account, amounts to more than twelve thousand souls. Having thus completed one of the most inhuman and apparently causeless transactions that ever disgraced a civilized people, they had the audacity to proclaim a public thanksgiving to the God of mercy for their happy deliverance from the hands of the heathen.

.   .   .   .

The private hours of a Javanese Prince are mostly passed in the society, or at least in the presence, of women. He feels himself, probably, more secure in their attendance than he would do in that of his own sex. He inlists as many into the number of his wives as he chuses. Polygamy is allowable to any extent, and the ladies take rank according to the priority of their introduction into the haram. The comparative estimation in which the sex is held is sufficiently declared in one of their laws, by which it is ordained that if a man, either by accident or design, shall kill his wife, he must pay to her relations the full value; but if the wife kill her husband, she must suffer death. Pecuniary compensations are fixed for theft and murder and almost every other crime, except treason against the Prince; and when the criminal is unable to pay the fine, he is usually sold as a slave. The power of a Javanese Prince over his subjects is very limited in some respects, in others it is absolute. By a sort of feudal right they are liable to become his slaves, in which situation he exercises over them an uncontrolled sway. When a man, for instance, dies and leaves behind him children that are either under age or unmarried, his wives, his children and property fall to the Prince, and are considered to be taken by him in lieu of the military service of the deceased, to which he had a claim. This right is not, however, generally exercised. The chief being considered as the sole proprietary of the soil, all lands are held of him under the tenure of military service, and a proportion of their produce; but since the settlement of the Dutch on Java, the several Princes not only oblige the peasantry to cultivate particular articles suitable for exportation, but take from them such proportion of the produce as will meet the terms on which they may have concluded their agreement with the Dutch. Formerly they exacted one half of the produce by way of rent, but they are now said to demand at least two thirds of the crop. Pepper and coffee are the two principal articles that are required to be cultivated, as best suiting the purpose of the Dutch, to whom they are delivered by the Javanese Princes at the low rate of about one penny a pound.

❧ VI ❧

WHEN THE WHITE MAN
WAS A BURDEN

IN THE century from the Battle of Waterloo in 1815 to the beginning of the First World War in 1914, Western man—or, to put it in the racist terms that he himself all too often used, the White Man—achieved almost complete ascendancy over Asia and the rest of the world. It took him another half century to lose it, but that, in the appropriate words of Kipling, is another story, which would make another, quite different but very interesting book.

In this full century the West advanced from the muzzle-loading musket to the breech-loading and then the repeating rifle, which gave explorers and the governments that backed them, or at least asked awkward questions if they came to a sticky end, a new authority. Never had so few had such a high prestige in the eyes of so many.

At the same time the factories of the industrial revolution were creating, in spite of all the suffering and exploitation that they caused, new young, wealthy, vigorous and enterprising societies, a new leadership, a new recognition of the economic rewards of science and technology, a new demand for education and a vast expansion of opportunities for educated men. Beginning with Britain, then spreading to France, Western Europe, North America, and Russia, new crops of adventurers and travelers began to appear around the edges of the safe and well paid jobs—mining prospectors, mercantile agents, religious missionaries, scientists, archaeologists, students of languages, decipherers of documents, sportsmen in search of new kinds of big game, officers on leave. It was an age in which it was assumed that any new bit of knowledge might be of value to somebody, that new resources might be discovered anywhere, that new bits of territory might be worth annexing. It was disputed whether trade followed the flag, or the flag followed trade, but any way you looked at it there was expansion and excitement.

Above all, it was an age in which the men of the West assumed that they had an inherent right to go anywhere. Moreover, not only did they have a right to discover and report, but by their mere presence "where no white man has ever been before," they somehow shed light on the benighted. It was exciting and sometimes dangerous, but not dangerous enough to make any journey impossible.

The white man's guns had everywhere made it known that the white man, if provoked, would come in force and lay down the law. This was known far beyond the most remote points to which military patrols had penetrated. In these outer zones, where the white man was known by repute before he had appeared in force, the right touch of bluff and assurance made it possible for the adventurous traveler to outstrip his predecessors and come back with reports of new discoveries. The occasional fatal casualty merely added romance to the reputations of those who came back safely.

The narratives of this age are near enough to us in mood to be easily understood, but far enough away to belong to "good old times" that will never return. There are so many of them, and so many of them are well written, that almost anyone could make his own selection and claim it to be better than the one we have given here. That is all to the good. We shall have done our part if what we print here leads others on to wider reading.

It will be noticed at once in our selection that there is more emphasis on China than on Japan and coastal Asia, and more emphasis on remote inland China and its Tibetan, Central Asian, and Mongolian fringes than on coastal China. We think this is in fact a fair emphasis, not a distortion. China, toward the end of the last century, was the one great landmass in Asia that had not quite been occupied and partitioned by the expanding empires of the West, though their shadows fell deeply over it. Moreover the West was well aware by this time that, while China had never been conquered by those who voyaged to it over the oceans, it had in the past been conquered by invaders from the landward side. This added an intriguing interest to the mysterious, imperfectly explored homelands of the Manchus, Mongols, Turks, and Tibetans. "The heart of Asia" is an expression frequent in the literature of the period, in many languages. The travelers we have selected are representative, in their widely varied origins and characters, of the diversity of the period.

Father Pereira's Journey [1]:
THOMAS PEREIRA, S.J.

[*When the Manchus took Peking in 1644 the Jesuits had already been established there for some time under the preceding Ming dynasty. They soon acquired even greater influence at the courts of the early Manchu emperors. Their knowledge of mathematics and astronomy enabled them to correct the Chinese calendar, and they helped to map the newly conquered empire, including Tibet. Much has been written, by the Jesuits themselves and by others, about their influence in China and the way in which they transmitted to Europe a knowledge of China based, for the first time, on the ability to read Chinese and Manchu. Through such European writers and savants as Voltaire and Leibniz, Jesuit ideas about China played a part in "modernizing" European thought. We have chosen here an excerpt which shows how, in an age of absolute monarchy, the Jesuits, by winning the personal favor of an emperor, were able to become so influential. The account also throws light on the still half-barbaric character of the Manchu court and aristocracy before they had fully transformed themselves into a "Chinese" dynasty and upper class.*]

Narrative of a Hunting Excursion performed by the present Emperor of China, beyond the Great Wall,

[1] From *History of the Two Tartar Conquerors of China*, by P. J. Orleans, S.J.

in the adjacent district of West Tartary, written by
Father Pereira from his personal observation:
from which the condition of these desert wastes
may be in some measure apprehended.

It was my original intention, in accordance with my custom, to be brief in my relation of Chinese matters: but, to satisfy the curious, I shall place before them a representation of the mountains which in the course of this my journey I closely observed. I shall, however, first relate the reasons for my undertaking of this journey, and thereafter the graciousness and respect which the emperor constantly evinced towards us. The emperor, learning that for some years past we had accomplished the manufacture of certain pipes or tubes, of various qualities of clay, which sometimes, by the intervention of men, and sometimes even without such, gave out in answer to each other musical sounds, sought to learn the theory and manner of this invention, and when he was made to understand it, proceeded to utter exclamations of astonishment, and to extol this our so successful contrivance.

The emperor, being a wise and far-seeing man, intelligent and good natured, readily acknowledged that to this hour the contrivance in question had been unknown to the Chinese. It was his pleasure to pass the summer season about and among the mountains of Tartary, for the benefit of the air. He announced this decision to me in words to this effect. "Now that I have attentively examined the art of your music it greatly pleases me. Your wisdom delights me. You must become the companion of my journey, that I may have the enjoyment of your skill while I am hunting." He desired to have books of science and such like translated into Chinese, saying that his people would study them with special application.

Father Ferdinand Verbiest being present when the emperor made this communication, foreseeing the inconvenience which awaited me, particularly from the scarcity of cold water, of which, by reason of an illness, I required a large supply (the Chinese drink no water which is not warmed), and representing this difficulty to his majesty, the latter answered that everything necessary should be provided. . . . On the following day he commanded his uncle and his father-in-law that they should take us in charge with due honour, and that raiment should be supplied to me from the imperial wardrobe, a thing hitherto unknown. He perhaps mislikes our poverty, which contrasts so strongly with the splendour of his court.

. . . The emperor further directed, in evidence of his good will and esteem, that two horses should be supplied daily from his own stable for my use. I, meanwhile, thus equipped, betook myself in all haste at midnight to the hills, the emperor being accustomed to choose that season for traveling, so as to avoid the heat, and to take up his abode on the mountains near the great Wall, which separates Tartary from China.

Since I have seen with my own eyes, to my great wonder, this Wall, which exceeds all others in length and breadth, some mention of it may not be unacceptable. It is a work of great excellence, which cost inconceivable labour, untold sums, and thousands of lives; and yet it is useless as a fortification for defence or security, wherefore its authors at this day enjoy but a poor reputation. I would here go through its history from beginning to end, had it not been so repeatedly furnished by other writers; so that I could say nothing new on the subject, especially of the three hundred miles at which its length is reckoned, which may in fact be more correctly stated at nine hundred, if we count the sinuosities and the course of the rampart round and over precipices and projecting rocks, in the which haunt great serpents, but no other wild animal as far as I have seen.

In the fields near this Wall tents or huts are raised, and in these we have to pass the nights; for the emperor is wont to encamp in these valleys and desert flats, near a river, that he may avoid becoming a burthen to the inhabitants and to the towns. When he thus halts for some days two tents are erected as palaces, the one for a dining-hall and for morning repose, the other for night repose: a very great work and perfect in all particulars, but composed of mats, yet worth some eight thousand ducats in value. The princes and grandees, on their part, are also very regularly lodged.

Admiration is excited when one considers the delicacies and fresh fruits which are conveyed hither from Pekin by divers messengers; and what care is taken meanwhile of the administration of justice, of which nothing is concealed from the emperor, but everything as well ordered as though he were present.

While these things were passing, the emperor was advised of an advantageous occurrence with the Russians touching a certain fortress, which, remaining in the hands of the latter, had been very prejudicial to the hunting and to the pearl fishery. There was much congratulation on the acquirement of this place, the more as it had occurred without much bloodshed. It gave occasion to the emperor to ask me many questions about the Russians.

On the third day, he called me to his presence that I might play him some music, in which art he takes special delight. I expounded it from its first elements, to the great satisfaction of all hearers, and to the utmost of my ability, and the emperor paid as much attention as if the fate of his empire were concerned; but when I had finished, his desires led him again to the chase.

On the fifth day we pursued our journey between mountains, which seemed to threaten us on either side. The precipices are fearful on account of the narrowness of the way, which, not without great cost and incomparable labour, has been so far improved, that not only access is afforded to the hunting grounds, but that many Chinese avail themselves of its facilities to establish themselves in the neighbourhood of the great wall; by which state policy the emperor not only extends his territory, but keeps at a respectful distance the Western Tartar tribes, who, were they strong enough, would act hostilely towards the Chinese.

When the emperor goes beyond the frontier, it is incredible how much cavalry he takes with him. Towards evening the camp of the soldiery was pitched in a level field, watered by four rivers, which descend from the mountains. This part of Tartary consists of high hills, which are clothed with wood, and would be agreeable if we could deprive them of the rudeness of their precipices.

Several races of people have established themselves in these districts by command of the emperor; and here dwell the Tartars, who are peculiarly addicted to the chase, building themselves huts, and enjoying a superfluity of wild animals, with the skins of which they clothe themselves. The soil here is very fertile, producing all kinds of grain. The forest super-abounds in fruitbearing trees; pears, apricots, apples and peaches, are in plenty. These afford not only food for foxes, wild swine, and other animals, but also profit to many who pluck these fruits for nothing, and sell them again dear enough. There are also other fruits not known among us, which are sold at high prices to those who pursue the chase in these mountains. When I was the companion of the emperor I followed his example in tasting these novel delicacies, and much relished them, especially some grapes of an extraordinary flavour. On account of the narrowness and steepness of the road, I dismounted and led my horse. The emperor and the princes of West Tartary in all this went on in advance, without regard to the danger. . . .

At this part of our journey we were obliged to halt some days, on account of the illness of a son of the emperor's by one of his queens, for whose carriage the road had been so carefully mended and also watered, that nothing more perfect could exist. It makes me ashamed to reflect how imperfect in comparison is my service to God the Lord of heaven and earth. When the patient's sickness had somewhat abated, the emperor returned from a visit which he had paid to him.

On the 25th day we girded ourselves again to our task, and crossed several rivers, bridges having been first laid over them. Every one made a push for the passage, although not free from danger, inasmuch as it was not safe to pass the night on the mountain, where tigers constantly abound. The spot which it was our object to reach at the end of this day's journey was four miles further on, and the day was nearly occupied with these passages of the rivers. After these had been effected the bridges were removed. They were made of heavy timbers like masts of ships, such as the timber traders on these rivers float down to the capital at Pekin, and receive there very high payment for the same. I stood amazed to behold such enormous trees, springing out of the bare rock.

We came finally to the appointed halting-place, near another great river, which descending southward, spreads itself out for a short space into a standing water. . . . Six sumptuous pavilions were erected, the first for the sole use of the emperor, the other for the queens, according to their rank, and for the prince, the eldest son, a successor to the throne, all alike of lacquer-work with tin lining, seven or eight ells in height, so that no one from without could look in. The entrance, after the fashion of the Chinese, faced the south, being guarded from the weather by curtains of the most costly silk damask.

On either side stood two tents for the princes and councillors of state, who wait upon the emperor twice a day; there is also another place for those with whom he has more private intimacy, among whom I was included, having liberty to go in and out at my pleasure; but this great privilege I was careful not to make too free use of. It behoved me to be cautious and circumspect, in order to avoid incurring disfavour from others.

Round the tents which I have described as thus magnificent, were magazines, and beyond these a net was drawn, made of thick and heavy cordage, seven feet high, which supplies the place of a second wall. In this there was a back entrance to the north, and another entrance to the south, at which were stationed troops of the body guard, and further inwards was the quarter of the halberdiers. Without this circle was another, formed of tents, adjusted so close to one another as to leave no interval, in which the soldiers kept guard for our greater security day and night. About two bowshots from this were encamped the princes and nobility, so near each other as to make a fourth wall. The common multitude lay without, in very good order, so that every one could without trouble find his own place. On each side of the river, for half a mile or a mile in extent, was a double row of tents, which served to secure the access on either bank to the stream. The princes of the West remained beyond this defence. The number of men was so great, that I should in vain attempt to state it, and am silent for fear of error and of contradicting other authorities.

The emperor, being minded to devote the day to the chase, required a double supply of horses and camels, and those which were needed for this purpose of his majesty's use were so quickly furnished, that he found everything in readiness at the appointed spot with as little confusion as if there were nothing to do, from which it is easy to infer the abundance of pasturage in the meadows on the banks of the river, but for which the proceeding would have been impossible.

Moving forward from this place on the thirtieth day, we came incontinently upon another very rapid river, at which the emperor, out of regard for our safety, made proclamation that not more than two horsemen at a time should ride over the bridge, which protracted the passage till evening, and caused many to remain on the hither side.

Some days after the chase, when everyone had risen before daylight, the emperor went forward in advance of all, and everyone took his meal when he chose, the hour of dinner being uncertain; and wheresoever half-cooked meat was served, of which these people are very fond, I was well content to get dry rice; wherefore the emperor's father-in-law, when he invited me to his table, gave orders that I should be abundantly supplied with cold water and dry rice.

After the table was over, it was my daily habit to attend the court, and when the emperor mounted his horse, I followed among his principal nobles till sunset, without food, unless that be called such which the wild fruits afforded and which I enjoyed with moderation. This mode of life I maintained for three months. In the woods I met with edible mushrooms as large as our hats. When, for the purpose of the chase, the low country has been left and the mountain has been ascended, a circle is formed far and wide to enclose the wild beasts, in the manner as follows.

When the cavalry has been arranged under its respective standards, then, at a given signal, two horsemen with blue flags are sent forward, the one of whom gallops off to the right flank and the other to the left to a certain limit, so as in short time to reach the appointed spots, about two miles distance from each other. Elevated above the circle, which, at a signal given to the horsemen, is then formed, stands another long row of horsemen, who are thus placed the better to discover the beasts among the brushwood; in the middle of this position is planted the emperor's standard, a flag made of tin, which is usually carried before him as he rides at the head of a company. He made me the associate of this his so agreeable occupation, his notice being attracted to me, as I suppose, by the length of my beard, which was conspicuous among so many shaven chins; this took place in the midst of a plain full of quails, of which he shot some twenty with arrows before my eyes. The first mentioned circle of horsemen is succeeded by another, whose office it is to kill the animals which have slipped through the hands of the former.

Between these first and last bands and the imperial standard, follows the entire train of courtiers on horseback, who are on the watch to catch the slightest sign of the emperor, so that among these rocks everything is at his hand the same as in the palace of Pekin. When the emperor moves to the higher ground, a fire is conveyed in an ingenious apparatus suspended between two horses, with a kettle containing Tartarian Cha or Teac, and warm water made from melted snow, with fresh fruits; and everything which can serve to excite the appetite is prepared with great expedition. At one time, when by accident a nest of tiger cubs had been discovered, some eunuchs in charge of the sheep loitered on their way, and occasioned the access to be left open. The culprit was immediately sentenced to walk on foot by the camels, which would have occasioned his death by fatigue, had not the emperor remitted the punishment; so heavy was the penalty ordained for so trifling an offence.

The last band is composed of the rabble, servants and attendants. The Western chieftains, as best accustomed to these forests, acted as commanders, allowing no one to leave his station. In the confined space the stags frequently put the riders in jeopardy, jumping six ells in distance. In these places are found the sweet mart (Martin cat), foxes, wolves, goats, sheep of various kinds, wild swine, roe deer, and other wild animals. Here also, as we have observed, are found tigers, against which the emperor is so incensed that he never spares them, but pursues them to the death; to which end he has proper weapons by him, and in particular two firelocks, which are always at hand. Wheresoever a river occurs abounding in fish, the chase is superseded, and all betake themselves to fishing; and for this purpose camels carry on their backs small boats made in separate pieces, which are put together and made available in an instant.

When the parties come in sight of the tents the circle is contracted round the beasts gradually, sometimes with the addition of two bands of horsemen, with blue flags, which is done by special command of the emperor. I, who had no other purpose but to drive the game within shot of the emperor, have nevertheless caught an animal between my legs, which much pleased the emperor. Nor is it unfrequent that the wildest animals are thus easily captured, when the circle has once closed in upon them. The horsemen then dismount, and leave their horses outside the circle, that they may keep closer together and repulse the animals, which would otherwise escape between the legs of the horses.

When the slaughter is over, camels are laden with the bodies, and hastily driven to the emperor, and there sentence is given as in a court of justice how the skins shall be removed, and the meat cut up in pieces fit to be dried in the sun and preserved against corruption. Laden with these spoils everyone towards evening betook himself to his tent, and by the following morning all were again in readiness. When the emperor occasionally dismounted for awhile, I used to allow myself a little sleep, not with an eye open, like the Chinese, who, when on horseback, are easily overtaken by slumber, but so that they seem to be awake.

It sometimes occurred, that when the emperor wished to show favour to some of his principal courtiers, he would cut some morsels of venison with his own hand from a stag's carcase for himself, and then would grant the same privilege to the favourites in question. Upon this each one would collect a bundle of faggots, and exhorted me to imitate their example, which, like another Diogenes, I performed, curious as to the purpose of the ceremony. And behold spits were produced, and large fires lighted, to which some held their portions of meat, others flung the pieces into the fire for a moment, and then swallowed them, still dripping with blood, with great relish. These were of the older mandarins, for the younger people born in China laughed at the proceeding, which I gazed at in silence and wonder. Some consider stag's flesh, with salt and vinegar, a great delicacy. The emperor looked on with satisfaction, as on a thing to which he was habituated.

In the thickets of this country there are many varieties of potherbs, namely, white and red onions, which I conjecture to have been brought from Egypt, much basilicum, but wild, and other vegetables, of which the names were unknown to us. Persian roses are as abundant as thistles or brambles with us; cloves flourish in great quantity, with four leaves, but without perfume; and many other things, more than I could mention without prolixity, albeit truly recounted. . . .

On the 29th of August we fell in with a flock of sheep, a sign of the proceedings of a company which the emperor had ordered on in advance, with the intent of killing the sheep by night, which was effected. These animals are altogether wild, and never check their flight till they are beyond sight of the hunter.

On this occasion the emperor was unwearied as another Hercules, killing, out of a second flock, mostly with his own spear, a thousand sheep. In these two flocks were captured two wolves, which kept company with the old sheep and fed on the young.

This chase being concluded we moved on, first to the north and then to the south, very desirous to fall in again with another flock, which had escaped us in the Pe Cha mountains. This we accomplished on the 8th of September, at a place where a river flows out of the mountain; and here lodges had been erected, according to orders of the emperor, for himself and others. When we had rested here some days the camp was again divided, one part following the march of the queens towards Pekin, the other attending the emperor towards the north-east, with the purpose of laying a new ambush against the stags, who for some months together make such a belling that the females hearing it resort to them, and their male rivals also seek an encounter. The consequence is, that running with great speed they fall into the hands of the hunters, which gave great contentment to the emperor. But this contentment lasted not long; for on the 16th and 17th of September fell a heavy snow, a not unusual circumstance for the season in this district, and threatened us with a failure of provision; which placed the emperor in great straights, and caused him to depart in haste towards Pekin. Before his departure, however, it pleased him to distribute among his great men the overplus of the spoil which had accumulated during his three months' hunting. I, unworthy as I was of such honour, received my share among the first, for which I made my humble acknowledgments, after the Chinese fashion.

Early on the morning of the 28th September the emperor, receiving accounts of the illness of his grandmother, pursued his way with all speed towards Pekin, and with him many of his court, the others following more slowly with the queens. Although the emperor, with excessive regard to my convenience, desired that I should be spared the fatigue of attending him, I considered myself, in return for his kindness, the more obliged to follow him. And thus, traveling day and night for fifty miles,

I reached a resting-place, so wearied that I could not bend a joint in my body. The labour, however great, had, as our experience showed, its reward; not only in an increase of the emperor's favour, but in the friendship, thus acquired, of many great men, with whom, but for this opportunity, we could have contracted no acquaintance. They discover that we are masters of all sciences, and question us on every subject.

Travels in Tartary, Thibet and China, 1844–1846 [2]:
HUC AND GABET

[*In the 1840's two missionary priests of the Lazarist order made a famous journey across Mongolia to Lhasa. The younger of the two, Abbé Huc, on their return, wrote an account of their journey that became a travel classic. The French sinologist Paul Pelliot, in an introduction, attributes its lasting success chiefly to the literary gifts of its author.*

[*"Huc had eyes to see and the power to recall what he had seen to life; but these very gifts have their counterpart in a somewhat ardent imagination, which led him on occasion to invent what he supposed himself to be merely reporting; he had the artist's instinct, which with a few lively touches heightens the color of reality, at times too drab. Some writers used to make this a pretext for denying the actuality of the journey itself; but there is no question that Huc and Gabet really did spend some time in Lhasa."*

[*At the beginning of his narrative Huc describes the difficulties and delays typical of the start of a long journey in that part of the world.*]

Towards the commencement of the year 1844, couriers arrived at Si-wan-a village north of the Great Wall. The prelate sent us instructions for an extended voyage we were to undertake for the purpose of studying the character and manner of the Tartars,

[2] From *Travels in Tartary, Thibet and China, 1844–1846*, by Huc and Gabet, translated by William Hazlitt.

and of ascertaining as far as possible the extent and limits of the Vicariat. This journey, then, which we had so long meditated was now determined upon; we sent a young Lama convert in search of some camels which we had put to pasture in the kingdom of Naiman. . . . The days passed away in futile expectation; the coolness of the autumn was becoming somewhat biting, and we feared that we should have to begin our journey across the deserts of Tartary during the frosts of winter.

We determined therefore to dispatch someone in quest of our camels and our Lama. A friendly catechist, a good walker and a man of expedition, proceeded on this mission. On the day fixed for that purpose he returned; his researches had been wholly without result. All he had ascertained was that our Lama had started several days before with our camels. The surprise of our courier was extreme when he found that the Lama had not yet reached us. "What!" exclaimed he, "are my legs quicker than a camel's! They left Naiman before me, and here I arrived before them! My spiritual fathers, have patience for another day. I'll answer that both Lama and camels will be here in that time."

Several days passed away. We once more despatched the courier in search of the Lama, enjoining him to proceed to the very place where the camels had been put to pasture—and not to trust to any statement that other people might make. . . . The day fixed for his return came and passed, and several others followed, but brought no camels, nor Lama, nor courier, which seemed to us most astonishing of all. . . .

[Our] project absolutely stupified our Christian friends; they could not comprehend how two Europeans should undertake by themselves a long journey through an unknown and inimical country: but we had reasons for abiding by our resolution. We did not desire that any Chinese should accompany us. It appeared to us absolutely necessary to throw aside the fetters with which the authorities had hitherto contrived to shackle missionaries in China. The excessive caution, or rather the imbecile pusillanimity of a Chinese catechist, was calculated rather to impede than to facilitate our progress in Tartary.

On the Sunday, the day preceding our arranged departure, every thing was ready; our small trunks were packed and padlocked, and the Christians had assembled to bid us adieu. On this very evening, to the infinite surprise of all of us, our courier arrived. As he advanced, his mournful countenance told us before he spoke, that his intelligence was unfavourable. "My spiritual fathers," said he, "all is lost; you have nothing to hope; in the kingdom of Naiman there no longer exist any camels of the Holy Church. The Lama doubtless has been killed; and I have no doubt the devil has had a direct hand in the matter."

. . . The intelligence thus received, though lamentable in itself, relieved us from our perplexity as to the past, without in any way altering our plan for the future. . . .

The night was far advanced, when suddenly numerous voices were heard outside our abode, and the door was shaken with loud and repeated knocks. We rose at once; the Lama, the camels, all had arrived; there was quite a little revolution. . . . We returned to our beds perfectly delighted; but we could not sleep, each of us occupying the remainder of the night with plans for effecting the equipment of the caravan in the most expeditious manner possible.

Next day, while we were making our preparations for departure, our Lama explained his extraordinary delay. First, he had undergone a long illness; then he had been occcupied a considerable time in pursuing a camel which had escaped into the desert; and, finally, he had to go before some tribunal, in order to procure the restitution of a mule which had been stolen from him. A law-suit, an illness, and a camel hunt were amply sufficient reasons for excusing the delay which had occurred. Our courier was the only person who did not participate in the general joy; he saw it must be evident to everyone that he had not fulfilled his mission with any sort of skill.

All Monday was occupied in the equipment of our caravan. Every person gave his assistance to this object. Some repaired our traveling-house, that is to say, mended or patched a great blue linen tent; others cut for us a supply of wooden tent pins; others mended the holes in our copper kettle, and renovated the broken leg of a joint stool; others prepared cords and put together the thousand and one pieces of a camel's pack. Tailors, carpenters, braziers, rope-makers, saddle-makers, people of all trades assembled in active co-operation in the court-yard of our humble abode. . . .

On Tuesday morning there remained nothing to be done but to perforate the nostrils of the camels, and to insert in the aperture a wooden peg, to use as a sort of bit. The arrangement of this was left to our Lama. The wild piercing cries of the poor animals pending the painful operation, soon collected together all the Christians of the village. At this moment, our Lama became exclusively the hero of the expedition. The crowd ranged themselves in a circle around him; everyone was curious to see how, by gently pulling the cord attached to the peg in its nose, our Lama could make the animal obey him, and kneel at his pleasure. . . .

The progress of our little caravan was not at first wholly successful. We were quite novices in the art of saddling and girthing camels, so that every five minutes we had to halt, either to re-arrange some cord or piece of wood that hurt and irritated the camels, or to consolidate upon their backs, as well as we could, the ill-packed baggage that threatened, ever and anon, to fall to the ground. We advanced, indeed despite all these delays, but still very slowly. After journeying about thirty-five *lis,* we quitted the cultivated district, and entered upon the Land of Grass. There we got on much better; the camels were more at their ease in the desert, and the pace became more rapid.

We ascended a high mountain, where the camels evinced a decided tendency to compensate themselves for their trouble by browsing, on either side, upon the tender stems of the elder tree or the green leaves of the wild rose. The shouts we were obliged to keep up, in order to urge forward the indolent beasts, alarmed infinite foxes, who issued from their holes, and rushed off in all directions. On attaining the summit of the rugged hill we saw in the hollow beneath the Christian inn of Yan-Pa-Eul [Yan-pa-êrh]. . . .

Inns of this description occur at intervals in the deserts of Tartary, along the confines of China. They consist almost universally of a large square enclosure, formed by high poles interlaced with brushwood. In the centre of this enclosure is a mudhouse, never more than ten feet high. With the exception of a few wretched rooms at each extremity, the entire structure consists of one large apartment, serving at once for cooking, eating, and sleeping; thoroughly dirty, and full of smoke and intolerable stench. Into this pleasant place all travelers, without distinction, are ushered, the portion of space applied to their accommodation being a long, wide *Kang* [*k'ang*], as it is called, . . . about four feet high, and the flat, smooth surface of which is covered with a reed mat, which the richer guests cover again with a traveling carpet of felt, or with furs. In front of it, three immense coppers set in glazed earth, serve for the preparation of the traveler's milk-broth. The apertures by which these . . . boilers are heated communicate with the interior of the *Kang* so that its temperature is constantly maintained at a high elevation even in the terrible cold of winter. Upon the arrival of guests the Comptroller of the Chest invites them to ascend the *Kang*, where they seat themselves, their legs crossed tailor-fashion, round a large table, not more than six inches high. The lower part of the room is reserved for the people of the inn, who there busy themselves in keeping up the fire under the cauldrons, boiling tea, and pounding oats and buck-wheat into flour for the repast of the travelers. The *Kang* of these Tartar-Chinese inns is, till evening, a stage full of animation, where the guests eat, drink, smoke, gamble, dispute, and fight: with night-fall, the refectory, tavern, and gambling-house of the day is suddenly converted into a dormitory. The travelers who have any bed-clothes unroll and arrange them; those who have none settle themselves as best they may in their personal attire, and lie down, side by side, round the table. When the guests are very numerous they arrange themselves in two circles, feet to feet. Thus reclined, those so disposed, sleep; others, awaiting sleep, smoke, drink tea, and gossip. The effect of the scene, dimly exhibited by an imperfect wick floating amid thick, dirty, stinking oil, whose receptacle is ordinarily a broken tea-cup, is fantastic, and to the stranger, fearful. . . .

We were on foot before daylight. Previous to our departure we had to perform an operation of considerable importance—no other than an entire change of costume, a complete metamorphosis. The missionaries who reside in China, all, without exception, wear the secular dress of the people, and are in no way distinguishable from them; they bear no outward sign of their religious character. . . .

We resolved to adopt the secular dress of the . . . Lamas; that is to say, the dress which they wear when not actually performing their idolatrous ministry in the Pagodas. The costume of the Thibetian Lamas suggested itself to our preference as being in unison with that worn by our young neophyte, Samdadchiemba.

We announced to the Christians of the inn that we . . . were about to cut off our long tails and to shave our heads. This intimation created great agitation: some of our disciples even wept; all sought by their eloquence to divert us from a resolution which seemed to them fraught with danger; but their pathetic remonstrances were of no avail; one touch of a razor, in the hands of Samdadchiemba, sufficed to sever the long tail of hair, which, to accommodate Chinese fashions, we had so carefully cultivated ever since our departure from France. We put on a long yellow robe, fastened at the right side with five gilt buttons, and round the waist by a long red sash; over this was a red jacket, with a collar of purple velvet; a yellow cap, surmounted by a red tuft, completed our new costume. Breakfast followed this decisive operation, but it was silent and sad. . . .

It was soon announced to us that everything was ready—so, mounting our respective animals, we proceeded on the road to Tolon-Noor, accompanied by Samdadchiemba.

We were now launched, alone and without a guide, amid a new world. . . .

As we have just observed, Samdadchiemba was our only traveling companion. This young man was neither Chinese, nor Tartar, nor Thibetian. Yet, at the first glance, it was easy to recognize in him the features characterizing that which naturalists call the Mongol race. A great flat nose, insolently turned up; a large mouth, slit in a perfectly straight line, thick, projecting lips, a deep bronze complexion, every feature contributed to give to his physiognomy a wild and scornful aspect. When his little eyes seemed starting out of his head from under their lids, wholly destitute of eyelash, and he looked at you wrinkling his brow, he inspired you at once with feelings of dread, and yet of confidence. . . .

At the age of eleven, Samdadchiemba had escaped from his Lamasery, in order to avoid the too frequent and too severe corrections of the master under whom he was more immediately placed. He afterwards passed the greater portion of his vagabond youth, sometimes in the Chinese towns, sometimes in the deserts of Tartary. It is easy to comprehend that this independent course of life had not tended to modify the natural asperity of his character; his intellect was entirely uncultivated; but, on the other hand, his muscular power was enormous, and he was not a little vain of this quality, which he took great pleasure in parading. . . .

He was, however, of no mortal service to us as a guide across the desert of Tartary, for he knew no more of the country than we knew ourselves. Our only informants were a compass, and the excellent map of the Chinese empire by Andriveau-Goujon. . . .

The sun had just set, and we were occupied inside the tent boiling our tea, when Arsalan warned us, by his barking, of the approach of some stranger. We soon heard the trot of a horse, and presently a mounted Tartar appeared at the door. *"Mendou"* he exclaimed, by way of respectful salutation to the supposed Lamas, raising his joined hands at the same time to his forehead. When we invited him to drink a cup of tea with us, he fastened his horse to one of the tent-pegs, and seated himself by the hearth. "Sirs Lamas," said he, "under what quarter of the heaven were you born?" "We are from the western heaven; and you, whence come you?" "My poor abode is towards the north, at the end of the valley you see there on the right." "Your country is a fine country." The Mongol shook his head sadly, and made no reply. "Brother," we proceeded, after a moment's silence, "the Land of Grass is still very extensive in the kingdom of Gechekten. Would it not be better to cultivate your plains? What good are these bare lands to you? Would not fine crops of corn be preferable to mere grass?" He replied, with a tone of deep and settled conviction, "We Mongols are formed for living in tents, and pasturing cattle. So long as we kept to that in the kingdom of Gechekten, we were rich and happy. Now, ever since the Mongols have set themselves to cultivating the land, and building houses, they have become poor. The Kitats (Chinese) have taken possession of the country; flocks, herds, lands, houses, all have passed into their hands. There remain to us only a few prairies, on which still live, under their tents, such of the Mongols as have not been forced by utter destitution to emigrate to other lands." "But if the Chinese are so baneful to you why did you let them penetrate into your country?" "Your words are the words of truth, Sirs Lamas; but you are aware that the Mongols are men of simple hearts. We took pity on these wicked Kitats, who came to us weeping, to solicit our charity. We allowed them, through pure compassion, to cultivate a few patches of land. The Mongols insensibly followed their example, and abandoned the nomadic life. They drank the wine of the Kitats, and smoked their tobacco, on credit; they bought their manufactures on credit at double the real value. When the day of payment came, there was no money ready, and the Mongols had to yield, to the violence of their creditors, houses, lands, flocks, everything." "But could you not seek justice from the tribunals?" "Justice from the tribunals! Oh, that is out of the question. The Kitats are skilful to talk and to lie. It is impossible for a Mongol to gain a suit against a Kitat. Sirs Lamas, the kingdom of Gechekten is undone!" So saying, the poor Mongol rose, bowed, mounted his horse, and rapidly disappeared in the desert.

We traveled two more days through this kingdom, and everywhere witnessed the poverty and wretchedness of its scattered inhabitants. Yet the country is naturally endowed with astonishing wealth, especially in gold and silver mines, which of themselves have occasioned many of its worst calamities. Notwithstanding the rigorous prohibition to work these mines, it sometimes happens that large bands of Chinese outlaws assemble together, and march, sword in hand, to dig into them. These are men professing to be endowed with a peculiar capacity for discovering the precious metals, guided, according to their own account, by the conformation of mountains, and the sorts of plants they produce. One single man, possessed of this fatal gift, will suffice to spread desolation over a whole district. He speedily finds himself at the head of thousands . . . of outcasts, who overspread the country, and render it the theatre of every crime. While some are occupied in working the mines others pillage the surrounding districts, sparing neither persons nor property, and committing excesses which the imagination could not conceive, and which continue until some mandarin, powerful and courageous enough to suppress them, is brought within their operation, and takes measures against them accordingly. . . .

We had just quitted the kingdom of Gechekten, and entered

that of Tchakar, when we came to a military encampment, where were stationed a party of Chinese soldiers charged with the preservation of the public safety. The hour of repose had arrived; but these soldiers, instead of giving us confidence by their presence, increased, on the contrary, our fears; for we knew that they were themselves the most daring robbers in the whole district. We turned aside, therefore, and ensconced ourselves between two rocks, where we found just space enough for our tent. We had scarcely set up our temporary abode, when we observed, in the distance, on the slope of the mountains, a numerous body of horsemen at full gallop. Their rapid but irregular evolutions seemed to indicate that they were pursuing something which constantly evaded them. By-and-by, two of the horsemen, perceiving us, dashed up to our tent, dismounted, and threw themselves on the ground at the door. They were Tartar-Mongols. "Men of prayer," said they, with voices full of emotion, "we come to ask you to draw our horoscope. We have this day had two horses stolen from us. We have fruitlessly sought traces of the robbers, and we therefore come to you, men whose power and learning is beyond all limit, to tell us where we shall find our property." "Brothers," said we; "we are not Lamas of Buddha; we do not believe in horoscopes. For a man to say that he can, by any such means, discover that which is stolen, is for them to put forth the words of falsehood and deception." The poor Tartars redoubled their solicitations; but when they found we were inflexible in our resolution, they remounted their horses, in order to return to the mountains.

Samdadchiemba, meanwhile, had been silent, apparently paying no attention to the incident, but fixed at the fire-place, with his bowl of tea to his lips. All of a sudden he knitted his brows, rose, and came to the door. The horsemen were at some distance; but the Dchiahour, by an exertion of his strong lungs, induced them to turn round in their saddles. He motioned to them, and they, supposing we had relented, and were willing to draw the desired horoscope, galloped once more towards us. When they had come within speaking distance:—"My Mongol brothers," cried Samdadchiemba, "in future be more careful; watch your herds well, and you won't be robbed. Retain these words of mine on your memory: they are worth all the horoscopes in the world." After this friendly address, he gravely re-entered the tent, and seating himself at the hearth, resumed his tea.

We were at first somewhat disconcerted by this singular proceeding; but as the horsemen themselves did not take the matter in ill part, but quietly rode off, we burst into a laugh. "Stupid Mongols!" grumbled Samdadchiemba; "they don't give themselves the trouble to watch their animals, and then, when they are stolen from them, they run about wanting people to draw horoscopes for them. After all, perhaps it's no wonder, for nobody but ourselves tells them the truth. The Lamas encourage them in their credulity; for they turn it into a source of income. It is difficult to deal with such people. If you tell them you can't draw a horoscope, they don't believe you, and merely suppose you don't choose to oblige them. To get rid of them, the best way is to give them an answer haphazard." And here Samdadchiemba laughed with such expansion, that his little eyes were completely buried. "Did you ever draw a horoscope?" asked we. "Yes," replied he, still laughing. "I was very young at the time, not more than fifteen. I was traveling through the Red Banner of Tchakar, when I was addressed by some Mongols who led me into their tent. There they entreated me to tell them, by means of divination, where a bull had strayed, which had been missing three days. It was to no purpose that I protested to them I could not perform divination, that I could not even read. 'You deceive us,' said they; 'you are a Dchiahour, and we know that the Western Lamas can all divine more or less.' As the only way of extricating myself from the dilemma, I resolved to imitate what I had seen the Lamas do in their divinations. I directed one person to collect eleven sheep's droppings, the dryest he could find. They were immediately brought. I then seated myself very gravely; I counted the droppings over and over; I arranged them in rows, and then counted them again; I rolled them up and down in threes; and then appeared to meditate. At last I said to the Mongols, who were impatiently awaiting the result of the horoscope: 'If you would find your bull, go seek him towards the north.' Before the words were well out of my mouth, four men were on horseback, galloping off towards the north. By the most curious chance in the world, they had not proceeded far before the missing animal made its appearance, quietly browsing. I at once got the character of a diviner of the first class, was entertained in the most liberal manner for a week, and when I departed had a stock of butter and tea given me enough for another week. Now that I belong to Holy Church I know that these things are wicked and prohibited; otherwise I would have given these horsemen a word or two of horoscope, which perhaps would have procured for us, in return, a good cup of tea with butter."

The stolen horses confirmed in our minds the ill reputation of the country in which we were now encamped; and we felt ourselves necessitated to take additional precautions. Before night-fall we brought in the horse and the mule, and fastened them by cords to pins at the door of our tent, and made the camels kneel by their side, so as to close up the entrance. By this arrangement no one could get near us without our having full warning given us by the camels, which, at the least noise, always make an outcry loud enough to awaken the deepest sleeper. Finally, having suspended from one of the tent-poles our traveling lantern, which we kept burning all the night, we endeavoured to obtain a little repose, but in vain; the night passed away without our getting a wink of sleep. As to the Dchiahour, whom nothing ever troubled, we heard him snoring with all the might of his lungs until daybreak. . . .

Our entrance into the city of Tolon-Noor was fatiguing and full of perplexity; for we knew not where to take up our abode. We wandered about a long time in a labyrinth of narrow, tortuous streets, encumbered with men and animals and goods. At last we found an inn. We unloaded our dromedaries, deposited the baggage in a small room, foddered the animals, and then, having affixed to the door of our room the padlock which, as is the custom, our landlord gave us for that purpose, we sallied forth in quest of dinner. A triangular flag floating before a house in the next street indicated to our joyful hearts an eating-house. A long passage led us into a spacious apartment, in which were symmetrically set forth a number of little tables. Seating ourselves at one of these, a tea-pot, the inevitable prelude in these countries to every meal, was set before each of us. You must swallow infinite tea, and that boiling hot, before they will consent to bring you anything else. At last, when they see you thus occupied, the Comptroller of the Table pays you his official visit, a personage of immensely elegant manners, and ceaseless volubility of tongue, who, after entertaining you with his views upon the affairs of the world in general, and each country in particular, concludes by announcing what there is to eat, and requesting your judgment thereupon. As you mention the dishes you desire, he repeats their names in a measured chant, for the information of the Governor of the Pot. Your dinner is served up with admirable promptitude; but before you commence the meal, etiquette requires that you rise from your seat, and invite all the other company present to partake. "Come," you say, with an engaging gesture, "come, my friends, come and drink a glass of wine with me; come and eat a plate of rice"; and so on. "No, thank you," replies everybody; "do you rather come and seat yourself at my table. It is I who invite you"; and so the matter ends. By this ceremony you have "manifested your honour," as the phrase runs, and you may now sit down and eat it in comfort, your character as a gentleman perfectly established.

When you rise to depart, the Comptroller of the Table again appears. As you cross the apartment with him, he chants over again the names of the dishes you have had, this time appending the prices, and terminating with the sum total, announced with special emphasis, which, proceeding to the counter, you then deposit in the money-box. In general, the Chinese restaurateurs are quite as skilful as those of France in exciting the vanity of the guests, and promoting the consumption of their commodities.

Two motives had induced us to direct our steps, in the first instance, to Tolon-Noor: we desired to make more purchases there to complete our traveling equipment, and, secondly, it appeared to us necessary to place ourselves in communication with the Lamas of the country, in order to obtain information from them as to the more important localities of Tartary. The purchases we needed to make gave us occasion to visit the different quarters of the town. . . .

Tolon-Noor is not a walled city, but a vast agglomeration of hideous houses, which seem to have been thrown together with a pitchfork. The carriage portion of the streets is a marsh of mud and putrid filth, deep enough to stifle and bury the smaller beasts of burden that not infrequently fall within it, and whose carcases remain to aggravate the general stench; while their loads become the prey of the innumerable thieves who are ever on the alert. The foot-path is a narrow, rugged, slippery line on either side, just wide enough to admit the passage of one person.

Yet, despite the nastiness of the town itself, the sterility of the environs, the excessive cold of its winter, and the intolerable heat of its summer, its population is immense, and its commerce enormous. Russian merchandise is brought hither in large quantities by the way of [Kiakhta]. The Tartars bring incessant herds of camels, oxen, and horses, and carry back in exchange tobacco, linen and tea. This constant arrival and departure of strangers communicates to the city an animated and varied aspect. All sorts of hawkers are at every corner offering their petty wares; the regular traders from behind their counters, invite, with honeyed words and tempting offers, the passers-by to come in and buy. The Lamas, in their red and yellow robes, gallop up and down, seeking admiration for . . . the skilful management of their fiery steeds.

The trade of Tolon-Noor is mostly in the hands of men from the provinces of Chan-Si [Shansi], who seldom establish themselves permanently in the town; but after a few years, when their money chest is filled, return to their own country. In this vast emporium, the Chinese invariably make fortunes, and the Tartars invariably are ruined. Tolon-Noor, in fact, is a sort of great pneumatic pump, constantly at work in emptying the pockets of the unlucky Mongols.

The magnificent statues, in bronze and brass, which issue from the great foundries of Tolon-Noor are celebrated not only throughout Tartary, but in the remotest districts of Thibet. Its immense workshops supply all the countries subject to the worship of Buddha with idols, bells, and vases employed in that idolatry. While we were in the town, a monster statue of Buddha, a present from a friend of Oudchou-Mourdchin [Ujumchin] to the Talé-Lama [Dalai-lama], was packed for Thibet, on the backs of six camels. The larger statues are cast in detail, the component parts being afterwards soldered together.

We availed ourselves of our stay at Tolon-Noor to have a figure of Christ constructed on the model of a bronze original which we had brought with us from France. The workmen so marvellously excelled, that it was difficult to distinguish the copy from the original. The Chinese work more rapidly and cheaply, and their complaisance contrasts most favourably with the tenacious self-opinion of their brethren in Europe.

During our stay at Tolon-Noor, we had frequent occasion to visit the Lamaseries, or Lama monasteries, and to converse with the idolatrous priests of Buddhism. The Lamas appeared to us persons of very limited information; and as to their symbolism, in general, it is little more refined or purer than the creed of the vulgar. Their doctrine is still undecided, fluctuating amidst a vast fanaticism of which they can give no intelligible account. When we asked them for some distinct, clear, positive idea what they meant, they were always thrown into utter embarrassment, and stared at one another. The disciples told us that their masters knew all about it; the masters referred us to the omniscience of the Grand Lamas; the Grand Lamas confessed themselves ignorant, but talked of some wonderful saint, in some Lamasery, at the other end of the country: *he* could explain the whole affair. However, all of them, disciples and masters, great Lamas and small, agreed in this, that their doctrine came from the West: "The nearer you approach the West," said they unanimously, "the purer and more luminous will the doctrine manifest itself.". . .

After maturely weighing the information we had obtained from the Lamas, it was decided that we should direct our steps towards the West. On October 1st we quitted Tolon-Noor; and it was not without infinite trouble that we managed to traverse the filthy town with our camels. The poor animals could only get through the quagmire streets by fits and starts; it was first a stumble, then a convulsive jump, then another stumble and another jump, and so on. Their loads shook on their backs, and at every step we expected to see the camel and camel-load prostrate in the mud. We considered ourselves lucky when, at distant intervals, we came to a comparatively dry spot, where the camels could travel, and we were thus enabled to re-adjust and tighten the baggage. Samdadchiemba got into a desperate ill-temper; he went on, and slipped, and went on again, without uttering a single word, restricting the visible manifestation of his wrath to a continuous biting of the lips.

Upon attaining at length the western extremity of the town, we got clear of the filth indeed, but found ourselves involved in another evil. Before us there was no road marked out, not the slightest trace of even a path. There is nothing but an apparently interminable chain of small hills, composed of fine, moving sand, over which it was impossible to advance at more than a snail's pace, and this only with extreme labour. Among these sand-hills, moreover, we were oppressed with an absolutely stifling heat. Our animals were covered with perspiration, ourselves devoured with a burning thirst; but it was in vain that we looked round in all directions, as we proceeded, for water; not a spring, not a pool, not a drop presented itself.

It was already late, and we began to fear we should find no spot favourable for the erection of our tent. The ground, however, grew by degrees firmer, and we at last discerned some sign of vegetation. By and by the sand almost disappeared, and our eyes were rejoiced with the sight of continuous verdure. On our left, at no great distance, we saw the opening of a defile. M. Gabet urged on his camel, and went to examine the spot. He soon made his appearance at the summit of a hill, and with voice and hand directed us to follow him. We hastened on, and found that Providence had led us to a favourable position. A small pool, the waters of which were half concealed by thick reeds and other marshy vegetation, some brushwood, a plot of grass: what could we under the circumstances desire more? Hungry, thirsty, weary, as we were, the place seemed a perfect Eden.

The camels were no sooner squatted, than we all three, with one accord, and without a word said, seized each man his wooden cup, and rushed to the pond to satisfy his thirst. The water was fresh enough; but it affected the nose violently with its strong muriatic odour. I remembered to have drunk water just like it in the Pyrenees, at the good town of Ax, and to have seen it for sale in the chemists' shops elsewhere in France: and I remembered, further, that by reason of its being particularly stinking and particularly nasty, it was sold there at fifteen sous per bottle.

After having quenched our thirst, our strength by degrees returned, and we were then able to fix our tent, and each man to set about his especial task. M. Gabet proceeded to cut some bundles of horn-beam wood; Samdadchiemba collected *argols* in the flap of his jacket; and M. Huc, seated at the entrance of the tent, tried his hand at drawing a fowl, a process which Arsalan, stretched at his side, watched with greedy eye, having immediate reference to the entrails in course of removal. We were resolved, for once and away, to have a little festival in the desert; and to take the opportunity to indulge our patriotism by initiating our Dchiahour in the luxury of a dish prepared accord-

ing to the rules of the *cuisinier Français*. The fowl, artistically
dismembered, was placed at the bottom of our great pot. A few
roots of synapia, prepared in salt water, some onions, a clove of
garlic, and some allspice, constituted the seasoning. The preparation was soon boiling, for we were that day rich in fuel. Samdadchiemba, by-and-by, plunged his hand into the pot, drew
out a limb of the fowl, and, after carefully inspecting it, pronounced supper to be ready. The pot was taken from the trivet,
and placed upon the grass. We all three seated ourselves around
it, so that our knees almost touched it, and each, armed with
two chopsticks, fished out the pieces he desired from the abundant broth before him.

When the meal was completed, and we had thanked God for
the repast he had thus provided us with in the desert, Samdadchiemba went and washed the cauldron in the pond. That done,
he brewed us some tea. The tea used by the Tartars is not prepared in the same way as that consumed by the Chinese. The
latter, it is known, merely employ the smaller and tenderer
leaves of the plant, which they simply infuse in boiling water,
so as to give it a golden tint; the coarser leaves, with which are
mixed up the smaller tendrils, are pressed together in a mould,
in the form and of the size of the ordinary house brick. Thus
prepared, it becomes an article of considerable commerce, under
the designation of Tartar-tea, the Tartars being its exclusive
consumers, with the exception of the Russians, who drink great
quantities of it. When required for use, a piece of the brick is
broken off, pulverised, and boiled in the kettle, until the water
assumes a reddish hue. Some salt is then thrown in, and efferves-
cence commences. When the liquid has become almost black,
milk is added, and the beverage, the grand luxury of the Tartars, is then transferred to the tea-pot. Samdadchiemba was a
perfect enthusiast of this tea. For our part, we drank it in
default of something better. . . .

We had not advanced an hour's journey on our way, when we
heard behind us the tramping of many horses, and the confused
sound of many voices. We looked back, and saw hastening in
our direction a numerous caravan. Three horsemen soon over-
took us, one of whom, whose costume bespoke him a Tartar
mandarin, addressed us with a loud voice, "Sirs, where is your
country?" "We come from the west." "Through what districts

has your beneficial shadow passed?" "We have last come from Tolon-Noor." "Has peace accompanied your progress?" "Hitherto we have journeyed in all tranquillity. And you: are you at peace? And what is your country?" "We are Khalkhas, of the kingdom of Mourguevan." "Have the rains been abundant? Are your flocks and herds flourishing?" "All goes well in our pasture-grounds." "Whither proceeds your caravan?" "We go to incline our foreheads before the Five Towers." The rest of the caravan had joined us in the course of this abrupt and hurried conversation. We were on the banks of a small stream, bordered with brushwood. The chief of the caravan ordered a halt, and the camels formed, as each came up, a circle, in the centre of which was drawn up a closed carriage upon four wheels. "*Sok! sok!*" cried the camel drivers, and at the word, and as with one motion, the entire circle of intelligent animals knelt. While numerous tents, taken from their backs, were set up, as it were, by enchantment, two mandarins, decorated with the blue button, approached the carriages, opened the door, and handed out a Tartar lady, covered with a long silk robe. She was the Queen of the Khalkhas repairing in pilgrimage to the famous Lamasery of the Five Towers, in the province of Chan-Si. When she saw us, she saluted us with the ordinary form of raising both her hands: "Sirs Lamas," she said, "is this place auspicious for an encampment?" "Royal Pilgrim of Mourguevan," we replied, "you may light your fires here in all security. For ourselves, we must proceed on our way, for the sun was already high when we folded our tent." And so saying, we took our leave of the Tartars of Mourguevan. . . .

At last, to complete our satisfaction, we entered upon the plains of the Red Banner, the most picturesque of the whole Tchakar. . . .

The Tchakar is divided into eight banners—in Chinese *Pa-Ki* —distinguished by the name of eight colours: white, blue, red, yellow, French white, light blue, pink, and light yellow. Each banner has its separate territory, and a tribunal . . . nominated and paid by the Emperor of China. In fact, the Tchakar is nothing more nor less than a vast camp, occupied by an army of reserve. In order, no doubt, that this army may be at all times ready to march at the first signal, the Tartars are severely prohibited to cultivate the land. They must live upon their pay, and upon the produce of their flocks and herds. The entire soil of the Eight Banners is inalienable. It sometimes happens that an individual sells his portion to some Chinese; but the sale is always declared null and void if it comes in any shape before the tribunals.

It is in these pasturages of the Tchakar that are found the numerous and magnificent herds and flocks of the Emperor, consisting of camels, horses, cattle, and sheep. There are 360 herds of horses alone, each numbering 1,200 horses. It is easy from this one detail to imagine the enormous extent of animals possessed here by the Emperor. A Tartar, decorated with the white button, has charge of each herd. At certain intervals, inspectors-general visit the herds, and if any deficiency in the number is discovered the chief herdsman has to make it good at his own cost. Notwithstanding this impending penalty, the Tartars do not fail to convert to their own use the wealth of the Sacred Master, by means of a fraudulent exchange. Whenever a Chinese has a broken-winded horse, or a lame ox, he takes it to the imperial herdsman, who, for a trifling consideration, allows him to select what animal he pleases in exchange, from among the imperial herds. Being thus always provided with the actual number of animals, they can benefit by their frauds in perfect security. . . .

You sometimes in Tartary come upon plains more animated than those you have just traversed; they are those, whither the greater supply of water and the choicest pastures have attracted for a time a number of nomadic families. There you see rising in all directions tents of various dimensions, looking like balloons newly inflated, and just about to take their flight into the air. Children, with a sort of hod at their backs, run about collecting *argols,* which they pile up in heaps around their respective tents. The matrons look after the calves, make tea in the open air, or prepare milk in various ways; the men, mounted on fiery horses, and armed with a long pole, gallop about, guiding to the best pastures the great herds of cattle which undulate, in the distance all around, like waves of the sea.

All of a sudden, these pictures, so full of animation, disappear, and you see nothing of that which of late was so full of life. Men, tents, herds, all have vanished in the twinkling of an eye. You merely see in the desert heaps of embers, half-extinguished fires, and a few bones, of which birds of prey are disputing the possession. Such are the sole vestiges which announce that a Mongol tribe has just passed that way. If you ask the reason of these abrupt migrations, it is simply this:—the animals having devoured all the grass that grew in the vicinity, the chief has given the signal for departure; and all the shepherds, folding their tents, had driven their herds before them, and proceeded, no matter whither, in search of fresh fields and pastures new.

After having journeyed the entire day through the delicious prairies of the Red Banner, we halted to encamp for the night in a valley that seemed full of people. We had scarcely alighted when a number of Tartars approached, and offered their services. After having assisted us to unload our camels, and set up our house of blue linen, they invited us to come and take tea in their tents. As it was late, however, we stayed at home, promising to pay them a visit next morning; for the hospitable invitation of our new neighbours determined us to remain for a day amongst them. . . .

Next morning, the time not appropriated to our little household cares, and the recitation of our Breviary, was devoted to visiting the Mongol tents, Samdadchiemba being left at home in charge of the tent.

We had to take especial care to the safety of our legs, menaced by a whole host of watchdogs. A small stick sufficed for the purpose; but Tartar etiquette required us to leave these weapons at the threshold of our host's abode. To enter a man's tent with a whip or a stick in your hand is as great an insult as you can offer to the family; and quite tantamount to saying, "You are all dogs."

Visiting among the Tartars is a frank, simple affair, altogether exempt from the endless formalities of Chinese gentility. On entering, you give the word of peace *amor* or *mendou,* to the company generally. You then seat yourself on the right of the head of the family, whom you find squatting on the floor, opposite the entrance. Next, everybody takes from a purse suspended at his girdle a little snuff-bottle, and mutual pinches accompany such phrases as these: "Is the pasturage with you rich and abundant?" "Are your herds in fine condition?" "Are your mares productive?" "Did you travel in peace?" "Does tranquillity prevail?" and so on. These questions and their answers being interchanged always with intense gravity on both sides, the mistress of the tent, without saying a word, holds out her hand to the visitor. He as silently takes from his breast-pocket the small wooden bowl, the indispensable vade-mecum of all Tartars, and presents it to his hostess, who fills it with tea and milk, and returns it. In the richer . . . families, visitors have a small table placed before them, on which is butter, oatmeal, grated millet, and bits of cheese, separately contained in little boxes of polished wood. These Tartar delicacies the visitors take mixed with their tea. Such as propose to treat their guests in a style of perfect magnificence make them partakers of a bottle of Mongol wine, warmed in the ashes. This wine is nothing more than skimmed milk, subjected for awhile to vinous fermentation, and distilled through a rude apparatus that does the office of an alembic. One must be a thorough Tartar to relish or even endure this beverage, the flavour and odour of which are alike insipid.

The Mongol tent, for about three feet from the ground, is cylindrical in form. It then becomes conical, like a pointed hat. The woodwork of the tent is composed below of a trellis-work of crossed bars which fold up and expand at pleasure. Above these, a circle of poles, fixed in the trellis-work, meets at the top, like the sticks of an umbrella. Over the woodwork is stretched, once or twice, a thick covering of coarse linen, and thus the tent is composed. The door, which is always a folding door, is low and narrow. A beam crosses it at the bottom by way of threshold, so that on entering you have at once to raise your feet and lower your head. Besides the door there is another opening at the top of the tent to let out the smoke. This opening can at any time be closed with a piece of felt fastened above it in the tent, and which can be pulled over it by means of a string, the end of which hangs by the door.

The interior is divided into two compartments; that on the left, as you enter, is reserved for the men, thither the visitors proceed. Any man who should enter on the right side would be considered excessively rude. The right compartment is occupied by the women, and there you will find the culinary utensils: large earthen vessels of glazed earth, wherein to keep the store of water; trunks of trees of different sizes, hollowed into the shape of pails, and destined to contain the preparations of milk, in the various forms which they make it undergo. In the centre of the tent is a large trivet, planted in the earth, and always ready to receive the large iron bell-shaped cauldron that stands by, ready for use.

Behind the hearth, and facing the door, is a kind of sofa, the most singular piece of furniture that we met with among the Tartars. At the two ends are two pillows, having at their extremity plates of copper, gilt, and skilfully engraved. There is probably not a single tent where you do not find this little couch, which seems to be an essential article of furniture; but, strange to say, during our long journey we never saw one of them which seemed to have been recently made. We had occasion to visit Mongol families where everything bore the mark of easy circumstances even of affluence, but everywhere alike this singular couch was shabby, and of ancient fabric. But yet it seems made to last for ever, and is regularly transmitted from generation to generation.

In the towns where Tartar commerce is carried on, you may hunt through every furniture shop, every broker's, every pawn-broker's, but you meet with not one of these pieces of furniture, new or old.

At the side of the couch, towards the men's quarters, there is ordinarily a small square press, which contains the various odds and ends that serve to set off the costume of this simple people. This chest serves likewise as an altar for a small image of Buddha. The divinity, in wood or copper, is usually in a sitting posture, the legs crossed, and enveloped up to the neck in a scarf of old yellow silk. Nine copper vases, of the size and form of our liqueur glasses, are symmetrically arranged before Buddha. It is in these small chalices that the Tartars daily make to their idol offerings of water, milk, butter and meal. A few Thibetian books, wrapped in yellow silk, perfect the decoration of the little pagoda. Those whose heads are shaved, and who observe celibacy, have alone the privilege of touching these prayer-books. A layman, who should venture to take them into his impure and profane hands, would commit a sacrilege.

A number of goats' horns, fixed in the woodwork of the tent, complete the furniture of the Mongol habitation. On these hang the joints of beef or mutton destined for the family's use; vessels filled with butter; bows, arrows and matchlocks; for there is scarcely a Tartar family which does not possess at least one fire-arm. . . .

The odour pervading the interior of the Mongol tents, is, to those not accustomed to it, disgusting and almost insupportable. This smell, so potent sometimes that it seems to make one's heart rise to one's throat, is occasioned by the mutton grease and butter with which everything on or about a Tartar is impregnated. It is on account of this habitual filth that they are called *Tsao-ta-Dze,* "Stinking Tartars," by the Chinese, themselves not altogether inodorous, or by any means particular about cleanliness.

Among the Tartars, household and family cares rest entirely upon the woman; it is she who milks the cows, and prepares the butter, cheese, etc.; who goes, no matter how far, to draw water; who collects the *argol* fuel, dries it, and piles it around the tent. The making of clothes, the tanning of skins, the fulling of cloth, all appertains to her; the sole assistance she obtains, in these various labours, being that of her sons, and then only while they are quite young.

The occupations of the men are of very limited range; they consist wholly in conducting the flocks and herds to pasture. This for men accustomed from their infancy to horseback is rather an amusement than a labour. In point of fact, the nearest approach to fatigue they ever incur is when some of their cattle escape; they then dash off at full gallop, in pursuit, up hill and down dale, until they have found the missing animals, and brought them back to the herd. The Tartars sometimes hunt; but it is rather with a view to what they can catch than from any amusement they derive from the exercise; the only occasions on which they go out with their bows and matchlocks are when they desire to shoot roebucks, deer, or pheasants, as presents for their chiefs. Foxes they always course. To shoot them, or take them in traps, would, they consider, injure their skin, which is held in high estimation among them. They ridicule the Chinese immensely on account of their trapping these animals at night. "We," said a famous hunter of the Red Banner to us, "set about the thing in an honest straightforward way. When we see a fox, we jump on horseback, and gallop after him till we have run him down."

With the exception of their equestrian exercises, the Mongol

Tartars pass their time in an absolute *far niente,* sleeping all night, and squatting all day in their tents, dozing, drinking tea, or smoking. At intervals, however, the Tartar conceives a fancy to take a lounge abroad; and his lounge is somewhat different from that of the Parisian idler; he needs neither cane nor quizzing glass; but when the fancy occurs, he takes down his whip from its place above the door, mounts his horse, always ready saddled outside the door, and dashes off into the desert, no matter whither. When he sees another horseman in the distance, he rides up to him; when he sees the smoke of a tent, he rides up to that; the only object in either case being to have a chat with some new person.

. . . .

Though it costs so little to keep, the camel is of an utility inconceivable to those who are not acquainted with the countries in which Providence has placed it. Its ordinary load is from 700 to 800 lbs., and it can carry this load ten leagues a day. Those, indeed, which are employed to carry dispatches are expected to travel eighty leagues per diem, but then they only carry the dispatch bearer. In several countries of Tartary the carriages of the kings and princes are drawn by camels, and sometimes they are harnessed to palanquins; but this can only be done in the level country. The fleshy nature of their feet does not permit them to climb mountains, when they have a carriage or litter of any sort to draw after them.

The training of the young camel is a business requiring great care and attention. For the first week of its life it can neither stand nor suck without some helping hand. Its long neck is then of such excessive flexibility and fragility that it runs the risk of dislocating it, unless someone is at hand to sustain the head while it sucks the teats of its dam. . . .

. . . You never see the young camel playing and frolicking about, as you see kids, colts, and other young animals. It is always grave, melancholy, and slow in its movements, which it never hastens, unless under compulsion. In the night and often in the day also, it sends forth a mournful cry, like that of an infant in pain. It seems to feel that joy or recreation are not within its portion; that its inevitable career is forced labour and long fastings, until death shall relieve it.

The maturation of the camel is a long affair. It cannot carry even a single rider, until its third year; and it is not in full vigour until it is eight years old. Its trainers then begin to try it with loads, gradually heavier and heavier. If it can rise with its burden, this is a proof that it can carry it throughout the journey. When that journey is only of brief duration, they sometimes load the animal in excess, and then they aid it to rise by means of bars and levers. The camel's capacity for labour endures for a long time. Provided that at certain periods of the year it is allowed a short holiday for pasturing at its leisure, it will continue its service for fully fifty years.

Nature has provided the camel with no means of defence against other animals, unless you may so consider its piercing, prolonged cry, and its huge, shapeless ugly frame, which resembles, at a distance, a heap of ruins. It seldom kicks, and when it does, it almost as seldom inflicts any injury. Its soft, fleshy foot cannot wound, or even bruise you; neither can the animal bite an antagonist. In fact, its only practical means of defence against man or beast is a sort of vehement sneeze, wherewith it discharges, from nose and mouth, a mass of filth against the object which it seeks to intimidate or to annoy.

Yet the entire [ungelded] male camels are very formidable during the twelfth moon, which is their rutting time. At this period, their eyes are inflamed; an oily, fetid humour exhales from their heads; their mouths are constantly foaming; and they eat and drink absolutely nothing whatever. In this state of excitement they rush at whatever presents itself, man or beast, with a fierceness of precipitation which it is impossible to avoid or to resist; and when they have overthrown the object they have pursued, they pound it beneath the weight of their bodies. The epoch passed, the camel resumes its ordinary gentleness, and the routine of its laborious career.

The females do not produce young until their sixth or seventh year; the period of gestation is fourteen months. The Tartars geld most of their male camels, which, by this operation, acquire a greater development of strength, height, and size. Their voices become at the same time thinner and lower, in some instances wholly lost; and the hair is shorter and finer than that of the entire camels.

The awkward aspect of the camel, the excessive stench of its breath, its heavy, ungracious movements, its projecting hare-lips, the callosities which disfigure various parts of its body, all contribute to render its appearance repulsive; yet its extreme gentleness and docility, and the services it renders to man, render it of permanent utility, and make us forget its deformity.

Notwithstanding the apparent softness of its feet, the camel can walk upon the most rugged ground, upon sharp flints, or thorns, or roots of trees, without wounding itself. Yet, if too long a journey is continuously imposed upon it, if after a certain march you do not give it a few days' rest, the outer skin wears off, the flesh is bared, and the blood flows. Under such distressing circumstances, the Tartars make sheep-skin shoes for it, but this assistance is unavailing without rest: for if you attempt to compel the animal to proceed, it lies down, and you are compelled either to remain with or to abandon it.

There is nothing which the camel so dreads as wet, marshy ground. The instant it places its feet upon anything like mud, it slips and slides, and generally, after staggering about like a drunken man, falls heavily on its sides.

When about to repose, it kneels down, folds its fore legs symmetrically under its body, and stretches out its long neck before it on the ground. In this position it looks just like a monstrous snail.

Every year, towards the close of spring, the camel sheds its hair, every individual bristle of which disappears before a single sprout of the new stock comes up. For twenty days the animal remains completely bare, as though it had been closely shaved all over, from the top of the head to the extremity of the tail. At this juncture, it is excessively sensitive to cold or wet; and you see it, at the slightest chillness in the air or the least drop of rain, shivering and shaking in every limb, like a man without clothes exposed in the snow. By degrees the new hair shows itself in the form of fine, soft, curling wool, which gradually becomes a long, thick fur, capable of resisting the extremest inclemency of the weather. The greatest delight of the animal is to walk in the teeth of the north wind, or to stand motionless on the summit of a hill, beaten by the storm and inhaling the icy wind. . . .

The hair of an ordinary camel weighs about ten pounds. It is sometimes finer than silk, and always longer than sheep's wool.

The hair growing below the neck and on the legs of the entire camels is rough, bushy, and in colour black, whereas that of the ordinary camel is red, grey, and white. The Tartars make no sort of use of it. In the places where the animals pasture, you see great sheets of it, looking like dirty rags, driven about by the wind, until they are collected in sheltered corners, in the hill sides. The utmost use the Tartars make of it is to twist some of it into cord, or into a sort of canvas, of which they construct sacks and carpets.

The milk of the camel is excellent, and supplies large quantities of butter and cheese. The flesh is hard, unsavoury, and little esteemed by the Tartars. They use the hump, however, which, cut into slices, and dissolved in tea, serves the purpose of butter.

. . . .

After eighteen months' struggle with sufferings and obstacles of infinite number and variety, we were at length arrived at the termination of our journey, though not at the close of our miseries. We had no longer, it is true, to fear death from famine or frost in this inhabited country; but trials and tribulations of a different character were no doubt about to assail us, amidst the infidel populations, to whom we desired to preach Christ crucified for the salvation of mankind.

The morning after our arrival at Lha-Ssa, we engaged a Thibetian guide, and visited the various quarters of the city, in search of a lodging. The houses at Lha-Ssa are for the most part several stories high, terminating in a terrace slightly sloped, in order to carry off the water; they are whitewashed all over, except the bordering round the doors and windows, which are painted red or yellow. The people of Lha-Ssa are in the habit of painting their houses once a year, so that they are always perfectly clean, and seem, in fact, just built; but the interior is by no means in harmony with the fine outside. The rooms are dirty, smoky, stinking, and encumbered with all sorts of utensils and furniture, thrown about in a most disgusting confusion. . . .

After a long search, we selected two rooms, in a large house, that contained in all fifty lodgers. Our humble abode was at the top of the house, and to reach it we had to ascend twenty-six wooden stairs, without railing, and so steep and narrow that in order to prevent the disagreeable incident of breaking our necks, we always found it prudent to use our hands as well as our feet. Our suite of apartments consisted of one great square room and one small closet. . . . The larger room was lighted . . . by a narrow window, provided with three thick wooden bars, and, above, by a small round skylight, which latter aperture served for a variety of purposes; first, it gave entrance to the light, the wind, the rain, and the snow; and secondly it gave issue to the smoke from our fire. To protect themselves from the winter's cold, the Thibetians place in the centre of their rooms a small vessel of glazed earth, in which they burn *argols*. As this combustible is extremely addicted to diffuse considerably more smoke than heat, those who desire to warm themselves find it of infinite advantage to have a hole in the ceiling, which enables them to light a fire without incurring the risk of being stifled by the smoke. You do, indeed, undergo the small inconvenience of receiving, from time to time, a fall of snow, or rain on your back: but those who have followed the nomadic life are not deterred by such trifles. The furniture of our larger apartment consisted of two goat-skins spread on the floor, right and left of the fire dish; of two saddles, our traveling tent, some old pairs of boots, two dilapidated trunks, three ragged robes, hanging from nails in the wall, our night things rolled together in a bundle, and a supply of *argols* in the corner. We were thus placed at once on the full level of Thibetian civilization. The closet, in which stood a large brick stove, served us for kitchen and pantry, and there we installed Samdadchiemba, who, having resigned his office of cameleer, now concentrated the functions of cook, steward and groom. Our two white steeds were accommodated in a corner of the court, where they reposed after their laborious but glorious campaign, until an opportunity should present itself of securing new masters; at present the poor beasts were so thoroughly worn down that we could not think of offering them for sale, until they had developed some little flesh between the bone and the skin.

As soon as we were settled in our new abode, we occupied ourselves with inspecting the capital of Thibet, and its population. Lha-Ssa is not a large town, its circuit being at the utmost two leagues. . ! .

Around the suburbs . . . are a great number of gardens, the large trees in which form, for the town, a magnificent wall of verdure. The principal streets of Lha-Ssa are broad, well-laid out, and tolerably clean, at least when it does not rain: but the suburbs are revoltingly filthy. The houses . . . are built some with stone, some with brick and some with mud, but they are all so elaborately covered with lime-wash that you can distinguish externally no difference in the material. In one of the suburban districts there is a locality where the houses are built with the horns of oxen and sheep. These singular constructions are of extreme solidity and look very well. The horns of the oxen being smooth and white, and those of the sheep, on the contrary, rough and black, these various materials are susceptible of infinite combinations, and are arranged accordingly, in all sorts of fantastic designs; the interstices are filled up with mortar. These houses are the only buildings that are not lime-washed; the Thibetians having taste enough to leave the materials in their natural aspect, without seeking to improve upon their wild and fantastic beauty. It is superfluous to add, that the inhabitants of Lha-Ssa consume an immense quantity of beef and mutton; their horn-houses incontestably demonstrate this fact.

The Buddhist temples are the most remarkable edifices in Lha-Ssa . . . larger, richer, and more profusely gilt than those of other towns.

The palace of the Talé-Lama merits, in every respect, the celebrity which it enjoys throughout the world. North of the town, at the distance of about a mile, there rises a rugged mountain, of slight elevation and of conical form . . . and upon this grand pedestal, the work of nature, the adorers of the Talé-Lama have raised the magnificent palace wherein their Living Divinity resides in the flesh. . . .

From the summit of this lofty sanctuary he can contemplate, at the great solemnities, his innumerable adorers advancing along the plain or prostrate at the foot of the divine mountain. The secondary palaces, grouped round the great temple, serve as residences for numerous Lamas, of every order, whose continual occupation it is to serve and do honour to the Living Buddha. Two fine avenues of magnificent trees lead from Lha-Ssa to the Buddha-La, and there you always find crowds of foreign pilgrims, telling the beads of their long Buddhist chaplets, and Lamas of the court, attired in rich costume, and mounted on horses splendidly caparisoned. Around the Buddha-La there is constant motion; but there is, at the same time, almost uninterrupted silence, religious meditations appearing to occupy all men's minds.

In the town itself the aspect of the population is quite different; there all is excitement, and noise, and pushing, and competition, every single soul in the place being ardently occupied in the grand business of buying and selling. Commerce and devotion incessantly attracting to Lha-Ssa an infinite number of strangers, render the place a rendezvous of all the Asiatic peoples; so that the streets, always crowded with pilgrims and traders, present a marvellous variety of physiognomies, costumes, and languages. This immense multitude is for the most part transitory; the fixed population of Lha-Ssa consists of Thibetians, Pebouns, Katchis . . . and Chinese.

The Thibetians belong to the great family which we are accustomed to designate by the term Mongol race; they have black eyes, a thin beard, small, contracted eyes, high cheekbones, pug noses, wide mouths and thin lips; the ordinary complexion is tawny, though, in the upper class, you find skins as white as those of Europeans. The Thibetians are of the middle height; and combine, with the agility and suppleness of the Chinese, the force and vigour of the Tartars. Gymnastic exercises of all sorts and dancing are very popular with them, and their movements are cadenced and easy. As they walk about, they are always humming some psalm or popular song; generosity and frankness enter largely into their character; brave in war, they face death fearlessly; they are as religious as the Tartars, but not so credulous. Cleanliness is of small estimation among them; but this does not prevent them from being very fond of display and rich sumptuous clothing.

The Thibetians do not shave the head, but let the hair flow over their shoulders, contenting themselves with clipping it, every now and then, with the scissors. The dandies of Lha-Ssa, indeed, have of late years adopted the custom of braiding their hair in the Chinese fashion, decorating the tresses with jewellery, precious stones and coral. The ordinary head-dress is a blue cap, with a broad border of black velvet surmounted with a red tuft; on high days and holidays they wear a great red hat, in form not unlike the Basquebarret cap, only larger and decorated at the rim with long, thick fringe. A full robe, fastened on the right side with four hooks, and girded round the waist by a red sash, red or purple cloth boots, complete the simple, yet graceful costume of the Thibetian men. Suspended from the sash is a green taffeta bag, containing their inseparable wooden cups, and two small purses, of an oval form and richly embroidered, which contain nothing at all, being designed merely for ornament.

The dress of the Thibetian women closely resembles that of the men; the main difference is, that over the robe, they add a short, many-coloured tunic, and that they divide their hair into two braids, one hanging down each shoulder. The women of the humbler classes wear a small yellow cap, like the cap of liberty that was in fashion in France at the time of our first republic. The head decoration of the ladies is a graceful crown composed of pearls. The Thibetian women submit, in their toilet, to a custom, or rather rule, doubtless quite unique, and altogether incredible to those who have not actually witnessed its operation: before going out of doors, they always rub their faces over with a sort of black, glutinous varnish, not unlike currant jelly; and the object being to render themselves as ugly and hideous as possible, they daub this disgusting composition over every feature, in such a manner as no longer to resemble human creatures. The origin of this monstrous practice was thus related to us: Nearly 200 years ago, the Nomekhan, a Lama king, who ruled over Hither Thibet, was a man of rigid and austere manners. At that period, the Thibetian women . . . were perfectly mad after all sorts of luxury and finery, whence arose fearful disorders, and immorality that knew no bounds. The contagion, by degrees, seized upon the holy family of the Lamas; the Buddhist monasteries relaxed their ancient and severe discipline, and were a prey to evils which menaced them with complete and rapid dissolution. In order to stay the progress of a libertinism which had become almost general, the Nomekhan published an edict, prohibiting women from appearing in public otherwise than with their faces bedaubed, in the manner we have described. . . .

In the country places the edict is observed with scrupulous

exactitude, and to the entire approbation of the censors; but at Lha-Ssa, it is not unusual to meet in the streets women, who, setting law and decency at defiance, actually have the impudence to show themselves in public with their faces unvarnished, and such as nature made them. Those, however, who permit themselves this license, are in very ill odour, and always take care to get out of the way of the police.

It is said that the edict of the Nomekhan has been greatly promotive of the public morality. We are not in a position to affirm the contrary, with decision, but we can affirm that the Thibetians are far indeed from being exemplary in the matter of morality. There is lamentable licentiousness amongst them, and we are disposed to believe that the blackest and ugliest varnish is powerless to make corrupt people virtuous. . . .

The women there enjoy very great liberty. Instead of vegetating, prisoners in the depths of their houses, they lead an active and laborious life. Besides fulfilling the various duties of the household, they concentrate in their own hands all the petty trade of the country, whether as hawkers, as stall-keepers in the streets, or in shops. In the rural districts, it is the women who perform most of the labours of agriculture.

The men, though less laborious and less active than the women, are still far from passing their lives in idleness. They occupy themselves especially with spinning and weaving wool. The stuffs they manufacture, which are called *poulou,* are of a very close and solid fabric; astonishingly various in quality, from the coarsest cloths to the finest possible merino. By a rule of reformed Buddhism, every Lama must be attired in red *poulou.* . . .

In Thibet, when you desire to salute anyone, you take off your hat, put out your tongue, and scratch the right ear, all three operations being performed simultaneously.

The Chinese you find at Lha-Ssa are for the most part soldiers or officers of the tribunal; those who fix their residence in this town are very few in number. At all times the Chinese and the Thibetians have had relations more or less important: they frequently have waged war against each other, and have tried to encroach upon one another's rights. The Tartar-Mantchou dynasty . . . saw from the commencement of their elevation the great importance of conciliating the friendship of the Talé-

Lama, whose influence is all-powerful over the Mongol tribes; consequently, they have never failed to retain at the court of Lha-Ssa two Grand Mandarins invested with the title of *Kin-Tchai*, which signifies ambassador, or envoy-extraordinary. The ostensible mission of these individuals is to present . . . the homage of the Chinese Emperor to the Talé-Lama, and to lend him the aid of China in any difficulties he may have with his neighbours.

.   .   .   .

. . . As soon as we had presented ourselves to the Thibetian authorities, declaring our characters and the object which had brought us to Lha-Ssa, we availed ourselves of the semi-official position we had thus taken, to enter into communication with the Thibetian and Tartar Lamas, and thus, at last, to begin our work as missionaries. One day, when we were sitting beside our modest hearth, . . . a Chinese dressed in exquisite style suddenly appeared before us, saying that he was a merchant and very desirous of buying our goods. We told him we had nothing to sell. "How, nothing to sell?" "Not anything, except indeed those two old saddles, which we do not want any longer." "Ah, exactly; that is just what I am looking for; I want saddles." Then, while he examined our poor merchandise, he addressed to us a thousand questions about our country and the places we had visited before we came to Lha-Ssa. Shortly afterwards there arrives a second Chinese, then a third, and at last two Lamas, in costly silk scarves. All these visitors insisted upon buying something from us; they overwhelmed us with questions, and seemed, at the same time, to scrutinize with distrust all the corners of our chamber.

We might say, as often as we liked, that we were not merchants—they insisted. In default of silk, drapery, or hardware, they would like our saddles; they turned them round and round in every way, finding them now perfectly magnificent, now abominable. At last, after long haggling and cross-questioning, they went off, promising to return.

The visit of these five individuals occasioned much serious reflection; their manner of acting and speaking was not at all natural. Although they came one after the other, yet they seemed perfectly to understand each other, and to aim at the same end by the same means. Their desire of buying something from us was evidently a mere pretext for disguising their intentions: These people were rather swindlers or spies, than real merchants. "Well," we said, "let us wait quietly; sooner or later we shall see clearly into this affair."

As it was dinner time, . . . we remained at the fireside, contemplating the pot, in which a good cut of beef had been boiling for some hours. Samdadchiemba, in his quality of steward, brought this to the surface of the liquid by means of a large wooden spoon, seized it with his nails, and threw it on the end of a board, where he cut it into three equal pieces; each then took his portion in his cup, and with the aid of a few rolls baked in the ashes, we tranquilly commenced our dinner without troubling ourselves very much about swindlers or spies. We were at our dessert—that is to say, we were about to rinse our cups with some buttered tea, when the two Lamas, the pretended merchants, made their re-appearance. "The Regent," they said "awaits you in his palace; he wants to speak to you." "But," cried we, "does the Regent, perchance, also want to buy our old saddles?" "It is not a question about either saddles or merchandise. Rise at once, and follow us to the Regent." The matter was now beyond a doubt; the government was desirous of meddling with us—to what end? . . .

After having dressed ourselves in our best, and put on our majestic caps of fox-skin, we said to our apparitor, "We are ready.". . .

We went at a rapid pace for about five or six minutes, and then arrived at the palace of the First *Kalon,* the Regent of Thibet. After having crossed a large courtyard, where were assembled a great number of Lamas and Chinese, who began to whisper when they saw us appear, we were stopped before a gilt door, the folds of which stood ajar; our leader passed through a small corridor on the left, and an instant after the door was opened. At the farther end of an apartment, simply furnished, we perceived a personage sitting with crossed legs on a thick cushion covered with a tiger's skin: it was the Regent. With his right hand he made us a sign to approach. We went close up to him, and saluted him by placing our caps under our arms. A bench covered with a red carpet stood on our right; on this we were invited to sit down. . . . Meantime the gilt

door was closed, and there remained in the saloon only the
Regent and seven individuals, who stood behind him—namely,
four Lamas of a modest and composed bearing, two sly-looking,
mischievous-eyed Chinese, and a person whom, by his long
beard, his turban and grave countenance, we recognized to be
a Mussulman. The Regent was a man of fifty years of age; his
large features, mild and remarkably pallid, breathed a truly
royal majesty; his dark eyes, shaded by long lashes, were intelligent and gentle. He was dressed in a yellow robe, edged with
sable; a ring, adorned with diamonds, hung from his left ear,
and his long, jet black hair was collected altogether at the top
of his head and fastened by three small gold combs. His large
red cap, set with pearls and surmounted by a coral ball, lay at
his side on a green cushion.

When we were seated, the Regent gazed at us for a long while
in silence, and with a minute attention. He turned his head
alternately to the right and left, and smiled at us in a half
mocking, half friendly manner. This sort of pantomime appeared to us at last so droll that we could not help laughing.
"Come," we said in French in an undertone; "this gentleman
seems a good fellow enough; our affair will go on very well."
"Ah!" said the Regent, in a very affable tone, "what language is
that you speak? I did not understand what you said?" "We
spoke the language of our country." "Well, repeat aloud what
you said just now." "We said, 'This gentleman seems a good-
natured fellow enough.'" The Regent, turning to those who
were standing behind him, said, "Do you understand this language?" They all bowed together, and answered that they did
not understand it. "You see, nobody here understands the
language of your country. Translate your words into the Thibetian." "We said, that in the physiognomy of the First *Kalon*
there was expressed much kindliness." "Ah! you think I have
much kindliness; yet I am very ill-natured. Is it not true that I
am very ill-natured?" he asked his attendants. They answered
merely by smiling. "You are right," continued the Regent; "I
am kind, for kindness is the duty of a *Kalon*. I must be kind
towards my people, and also towards strangers." He then addressed to us a long harangue, of which we could comprehend
only a few sentences. When he had finished, we told him that,
not being much accustomed to the Thibetian language, we

had not fully penetrated the sense of his words. The Regent signed to a Chinese, who, stepping forward, translated to us his harangue, of which the following is the outline. We had been summoned without the slightest idea of being molested. The contradictory reports that had circulated respecting us since our arrival at Lha-Ssa had induced the Regent to question us himself, in order to know where we came from. "We are from the western sky," we said to the Regent. "From Calcutta?" "No; our country is called France." "You are, doubtless, Peling?" "No, we are Frenchmen." "Can you write?" "Better than speak." The Regent, turning round, addressed some words to a Lama, who disappearing, returned in a moment with paper, ink, and a bamboo point. "Here is paper," said the Regent; "write something." "In what language—in Thibetian?" "No, write some letters in your own country's language." One of us took the paper on his knees and wrote this sentence: "What avails it to man to conquer the whole world, if he lose his soul?" "Ah, here are characters of your country! I never saw any like them; and what is the meaning of that?" We wrote the translation in Thibetian, Tartar, and Chinese, and handed it to him. "I have not been deceived," he said; "you are men of great knowledge. You can write in all languages, and you express thoughts as profound as those we find in the prayer-books." He then repeated, slowly moving his head to and fro, "what avails it to man to conquer the whole world if he lose his own soul."

.   .   .   .

The conversation extended far into the night. At last the Regent rose, and asked us whether we did not feel in want of a little repose. "We only awaited," we answered, "for the permission of the *Kalon,* to return to our lodgings." "Your lodgings! I have ordered an apartment to be prepared for you in my palace; you will sleep here to-night: to-morrow, you can return to your house." We sought to excuse ourselves from accepting the kind offer of the Regent; but soon became aware that we were not at liberty to refuse what we had been simple enough to consider a compliment. We were regular prisoners. We took leave of the Regent rather coolly, and followed an individual, who, after crossing a great many rooms and corridors, ushered us into a sort of closet, which we might fairly call a prison, as we were not permitted to leave it for any other place.

. . . Lamas and attendants of the Regent came in great numbers to see us. Those who had gone to bed got up, and soon we heard, in this vast palace, lately so calm and silent, doors opened and shut, and the rapid steps of the curious sounding in the passages. Crowds thronged around us and examined us with insupportable avidity. In all those eyes staring at us there was neither sympathy nor ill-will; they simply expressed vapid curiosity. To all these individuals around us, we represented merely a kind of zoological phenomenon. Oh, how hard it is to be exposed thus to an indifferent multitude! When we thought that these troublesome people had sufficiently stared and whispered, and ought now to be satisfied, we informed them that we were going to bed, and that we should feel extremely obliged if they would be kind enough to retire. Everyone bowed: some of them even were polite enough to put out their tongues at us; but nobody stirred. It was evident that they had a mind to know how we should behave on going to bed. This desire seemed to us somewhat misplaced; but we thought we would submit to it up to a certain point. Accordingly, we knelt down, made the sign of the cross, and recited, aloud, our evening prayer. As soon as we commenced, the whispering ceased, and a religious silence prevailed. When the prayer was finished, we once more invited the crowd to leave us, and, in order to add efficacy to our words, we extinguished the light. The crowd, thus plunged into deep darkness, adopted the course of first having a hearty laugh, and then retiring gropingly. We closed the door of our prison and laid down to rest.

When stretched on the beds of the First *Kalon,* we felt much more disposed to talk than to sleep. We experienced a certain pleasure in recapitulating the adventures of the day. The feigned merchants who wanted to purchase our saddles, our appearance before the Regent, the examination we had undergone by the ambassador, Ki-Chan, our supper at the expense of the public treasury, our long conversation with the Regent: all this appeared to us a phantasmagoria.

. . . As soon as dawn appeared, the door of our cell was gently opened, and the governor of the Katchi entered. He took a seat at our side, between the two couches, and asked us in kind, affectionate tones, whether we had spent a good night. He then presented to us a basket of cakes, made by his family, and some dried fruits from Ladak. We were deeply touched by this attention, which seemed to announce that we had met with a sincere and devoted friend.

The governor of the Katchi was thirty-two years old: his face, full of nobleness and majesty, breathed at the same time a kindness and candour well calculated to arouse our confidence. His looks, his words, his deportment, everything about him, seemed to express that he felt a very lively interest in us. He had come to acquaint us with what would be done during the day. . . . "In the morning," he said, "the Thibetian authorities will go with you to your lodgings. They will put a seal upon all your effects, which will then be brought before the tribunal, and be examined by the Regent and the Chinese ambassador, in your presence. If you have no manuscript maps in your baggage you need fear nothing; you will not be molested in any way. If, on the contrary, you have any such maps, you would do well to let me know beforehand, as in this case, we may perhaps find some way to arrange the affair. I am very intimate with the Regent, . . . and it is he himself who directed me to make to you this confidential communication." He then added, in an under voice, that all these difficulties were got up against us by the Chinese, against the will of the Thibetian government. We answered the governor of Katchi, that we had not a single manuscript map; and we then gave him, in detail, a statement of all the articles that were in our trunks. "Since they are to be examined to-day, you will judge for yourself whether we are people to be believed." The countenance of the Mussulman brightened. "Your words," he said, "quite reassure me. None of the articles you have described can at all compromise you. Maps are feared in this country—extremely feared, indeed; especially since the affair of a certain Englishman named Moorcroft, who introduced himself into Lha-Ssa, under the pretence of being a Cashmerian. After a sojourn there of twelve years, he departed; but he was murdered on his way to Ladak. Amongst his effects they found a numerous collection of maps and plans, which he had drawn during his stay at Lha-Ssa. This circumstance has made the Chinese authorities very suspicious on this subject. As you do not draw maps, that is all right; I will now go and tell the Regent what I have heard from you."

When the governor of Katchi had left us, we rose, for we

had remained in bed, without ceremony, during his long visit. After having offered up our morning prayer, and prepared our hearts to patience and resignation, we ate the breakfast which had been sent to us by order of the Regent. It consisted of a plate of rolls stuffed with sugar and minced meat, and a pot of richly-buttered tea. . . .

Three Lama ushers soon came and announced to us . . . that our luggage was to be inspected. We submitted respectfully to the order of the Thibetian authority, and proceeded to our lodgings, accompanied by a numerous escort all the way. From the palace of the Regent to our habitation we observed great excitement; they were sweeping the streets, removing the dirt, and decorating the fronts of the houses with large strips of *poulou* (woollen cloth), yellow and red. We asked ourselves what all this meant? for whom were all these demonstrations of honour and respect? Suddenly we heard behind us loud acclamations, and turning round we saw the Regent, who was advancing, mounted on a magnificent white charger, and surrounded by numerous horsemen. We arrived at our lodgings nearly at the same time with him. We opened the padlock by which the door was fastened, and requested the Regent to honour us by entering the apartments of the French missionaries. . . .

The Regent took a seat in the middle of our room on a gilded chair, which had been brought from the palace for this purpose, and asked whether what he saw in our room was all we possessed? "Yes; that is all we possess; neither more nor less. These are all our resources for invading Thibet." "There is satire in your words," said the Regent; "I never fancied you such dangerous people. What is that?" he added, pointing to a crucifix we had fixed against the wall. "Ah, if you really knew what that was, you would not say that we were not formidable; for by that we design to conquer China, Tartary, and Thibet." The Regent laughed, for he only saw a joke in our words, which yet were so real and serious.

A scribe sat down at the feet of the Regent, and made an inventory of our trunks, clothes and kitchen implements. A lighted lamp was brought, and the Regent took from a small purse which hung from his neck, a golden seal, which was applied to all our baggage. Nothing was omitted; our old boots, the very pins of our traveling tent, were all daubed with red wax and solemnly marked with the seal of the Talé-Lama.

When this long ceremony was completed, the Regent informed us that we must now proceed to the tribunal. Some porters were sent for, and found in very brief time. A Lama of the police had only to present himself in the street and summon, in the name of the law, all the passers by, men, women, and children, to come into the house immediately and assist the government. At Lha-Ssa the system of enforced labour is in a most prosperous and flourishing state; the Thibetians coming into it with entire willingness and good grace.

When enough labourers were collected, all our goods were distributed among them, and the room was completely cleared, and the procession to the tribunal set out with great pomp. A Thibetian horse soldier, his drawn sword in hand, and his fusil at his side, opened the procession; after him came the troop of porters, marching between two lines of Lama satellites; the Regent, on his white charger, surrounded by a mounted guard of honour, followed our baggage; and last, behind the Regent, marched the two poor French missionaries, who had, by way of suite, a not very agreeable crowd of gapers. Our mien was not particularly imposing. Led like malefactors, or, at least, like suspected persons, we could only lower our eyes, and modestly pass through the numerous crowd that thronged on our way. . . .

When we arrived at the tribunal, the Chinese ambassador attended by his staff, was already in his place. The Regent addressed him: "You want to examine the effects of these strangers; here they are; examine them. These men are neither rich, nor powerful, as you suppose." There was vexation in the tone of the Regent, and, at bottom, he was naturally enough annoyed at this part of policeman which he had to play. Ki-Chan asked us if we had no more than two trunks. "Only two; everything has been brought here; there remains in our house not a rag, not a bit of paper." "What have you got in your two trunks?" "Here are the keys; open them, empty them, and examine them at your pleasure." Ki-Chan blushed, and moved back. His Chinese delicacy was touched. "Do these trunks belong to me?" he said with emotion. "Have I the right to open them? If anything should be missed afterwards, what would you say?" "You need not be afraid; our religion forbids us rashly to judge our neighbour." "Open your trunks yourselves; I want to know what they contain; it is my duty to do so; but you alone have the right to touch what belongs to you."

We broke the seal of the Talé-Lama, the padlock was removed, and these two trunks, which had been pierced by all eyes for a long time past, were at last opened to the general gaze. We took out the contents, one after another, and displayed them on a large table. First came some French and Latin volumes, then some Chinese and Tartar books, church linen, ornaments, sacred vases, rosaries, crosses, medals, and a magnificent collection of lithographs. All the spectators were lost in contemplation of this small European museum. They opened large eyes, touched each other with the elbow, and smacked their tongues in token of admiration. None of them had ever seen anything so beautiful, so rich, so marvellous. Everything white they considered silver, everything yellow, gold. The faces of all brightened up and they seemed entirely to forget that we were suspected and dangerous people. The Thibetians put out their tongues and scratched their ears at us; and the Chinese made us the most sentimental bows. Our bags of medals, especially, attracted attention, and it seemed to be anticipated that, before we left the court, we should make a large distribution of these dazzling gold pieces.

The Regent and Ki-Chan, whose minds were elevated above those of the vulgar, and who certainly did not covet our treasure, nevertheless forgot their character as judges. The sight of our beautiful coloured pictures transported them quite out of themselves. The Regent kept his hands joined, and preserved a continuous stare with his mouth open, whilst Ki-Chan, showing off his knowledge, explained how the French were the most distinguished artists in the world. . . . Ki-Chan asked us if we had not watches, telescopes, magic-lanterns, etc. etc. We thereupon opened a small box which no one had hitherto remarked, and which contained a microscope. We adjusted its various parts, and no one had eyes but for this singular machine, in pure gold, as they took it to be, and which, certainly, was about to perform wondrous things. Ki-Chan alone knew what a microscope was. He gave an explanation of it to the public, with great pretension and vanity. He then asked us to put

some animalculae on the glass. We looked at his excellency
out of the corner of the eye, and then took the microscope to
pieces, joint by joint, and put it in the box. "We thought," said
we to Ki-Chan, with a formal air, "we thought that we came
here to undergo judgment, and not to play a comedy." "What
judgment!" exclaimed he, abruptly; "we wished to examine
your effects, ascertain really who you were, and that is all."
"And the maps: you do not mention them." "Oh, yes—yes! that
is the great point; where are your maps?" "Here they are," and
we displayed the three maps we had: a map of the world, the
two hemispheres upon the projection of Mercator, and a Chinese
empire.

The appearance of these maps seemed to the Regent a clap of
thunder; the poor man changed colour three or four times in
the course of a minute, as if we had shown our death warrant.
"It is fortunate for us," said we to Ki-Chan, "that we have met
with you in this country. If, by ill luck, you had not been here,
we should have been utterly unable to convince the Thibetian
authorities that these maps are not our own drawing. But an
instructed man like yourself, conversant with European matters,
will at once see that these maps are not our own work." Ki-Chan
was evidently much flattered by the compliment. "Oh, it is
evident," said he, at the first glance, "that these maps are
printed. Look here," said he to the Regent; "these maps are not
drawn by these men; they were printed in the kingdom of
France. You cannot distinguish that, but I have been long used
to objects, the productions of the Western Heaven." These
words produced a magical effect on the Regent. His face became
radiant, and he looked at us with a look of satisfaction, and
made a gracious movement with his head, as much as to say,
"It is well, you are honest people."

We could not get off without a little geographical lecture.
We yielded charitably to the wishes of the Regent and the
Chinese ambassador. We indicated with our fingers on the map
of Mercator, China, Tartary, and Thibet, and all the other
countries of the globe. . . .

After recognizing the principal points of Thibet, the Regent
inquired whereabouts was Calcutta? "Here," we said, pointing
to a little round speck on the borders of the sea. "And Lha-Ssa:
where then is Lha-Ssa?" "Here it is." The eyes and finger of

the Regent went from Lha-Ssa to Calcutta, and from Calcutta to Lha-Ssa. "The Pelings of Calcutta are very near our frontiers," said he, making a grimace, and shaking his head. "No matter," he added, "here are the Himalaya mountains."

The worthy Regent was all joyous and triumphant, when he saw that we had nothing in our possession calculated to compromise us. "Well," said he to the Chinese ambassador with a sneer, "what do you think of these men? What must we do with them? These men are Frenchmen, they are ministers of the religion of the Lord of Heaven, they are honest men; we must leave them in peace.". . .

The porters shouldered our luggage, and we returned to our lodging with undoubtedly greater alacrity and lighter hearts than when we had left it. The news of our reinstatement soon spread through the town, and the Thibetian people hastened from all quarters to congratulate us. They saluted us heartily, and the French name was in everyone's mouth. Thenceforward the white Azaras were entirely forgotten.

When we had refurnished our apartments we gave some *Tchang-Ka* to the porters, in order that they might drink our health in a pot of Thibetian small beer, and appreciate the magnanimity of the French, in not making people work for nothing.

Everyone having gone away, we resumed our accustomed solitude; and solitude inducing reflection, we discovered two important things. In the first place, that we had not yet dined, and in the second, that our horses were no longer in the stable. Whilst we were considering how to get something quickly cooked, and how to find where our horses were, we saw at the threshold of our door the governor of the Katchi, who relieved us from the double embarrassment. This excellent man, having foreseen that our attendance at the court of inquiry would not allow us time to make our pot boil, came, followed by two servants carrying a basket of provisions, with an ovation he had prepared for us. "And our horses—can you give us any information about them? We no longer see them in the court?" "I was going to tell you about them; they have been since yesterday evening in the Regent's stables. During your absence they have felt neither hunger nor thirst. I heard you say you intended to sell them—is that so?" "Oh, quite so, these animals ruin us: and yet they are so thin, no one will buy them." "The Regent wants to buy them." "The Regent!" "Yes, the Regent himself. Do not smile, it is no jest." "How much do you want for them?" "Oh, whatever he likes to give." "Well, then, your horses are purchased," and so saying, the Cashmerian unrolled a small packet he had under his arm, and laid upon the table two silver ingots, weighing ten ounces each. "Here," said he, "is the price of your two horses." We thought our beasts, worn and attenuated as they were, not worth the money, and we conscientiously said so to the governor of the Katchi; but it was impossible to modify the transaction which had been all settled and concluded beforehand. The Regent made out that our horses, although thin, were of an excellent breed, since they had not succumbed beneath the fatigues of our long journey. Besides, they had, in his eyes, a special value, because they had passed through many countries, and particularly because they had fed on the pastures of Kounboum, the native place of Tsong-Kaba. Twenty extra ounces of silver in our low purse was almost a fortune. We could be generous with it; so, on the spot, we took one of the ingots and placed it on Samdadchiemba's knees. "This is for you," we said, "you will be able with it to clothe yourself in holiday dress from head to foot." Samdadchiemba thanked us coldly and awkwardly; then the muscles of his face became distended, his nostrils swelled, and his large mouth assumed a smile. At last he could not restrain his joy; he rose and made his ingot leap in the air twice or thrice, crying, "This is a famous day!" And Samdadchiemba was right. This day, so sadly begun, had been fortunate beyond anything we could have expected. We had now, at Lha-Ssa, an honourable position, and we were to be allowed to labour freely in the propagation of the gospel.

The next day was still more lucky for us than its predecessor; putting, as it were, a climax to our prosperity. In the morning we proceeded . . . to the palace of the Regent, to whom we desired to express our gratitude for the manifestations of interest with which he had honoured us. We were received with kindness and cordiality. He told us, in confidence, that the Chinese were jealous of our being at Lha-Ssa; but that we might count on his protection, and reside freely in the country, without any one having a right to interfere with us. "You are very badly lodged," added he; "your room seemed to me dirty, small, and uncomfortable. I would have strangers like you, men come from so great a distance, well treated at Lha-Ssa. Strangers are guests; you must leave your present abode; I have ordered a suitable lodging to be prepared for you in one of my houses." We accepted this generous offer with grateful thanks. To be lodged comfortably and free of expense was not a thing for men in our position to despise; but we appreciated, above all, the advantage of residing in one of the Regent's own houses. So signal a favour, such emphatic protection, on the part of the Thibetian authorities, could not but give us with the inhabitants of Lha-Ssa great moral influence, and facilitate our apostolic mission.

On leaving the palace, we proceeded, without loss of time, to visit the house which had been assigned to us; it was superb—charming. The same evening we effected our removal, and took possession of our new dwelling.

The Heart of a Continent [3] :
SIR FRANCIS E. YOUNGHUSBAND

[Francis E. Younghusband, who began his career as a young cavalry officer in India, was the nephew of Robert Shaw, a former tea-planter in the Himalayan foothills who had become a British political officer dealing with the Central Asian adventurer Yakub Beg in Kashgar. Younghusband accompanied an expedition led by H. E. M. James in the 1880s to explore Manchuria, and was granted permission to return to India not by sea, but by traveling through Mongolia and Sinkiang. He became the youngest man (until then) ever to be awarded a gold medal by the Royal Geographical Society and went on to become prominent in the rival British and Russian exploration of the "roof of the world" mountain frontier in the Pamirs and Karakoram, and to lead the British expedition that marched to Lhasa in 1904 and drove the Dalai Lama into flight and exile, for a period, in China and Mongolia.]

[3] From The Heart of a Continent, by Sir Francis E. Younghusband.

Across the Gobi Desert

"But here—above, around, below,
  On mountain or on glen,
Nor tree, nor shrub, nor plant, nor flower,
  The weary eye may ken."

SCOTT

The auspicious day, April 26, having at length arrived, I had reluctantly to say good-bye to my kind and hospitable friends—the last of my countrymen I should see for many a month to come—and take my plunge into the Gobi and the far unknown beyond. . . . Ours was a compact little party—the camel-man, who acted as guide, a Mongol assistant, my Chinese "boy," eight camels, and myself. Chang-san, the interpreter, had gone back to Peking, feeling himself unable to face the journey before us, and so I was left to get on as best I could, in half-English, half-Chinese, with the boy, Liu-san. The guide was a doubled-up little man, whose eyes were not generally visible, though they sometimes beamed out from behind his wrinkles and pierced one like a gimlet. . . . The way in which he remembered where the wells were, at each march in the desert, was simply marvellous. He would be fast asleep on the back of a camel, leaning right over with his head either resting on the camel's hump, or dangling about beside it, when he would suddenly wake up, look first at the stars, by which he could tell the time to a quarter of an hour, and then at as much of the country as he could see in the dark. After a time he would turn the camel off the track a little, and sure enough we would find ourselves at a well. . . . As a rule no track at all could be seen, especially in the sandy districts; but he used to lead us somehow or other, generally by the droppings of the camels of previous caravans, and often by tracks which they had made, which were so faint that I could not distinguish them myself even when pointed out to me. A camel does not leave much of an impression upon gravel, like a beaten-down path in a garden; but the guide, from indications here and there, managed to make out their tracks even in the dark. Another curious thing about him was the way he used to go to sleep walking. His natural mode of progression was by bending right forward, and this seemed to keep him in motion without any trouble to himself, and he might be seen mooning along fast asleep. He had, however, one failing—he was a confirmed opium-smoker; directly camp was pitched he would have out his opium pipe, and he used to smoke off and on till we started again. I was obliged occasionally to differ in opinion from this gentleman, as will be seen further on; but, on the whole, we got on well together, and my feelings towards him at parting were more of sorrow than of anger, for he had a hard life of it going backwards and forwards up and down across the desert almost continuously for twenty years; and his inveterate habit of opium-smoking had used up all the savings he ought to have accumulated after his hard life.

The Mongol assistant, whose name was Ma-te-la, was a careless, good-natured fellow, always whistling or singing, and bursting out into roars of laughter at the slightest thing, especially at any little mishap. He used to think it the best possible joke if a camel deposited one of my boxes on to the ground and knocked the lid off. He never ceased wondering at all my things, and was as pleased as a child with a new toy when I gave him an empty corned-beef tin when he left me.

Poor Ma-te-la had to do a most prodigious amount of work. He had to walk the whole—or very nearly the whole—of each march, leading the first camel; then, after unloading the camels, and helping to pitch the tents, he would have to scour the country round for the argals or droppings of camels, which were generally the only thing we could get for fuel. By about two in the morning he could probably get some sleep; but he had to lie down amongst the camels in order to watch them, and directly day dawned he would get up and take them off to graze. This meant wandering for miles and miles over the plain, as the camels are obliged to pick up a mouthful of scrub, here and there, where they can, and consequently range over a considerable extent of ground. He would come into camp again for a short time for his dinner, and then go off again, and gradually drive the camels up to be ready for the start; then he would have to help to load them, and start off on the march again. . . .

There were eight camels. I rode one myself, four others carried my baggage and stores, and my servant rode on the top of one of these baggage camels; of the remaining three, one carried the water, one was laden with brick tea, which is used in place of money for buying things from the Mongols, and the third was loaded with the men's things. . . .

We left Kwei-hwa-cheng by the north gate of the town, and, after passing for some five miles over a well-cultivated plain, began to ascend the great buttress range on to the Mongolian plateau. . . . Crossing these mountains the following day, we afterwards entered an undulating hilly country, inhabited principally by Chinese. Villages were numerous, cart-tracks led in every direction, and the valleys were well cultivated. There were also large meadows of good grass, where immense flocks of sheep were feeding; but I was astonished to see that, although we were now in Mongolia, the largest and best flocks were tended by and belonged to Chinese, who have completely ousted the Mongols in the very thing which, above all, ought to be their speciality. It is really a fact that the Chinese come all the way from the province of Shantung to these Mongolian pasture-lands to fatten sheep for the Peking market. Here is another instance of the manner in which the pushing and industrious Chinaman is forcing his way, and gradually driving back the less persevering inhabitants of the country on which he encroaches; and it seems probable that the Chinese from the south, and the Russians from the north, will, in course of time, gradually force the poor Mongols into the depth of the desert.

. . . .

On May 7 we emerged from the undulating hilly country, and, after crossing a small stream called the Moli-ho, came on to an extensive plain bounded on the north, at a distance of five or six miles, by a barren, rugged range of hills, at the foot of which could be seen some Mongol yurts, and a conspicuous white temple; while to the south, at a distance of about twenty miles, were the Sheitung-ula Mountains, . . . which lie along the north bank of the Yellow river, and were explored in 1873 by Prjevalsky. . . .

A caravan from Guchen passed us on the 8th. There were about a hundred and fifty camels, mostly unladen, but several carried boxes of silver. This was the only caravan we met coming from the west; it had left Guchen sixty days previously.

The following day we passed close by a spur from the northern range of hills, which appeared to be of volcanic origin. The range presented a most fantastic appearance, rising in sharp rugged peaks. It consists of a series of sharp parallel ridges with intervening strips of plain, perhaps a quarter of a mile wide.

A small stream—here a few inches deep only, flowing over a wide pebbly bed—runs down from these hills. . . . We encamped near it on the 10th, in a spot bounded on the south by a low round range of hills, or rather undulations. During the morning I set off to look at this, thinking it was a couple of miles or so distant, but the distances are most deceptive here, and I found myself at the top in ten minutes. . . . A few days previously I had strolled out casually to a hill which appeared to be about five minutes' walk off, but was obliged to walk fast for half an hour before I got there. There is nothing to guide the eye—no objects, as men or trees, to judge by; only a bare plain and a bare smooth hillside are to be seen in front, and it is hard to say whether a hill is half a mile or two miles distant. . . . We were between two parallel ranges. The intervening country is undulating, the depressions being generally sandy, while the slopes are of alluvial deposit, covered with a reddish clay, which supports a scanty crop of coarse grass and scrubby plants. A few flowers of stunted growth appear occasionally, but they evidently have a hard struggle for existence with the severe climate of these deserts. The flower that flourishes most in this region is the iris, which does not, however, attain a greater height than six or eight inches, though occasionally it is seen in clumps growing to a height of one or one and a half feet. In the next march I climbed a small rocky hill, on which I found wild peach in full bloom, growing luxuriantly in the clefts, and also yellow roses. Later on, among the lower ridges of the Altai Mountains, I found white roses.

We were now gradually approaching the heart of the Gobi, and the aspect of the country became more and more barren; the streams disappeared, and water could only be obtained from the rough wells or water-holes dug by former caravans. No grass could be seen, and in its place the country was covered with dry and stunted plants, burnt brown by the sun by day and nipped by the frost by night. Not a sound would be heard, and scarcely a living thing seen, as we plodded along slowly, yet steadily, over those seemingly interminable plains. Sometimes I would strike off from the road, and ascend some rising ground to take a look round. To the right and left would be ranges of bare hills, very much resembling those seen in the Gulf of Suez, with rugged summits and long even slopes of gravel running down to the plain, which extended apparently without limit in front of me. And there beneath was my small caravan, mere specks on that vast expanse of desolation, and moving so slowly that it seemed impossible that it could ever accomplish the great distance which had to be passed before Hami could be reached.

Our usual plan was to start at about three in the afternoon, and travel on till midnight or sometimes later. This was done partly to avoid the heat of the day, which is very trying to the loaded camels, but chiefly to let the camels feed by daylight, as they cannot be let loose to feed at night for fear of their wandering too far and being lost. Any one can imagine the fearful monotony of those long dreary marches seated on the back of a slow and silently moving camel. While it was light I would read and even write; but soon the sun would set before us, the stars would appear one by one, and through the long dark hours we would go silently on, often finding our way by the aid of the stars alone, and marking each as it sank below the horizon, indicating how far the night was advanced. At length the guide would give the signal to halt, and the camels, with an unmistakable sigh of relief, would sink to the ground; their loads would quickly be taken off; before long camp would be pitched, and we would turn in to enjoy a well-earned sleep, with the satisfaction of having accomplished one more march on that long desert journey.

Camp was astir again, however, early in the morning, and by eight I used to get up, and after breakfast stroll about to see what was to be seen, then write up my diary, plot out the map, have dinner at one or two, and then prepare for the next march. And so the days wore on with monotonous regularity for ten whole weeks.

But though these marches were very monotonous, yet the nights were often extremely beautiful, for the stars shone out with a magnificence I have never seen equalled even in the heights of the Himalayas. Venus was a resplendent object, and it guided us over many a mile of that desert. The Milky Way, too, was so bright that it looked like a bright phosphorescent cloud, or as a light cloud with the moon behind it. This clearness of the atmosphere was probably due to its being so remarkably dry. Everything became parched up, and so charged with electricity, that in opening out a sheepskin coat or a blanket a loud cracking noise would be given out, accompanied by a sheet of fire. . . .

The temperature used to vary very considerably. Frosts continued to the end of May, but the days were often very hot, and were frequently hottest at nine or ten in the morning, for later on a strong wind would usually spring up, blowing sometimes with extreme violence, up till sunset, when it generally subsided again. If this wind was from the north, the weather was fine but cold. If it was from the south, it would be warmer, but clouds would collect and rain would sometimes fall; generally, however, the rain would pass off into steam before reaching the ground. Ahead of us we would see rain falling heavily, but before it reached the ground it would gradually disappear—vanish away—and when we reached the spot over which the rain had been falling, there would not be a sign of moisture on the ground.

.   .   .   .

After crossing the connecting ridge between Sheitung-ula and the mountains, we passed through some very dreary country —a plain between parallel ranges of hills. The soil was either sandy or covered with small pebbles, and was dotted over with clumps of furze, which flowered almost exclusively on the southern side, the cold blast of the north wind nipping the flowers in the bud on the northern side. Extracts from my diary will best illustrate the description of country we now passed through.

May 13.—A very disagreeable windy day. The sand penetrates everywhere; you do not see the sand in the air, but everything in the tent gradually gets covered with a coating of it. The country is extremely dreary looking—nothing but sandhills everywhere, and the air hazy with the particles of sand. Every evening about five we see herds and flocks slowly wending their way over the plain and converging on the water near the camp, but only the sheep seem to be attended by any one, and there is scarcely ever a yurt in sight.

The ponies go about in a semi-wild state, in troops of about twenty mares, under the guardianship of one or more stallions, who drive them about from place to place seeking something to graze on. They are entirely free, and every evening at sunset they march slowly back to the Mongol yurt. The Mongols have great difficulty in getting hold of one when they want it. They chevy the selected pony, riding after him with a long pole having a noose at the end, which they at last succeed in throwing over his head.

. . . We passed through some low hills, and then descended a valley in which were some gnarled and stunted elm trees—the first trees I have seen in Mongolia. They were about thirty feet high, and evidently very old. We then passed over a sandy, barren waste, the beginning of the Galpin Gobi, the very worst part of the whole desert. We met a small caravan of Mongols, and passed the encampment of a large caravan going from Bautu to Guchen.

In my diary I apparently have merely recorded the fact that we halted and camped, but I remember well how hard it was to camp that night. The darkness was so great that we could not see a yard in front of us, a regular hurricane was blowing, and heavy bursts of drenching rain kept falling at intervals. The lantern could not be lighted, on account of the violence of the wind, and we had to grope about amongst the camels, get the loads off, feel for the tent, and then get that up as best we could—which was no easy matter, for the wind blowing against it nearly blew us off our legs, and it was all we could do to prevent the whole thing from being carried away.

.   .   .   .

May 17.—We continued over the plain, which was covered with scrub, but there were a few tufts of coarse grass. A good many herds of camels were seen, and some ponies and sheep. Quantities of partridges rose from the scrub—many so tame that I used to chevy them running along the ground. . . . Putting up a tent in a sandstorm is one of the most irritating things I know of. No sooner do you hammer a peg in than it is pulled up again by the force of the wind; the sand gets driven into your eyes as you kneel to drive in the pegs; and to add to it all, it was pitch dark, and heavy spurts of rain would come driving down at intervals. . . . Two Mongols encamped with us. They slept in a makeshift tent of felts supported by sticks, leaving just room enough for the men to lie down with a fire between them.

May 20.—A really delightful morning. The desert is not so dreary after all; for no artist could wish for a finer display of colouring than the scene presents this morning. Overhead is a spotless, clear blue sky, and beneath it the plain has lost its dull monotonous aspect, fading away in various shades of blue, each getting deeper and deeper, till the hills are reached; and these again, in their rugged outline, present many a pleasing variety of colour, all softened down with a hazy bluish tinge; while the deceitful mirage makes up for the absence of water in the scene, and the hills are reflected again in what appear to be lovely lakes of clear, still water.

For two marches we kept gradually ascending towards a watershed, connecting the Hurku with a similar but somewhat lower range running parallel to the road, eight or ten miles to the south. Crossing this connecting ridge, we arrived at the Bortson well in the early hours of the morning of the 22nd.

There were a few Mongol yurts here on the banks of some small trickles of water, running down from the Hurku Hills to the north. . . . .

.   .   .   .

We passed several Mongol encampments, and one day a Mongol official came to visit me. He was an old man, and not interesting, showing no signs of ordinary intelligence. He had bad eyes, and I gave him some of Calvert's carbolic ointment to rub on the eyelids, for which he did not appear at all thankful. He fished about in the leg of his long boot, and produced from it a miscellaneous collection of articles—a pipe, a small piece of string, some camel's wool, a piece of paper, and various odds and ends, and eventually my ointment was done up in a suitable packet to his satisfaction, and stowed away again in the leg of his boot.

The Mongols carry about half their personal effects in their boots, and my man, Ma-te-la, one day produced from his boots

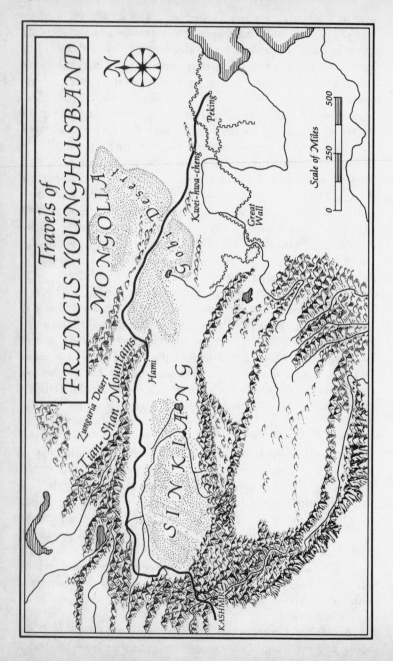

Travels of
FRANCIS YOUNGHUSBAND

MONGOLIA

Gobi Desert

1905

Zungaria Desert

Tian-Shan Mountains

Hami

SINKIANG

Kwei-hwa-cheng

Peking

Great Wall

KASHMIR

Scale of Miles

0   250   500

every little scrap that I had thrown away during the march, such as bits of paper, ends of string, a worn-out sock, and numerous other trifles. Everything is so precious to these Mongols in the desert that they never waste anything, and I soon learnt the value they put on every little article.

Liu-san one day took me to task severely for giving away an old lime-juice bottle to an ordinary Mongol. He said such valuable gifts ought to be reserved for the big men. . . . As we passed Mongol encampments, men used to come galloping over the plain to know if we had anything for sale, and to beg some tobacco of us. The Chinese guide would never give them any, although he had plenty; but poor Ma-te-la always used to give them a pinch or two, or, at any rate, a piece of brown paper—which he would produce from his boot, and which was probably a relic of something I had thrown away.

On June 3, just as we were preparing to start, we saw a great dark cloud away in the distance over the plain. It was a dust storm coming towards us. Where we were it was quite still, and the sky was bright overhead, and perfectly clear, but away to the west we saw the dark clouds—as black as night. Gradually they overspread the whole sky, and as the storm came nearer we heard a rumbling sound, and then it burst upon us with terrific force, so that we were obliged to lie at full length on the ground behind our baggage. There was fortunately no sand about—we were on a gravel plain—but the small pebbles were being driven before the wind with great velocity, and hurt us considerably. The storm lasted for half an hour, and it was then as calm and bright as before, and much cooler.

.   .   .   .

June 14.—A fine, bright day. The sun was very hot, but a cool breeze blew from the east.

We started at 4.20, still passing over the plain, and at ten entered some low hills. I had a long conversation with my boy in Chinese, helped out occasionally by English. His brother is an importer of racing ponies to Shanghai, and he says they all come from Jehol-Lamamiau. They are driven down to Tientsin and shipped in foreign steamers at fifteen dollars a head, or three ponies with a man for thirty-six dollars. He has been a riding-boy himself at Shanghai, and is a pretty smart

fellow at times, when he likes, and on the whole is a satisfactory boy for the trip. His English has improved a good deal,
and, with my small knowledge of Chinese, we manage to understand each other all right. Now and then I am astonished to
hear him come out with a choice selection of English swearing,
to supplement his stock of Chinese oaths, when he is having a
row with the guide.

We camped at 11.35 at Liang-ko-ba, a collection of four
Mongol yurts on the plain, round a patch of green.

We changed two camels here; one had gone lame, and the
other could scarcely move. I bought a sheep for three bricks of
tea for which I had paid a tael in Kwei-hwa-cheng. There
were some ponies feeding about. They were strong, well-shaped
animals, but in bad condition. I rode one which a Mongol had
ridden to our tent. It was very different from the clumsy ponies
of Peking. . . .

On the 17th we emerged from the hills again, on to another
great plain running between two parallel ranges of bare hills.
On this plain we saw some more wild asses or horses, which I
had good opportunity of examining with my telescope. They
have large heads and ears, and thick, rather short, full, round
bodies, legs well in proportion to their bodies, long tails reaching nearly to the ground, and thin like a mule's or donkey's.
As far as I can see, they have no mane, or only a very short one.
The guide calls them mules, and says they are from wild she-
asses.

The following day we continued over the plain, but after
sunset it became extremely dark, the sky being covered with
heavy rain-clouds. About eleven the camels began floundering
about, and we found we were in a bog. There had been heavy
rain here during the day; the soil was a very slimy clay, and the
ground broken up into hillocks. The guide was with difficulty
persuaded to light a lantern, as he says that it frightens the
camels, and they see their way better without it.

When it was lighted, the position did not look cheerful. The
camels were each perched up on a little hillock, separated from
each other by pools of water and slimy clay. The guide, the two
Mongols, and my boy were pulling away at their nose-strings, till
I thought their whole noses would be pulled off, but they would
not budge. Beating them behind was next tried, but that also
failed. At last they tried pulling them backwards, and this had

the desired effect—they were started, and once they were in motion they were kept going, although they nearly fell or split themselves up at every step. But now the path had disappeared, it began to rain, and I thought we were in for a night on the swamp, which would probably have been our fate had not my compass shown that we were going off in the wrong direction, there being no signs of a star for the guide to follow. At last we came upon sand, found a path, and very soon after a patch of gravel, on which we pitched camp.

One evening Ma-te-la, the Mongol assistant, was suddenly seen to shoot ahead at a great pace, and, on asking, I found he was going home. On he went, far away over the plain, till he became a mere dot in the distance, and I could not help envying him. In the same direction, and with nothing apparently between me and it but distance, was my home, and I felt myself struggling to pierce through space, and see myself returning, like Ma-te-la, home. But the dull reality was that I was trudging along beside a string of heavy, silent, slow-going camels, and on I had to go, for hour after hour through the night with monotonous regularity.

Suddenly, after traveling for nine hours, the gravel plain ended, and we passed over a stretch of grass and halted by a small stream. Close by were pitched four tents (yurts), and this was Ma-te-la's home.

He came to me the next day, saying the guide could not pay him all his wages, and asked me to lend the guide four taels, which I did. He has served the guide for two years, and the guide has now given him only fifteen taels (£3 15s). That guide is a regular scoundrel. Poor Ma-te-la had to work night and day, collect fuel, fetch water, look after the camels grazing, and then have to walk the whole march. In spite of this he was always perfectly happy, and used to sing and whistle the whole march, and would laugh at everything—if you even looked at him you saw a grin overspread his whole countenance. And now, for all his two years of hard work in this frightful desert, in the arctic cold of winter and the tropical heat of summer, he got fifteen taels—about a penny a day.

Started at 3.10 P.M., and passed over the gravelly plain again. The sunset was most wonderful. Even in the Indian hills during the rains I have never seen such a peculiar red tinge as the clouds had to-night. It was not red, it was not purple, but a mixture between the two—very deep, and at the same time shining very brightly. . . . An hour and a half later, when it was nearly dark, a very light, phosphorescent-looking cloud hung over the place of sunset.

June 23.—The gravel plain gradually gave way to a light clay soil, with plenty of bushes; and a little further we came on a regular meadow, with herds of cattle, sheep, and ponies, and several Mongol tents. We even saw patches of cultivation and trees, and water was plentiful, and was led on to the fields by irrigation ducts. Wheat was the only crop grown. The Mongol is evidently not fitted for agriculture, for the plots of cultivation were in the most untidy state. There were no signs of furrows, and the seed had evidently been thrown broadcast over the land; in some places it was very thick, and in others very thin. This was the first real oasis we had come across. It is in a depression between the range of hills, the ground gently sloping down to it from every side.

The name of this oasis is Ya-hu. It is about five miles in extent from west to east, and rather more from north to south. Some twelve miles to the west is a remarkable hill, called by the guide Ho-ya-shan. It rises very abruptly out of the plain to a height of about two thousand feet, and is a perfectly solid mass of rock of a light colour. There is said to be water on the summit, possibly in the crater of an old volcano, as in the Pei-shan in Manchuria.

On June 25 we reached Ula-khutun, where the road to Hami leaves the road to Guchen. . . .

We camped at 6.30 by a spring and some good grass, which the camels have not had for some time. I climbed one of the highest hills to have a look round. There were plenty of white soft clouds about, but suddenly my eye rested on what I felt sure was a great snowy range. I had out my telescope, and there, far away in the distance, were the real Tian-shan, only just distinguishable from the clouds. My delight was unbounded, and for long I feasted my eyes on those "Heavenly Mountains," as the Chinese call them, for they marked the end of my long desert journey.

Our next march, however, was the most trying of all, for we had to cross the branch of the Gobi which is called the desert of Zungaria, one of the most absolutely sterile parts of the whole

Gobi. We started at eleven in the morning, passing at first through the low hills, which were perfectly barren, but the hollows had a few tufts of bushes, and one hollow was filled with white roses. After seven and a half miles we left the hills, and entered a gravel plain covered with coarse bushes, but no grass. There was no path, and we headed straight for the end of the Tian-shan range. After passing over the plain for fifteen miles, we struck a path and followed it along till 11.30 P.M., when we halted to cook some food and rest the camels. It was of no use pitching camp, for there was neither water, fuel, nor grass; not a bush, nor a plant, nor a blade of grass—absolutely nothing but gravel. I lay down on the ground and slept till Liu-san brought me some soup and tinned beef. We started again at 4 A.M., and marched till 3.15 P.M. through the most desolate country I have ever seen. Nothing we have passed hitherto can compare with it—a succession of gravel ranges without any sign of life, animal, or vegetable, and not a drop of water. We were gradually descending to a very low level, the sun was getting higher and higher, and the wind hotter and hotter, until I shrank from it as from the blast of a furnace. Only the hot winds of the Punjab can be likened to it. Fortunately we still had some water in the casks, brought from our last camping-ground, and we had some bread, so we were not on our last legs; but it was a trying enough march for the men, and much more so for the camels, for they had nothing to eat or drink, and the heat both days was extreme. We at last reached a well among some trees. The guide called the distance two hundred and thirty *li,* and I reckon it at about seventy miles. We were twenty-seven hours and three-quarters from camp, including the halt of four and a half hours. We had descended nearly four thousand feet, and the heat down here was very much greater than we had yet experienced. We were encamped on the dry bed of a river, on the skirts of what looked like a regular park—the country being covered with trees, and the ground with long coarse grass. It was most striking, as on the other bank of the river there was not a vestige of vegetation.

.   .   .   .

About ten at night we suddenly found ourselves going over turf, with bushes and trees on either side, and a shrill clear voice hailed us from the distance. We halted, and the guide answered, and the stranger came up and turned out to be a Turki woman, who led us through the bushes over some cultivated ground to a house, the first I had seen for nearly a thousand miles.

It was the first sign that I had entered a new land—Turkestan —the mysterious land which I had longed for many a day to see. Flowing by the house was a little stream of the most delicious water. It was scarcely a yard broad, but it was not a mere trickle like the others we had passed in the Gobi, but was flowing rapidly, with a delightful gurgling noise, and was deep enough for me to scoop up water between my two hands. I gulped down mouthful after mouthful of it, and enjoyed such a drink as I had not had for many a long day, and as I lay down on the grass on its bank while the water-casks were being filled, I thought the trials of the desert journey were nearly over. But they were not quite; hardly fifty yards from the stream the vegetation disappeared, and we were again on gravel desert, and we had still to travel for five hours, gradually ascending as before—at twelve passing through a gorge two and a half miles long, in a range of little hills running parallel to the slope. We halted as the day was dawning, on a part of the slope where there was enough scrub for fuel and for the animals to eat. No water.

Next day we continued to ascend the long lower slopes of the Tian-shan, gradually rounding the eastern extremity of these mountains.

. . . The going was bad on account of the stones, and because the whole slope was cut up by dry water-courses. These were seldom more than a foot deep, but the slope was covered with them. They were formed by the natural drainage from the mountains, which, instead of running in deep valleys, spreads over the slope. The whole country was still barren, being covered with scrub only; but in the depression at the foot of the slope was a small Turki village, surrounded with trees and cultivation.

That night we encamped near a Turki house called Morgai, surrounded with fields of wheat and rice, watered from a small stream which appeared above the surface just here, and which, lower down, spread out and was swallowed in the pebbly slopes of the mountain.

The following morning I, for the first time, had an opportunity of examining more closely one of this new race of people through whose country I was about to travel for fifteen hundred miles or so. The men were tall and fine-looking, with more of the Mongol caste of feature about them than I had expected. Their faces, however, though somewhat round, were slightly more elongated than the Mongols, and there was considerably more intelligence about them. But there was more roundness and less intelligence, less sharpness in the outlines than is seen in the inhabitants of the districts about Kashgar and Yarkand. In fact, afterwards, in the bazaar at Hami, I could easily distinguish a Kashgari from an inhabitant of the eastern end of Turkestan.

Here at Morgai, too, I saw the Turki women. Very different they were from the doll-like Chinese women, with painted faces, waddling about on contorted feet; from the sturdy, bustling Manchu women, and from the simple, silly Mongol girls with their great red cheeks and dirty, unintelligent faces. These Turkis were fine, handsome women, with complexions not much darker than Greeks or Spaniards. They had good colour on their cheeks, and their eyes were dark and full. Their whole appearance was most picturesque, for they had a fine, dignified bearing, and were dressed in a long loose robe not confined at the waist, their long black tresses allowed to fall over their shoulders, only fastened at the ends into two thick plaits; on their head, slightly inclined backwards, they wore a bright red cap, which set off their whole appearance very effectively.

They stared with great astonishment at the sudden appearance of a white man (though I fancy at that time my face was not quite as white as an Englishman's generally is). But we had not much time to examine each other's charms, for I had that day to cross the Tian-shan.

Starting early, we ascended the stream, but it soon disappeared again, and we saw nothing more of it. The hillsides were at first rather bare, but the higher we got the greener they became; and after five or six miles were covered with rich green turf, most delightful to look upon after the bare hills of the Gobi; while here and there through an opening in the hills we could catch a glimpse of the snowy peaks above. There are, however, no trees nor even bushes, either on the hills or in the valleys.

We crossed the range at a height of eight thousand feet. Except the last half-mile the ascent was not steep, but led gradually up a narrow valley. The last mile or two was over soft green turf, and near the summit there was a perfect mass of flowers, chiefly forget-me-nots; and I am sure I shall not forget for a very long time the pleasure it was, seeing all this rich profusion of flowers and grass, in place of those dreary gravel slopes of the Gobi Desert. . . .

There were still no trees to be seen, and a curious characteristic of these hills is that there is absolutely no water. For twelve miles from Morgai to the summit of the pass we had not seen a drop of water. From this absence of water the valleys were not deep—not more than five or six hundred feet below the summit of the hills on either side—nor were the hillsides remarkably steep, as in the Himalayas. They are grassy slopes with rocks cropping out at their summits, and here and there on their sides. Five miles on the southern side a small stream appeared, and the valley bottom was partitioned off into fields, round which irrigation ducts had been led; but these were all now deserted, and the water was wasted in flowing over uncultivated fields. Trees now began to appear near the stream, and at 11.10 P.M. we pitched camp on a little grassy plot near a stream of cold clear water, and under a small grove of trees. It really seemed the height of bliss—a perfect paradise, and the desert journey a terrible nightmare behind me. The singing of the birds, too, struck me very much; for in the Gobi there was always a death-like silence, and so I noticed the continued twitter which the birds kept up. Trees were more numerous now, and on the northern slopes of some of the hills I even saw some patches of pine forests.

The Japan Expedition [4]:
JAMES WILLETT SPALDING

[*James Willett Spalding seems hesitant to tell us anything personal about himself in his book and reference works of the period present equally meager results. He was born in Richmond, Virginia, in 1827 and between 1852–55 served as captain's clerk*

[4] From *The Japan Expedition*, by J. Willett Spalding.

*aboard Commodore Matthew Calbraith Perry's steam frigate
flagship, the* Mississippi, *during its famous "opening of Japan"
expedition. His book is an account of this famous event. It produced a scathing review in the London* Atheneum *in 1855
which considered his anti-British bias so strong that the re-
viewer was not surprised to find him, as a result, treating the
English language unhandsomely, but was at a loss to understand
why he was equally hard on the Latin and Hindustani languages. Not without quiet glee, a generous sampling of his mis-
takes is given. "It is to be regretted that an expedition of such
undeniable interest as that of the* Mississippi *should not have
been chronicled with more ability and less flippancy and malev-
olence." However superior the British felt about Spalding's
book, in many ways it is a typically U.S. production, being
lively, gossipy, uninhibited and frankly displaying all the prejudices of his time, some of which may provide insight into the
current lack of love for the United States throughout Asia.*]

"Strange and singular as everything we have heard about
Japan undoubtedly is, nothing is so strange or so singular as the
determination of the inhabitants to resist all intercourse with
their fellow-creatures, except it be the fact that they have been
able to act upon the resolution with effect during two centuries.
It is this consideration which sheds a tinge of romance about the
operations of the American squadron. The attack upon Japan
is more than an expedition, it is an adventure. . . .

"The flavor of forbidden fruit has smacked racily on mortal
lips from the days of Eve downward. Be the impulse right or
wrong it exists, and as it will most surely be acted on, it must
not be ignored. The affair, however, is one of far too vital importance to be treated in a light or jesting spirit, for we have
every reason to suppose, and to fear, that the resistance of the
Japanese to the invaders will be of the most determined character. Great bloodshed and great misery will probably precede
the opening up of Japan. However necessary, and however jus-
tifiable such a step may be, we are not of those who can contemplate the slaughter of a gallant people, however mistaken their
cause, without a pang of regret."

The cruel treatment which had long been practised by that

singular and secluded people, the Japanese, toward American whalers who were thrown by the misfortune of shipwreck upon their coasts, the incentive of mercantile cupidity, and the urgency of personal ambition, induced the government of the United States, in 1852, to project an expedition to Japan, to obtain some assurance from the government of the country against a continuance or repetition of the inhospitality and cruelty inflicted upon our unfortunate citizens, and, if possible, to open the sources of trade. The East India squadron was accordingly augmented for this purpose, and Commodore Matthew Calbraith Perry was invested with the command, and charged with the performance of the duty.

After almost conjugating delay in all its moods and tenses, induced by the failure of the boilers of the unfortunate *Princeton,* and other causes, his flag-ship was ready for sea in November, 1852; and on the 24th of this month and year, with a desire to visit the hermetic empire, whetted by reading the Dutch historians, I found myself, as commander's clerk, on board of her. At midday we had dropped, not below the "kirk or hill," but below the hospital at Norfolk, and night found us ploughing deeply the ocean in the direction of Madeira; and before a very late hour the gleams from the Cape Henry lighthouse disappeared altogether.

The ship was the old steam-frigate *Mississippi,* which, as her name is a synonyme for the "father of waters," may be termed the father of our war-steamers, having been the consort of the pioneer ship, the *Missouri,* destroyed by fire on her first cruise, under the rock of Gibraltar. She had been engaged unremittingly since she first slid from her ways . . . and now the old *Mississippi* was leaving her own country, bound to the other side of the great globe, bearing the hopes of many, and embarked in a mission which might be successful—which might, perhaps, come to naught.

I said she ploughed deeply on getting beyond the Capes, because, with the considerate intelligence and humanity which preside over our naval affairs, sending boxes of guns to sea with national names, bringing about such sad losses as those of the *Albany* and the *Porpoise,* the *Mississippi,* designed by her constructor to draw eighteen feet of water, and to carry four hundred and fifty tons of coal, has her bunkers enlarged to the capacity of six hundred tons, additional lines of copper put upon her, and goes out drawing twenty-one feet, her guards but a short distance from the water. In this state we left the United States; her decks not yet cleared of the stores hastily put aboard for the different messes; the lengthened visage of sad people all around, thinking whether they had omitted anything in their notes of last adieu. . . .

Before reaching the bay of Yedo, sounding-spars had been rigged out from the end of the bowsprit of each steamer, from which depended sounding-leads, that were kept constantly going as well as the leadsmen in the "chains." As previous knowledge of the water was rather defective, the ships proceeded in with caution. The sweep of the bay is a noble one, as you approach, and the morning being a clear and lovely one, every object, from the strange-looking crafts coming continually in sight, to the summits of the high shores, and bold bluffs, were sharply defined. Then too, simultaneously with our first sight of the *nolli me tangere,* we got our first sight of *the* mountain of Japan —*Foogee Yama [Fujiyama].*

Perhaps the incidents which transpired during our first short visit to Japan, can be better conveyed by giving them as jotted down at the time.

July 8.—Ship cleared for action; fore and bowrails and iron stancheons taken down and stowed away; ports let down, guns run out into position and shotted. Flag-ship made signal, "Have no communication with shore; allow none from shore." Nine o'clock—standing up the outer bay of Yedo; a number of Japanese junks in sight. Smaller boats, in considerable numbers, making for the ships, and crossing their bows; but the sight of the revolving-wheels makes them haul up, and they give us a wide berth as we hold our way past them. To those in the boats who never before saw a steamship, particularly two large war-steamers, towing sloops-of-war through the water at a fast rate, how wonderful must be the sight! As the ships approached the town of Uragawa, or Uraga (about three o'clock), a fort, situated on a high hill, sent up a shell high into the air; and in a little while after we heard the explosion of another. As they did not appear to be aimed at us, but probably intended as signals, or to warn us not to come to anchor in their bay, we kept on. A few moments after stopping our wheels, long sharp-built boats of pine, fastened with copper, and ornamented at the prow with a black tassel, that had not been previously observed under the shadow of a high bluff, swarmed off under oar and sail, and surrounded the ships. They were all fully manned with men in uniform, and an old chap leaned over a rail in the stern. One of the boats that reached us first, contained a mandarin with two swords, who shook a letter at us, and then attempted to board us on the port bow, but the presentation of a loaded musket, by a sentinel, made him think a little while about it. He became much enraged, turned almost white with anger, his crew keeping up the while an awful pow-wow and noise; and, with them, he tries to board again, where our rail was down, but a division of pikes staring them in the face, and a steamer's wheels kept revolving (rather ugly things for a boat to get under), made them adjourn their determination. Drifting aft to our port-gangway and finding the prospect no better, he put off for shore, pointing to, and motioning that we must not let go our anchor, drawing and sheathing his swords, and holding up a letter. (One of these letters was thrown aboard of the *Plymouth,* written in French and Dutch, warning us, if we anchored there, we did it at our "peril.") But our ships went in under their guns and let go their anchors, forming a line broadside to shore, as previously ordered by diagram from Commodore Perry. Boats continued to circle around us, the occupants of some of them appearing to be making drawings of us, but they took care to keep at a respectable distance. In the evening, the lieutenant-governor of the province, Kayama Yesaimon, came off in a boat with streamers, and his rank being announced, he was allowed to come on board the flag-ship. The commodore would not receive him, but turned him over to his flag-lieutenant. In the meantime they commenced the formation of a cordon of boats around the ships. The Japanese functionary was first asked why this was being done. He said it was Japanese "custom." He was at once told that it was an *American* "custom" not to allow any such thing; that these boats must be sent away, not only from the flag, but the other ships; and if not away in fifteen minutes, they would be fired into. The boats left for shore. The governor wished to know what these ships had come there for. He was told that our commodore had a letter from our chief magistrate to his emperor. He said that their laws would only allow them to receive the letter at Nangasaki; that he would inform the authorities at Yedo of the arrival of the ships and of the letter; and that it would be four days before any answer could be received. The commodore directed it to be told him that he would wait three days and a half, and if, at the end of that time, there was not some one to receive our president's letter, that with five hundred men he would land, and deliver the letter himself. The governor then went ashore. In the evening the steam-chimney was ordered to be kept protected; no coal to be taken from the bunkers so as to expose the engines; steam to be kept up, and every suitable person on board ship directed to stand strict guard during the night, armed with cutlass, carbine, &c., and blue and red signal lights agreed upon between the ships, to be hoisted upon the appearance of any burning junks sent down upon us, or other danger during the night.

July 9.—Still at anchor off the harbor and town of Uraga, each ship with springs on her cable. Uraga is the seaport of Yedo, and said to contain twenty thousand inhabitants. Innumerable junks, with white-laced sails, have been continually arriving and departing since we have been here, having to be examined by officers of the customs, both going up and coming down. We can only see a portion of the town, the remainder being shut in by the narrow entrance to its harbor. During my mid-watch, last night, the Japanese ashore were striking, at intervals, a sweet and deep-toned bell, probably as a tocsin; while from the stern of each of the immense number of boats, anchored side by side, in shore, shone bright lights through lanterns of every color, making one long necklace of light, in front of the town of Humai, situated in the midst of forts and water-batteries. At sunrise, through a spy-glass could be discerned a number of fortifications along shore, extending up to a point which marks the entrance to the inner bay. There was also visible a number of long striped-cloth curtains, containing armorial figures of the different princes of the empire, the encampment of whose soldiers they are designed to mark out. The soldiers, like those previously seen in the boats, wear loose sacks of red, green, or blue, unconfined in front, and having in white on their backs the insignia of the prince whom they serve. There was a great deal of marching and countermarching, with gay banners, &c., between the different forts. The calibre of the guns in the embrasures, could not be made out, being kept under cover, or, as the sailors say, in "petticoats." On a very well-designed fort, circular in plan, intended to protect the entrance to the harbor of Uraga, were a number of the natives at work. About nine o'clock, boats well-armed were sent from each ship, with lead-lines, to ascertain the depth of water between the ships and the shore. These boats pulled as high as the upper fort, where the uppermost one was surrounded by Japanese guard-boats, who ordered them back, but did not attempt anything else, some of our oars being trailed, and the curtains over the muskets raised up for their edification. Our boats paid no further attention to them, but continued to stand in and pull close down the shore, getting soundings as they went, and at the same time making a rather bold reconnoissance of their guns and forts, who did not fire upon them, as many watching from the ships, at one time thought they would do.

July 10—Sunday.—A number of boats came off and rowed around the ship; troops, apparently, collecting on shore. Japanese at work on a fort just opposite to us. Weather clear. The steep shores, well-wooded, looking fine as they are brightened by the sun-light. Evening—A whale blowed not far from the ship. Foogee Yama obscured by cloud. During the day, the capstan having been dressed as usual, and books distributed, the chaplain gave out the hymn, commencing—

> "Before Jehovah's awful throne,
>   Ye nations, bow with sacred joy,"

and with the aid of many of the fine voices of the crew, and the assistance of the bass instruments of the band, in sight of heathen temples, and, perhaps, in the hearing of their worshippers, swelled up "Old Hundred" like a deep diapason of old ocean.

July 11.—By order of the commodore, the *Mississippi* was ordered to get under way, and stood up the straits, following slowly after our boats sent to sound the inner bay, to ascertain the practicality of reaching the capital, our present anchorage being twenty-five miles from the city of Yedo. Passed close in under the chief fort, on the point beyond which no "barbarian" ship had ever been permitted to go. Fort did not fire.

On debouching we entered a magnificent bay, of great extent, bounded on its western side by picturesque slopes, bold bluffs, with here and there a village between them, deeply indented coves, and a well-wooded island, crowned with a three-gun battery, which on our survey chart was called "Perry island." Our boats continued to sound ahead during the day, the Japanese guard-boats enveloping them and attempting to impede their progress by getting across their track, but attempted nothing further. Two little brass howitzers, on each of our forward guards, loaded with grape and cannister, would probably have caused some dancing among them if they had. On the east of us, on a long low sand beach, through a spy-glass could be seen an encampment of Japanese troops, near a breastwork, dressed in black figured clothes, and surmounted with banners. This was probably an "army of observation." We continued to hold our way up the bay until a late hour, as far as a high bluff of clay-stone, which was named "Mississippi bluff," as a token that it was nearer to the palace of the ziogoon of Japan than any foreign ship had ventured to go before. Our boats were then taken in tow, and we started on our return to the anchorage we had left in the morning. A two-sworded mandarin attempted to make his boat fast to one of our boats astern, that he might get a tow back, and I was surprised to hear him ask in English, "Are you going back?" The sailors in the boats were ordered to cut his line if he made fast to them. He was much angered as our wheels left him in the distance. We regarded his proposition for a tow, as cool as a fellow who would play spy on you all day, and then ask you to take him home in a carriage at night. On our way back we passed through a flotilla of their boats, when our chief engineer opened our steam-whistle. Never were human beings more astounded, when the unearthly noise reached their ears, the fellows at the sculls dropped their oars and stood aghast. To all of the day's doings the inhabitants of the different towns, and the troops strung along shore, have been constant and watchful observers. They could not understand what our movements meant. Jonathan's boldness had dumbfounded them.

July 12.—Governor of Uraga came aboard and urged Nanga-saki as the proper place at which Japan could receive foreign communications. Commodore Perry replied that his government had sent him to *Yedo,* and that he would go nowhere else to deliver his letter. The Japanese officials then pretended to hold a conference ashore, and afterward brought off word that they would receive the letter at a point which they would make known. It was afterward arranged that the reception of the letter was to be by a high officer, sent from the capital for the especial purpose; the place, a bay below the town of Uraga, and that it would take two days for them to get up a building for the ceremony. They said they had selected this spot for its privacy, that their rabble population might not be present; and as the whole thing was without precedent with them, and against their laws; —also, probably, because they did not wish us to get a sight of their towns, or a nearer view of their forts. The governor and his two interpreters at this interview remained aboard some time, and were very observant of everything, and evinced more information than could have been expected. The engine-room astonished them, though with Japanese self-possession they concealed much. They laughed, and were untiring in their attention to cherry brandy. On being shown a daguerreotype, they immediately called its name. On a globe they pointed out Boston, New York, Philadelphia, New Orleans, &c.; gave the boundaries of Mexico, and said our country had a part of Mexico; if our mission was a peaceful one, why did we have *four* ships-of-war to bring *one* letter? (Commodore told them that it was a greater compliment to their emperor—probably!) Wished to know why the steam-vessel *Mississippi* went up the inner bay so far? It was replied that the commodore had more ships in these waters, and if they should render it necessary that they would all come with him, the next time he came; he desired an anchorage less exposed than the one we were then lying at.

July 13.—Some little suspicion of treachery ashore; much conference going on among chief mandarins. Boats were sent from the ships to go and sound off the mouth of the appointed place, to see whether any of the ships could get in sufficiently near to cover and protect the landing of the boats; orders issued prescribing who were to compose the landing party; some will have to stay on board the ships; poor fellows! Bad day for Japanese to-morrow, if they attempt with us the treacherous game that they played upon Golownin:—

"The Americans must not quit their wooden walls."

—*London Press.*

July 14.—Bright and beautiful day. Much activity and preparation for the landing; boats being lowered away, percussion-
caps distributed, and twenty rounds of ball-cartridges delivered
to each man; officers rigging in undress uniforms, and arming
mostly with cutlasses and Colt's six-shooters. Quartermasters
fastening American ensigns on pikes. General orders received
early in the morning. . . .

The ships will watch the proceedings on shore, having their
guns primed and pointed, and their remaining boats alongside,
with arms in them, ready in a moment to shove ashore, if the
commanding officers think there is need of them. . . .

At daybreak the *Susquehanna* and *Mississippi* steam-frigates
tripped their anchors, dropped down, and anchored immediately
across the entrance of the bay where we were to land, to protect
and cover the landing, having springs on their cables, that their
broadside of guns might be trained on the shore. After some
delay the boats moved ashore. The captain of the *Susquehanna*
and officers, leading; Captain Walker of the *Saratoga* and officers next, then the *Mississippi's* boats, in the first of which I was,
under Lieutenant Taylor. Following in line came the remaining
boats of all the ships, with sailors, marines, two bands, &c.

The place selected by the Japanese for the delivery of the letter, was a bay of some mile and a quarter in depth, surrounded
by an amphitheatre of bold hills, its entrance being narrow, and
defended by forts on either side. At the head of this bay, following the line of a crescent beach of black and white sand, ankle-
deep, is the town of Gorihama. In the distance, with its veil of
blue, and patches of snow, towering up fifteen thousand feet,
shone the extinct volcano of Foogee. The boats, as they pulled
in, presented a fine sight; the "flower-flag," as the Chinese call
it, waving gracefully from the stern of each boat; the bright
muskets shining in the sun, and the epaulettes glistening. The
landing was done in fine order, and with great promptitude,
under the command of Major Zeilen, of the marine corps. Each
man, as the boat touched the beach, jumped ashore, and took
his proper place in line, which, when formed, presented a bold
front, notwithstanding officers and men all told, it scarcely exceeded four hundred men; and encircling them a few paces in
rear, and as far as one could see, on either hand, in horseshoe
form, were Japanese troops, who had been collected there for
the occasion, armed with spears and bows, long bayonet brass-

mounted muskets, and match-locks, with ready fuses, coiled on their right arms. In their front, equi-distant, sat their officers on stools, armed with two swords. Near by, not very large, were a number of horses richly caparisoned about the head, and with gaudy housings, belonging to the officers. Extending all around were canvass curtains supported by stakes driven in the ground, with different insignias painted on the front, and festooned with blue cords and tassels; at the termination of each one floated the colored flag of each particular prince, whose men were present. The shining and gilded lacquered broad-brims of the Japanese; the varied costumes, brilliant colors, flapping flags, and curtain enclosures, all overhung by a dense green of trees, as the eye took them in, made one think that he had come to be a specta-tor of some joust or tourney. The Japanese say they had five thousand men present, but I hardly think there were as many, unless some were hid in the town, whose houses in our direction were concealed behind temporary walls of thatching straw.

A salute of thirteen guns from the flag-ship, which caused some little stir among the Japanese troops, who did not seem exactly to understand it, announced that the commodore and his immediate suite had left, in his barge, for shore. In a little while he landed on a small jetty, made of rice-straw and sand, passing through a street formed of his own officers, to his place in line, when the squadron band struck up "Hail Columbia" in a style, and with a force that made the Japanese open their ears (they may have to listen to it again), and the hills around sent each note of "Hail Columbia" back again. "Hail Columbia" never sounded better. The column of escort with the marines in front, a stalwart sailor with the broad pennant; commodore and staff; suite of officers; boxes containing president's letter, &c.; two men over six feet high, each, with pikes upon which American ensigns were fastened, with revolving rifles slung across their shoulders; sailors with bronzed muskets; *Missis-sippi's* band, &c.; and marines then marched to the building for the ceremony; shown the way by two Japanese officials. The sailors were in blue trousers and white frocks, prettily bisected with the slings of their cartridge boxes, and wore blue cloth caps, with bands of red, white, and blue, ornamented with thirteen stars in white. The marines were in full uniform. The room of ceremony was reached by passing through a small canopied court, enclosed with primitive landscape screens, the floor of which was covered with matting. The place of audience was a room in a thatched building, limited in space, and entirely open in the direction of the court, ornamented with gauze curtains as drapery. At the back of the room were representations of shrubbery, and of cranes wheeling in flight over it, while on the two remaining sides, were hung large blue flags, having in the centre one large and eight smaller satellite representations. Overhead you looked up to thatching, and each rafter was marked with Japanese characters, as if the building had been originally constructed at some other place, probably at Yedo, and sent down for erection. On the left of the room as you entered by ascending one step, was seated the chief Japanese functionary, appointed by the emperor to receive the president's letter, the prince of Idzoo; beside him was the prince of the province of Iwami; behind him quite a number of two-sworded mandarins. The chief man was attired in a maroon silk robe, with an over-garment of red, blue cloth socks, with places left for the great toe. On the back of the red over-garment, were figures worked in white, some resembling cornucopias. His suite were attired in the same manner with slight exceptions. On the other side of the room were placed ornamental chairs, with well-designed arm-rests, in which were seated Commodore Perry and suite.

Dr. Williams, of Canton, was present as interpreter of the Japanese language; although his services were not called into requisition. Mr. A. L. C. Portman, the commodore's clerk, as it was most agreeable to the Japanese, acted as interpreter in the Dutch language. The floor of the chamber was covered with mats, having spread over them in the centre of the room, cloths resembling red felt blankets, indifferently dyed. After the manner of the Japanese, two interpreters were in attendance on the prince, one of them squatted on the floor near our interpreter, partially facing the chief and another (Kayama Yesaimon, governor of Uraga) on his haunches immediately in front of him. Midway, in rear of the room, was placed a brightly-lacquered red chest, resting upon eight feet, with its deep and projecting lid, confined by tasselled cords of blue. The gilt ornamental design in front resembled the rose of the Gothic style. The officers of the ships occupied the court facing the platform.

Everything being announced ready, and obeisance interchanged between the prince and commodore, beautiful rose-
wood-boxes, hinged, clamped, and clasped with gold, having
inscriptions with German-text letters, let in with gold on their
tops, which had been carried by side-boys, were then brought
in, and displayed upon the chest. Mr. Portman opened them to
assure the Japanese of the presence of the letters; and the interpreter was directed to inform the prince, which was done, one
interpreter whispering to the other, that in the boxes were also
translations of our president's letter, in Dutch and Chinese. The
credentials from the emperor empowering the prince of Idzoo
to receive the letter, were then handed over by the prince, and
taken charge of by the flag-lieutenant, having been duly examined the day before on shipboard.

.   .   .   .

A brief pause followed the delivery of the letters, the Japanese appearing dispirited, and their prince as if the day's doings
might result to him in being compelled to perform the "Happy
Despatch" of his country; the commodore directed the interpreter to say, that as it would take some time to deliberate on
the letter of the president, he should not wait for an answer,
but would return in the spring; that he would leave in a few
days for Canton, by way of the great Loo-Choo island, and would
be happy to take any commands they might have. . . . The
governor of Uraga then rose, placed the president's letter in the
lacquered chest, and tied the cords; then, turning, bowed very
low, intimating that the audience was concluded; the prince
rising and saluting as we retired.

The column of escort then reformed, and returned to the
beach where we landed, in the same order in which we had
come, passing down the front of the line of Japanese soldiers,
many a scowling fellow meanwhile looking daggers at us; and
their officers, affecting an indifference to the scene, which they
could not have felt, perhaps thinking how agreeable a thing it
would be, to hold one of those Americans on the end of one of
their blades, as a fork, and hack him with the other as a knife;
if they only dared to try. So closed the day that is to mark the
opening of Japan to the world. America has said, "Open,
sesame!"

I said to Major Zeilen, of the marine corps (a fine old soldier), the day before we landed, "Well, major, they have our cages ashore?" "No, sir; no caging to-morrow," said he, "it will be fight to the death!" Our men marched past the Japanese troops with the greatest indifference, making such remarks as "Jack, give us a chaw of tobacco." "Robinson," said the officer of the deck to a six-foot quartermaster who was to carry an American ensign, "don't you let them take that away from you, to-day." Robinson said, "Well, sir, they may do it, but the man who takes it *wont be able to carry it after* he gets it."

In the afternoon, of the day of the landing, the steamers got underway, passed the point or "Rubicon Fort," as it was named, and went into anchorage in the inner bay, which had been sounded out by boats under cover of the *Mississippi,* three days before. In doing so we got the best view of the line of fortifications, which extend from a point on the western side, marking the narrowest part of the outer, or entrance to the inner bay, down to the city of Uraga. . . .

We had now been in their waters about eight days, during which we had only one opportunity of noticing things and people, near by on shore, and then for not a very long time. But what we had been able to observe, assured us that the Japanese were a superior race, though they might belong to the same variety of the human family as their pig-tail neighbors. Their complexions were better, their features more regular, they had not a great obliquity of eye; their manners were more collected and impressive, their bearing more dignified, their costume less sacerdotal; and their crowns, instead of displaying a patch of hair the size of a dinner-plate behind, with a pendent plait, were shaven in an oval on the top, around which the hair was brushed perpendicularly, and pomatumed, terminating in a tie, from which the united ends, adhering together with the pomatum, laid like a cheroot-cigar in form, the end pointing to the brow, in the centre of the place that the razor has denuded. They look like the literary gentlemen whose bald heads cause their foreheads to run back nearly to their coat-collar. Certain it is that they can hardly be deemed descendants of the son of Manoah, of whom it was prophesied—*"and no razor shall come on his head."*

Their boats were sharp, and by the continued action of the

sculls—instead of rowing on their sides—were impelled with greater speed than the boats of the celestials; while the nice bows to their junks indicated great superiority, and the single white canvass sail, stretched by a yard from their enormous mast, was far more pleasant to the eye and sensible than the dingy mat-sail of the Chinaman. Their plan of reducing sail is singular: instead of lessening the hoist of the sail as other nations do, as in reefing, they reduce the width of their sail by unlacing a cloth from either side. We did not on this visit get in the vicinity of the large capital but could form some idea of its consumption by the immense number of coasting-junks for ever going up and returning, keeping white the bay, with their singular sails, in centre of which black characters told the district they were from, or it was indicated by strips of black cloth hanging on either end of the yard. It was soon apparent, and the Japanese were no doubt aware that we knew it, that if it should become necessary to resort to offensive measures, that the blockading of the custom-port of Uraga, and the stoppage of the passage of their junks with their supplies to the immense city, would make them very effective. Their forts would not have been able to have raised the blockade; we could have kept out of the reach of their guns, and peppered them with the long range of our own.

On Sunday morning, July 17, at daybreak, we lifted anchor, and the *Susquehanna* with the *Saratoga* in tow, and the *Mississippi* towing the *Plymouth,* we proceeded down the outer bay, and left for a time the waters of Japan, numbers on shore and the troops on the parapets of the forts of Kami Saki looking at us, and apparently much pleased with the movement.

. . . .

We entered the bay of Yedo in the morning of the 13th of February, the *Susquehanna* towing the *Vandalia;* the *Powhatan,* the *Lexington;* and the *Mississippi,* having more towing-power from greater face of wheel and immersion of paddle, the *Macedonian.* As before, the batteries were ready, and guns shotted; but instead of proceeding cautiously, as on the occasion of our former visit, the line of ships ran directly past their forts and into their inner bay, not stopping until reaching what had been called "American anchorage," on our first reconnoissance, about ten miles above the port of Uraga, off the island of Natse. The storeship *Southampton* had arrived there some days before. We had scarcely anchored when some Japanese officials came off to the flag-ship to welcome the commodore and officers back to Japan. They verified the intelligence we had received through the Russians before leaving China—that of the death of the emperor *Minamoto Jyekosi,* and the accession to the throne of his son, with the title *Minamoto Yosisaki-sei-tai-seogun.* It was very soon discovered from them, to our surprise, that their government was prepared to return an affirmative response to the demands and requests contained in the letter of our president. They informed the commodore that a building had been erected, and preparations made to receive him at Uraga, where they said was a high functionary who would deliver to him the imperial answer to the president's letter, and begged that he would move his squadron down to that place.

The commodore, through his captain of the fleet, peremptorily refused to accede to this request, on the ground that the anchorage there was too much exposed at that season of the year; and requested them to inform their government that a suitable place for his interviews with those appointed to confer with him, must be selected in the vicinity of the then anchorage of his squadron, otherwise, if he moved at all, it would be to ascend the bay in the direction of Yedo.

Several days were allowed to elapse before the Japanese consented to change the location for the negotiations. . . .

The spot selected for the erection of the buildings for the conferences, was on the beach of the village of Yokohama, or compost town, in the small bight of Kawa-saki, and separated from the city of Kanagawa by the little river Kana. This place was quite sheltered by a projecting bluff below. The Japanese, as could be seen through a glass at two and a half miles distant, set to work in the erection of the buildings on shore, with a Babel-like activity; and the ships of the squadron moved in closer and formed a crescent line in their anchorage, agreeably to buoys previously established.

While the buildings were being gotten ready, a number of their fast-sailing, sharp, copperplated and tassel-prowed boats, some quite ornamentally painted, came off and moved round the ships, their inmates not being allowed to come alongside by their government's cruisers, peering all they could. The sterns of these boats are open, or indented to the distance of a foot or so in their build, they believing, perhaps, that the eddying water at this point serves to propel the craft. The tall, square masts of their boats, when not under sail, rests on a kind of gallows at the stern. At one corner of the stern is an upright bamboo-pole to which, like a tavern-keeper's sign, is attached by strips, a cotton or provincial flag; if it be a government or customhouse boat, the flag is of white cotton with a horizontal black stripe through the centre of it. On the other corner is a similar arrangement, from which is suspended the universal paper lantern, differing from the Chinese in lifting up, instead of opening out like an umbrella. The rowers of these boats are athletic men, who appear very indifferent to cold, and in the chilliest weather their cotton garments are most epigrammatic in character.

The Japanese officials, or gentlemen, who came off to the ships were politely received and kindly entertained, at which they seemed gratified, and, after the manner of their land, indicated their appreciation by bringing from time to time little presents of lacquered-ware, &c. I don't remember to have seen anything else but the most quiet and gentle manner in any of these visiters, except in the case of an impertinent little officer of artillery, who it would have been as well to have shown the gangway. This fussy little animal, who rejoiced in a flaming pair of big brocade breeches, being a consumptive, according to the Aesculapian theory of his country, left all "the hair on the top of his head," which according to our theory is the "place where hair ought to be." He had, however, the cheroot-cigar-looking tuft of hair laying horizontal, and end pointing forward. This fussy little person pryed into everything about the ship with rude curiosity. He came and went from the cabin without decorum, and examined huffily officers' state-rooms, without solicitation. The only point of interest in the diminutive animal was, that he appeared to understand quite well, how a howitzer in battery should be worked.

A dinner was given on the *Susquehanna,* by her commander, to Yezimon, governor of the province of Uraga, and a suite of ten others, among whom was the little peripatetic consumptive of the artillery. The Japanese being accustomed to the use of the chopsticks at their meals—which are not of ivory as the Chinese, but lacquered black—were a little awkward at first in the use of the Christian assistants of knife and fork, but it did not take them long to acquire the requisite facility, when they made up for lost time. The cherry cordial, of which they are very fond, did not go untasted, and champaigne was by no means neglected by them. . . .

They remained at the table some two hours, during which time one of their number present, "by request," sang a Japanese song—if a kind of a cross between the half wail, half-vocal screech of the Chinese, a boy dragging a stick over the palings after him, and a severe asthma, may be called a song. . . .

Yezimon, on leaving the ship where he had been so handsomely entertained, remarked that he hoped he would have the opportunity of reciprocating the courtesies which had been shown them, when the friendship (treaty) had been made; they would then see more of us, and we more of them and their towns. As customary, they left a number of little presents, consisting of confections in small wooden boxes, and flowers, and little birds on miniature trees, made with shells. . . .

While at dinner, they laid aside their two swords. I had a very good opportunity of examining them in the cabin of the *Mississippi*. The *Damascus* may not equal them; but they evinced much surprise when I showed them the temper of this far-famed blade, by an engraving, in which the point of one appeared so bent as to be put through the guard. The Japanese blade is of the most magnificent steel; it has the back shaped like that of a razor, and the edge is equally as sharp, and so highly polished that they look black instead of bright, and the breath disappears from their surface, as from the face of the finest mirror. The hilts were without "basket" of any kind, and about a foot in length, intended to be grasped, when in use, with both hands. They were covered with the skin of the shark, or the corrugated plaice, wrapped in silk cord in diamond shapes, and ornamented with amulets in the shape of small animals, made of gold, boxwood, red coral, or bronze. The guard, which was a circle of bronze, was decussated, and frequently had an image of a fly entangled in a web. The blade has little curve, and is contained in a scabbard of wood finely lacquered, and ornamented with purple cord.

The Japanese interpreter present spoke English tolerably; said he had learned it from an American at Nangasaki, but took good care not to mention that this American was one of the sailors whom the United States ship *Preble* took from them in 1849, who had been held by them in captivity. They were very desirous of getting dictionaries and grammars in English. They were offered a passage to the United States in one of the steamers; they said "No; they would come when they could build ships"—indicating the three masts with their fingers, and the yards by crossing them. Two of the party ascended as high as the main-top.

The houses on shore progressed, and were being built without any palisade enclosure, as had been agreed on. On the 4th of March we had a slight fall of snow, and the air was cool. The Japanese, with the ships' casks, brought off in their boats, from some place of their river, water to fill our tanks. They brought two kinds, and desired us to choose between them. Everything in Japan having any connection with strangers, is deemed a matter of such importance, that the water-boats were always accompanied by others with municipal officials. They were entertained with cakes and tea and wine; and were quite curious in examining each portion of the ship. They did not understand why we should have brought so many vessels. They told us that the Russian squadron had been at Nangasaki, and left there on the 12th of February. At that time they declared their intention of making a treaty with the "American States" alone. . . .

About 11 o'clock in the morning of the 8th, preparation being complete, twenty-nine boats of the different ships, with officers and crews armed and equipped agreeably to the order, were formed in a line abreast according to rank of commanders, and pulled ashore, presenting a beautiful sight. The number landing, including officers, was about five hundred. The commodore not long after, left the flag-ship in a white barge, under a minister's salute of seventeen great guns from the *Macedonian,* he going ashore in the capacity of "Special Ambassador." On reaching the beach, as before, he was received by his officers, and with American national airs from the bands. The column of escort was then formed, and all marched to the reception-house—a short distance. A large field around the buildings had been screened off with striped cotton cloth, of black and white, while the common people of the village were kept back by ropes, extending from a growth of fine trees to the water's edge. A Japanese guard of honor with lances, were drawn up on the right in rear of our line of marines and sailors, and a cordon of the sharp government boats lined the beach to the left.

On entering the hall, the commodore was received by the five commissioners. The party being seated, the flag of Japan was run up on board the *Powhatan,* and saluted with twenty-one guns from the launches, after which another salute of seventeen guns was given to the Japanese high commissioners, which the Japanese say, they took as a great compliment.

The room of reception and audience was in a white pine-building, unpainted. You entered by a flight of three steps. On either side the room was lighted through white oiled paper in the place of glass, placed in frames resembling sash-work. The extreme end of the room was concealed by a large blue flag, having in its centre in white, the Japanese coat-of-arms, composed of three quarter-moons, whose horns unite so as to form a circle, around which at intervals, was entwined a small wreath. The walls of the entrance were covered with paper screens, having on them the Japanese deified or sacred bird, the crane, perched on leafless trees. The floor was covered with mats, or rather straw-cushions, they being some three inches thick, bound on the edges, and very springy, when walked on. Along the entire length of the room, were placed low benches for seats, in front of which nearly as low, were narrow tables covered with red cotton cloth. The temperature of the room was regulated by charcoal in full heat, placed in copper-pans as "braziers," resting in lacquered stands with gilt and ornamental legs, distributed along the centre of the floor. The company being seated— the Americans on the left and the Japanese functionaries on the right, the Japanese interpreter received a message from his prince, with his nose about two inches from the matting, and then dragging or sliding himself *à la Turk* by the use of his arms, to where the commodore was seated, told Mr. Portman, his clerk, in Dutch, to say to the commodore, that the prince was glad to see him, and hoped his health was better. This civility was returned in like manner. They then went to business: they desired to know what number of persons the commodore wished to have retire with him in the conference: commodore said, he wished a room for five, and named the captain of the fleet, Mr. S. W. Williams of Canton, author of the "Middle kingdom," his son—his secretary, and Mr. Portman, who interpreted in Dutch. They retired into another room in the rear, whose entrance was concealed by a purple flag. The interview lasted some three hours, during which time the following answer to the president's letter was received:—

The return of your Excellency as Ambassador from the United States to this Empire, has been expected, according to the letter of his Majesty the President; which letter your excellency delivered last year to his Majesty the Emperor of Japan. It is quite impossible to give satisfactory answers at once to all the proposals of your government, since those points are most positively forbidden by the laws of our imperial house; but for us to continue bigotedly attached to the ancient laws, seems to misunderstand the spirit of the age, and we wish rather to conform to what necessity requires.

At the visit of your excellency last year, his Majesty, the former Emperor, was sick, and is now dead. Since his Majesty, the present Emperor, has ascended the throne, the many occupations demanding his care, in consequence thereof are not yet finished, and there is no time to settle other business thoroughly; moreover, his Majesty the new Emperor, at his accession to the throne promises to the Princes and high officers of the Empire to observe the laws. It is therefore evident, that he can not now bring about any alteration in the ancient laws.

Last Autumn at the departure of the Dutch ship, the superintendent of the Dutch trade in Japan was requested to inform your government of this event, and a reply in writing has been received.

At Nangasaki, the Russian Ambassador recently arrived to communicate a wish of his government; he has since left that place, because no answer would be given to any nation that might communicate similar wishes.

However, we admit the urgency, and shall entirely comply with the proposals of your government, concerning, wood, water, provisions, and the saving of ships and their crews in distress. After being informed, which harbor your Excellency has selected, that harbor shall be prepared, and this preparation, it is estimated, will take about five years. Meanwhile a commencement can be made with the coal at Nangasaki by the beginning of the next Japanese year [10th of February, 1855].

Having no precedent with respect to coal, we request your Excellency to furnish us with an estimate, and upon due consideration this will be complied with, if not in opposition to our laws. What do you understand by provisions? and how much coal?

Finally, anything ships may be in want of, that can be furnished from the productions of this Empire shall be supplied; the prices of merchandise and articles of barter to be fixed by Kuro-kawa Kahei, and Moriyama Yenoske. After settling the point before mentioned, the treaty can be concluded, and signed at the next interview.

Seal attached by order of the Imperial Commissioners.

      (L. S.)   MORIYAMA YENOSKE.

Kayei, 7th year, 1st moon, 26th day.

   [February 23d, 1854.]

The commissioners expressed themselves prepared to commence discussions upon the various points contained in the letter from the president, presented last year, and also to receive any further propositions that the commodore might wish to make—that in the determination of the emperor to make some modification in their laws of seclusion, he relied upon the friendly disposition of the Americans toward Japan; and as such negotiations were entirely novel to them, they would trust with confidence to the commodore's superior experience, to his generosity, and his sense of justice.

Commodore Perry was fully satisfied on all points suggested by him, which were in accordance with Mr. Webster's letter of instructions to Commodore Aulick, accompanying the first letter to the emperor. A draft treaty, in English, Dutch, Chinese, and Japanese, was put into the hands of the Japanese commissioners, who said that it would receive due consideration; but the old emperor had died since Commodore Perry was there last year, and his successor was a young man, who would require to consult his council before coming to a determination, and the commodore was reminded that the Japanese did not act with the same rapidity as Americans did.

When the commissioners and commodore retired, the officers

of the escort, who remained, were treated with tea and confections. After these thin-cooked meats, some bearing great favor to fried snakes, cut in slips so thin that the hinges of one's jaw would become tired, long before his appetite became satisfied, were placed before them on lacquered plates. This repast produced much disappointment with the officers; they had paid two official visits to the prince-regent of Loo-Choo island—a dependency of Japan, and on one occasion were entertained by him with as many as thirteen different soups at one feast, and arguing from "man to master," they anticipated twenty-six different kinds of soups, when they got their knees under Japanese pine. To those who were sharp-set, the entertainment of Timon of Athens could not have been much less satisfactory.

Equi-distant on the tables, were lacquered trays supported with feet, on which were placed of the same material, heavy ornamental silver "tea-pots," containing saki, while the tea was served in thin-lacquered cups, resting—to keep the heat from the hand—on circular pieces of bamboo, resembling the dice-box of a backgammon-board. The Japan lacquer—and this being a part of the "service" of royalty, must have been a fair specimen of it, did not strike me as being incomparably superior to that of the Chinese, as I had supposed.

When the repast was concluded some Japanese amateur-artists from Yedo, who had come down from the city in the suite of the commissioners, made crayon sketches of many of the officers, and seemed to labor under the impression, that the only thing necessary to make a good American portrait was to draw a large nose, and sketch the balance of the features around it. Their essays at representing flowers—the Japonica for instance, were much better.

In the interview, the subject of supplying us with coal was broached, which they gave a favorable response to, and promised to have some specimen, of what coal they had, ready for inspection in a short time. This contrasted strongly with the dissimulation practised by them during the stay of the *Preble* at Nangasaki in 1849. Then, those Japanese who came on board, affected the greatest curiosity in looking at the coal in the armorer's forge; they were much surprised at the heated rocks, and one of them asked permission to take ashore a piece of the coal, which he carefully wrapped in paper.

The next day Japanese officials were aboard of the *Mississippi*, and held interviews there with the captain of the fleet, with regard to furnishing fresh provisions to the ships. . . .

Negotiations having progressed harmoniously, on the 13th of March launches were sent alongside of the storeships, and the presents for the Japanese being put in them, the captain of the *Macedonian* with a suite of officers, pulled ashore, and delivered them *pro forma* to the authorities. They were afterward pleasantly entertained by them. The Japanese must have formed a rather exaggerated opinion of the quantity of the presents intended for them by the Americans—judging from the size of the room set apart for their reception. They were given to understand that these were tokens of amity, not a tribute.

The presents for the emperor consisted of, among other things:—

A railway with steam-engine; a magnetic telegraph; a surf-boat; a life-boat; a printing-press; a fine lorgnette; a set of Audubon's American Ornothology, splendidly bound; plates of American Indians; maps of different states of America; agricultural implements, with all the modern improvements; a piece of cloth; a bale of cotton; a stove; rifles, pistols, and swords; champagne, cordials, and American whiskey.

And for the empress (presuming there was one):—

A telescope; a lorgnette in a gilded case; a lady's toilet-box, gilded; a scarlet velvet dress; a changeable silk dress flowered; a splendid robe; Audubon's illustrated works; a handsome set of China; a mantelpiece clock; a parlor stove; a box of fine wines; a box of perfumery; a box of fancy soaps.

Among the presents, perhaps the one most valued, was a copy of Webster's complete dictionary, to the imperial interpreter. To the high officers were given books, rifles, pistols, swords, wines, cloths, maps, stoves, clocks, and cordials, the latter of which they fully appreciated; and as regards clocks, when it was proposed to bring an engineer from shipboard to set them agoing, the Japanese said there was no occasion for that, for they had clockmakers in Yedo who understood them perfectly. They were curious to know, however, if Ericsson's caloric engine, of which they had heard, had been successful. There were also given them a quantity of Irish potatoes, and an hydraulic-ram.

The Land of the Lamas [5]:

WILLIAM W. ROCKHILL

[*William W. Rockhill (1854–1914) was an American to match the British pattern of eccentric careers. He studied at St. Cyr, the French military academy, served as an officer in the Foreign Legion, then entered the American diplomatic service. During four years at the American Legation in Peking he studied Tibetan as well as Chinese and learned as much as he could from Chinese literature and from natives from various parts of Tibet about that little known country. Then, in 1888, he started out on the adventurous journey described below of several thousand miles through Kokonor, Ts'ai-dam and Eastern Tibet. Later he studied the history of Chinese population growth and census-taking, and some of his scholarly work was (for lack of sufficient interest in America) published in Russia.*]

Tibet has been my life hobby. I began while at college to study the few works written by Europeans on this subject, and was later on led to learn Chinese as a means of gaining further information about the country and its inhabitants. In 1884 I was attached to the United States Legation at Peking, and it seemed then as if I might be able to carry out cherished schemes of exploration in Tibet if I could but learn the spoken language, a knowledge which, from the first, I held to be an absolute requisite of success. No foreigner could help me, for none spoke the language, and none of the natives whom I at first met would consent to teach me, being suspicious of the use I might make of my knowledge. I finally gained the friendship of an intelligent lama from Lh'asa, and with him for the next four years I studied Tibetan, giving also some time to the study of Chinese.

European travelers who had attempted to enter Tibet had usually done so from either India or western China. The fron-

[5] From *The Land of the Lamas,* by William W. Rockhill.

tiers along both these countries are thickly inhabited, or rather the only practicable roads through these border-lands pass by large towns and villages, and so those travelers had found themselves confronted on the very threshold with the one serious obstacle to ingress to the country, a suspicious people, who see in every stranger desirous of visiting their country a dangerous interloper, whose sole purpose is to steal the treasures with which they think their land is teeming, and a possible forerunner of invading armies.

To the north, Tibet is composed of high plateaux intersected by numerous chains of mountains running from east to west, a bleak, arid country, either desert or inhabited by a scattered population of nomads. To the south of these pastoral tribes, and then only in the larger valleys, live a sedentary people who cultivate the soil. Hence it appears that a traveler, coming from the north, can advance much farther into the country without having to fear serious opposition by the people than from any other side.

These considerations and the further fact that the only serious attempt to enter Tibet from the north, that of Fathers Huc and Gabet in 1845, had proved successful, made me choose this route as the one I would follow.

In the winter of 1888, having resigned my post of Secretary of Legation, I made preparations for my journey. The route selected was the highway, which, passing by Hsi-an Fu and Lan-chou Fu, leads to Hsi-ning Fu near the Koko-nor, and which from that point is known as the northern route to Lh'asa. My outfit was simple and inexpensive, for, dressing and living like a Chinaman, I was incumbered neither with clothes nor foreign stores, bedding, tubs, medicines, nor any of the other endless impedimenta which so many travelers consider absolute necessities.

The most rapid and on the whole the most convenient way to travel in northern China is by cart; each will carry about 300 pounds of goods, and still leave room enough for a passenger and driver, and the tighter one is packed in one of these primitive conveyances the more comfortably will one ride, for, as these carts are innocent of springs or seats, the jogging when they are empty is dreadful. I made a contract with a cart firm to supply me with two carts, with two mules to each, to take me to Lan-chou Fu, the capital of the province of Kan-su, in thirty-four days. For every day over this they were to pay me Tls. 2, I giving them the same amount for every day gained on the time agreed upon. This arrangement worked admirably, and I reached my destination two days ahead of time.

.   .   .   .

Chinese New-year was so near at hand when I reached Lan-chou that I had to defer my departure for Hsi-ning until the festivities were over.

Finally . . . having hired three mules to carry my luggage and bought a pony for myself, I left on the third of the first moon (February 3d) for Lusar, a small village about twenty miles south of Hsi-ning, where I hoped to be able to organize a little caravan, and strike out through the Koko-nor steppe towards Tibet.

It was most delightful to feel one's self free in movement and in the saddle—no longer cramped up in a small cart—and the ride to Hsin ch'eng, a village some thirty miles west of Lan-chou and on the Yellow River, was a most agreeable one. . . . The bottom of the valley was stony, and, in most places, unfit for culture, or even for habitation. The land on the hillsides was tilled, however, and irrigation ditches carried the river water all over it. The water is raised by immense wheels, gen-erally fifty to sixty feet in diameter; they belong to villages, and in a few cases to individuals, who, for a small consideration, sell the water to the peasants. The price is calculated by the quan-tity which flows from the wheel while a given length of joss-stick burns. . . .

At Hsin-ch'eng a branch of the Great wall crosses the Yellow River, and follows the right bank for some miles southward; it is like every part of the wall I have seen west of Chih-li, which as said before is made of earth, without any brickwork, and it has a ditch along its front. Some nine miles farther, in a south-erly direction, through a gorge of red sandstone formation, we came to the mouth of the Hsi-ning ho, where in a little ferry-boat we crossed the Yellow River. . . .

From here to Lusar I journeyed in company with a large party of Khalkha Mongols from Urga, near the Russian frontier. Their tribe is the richest in the empire, and numbers of this people may be seen during the winter months at all the great lamaist sanctuaries in northern China, Mongolia, or Tibet, where they nearly always bring presents of considerable value, horses, camels, silver, satins, etc.

When about eleven miles from Hsi-ning we passed through the "little gorge" (*Hsiao hsia*), first crossing the river by a substantial bridge of heavy logs, constructed somewhat on the cantilever system. . . .

From here I could see in the distance the walls of Hsi-ning, and shortly afterward I entered the town, and put up in a large inn in the eastern suburb. The sole suburb is on the eastern side and is half a mile long, but has only one important street, in which are a great number of inns, eating-houses, butcheries, bakeries, and other stores. The population of Hsi-ning is probably between 30,000 and 40,000, a large proportion of which is Mohammedan.

While many of the people of Hsi-ning show by their features traces of their foreign lineage, a number of their customs point even more clearly to the same fact. Here, for the first time, I saw women wearing a dark blue or black veil across the lower part of the face when on the street, in fact a decent Mohammedan woman would not venture out without one. Sending a guest repeated presents of food, drinking wine with him from one cup, leading his horse on his arrival and departure, holding the stirrup, and assisting him into the saddle, are all customs foreign to the Chinese, as far as my observation goes.

. . . .

I had not been in my inn half an hour before two or three policemen made their appearance, and told me that I must send my name to the magistrate, let him know whence I came, where I was going, what was my business, etc., none of which did I care in the least to tell, especially where I was going. I consequently made up my mind not to remain longer in town than the morrow, and to go at once to Lusar where I knew there were no inquisitive officials. . . .

The next morning at daylight, having donned a big Mongol gown and fur cap, and with clean-shaved head and face, I left with the Khalkhas I had met near Nienpei, and rode to Lusar. Passing through the cemetery outside of the city, and crossing the hills, we soon found ourselves in the valley of the Nanch'uan. Hardly had we lost sight of Hsi-ning than we seemed to have suddenly left China and its people far behind, so great were the changes that everywhere met us. No longer were all the passers-by blue-gowned and long-queued Chinese, but people of different languages, and various costumes. There were Mongols, mounted on camels or horses, and clothed in sheepskin gowns and big fur caps, or else in yellow or red lama robes—the women hardly distinguishable from the men, save those who, from coquetry, had put on their green satin gowns and silver head and neck ornaments, to produce a sensation on entering Lusar or Kumbum. There were parties of pilgrims, tramping along in single file, and dressed in white woolen gowns pulled up to the knee, each one with a little load, held by a light wooden framework, fastened to his back. They belonged to some of the Tibetan tribes living in the valleys to the north of Hsi-ning. . . .

Our road led us towards a high, black line of nude and jagged peaks, rising like a wall across the southern extremity of the valley, and called on our maps South Koko-nor range, through a well-cultivated country dotted with numerous villages, inhabited by Chinese, and T'u-ssŭ, agricultural tribes of mixed Chinese, Tibetan and Turkish descent. When about fifteen miles up the Nanch'uan, we turned to the southwest, and, crossing the low hills which here border it, we looked down into a vale of loess formation, lying at our feet, and saw a straggling village built on the side of a hill, at whose base two small streams met. Here was a grove of slender poplar saplings, black with flocks of croaking ravens and small, yellow-billed crows; and shaggy, grunting yak, camels with gurgling moans, and little, rough ponies, led by their wild-looking masters, were drinking in the stream. On the flat roofs of the village houses were men and women, gossiping, spinning yarn, or spreading out manure to dry. This was Lusar. I looked to the left and there were the golden roofs and spires of the temples of Kumbum, with walls of green and red; and over the hillside roundabout, long, irregular lines of low, flat-roofed houses, partly hid behind clean, whitewashed walls, the homes of the 3,000 odd lamas who live at this great sanctuary of the Tibetan and Mongol faith. On the hill-slope, between the village and the lamasery, was the fair-ground, where a motley crowd was moving to and fro, where droves of yak and strings of camels were continually passing; and scattered about in the distance were the traveling tents of those who preferred their ordinary dwellings to the small, dingy rooms for rent in the lamasery or at Lusar.

.   .   .   .

The day after my arrival was the 12th of the first moon, when the Chinese in every village and town of the empire celebrate the dragon festival. Lusar had its share of the feast, and I went to see the fun. The street of the little village was filled with a gaily dressed and motley crowd, all pressing on towards the small Chinese temple . . . at the foot of the hill, where the theatrical representation was to begin. . . .

The Tibetans, both men and women, wore high-collared gowns of sheepskin or undyed cloth, reaching barely to the knee, and hanging very full about the waist. On their shaved heads the men had little pointed red caps trimmed with lambskin, big clumsy foxskin hats, or else dark-red turbans. The gowns of the "swells" were of garnet-colored cloth, trimmed along the bottom and on the collar with leopard, otter, or tiger skin, and those of the fashionable women, with broad bands of red black and green stuff around the hem. Most of the men had a large circular silver ring, set with turquoise and coral beads, in the left ear; and the women wore heavy silver pendants, also set with coral beads, in both of theirs. But the principal distinction in the dress of the women consisted in their fashion of wearing the hair. It was plaited in innumerable little tresses from the crown of the head, and hung down over their shoulders and back like a cloak. Three broad bands of red satin or cloth, to which were attached embossed silver plates, or cowry shells, pieces of chank-shell, turquoise, coral, or glass beads, were fastened to the hair, two depending from that which fell to the shoulders, one from that which fell to the waist. Nearly all, men and women, wore copper or silver charm-boxes (gawo) around their necks, from which also hung their prayer-beads.

The T'u-ssu, or agricultural aborigines, were dressed very much like the Chinese, their gowns being a little shorter and fuller; most of their women had red handkerchiefs tied around their heads, and wore violet silk gowns of Chinese pattern.

But the wildest figures among them all were the Hung

mao-tzŭ, the K'amba of eastern Tibet, with long, matted hair cut in a fringe over the eyes, dirty sheepskin gowns pulled up above the knee, and boots with rawhide soles and red or variegated cloth tops fastened below the knee with a broad garter. In their belts were long, straight swords, and hanging around their necks were charm-boxes and prayer-beads. The day was warm, and they had slipped their right arms out of their gowns, which hung loosely on the left shoulders, and their hands rested defiantly on the hilts of their swords.

There were also at the play Tibetans from Lh'asa, . . . tall men with swarthy complexions, and many of them with angular features. They wore the Chinese queue, and dark violet gowns, trimmed with leopard skin; and their speech was softer than that of their eastern compatriots.

Lamas in red cloth, with bare right arms, and shawls thrown over their shaven pates to shade them from the sun, were everywhere, in the shops or on the street, walking about in company with friends and relatives, many of whom had come a month's journey to see them and attend the fair.

.   .   .   .

For three or four hours I wandered about, no one paying any special attention to me; some took me for a Mongol, others for a Turk, and a few for a foreigner (*Olossu*). All the questions I asked were answered politely, and not an ungracious remark was made to, or, as far as I could hear, about me. I certainly should not have fared so well in any Chinese town I have ever seen; but the Chinese showed themselves most kind during my sojourn of a month and a half at Lusar, confirming the excellent opinion I had already formed of the Kan-su people. Most of them were conversant with Mongol and Tibetan, and had traveled extensively among the border-tribes, so I had an excellent opportunity of acquiring a knowledge of those peoples, and of finding good men to accompany me westward.

Though the streets of Lusar were gay and full of life, it was within the temple grounds, about a quarter of a mile off, that the principal attractions of the fair centered. Following the crowd which was going in that direction to trade, and, *en passant,* to do a little praying at the temple, I walked over the hillside covered with open-air restaurants, butchers' and bakers' stalls, dealers in hides and peltries, peep-shows, in which, I am sorry to say, European obscene pictures were the cynosure, gambling tables, and all the endless variety of trades and peoples met with at such fairs in China.

The food of the Koko-nor Tibetans, and also of the eastern Tibetans, consists principally of tea and parched barley or *tsamba*. To this Spartan diet they occasionally add vermicelli (*kua-mien*), sour milk (*djo*), granulated cheese (*ch'ura*), *choma* (*Potentilla anserina*) or boiled mutton. The tea, previously reduced to powder, is put in the kettle when the water is hot and is left to boil for about five minutes, a little salt or soda being added. Then it is placed before the inmates of the tent, squatting in a circle. Each one draws from the bosom of his gown a little wooden bowl, also used on very rare occasions as a washbowl, and fills it. Taking with his fingers a chunk of butter from a sheep's paunch filled with it, which has also been set before them, he lets it melt in his bowl, drinking some of the tea and blowing the melted butter to one side; and then adds a handful of tsamba from the small ornamented bag in which it is kept. He deftly works with his right hand the tea, butter, and tsamba into a ball of brown dough which he eats, drinking as much tea as is necessary to wash down the sodden lump. When ch'ura is eaten it is allowed to soften in the cup, and is afterward worked up with the tsamba and butter. Such is the daily food of this people and also of the Mongols. There are naturally no regular meals; the kettle is always kept full, and each one eats when hungry. When one has eaten sour-milk or anything which soils the bowl, it is customary to lick this clean, and, without further ado, put it back in the gown. If any mutton is to be eaten it is boiled in the teakettle, and each one picks out a piece from the pot and eats it literally *"sur le pouce,"* using his sheath-knife to remove every particle of meat from the bone, which is always cracked if it contains marrow; and, if a shoulder-blade, is put away for fortune-telling. . . . The greasy hands are wiped over the face, or the boots if they require grease rather than the skin.

The preponderance of testimony tends to prove that monogamy is the rule, and polygamy the exception, among the Koko-nor Tibetans. I believe this is the case among all nomadic Tibetans. Wives are bought from the parents by a go-between, and a man is frequently obliged to give as much as 300 sheep, 10 horses, and 10 yak for a fine-looking girl; so the parents of two or three pretty and clever girls are sure of making their fortune. On marrying, and then only, does a man leave his parents' tent and start one for himself, although he may previously have had horses and cattle of his own. Families are small; two or three children are the most I have ever seen in any of their tents.

This people sets little store on chastity in women, married or unmarried, as the existence of the following custom proves. In lamaseries in Amdo, there is held at different times a feast known to the Chinese as *t'iao mao hui*, "the hat-choosing festival." During the two or three days the feast lasts a man may carry off the cap of any girl or woman he meets in the temple grounds who pleases him, and she is obliged to come at night and redeem the pledge. Chinese are not admitted to play at this game of forfeits, or allowed any of the privileges of this *fête d'amour*.

The old are but little respected, and it often occurs that a son kills his father when he has become a burden to him. The present Konsa lama is said to have disposed of his father for this reason. It also frequently happens that when a person is dying a relative or friend asks him, "Will you come back, or will you not?" If he replies that he will, they pull a leather bag over his head and smother him; if he says he will not, he is let die in peace. The probable explanation of this custom is a fear that the spirit of the dead will haunt its former abode.

The remains of the dead are exposed on the hillsides in spots selected by lamas; if the body is rapidly devoured by wild beasts and birds of prey, the righteousness of the deceased is held to be evident, but if it remains a long time undevoured, his wickedness is proved.

.   .   .   .

The Koko-nor ponies are celebrated all over Mongolia and northern China, as much on account of their speed as for their wonderful endurance. While I do not believe that they are faster than the eastern Mongol horses, their powers of endurance are certainly wonderful. They average, probably, thirteen hands high, and are mostly light gray or black. The Tibetans never feed them, even when traveling, nor at that time are the saddles ever removed from their backs. When horses have been ridden too hard and are greatly fatigued, they doctor them with dried meat powdered, or else tea-leaves mixed with tsamba and butter. When on a journey, they hobble and side-line them during the day, and at night attach them by one foot to a rope made fast to the ground with pegs, and only a few feet away from their camp-fire. These horses are never shod on the hind feet, and but seldom even on the fore feet.

The most influential and wealthy portion of the Koko-nor Tibetans is the lama class. . . .

The non-official lamas are divided into two classes. The first are those who have simply shaved their heads, taken the five minor vows, put on the red gown and made their home in a lamasery; these are usually called *Draba*. They do all such work as printing books, looking after the horses and cattle, gathering cattle dung, cooking, sweeping the temples, and trimming the lamps. The second class are those who have studied the sacred books and have been ordained *gélong*, taking on them vows of chastity, poverty, abstinence from tobacco, liquor, gaming, etc. From their number all the lama officials are chosen. Among the Tibetans and Mongols of the Koko-nor lamas are addressed as *Aka*, the title *Lama* (Sanskrit *guru*) being reserved for those of high degree and of known saintliness.

The *Draba* are not even bound to celibacy in this part of the empire; at certain seasons of the year they can obtain leave of absence and return to their families; but they must not show themselves in the company of their wives within the convent. Among the Mongol lamas from the Ts'aidam and the Koko-nor, nearly all are married, the *Gélong*, of course, excepted.

I have frequently been questioned as to the morality of the lamas of Mongolia and Tibet, and I can only answer that, while I do not believe that the standard attained by those persons would be considered very high by us, there are large numbers of them and even of the laity who observe their moral laws, and there are undoubtedly not a few men among the *Gélong* who strictly adhere to the vows of chastity, poverty, truthfulness, and all the other obligations they have taken upon themselves in entering the order.

.   .   .   .

My life at Lusar was monotonous in the extreme. At dawn an old lama, who lived in a watch-tower on the top of the hill overlooking the village, heralded in the day by blowing on a conch-shell. After seeing to the ponies, and killing as much time as possible over my breakfast, I strolled about from shop to shop talking and asking questions about the strange peoples and countries the shopkeepers had visited, or else I took a walk over to Kumbum to see some lama. When the sun had risen above the high hills which surrounded the village, I climbed on to the broad, flat roof of my dwelling where the tent-makers were at work, and basked in the sun. The weather was generally delightful, the nights never very cold, and in the daytime the thermometer frequently stood at 60° F. in the sun. Now and then a little snow fell, but it melted in the first warm rays of the sun, and vanished in heavy mists which rolled up the mountain side. The only really cold weather was when the sky became cloudy, and I learned that this was always the case. The wind seldom blew, and before the middle of March all the fields had been plowed, and sown with grain.

Sand Buried Ruins of Khotan [6]:

SIR MARK AUREL STEIN

[*Sir Mark Aurel Stein (1862–1943) was the most prodigious combination of scholar, explorer, archeologist and geographer of his generation. Born in Hungary, and educated there and in Germany and Austria, he went to England in 1884, working at Oxford and the British Museum. In his mid-twenties he went to India, where he became principal of Oriental College and registrar of Punjab University. In 1900–01, at the age of thirty-seven, he made his first expedition to Sinkiang. The sensational importance of his first discoveries was immediately recognized, and from then on, for 40 years, he never ceased to travel, excavate, and publish. He had a deep knowledge of Sanskrit and Pali, and of course of Latin and Greek, and was fluent in several modern Indian languages, Central Asian Turkish, and Persian, needing an interpreter only for Chinese.*

[6] From *Sand Buried Ruins of Khotan,* by Sir Mark Aurel Stein.

[*At the age of eighty, after many years of trying, he finally obtained permission to explore Afghanistan, with the help of the U. S. Minister to that country. He arrived at Kabul to begin his journey, was taken ill and died at the U. S. Legation.*

[Sand Buried Ruins of Khotan, *from which we quote, describes the first of his many expeditions.*]

Calcutta to Kashmir

It was from the Alpine plateau of Mohand Marg, my beloved camping-ground for three Kashmir summers, that I had in June, 1898, submitted to the Indian Government the first scheme of the explorations which were to take me across the great mountain barriers northward and into the distant deserts of Khotan. Almost two years had passed when I found myself, early in May, 1900, again in Kashmir and within sight of Mohand Marg. With a glow of satisfaction I could look up to the crest of the high spur, some 10,000 feet above the sea and still covered with snow, on which my tent had stood, and where my plans had been formed. It had taken two years, and bulky files of correspondence; but at last I had secured what was needed—freedom to move, and the means requisite for my journey.

In the meantime official duty, and minor archaeological tours to which I devoted my vacations, had taken me over widely different parts of India. . . . The thought of the task which was drawing me beyond the Himalaya had followed me everywhere. But it was only when the final sanction for my proposals reached me on a sultry monsoon night down in Calcutta that I had been able to start some of the multifarious preparations which the journey demanded. . . . The tents which I had ordered from the Cawnpore Elgin Mills; the galvanised iron water-tanks, made at Calcutta workshops, that were to serve in the desert; the stores of condensed food, the photographic outfit, and the semi-arctic winter clothing which I had indented for from London—all were slowly moving up to Srinagar, whence my little expedition was to start. . . .

On the 25th of April I passed once more into the Kashmir Valley by the gorge of Baramula, now as in ancient days the "Western Gate of the Kingdom." The snow still lay low down the mighty Pir Pantsal range which forms the southern rampart between Kashmir and the outer world. But the great riverine plain which opens out just beyond Baramula was decked in all the gay colours of a Kashmir spring, blue and white irises growing in profusion over village cemeteries and other waste spaces. At Baramula, where my servants, sent ahead with the heavy baggage, awaited me, I took to boats for the remaining journey to Srinagar; for old experience had shown me the convenience and attractions of river communication in Kashmir. The day I spent gliding in my comfortable "Dunga" through the limpid water of the great lagoons which fringe the Volur Lake, and along the winding course of the Jhelam, gave delightful repose such as did not again fall to my share for many months. . . . The floating meadows of water-lilies and other aquatic plants which cover the marshes; the vivid foliage of the great Chinar trees which shade all hamlets and Ghats along the river banks; the brilliant snowfields on the Pir Pantsal, and the higher ranges to the north over which my road was soon to lead—these and all the other splendours of Kashmir spring scenery will never lose their charm for me.

During the second night the boat passed the winding reaches in which the river traverses Srinagar, and the next morning found me once more in the Chinar Bagh, my old camping-ground in the Kashmir capital. With the increasing crowd of European visitors from the Indian plains, the shady grove by the side of the "Apple Tree Canal" has long ago ceased to be a place suited for work or even quiet enjoyment. But haunted as it is at all hours of the day by the versatile Kashmir traders and craftsmen who provide for the Sahibs' camping requirements, it was just the place adapted for the purpose of my first stay at Srinagar. There were plenty of orders to give for mule trunks and leather-covered baskets or "Kiltas," in which stores, instruments, etc., were to be packed. Fur coats and warm winter clothing of all sorts had to be provided to protect myself and my followers against the cold of the Pamirs and the Turkestan winter; bags to carry provisions, and all the other paraphernalia which my previous experience showed to be necessary for a protracted campaign in the mountains. . . .

The Government of India in the Foreign Department had granted me permission to use the Gilgit-Hunza route for my journey to Kashgar. The special conditions prevailing along the

"Gilgit Transport Road" made it necessary to give timely and exact intimation as to the amount of transport required, the number of followers, etc., all the more as the time I had fixed for my start, the end of May, was in advance of the regular transport season. Luckily, Captain G. H. Bretherton, D.S.O., Assistant Commissary-General for Kashmir, to whom I had to apply in the matter of these arrangements, proved exceptionally able and willing to afford information. Guided by his experience, I was soon in a position to prepare with fair accuracy my estimates as to the time, means of transport, and supplies needed not only up to Hunza, but also beyond towards the Chinese frontier. It was no small advantage to obtain quickly a clear working plan of these practical details. For upon the exact information which I could send ahead to Gilgit and Kashgar depended my hope of securing, without loss of time, all that was was needful for the onward journey.

. . . Knowing that no European traveler in the parts I was bound for could wholly refuse the *rôle* of the "Hakim" forced upon him by popular belief, I had early ordered my medicine case from Messrs. Burroughs Wellcome & Co., the great London firm of "Tabloid" fame, . . . but its power cannot level mountains, and as the transport of heavy articles across the snow-covered passes was not to begin till later in the season, there seemed little chance of that eagerly looked-for case ever catching me up if not received before my start from Srinagar.

Fortune seemed to offer a small mark of favour at least in this direction. For when, on the evening of the 29th of May, the time of departure fixed weeks before, my little flotilla of boats was lying opposite to the Srinagar Post Office, . . . the attentive postmaster triumphantly reported the arrival of the box. When it was at last safely deposited in my hands it was time to set out from the Venice of India. Gliding down the dark river under the seven bridges which have spanned it since early times, and between the massive embankments built with the slabs of ruined temples, . . . it was midnight before I had seen the last of my old Pandit friends, who were waiting each at the Ghat nearest to his home to bid me farewell.

The road, after leaving the straggling line of wooden huts which form the Bazar of Bandipur, leads for about four miles up the open valley of the Madhumati stream. In the irrigated fields the fresh green of the young rice-shoots was just appearing, while the hamlets on either side were half hidden under the rich foliage of their Chinars and walnut-trees. . . . Near the village of Matargom the road turns to the north to ascend in long zigzags the range which forms the watershed between Kashmir and the valley of the Kishanganga. From the spur up which the road winds I had a splendid view of the Volur Lake and the snow-covered mountains to the east which encircle the hoary Haramukh Peaks. At a height of about 9,000 feet a fine forest of pines covers the spur and encloses a narrow glade known as Tragbal. Here the snow had just disappeared, and I found the damp ground strewn with the first carpet of Alpine flowers.

A rude wooden rest-house begrimed with smoke and mould gave shelter for the night, doubly welcome, as a storm broke soon after it got dark. The storm brought fresh snow, and as this was sure to make the crossing of the pass above more difficult I started before daybreak on the 1st of June. A steep ascent of some two thousand feet leads to the open ridge which the road follows for several miles. Exposed as this ridge is to all the winds, I was not surprised to find it still covered with deep snowdrifts, below which all trace of the road disappeared. Heavy clouds hung around, and keeping off the rays of the sun let the snow remain fairly hard. Soon, however, it began to snow, and the icy wind which swept the ridge made me and my men push eagerly forward to the shelter offered by a Dak runners' hut. The storm cleared before long, but it sufficed to show how well deserved is the bad repute which the Tragbal (11,900 feet above the sea) enjoys among Kashmirian passes.

For the descent from the pass I was induced by the "Marko-bans" owning the ponies to utilise the winter route which leads steeply down into a narrow snow-filled nullah.

   .   .   .   .

Some four miles lower down I reached the main valley of the Kishanganga, and in it the first Dard village. Another ten miles' march up the valley brought me to Gurez, a collection of villages at a point where the valley widens to a little plain, about a mile broad.

Sombre and forbidding the valley looked between its high pine-covered mountains and under a dark, rainy sky. The effect was heightened by the miserable appearance of the rude log-built dwellings scattered here and there along the slopes, and by the dark-coloured sand in the bed of the river. . . .

Gurez was once the chief place of a little Dard kingdom which often harassed the rulers of old Kashmir. But I confess, when I approached it at the close of my fatiguing double march, this antiquarian fact interested me less than the comfortable shelter which I found for my men and myself in Mr. Mitchell's new bungalow. . . .

The close contact with the Far West into which modern political conditions have brought these once secluded valleys was illustrated by the fact that I could read at Captain Manners Smith's table the latest Reuter telegrams just as if it had been in the Club at Lahore. But the presence in camp of my host's pretty little children offered an even more convincing indication how far European influence has penetrated across the mountains. Bright and rosy-cheeked, they were worthy representatives of the British Baby which in the borderlands of India has always appeared to me as the true pioneer of civilization. I have come across it in many a strange place, and its manifest happiness amongst surroundings which often seemed incongruous with the idea of a nursery has ever forced me to admiration. The British Baby has never been slow to follow the advance of British arms in India. Occasionally it has come early enough to see some fighting: witness Fort Lockhart and the Malakand. But on the whole its appearance on the scene marks the establishment of the pax britannica, and for this mission of peace and security it well deserves that thriving condition which it usually enjoys in the mountains around Kashmir.

For afternoon tea my hosts took me to a pretty "Marg" on the top of the ridge above their camp. From this height the Indus Valley, in its barrenness of rock and sand, could be seen descending far away towards Chilas and Darel. The day will come when this natural route to the Indian plains will be open again as it was in old times. Then the last bit of terra incognita along the Indus, which now extends from Chilas down to Amb, will be accessible, while the difficulties inseparable from a line of transport crossing the great barriers of the Kashmir ranges will no longer have to be faced.

On the morning of the 10th of June I took leave of my kind

hosts and hurried down towards Bunji to catch up my camp.
As I descended the defile of the Astor River, where the road
leads along precipitous cliffs and past shingly ravines, the heat
rose in a marked degree. . . . On the eleven miles which
brought me down to the level of the Indus close to the point
where the Astor River joins it, I did not meet with a single
traveler. Equally desolate was the ride from Ramghat, where
the road crosses the Astor River, to Bunji, some eight miles
higher up on the Indus. The broad rocky plain which stretches
from the bank of the great river to the foot of the mountains
showed scarcely a trace of vegetation. The radiation of the sun's
rays was intense, and I was glad to reach by one P.M. the shelter
of the Bunji Bungalow. The neighbouring fort is still held by
some detachments of Kashmir troops, though the ferry over the
Indus which it once guarded has become disused since the
construction of the new road. During the hot hours I spent at
Bunji there was little to tempt me outside. A hazy atmosphere
hung over the valley and deprived me of the hoped-for view
of Nangaparbat, which, rising fully 22,000 feet above the level
of the Indus, dominates the whole scenery in clear weather. A
strong wind blowing down the valley carried the fine sand of
the river-bed even into the closed rooms.

Fodder is practically not to be got at Bunji, and this accounts
for the difficulty I found in procuring a pony that was to take
me in the evening to the next stage where my baggage had
marched ahead. At last the local Tahsildar had to lend me his
mount, but it was already evening before I could set out. A
lonely ride across a sandy plain brought me to the imposing
suspension bridge which spans the Indus, just as it was getting
dark. In the dim light of the moon which was then emerging
for a time from the clouds the deep, rockbound gorge of the
river looked quite fantastic. And so did the rugged mountains
further east through which the Gilgit River comes down to
meet the Indus. To ride along the face of the rocky spur which
rises in the angle of the two rivers was slow work in the scanty
light of a fitful moon, and by the time I had turned fully into
the Gilgit Valley, and reached safer ground, rain came on and
brought complete darkness. Mile after mile passed without my
coming upon the longed-for rest-house where I could rejoin my
camp. At last it became clear that I must have passed it by, and

I had only the choice of continuing my ride straight into Gilgit or returning to search for the missed bungalow. Dark as it was I preferred the latter course, and ultimately discovered a side path which brought me to the expected shelter fully half a mile away from the main road. It was close on midnight when I sat down to the dinner which my servants had duly kept ready for me, though it had never struck them that I might require a light to show me the way to it.

Pari, where I spent what remained of the night, proved in the morning a desolate spot by the sandy bank of the river, enclosed by an amphitheatre of bare reddish-brown mountains. The scenery remained the same for the next nine miles or so until after rounding one of the countless spurs along which the road winds the open part of the great Gilgit Valley came into view. Minaur is the first village where cultivated ground is again reached, and thereafter every alluvial fan on the left bank was green with carefully terraced and irrigated fields. A few miles further on the valley of the Hunza River opens from the north, and beyond it stretches the collection of hamlets to which the name Gilgit properly applies. It was a cheerful sight to view this expanse of fertile fields and orchards from the height of an old moraine issuing from a side valley. While riding through it I was met by a note from Captain H. Burden, I.M.S., the Agency Surgeon, offering me that hospitable reception for which Captain Manners Smith's kindness had prepared me.

I soon was installed in a comfortable set of rooms, and realised that for my stay at Gilgit I was to be the guest of the officers remaining at the headquarters of the Agency. Small as their number was I found among them most attractive and congenial company. Each of them, whether in charge of the Kashmir Imperial Service troops supplying the local garrisons, or of the Commissariat, the Public Works, or the hospitals of Gilgit, showed plainly that he knew and liked these hills. For each the semi-independence secured by the arrangements of an out-lying frontier tract under "political" management had been a source of increased activity and consequent experience in his own sphere. That the political interests which necessitated the garrisoning of Gilgit with Imperial officers and troops have benefited this region in more ways than one was apparent from a stroll through the little "station." I found there a well-built hospital, neat offices for the various departments of the administration, a clean and airy bazar, and even substantial buildings for a school and a zenana hospital. Small but comfortable bungalows have been built for the European officers on the terraced slopes overlooking the valley, and in their midst there has quite recently risen even a substantial club with an excellent though necessarily select library. It is only some eleven years since the new era set in for Gilgit, and yet it is already difficult to trace the conditions which preceded it. The fort, built of rubble with a wooden framework, after the usual Sikh fashion, alone reminds one of the days when Gilgit was the prey of an ill-paid and badly disciplined soldiery, when years of unabated exactions had laid great parts of the cultivable land waste and driven the now peaceful Dards into violent rebellions.

I had originally intended to stop only one day at Gilgit in order to give my men a much-needed rest and to effect some repairs in the equipment. But difficulty arose about getting fresh transport for the march to Hunza, and my stay was of necessity extended to three days. Ample work and the amiable attention of my hosts scarcely allowed me to notice the delay. Though all Government transport was occupied in out-lying camps, and the local ponies were grazing far away in distant nullahs, Captain E. A. R. Howell, the energetic Commissariat Officer, provided by the third day a train of excellent animals to which I could safely trust my baggage up to Hunza. Little defects in my outfit which the experience of the previous marches had brought to light were easily made good in the interval, since every member of the "station" offered kind help. While the Commissariat Stores supplied what was needed in the way of followers' warm clothing, foodstuffs, etc., Mrs. W., the only lady left in the "station," kindly offered threads of her own fair hair for use in the photo-theodolite. How often had I occasion to feel grateful thereafter for this much-needed reserve store when handling that delicate instrument with half-be-numbed fingers on wind-swept mountain-tops!

Through Hunza

On the afternoon of the 15th of June I left Gilgit. . . . The first march of eighteen miles was to Nomal, a green oasis in the otherwise barren valley of the river which comes from Hunza. . . . Since the little war of 1891, which had asserted British authority in Hunza, the road up the valley has been greatly improved. Nevertheless, it is but a narrow bridle path, and as it winds along precipitous spurs many hundred feet above the stream, it required such a steady hill pony as that kindly lent to me by Major E. J. Medley, of the 17th Bengal Lancers, then Commanding the Force in Gilgit, to ride with any feeling of comfort.

From Nomal and upwards the river has cut its way through a succession of deep gorges, lined often with almost perpendicular cliffs. The path is carried in long zigzags over the projecting cross-ridges, and more than once traverses their face by means of galleries built out from the rock. At Chalt, the end point of my second day's march, I reached the limit of Gilgit territory. . . . As a reminiscence of an earlier state of things the place is garrisoned with a company of Kashmir Imperial Service troops. Their commandant . . . came to call on me soon after I had arrived at the comfortable bungalow of the Military Works Department. In the course of our long conversation he gave me graphic accounts of what Gilgit meant to the Kashmir troops twenty and thirty years ago; of the hardships which the want of commissariat arrangements caused both to the soldiers and the inhabitants. From the description of these sufferings it was pleasant to turn to other aspects of soldiering in the old Dogra service, *e.g.*, the quaint Sanskrit words of command concocted under Maharaja Ranbir Singh, and still in use not many years ago.

On the 17th I intended to make a double march, pushing on straight to the centre of the Hunza valley, where baggage animals were to be left behind and coolies taken for the rest of the journey to the Taghdumbash Pamir. After leaving Chalt the road crosses to the left bank of the river by a fine suspension bridge, hung like the rest of the more important bridges on the route from Kashmir, from ropes made of telegraph-wires. This mode of construction, first tried in these parts by Colonel Aylmer, of the Royal Engineers, has proved everywhere a signal success; its advantages are easily appreciated in a country where other suitable materials could scarcely be carried to the spot.

. . . After rounding a long massive spur which causes a great bend in the river-bed . . . I first beheld the ice-clad peaks of Mount Rakiposhi in their glory. The weather had been too cloudy during the preceding days to see much of this giant of mountains while I was marching in the valleys which flank it to the south and west. Now that I had got to its north side a day of spotless clearness set in, and the dazzling mass of snow and ice stood up sharp against the blue sky. Rakiposhi, with its towering height of over 25,500 feet, commands completely the scenery in the Upper Hunza Valley. Though several peaks run it close in point of elevation, none can equal it in boldness of shape and noble isolation. All day long I revelled in this grand sight, hidden only for short distances by the spurs which Rakiposhi sends down into the valley. Between them lie deep-cut side valleys through which the streams fed from the glaciers of Rakiposhi make their way to the main stream. The ample moisture supplied by the eternal snows of the higher slopes has not only brought verdure to the cultivated terraces in the valley. High above the walls of bare rock which bound the latter, patches of pine forest and green slopes of grazing land can be seen stretching up to the edge of the snow line. Glaciers, of spotless white on their higher parts, but grey with detritus below, furrow the flanks of the mountain mass and push their tongues almost down to the level of the main valley which here rises from six to seven thousand feet above the sea.

At Nilth, some eight miles above Chalt, the first Nagir village is reached. It was the scene of the notable fight which decided in 1891 the fate of Hunza and Nagir. The two little hill states which divide between them the right and left sides of the valley jointly known as Kanjut, had stoutly maintained their independence against all Dogra attempts at conquest. No wonder that people to whom their own mountains offer so scanty room and sustenance proved troublesome neighbours. Slave raiding into the lower valleys had for a long time been a regular source of revenue for the chiefs or Mirs of Hunza. . . .

[*Sir Aurel Stein's account brings out the differences between the difficulties of the high mountain masses between India and China, and those of the heavy going in the sands of the great Taklamakan desert of Sinkiang. O.L.*]

Marching in the drift sand was slow work, though the dunes were low, rising only to 6 to 10 feet in the area crossed during the first two days. The feet of men and animals sank deep at every step into the fine sand, and the progress of the heavily laden camels was reduced to about 1¼ miles per hour. In view of the want of sufficient fodder and water, it was essential to save them all over-exertion; hence I soon found that the direct distance covered by a day's march could rarely exceed 9 to 10 miles. The tamarisk and "Kumush" scrub which was plentiful at first, grew rare in the course of our second march, while the wild poplars or "Toghraks" disappeared altogether as living trees.

Luckily amidst the bare dunes there rose at intervals small conical hillocks thickly covered with tamarisk scrub, the decayed roots of which supplied excellent fuel. Close to these hillocks there were usually to be found hollows scooped out of the loess soil, evidently by the erosive action of wind. These hollows, which reach down to at least 10 to 15 feet below the level of the little valleys separating the neighbouring sand dunes, offer of course the nearest approach to the sub-soil water. It was accordingly invariably in these depressions that Kasim's advance party had dug their wells; which we also chose for our camping places. The water, which was reached after digging to an average depth of 5 to 7 feet, was very bitter at the first two camps and scarcely fit for human consumption. But as we moved further away from the Khotan River it became comparatively sweet. I have no doubt that geology would furnish a satisfactory explanation for this observation, which was well known to my guides as generally applicable to these parts of the Taklamakan and has been noticed already by Dr. Hedin. The supply of water furnished by these wells was decidedly scanty for so large a party as mine; and as it was stopped altogether by the damp soil getting frozen overnight, men had in the evening to be detailed gradually to collect spare water in two of my iron tanks where it could be stored as ice for use on the next day.

The winter of the desert had now set in with full vigour. In daytime while on the march there was little to complain of; for though the temperature in the shade never rose above freezing point, yet there was no wind, and I could enjoy without discomfort the delightfully pure air of the desert and its repose which nothing living disturbs. But at night, when the thermometer would go down to minimum temperatures from 0° to 10° Fahr. below zero, my little Kabul tent, notwithstanding its extra serge lining, was a terribly cold abode. The "Stormont-Murphy Arctic Stove" which was fed with small compressed fuel cakes (from London!) steeped in paraffin proved very useful; yet its warmth was not sufficient to permit my discarding the heavy winter garb, including fur-lined overcoat and boots, which protected me in the open. The costume I wore would, together with the beard I was obliged to allow to grow, have made me unrecognisable even to my best friends in Europe. When the temperature had gone down in the tent to about 6° Fahr. below freezing-point, reading or writing became impossible, and I had to retire among the heavy blankets and rugs of my bed. There "Yolchi Beg" had usually long before sought a refuge, though he too was in possession of a comfortable fur coat of Kashmirian make, from which he scarcely ever emerged between December and March.

To protect one's head at night from the intense cold while retaining free respiration, was one of the small domestic problems which had to be faced from the start of this winter campaign in the desert. To the knitted Shetland cap which covered the head but left the face bare, I had soon to add the fur-lined cap of Balaclava shape made in Kashmir, which with its flaps and peak pulled down gave additional protection for everything except nose and cheeks. Still it was uncomfortable to wake up with one's moustache hard frozen with the respiration that had passed over it. Ultimately I had to adopt the device of pulling the end of my fur-coat over my head and breathing through its sleeve!

From A Journey in Southern Siberia [7]:
JEREMIAH CURTIN

[*Jeremiah Curtin (1838 or 1840–1906) was a facile linguist. He liked to study a language in the winter, and travel the next summer in the country where it was spoken. President Charles Eliot of Harvard, in his introduction to Curtin's A* Journey in Southern Siberia, *states that he knew more than sixty languages and dialects; the* Dictionary of American Biography *puts the number at seventy! In any case there is no doubt that he was a genius at learning languages and apparently could do it as easily at sixty as when he was a Harvard student. He mastered the European languages first and then branched out, finally making his most important contributions in three linguistic areas, the Irish, Slavonic and American Indian. He was the first to translate and popularize the work of the Polish novelist, Sienkiewicz (Quo Vadis?). His gifts were appreciated and utilized. The U.S. made him Secretary of the Legation in Russia from 1864 to 1870, and later found his services invaluable.*

[*It was Curtin's habit after he learned a new language to learn the history, achievements, folk and religious beliefs of those who spoke the language. He felt the importance of folklore could not be overestimated because it "furnishes us with a documentary history of the human mind." In this connection he decided after studying Mongol to visit what he thought was the birthplace of the Mongol people, the region of Lake Baikal in central southern Siberia. Here he would study the people he thought were the surviving Mongols of today, the Buriats, who inhabit three sides of Baikal, the deepest freshwater lake in the world and the largest in the Old World.*

[*Curtin made his journey between the 19th of July and the 15th of September in 1900. It may be that, like other facile linguists, he did not have a thorough command of every language he knew. There are suggestions, in his own account, that he may have worked as much through Russian-speaking Buriats*

[7] From *A Journey in Southern Siberia*, by Jeremiah Curtin.

*as through the Buriat-Mongol language itself. The fact remains
that he succeeded in bringing home linguistic as well as anthro-
pological and folklore-historical material.*]

Collecting Myths

The day following the wedding Andrei Mihailovitch came
over from his summer place. He was supposed to remain at
home for nine days, still he came. After a while he invited me
to walk along the street with him. We went the whole length
of the village. He met a number of people, who showed immense respect for him; he kissed one man, but there was much
condescension in his kiss. The grandeur of the old Buriat as he
led me, an American, on exhibition through the town, was
truly fine.

We stood for a time on the long bridge across the Kudá,
talked a little, and looked at the river, the country, and the
Russian Mission Church.

"Bishops and priests," said Mihailovitch, "have asked me to
be baptized, but I would not. I will stay with the beliefs into
which I was born."

Just then a man appeared, racing on horseback at the highest
speed. There seemed to be in the horse and man a peculiar
impetus and internal force. Without decreasing the pace of the
horse the man turned toward Andrei Mihailovitch, and, during the instant in which he was passing, saluted him with the
highest respect. Soon the man was beyond the Mission Church,
and next he was a speck on the horizon.

"Think," said I to my host as I watched the horseman, "of
the time when Jinghis Khan had a cavalry of one hundred thousand men like that man and more than two hundred thousand
horses swifter than that horse."

"Oh," replied he, "there was never on earth anything to
equal the cavalry of Jinghis Khan. It swept everything down
before it! What have we now?—Nothing. We were great once,
we conquered many countries, we ruled many peoples. China
and Russia overpowered us, but our turn will come again."

We went back to the balcony and talked long over the question of finding men who could tell the ancient myths and explain the customs and beliefs of the Buriats. A list was made,

and that afternoon the search began. Messengers were sent to surrounding villages to look for wise men. Those who were able were to be brought to Usturdi, if possible. In case they were old and decrepit I could go to them. The first and most important step was to find persons who knew what I wanted and would tell it.

The number found was small. Some had gone on visits to distant places and were inaccessible, others had known much years before, but had forgotten almost everything. In the first attempt only two old men were discovered. These two promised to come the following day. They came, gave some information, told one story, good as far as it went, but told too briefly. The story was of Esege Malan, or Father Bald Head (Father Bald Head is the highest heaven itself), and Ehé Tazar, Mother Earth.

Other men were found after those two, but none came who were at all satisfactory till Manshut appeared. He told three stories: Gesir Bogdo, Ashir Bogdo, and The Iron Hero.

When Manshut had finished these three stories he declared that he was forced to go home. I was greatly disappointed, for I was convinced that he knew more myths. Though he promised earnestly to come again and tell me all that he could remember I was doubtful about his return, for he was a restless man and seemed to dislike anything that required concentrated attention. He was a great lover of the pipe and smoked continually, drew whiffs between sentences, even between words. As talking seemed to interrupt his smoking, at least to a certain extent, I felt that I should not see him again until he needed more money for tobacco.

Early in the morning of July 30th a procession of long-bodied one-horse wagons crowded with men and women passed through the main street of Usturdi. These men and women were convicts from Russia, and a stalwart soldier, carrying a rifle, walked by the side of each wagon.

A halt was called on the first open field beyond the village. The dusty wagons were at once abandoned, and the crowd of convicts, falling into groups, began to build fires and prepare tea. Meanwhile the soldiers formed a circle around the entire party and stood on guard.

There were two hundred and seventy-four of these men and women. They were on the way to the Lena River, and farther north to the frozen Yakuts country. They had received sentence before the ukas abolishing exile to Siberia had been issued, and were specially interesting as being, perhaps, the last group of prisoners to be sent into that country, which has so long been used as a place for exile and punishment. Following the convicts came a small party of political prisoners, but they were allowed to stop at the post station for rest and refreshment.

The crowd sitting on the ground ate brown bread and drank tea with great relish. The soldiers conducting the prisoners did not fare better than the prisoners, in fact they did not fare as well, for I saw them receive merely large pieces of rye bread; at this halt they were not given tea. It seemed to me that by united action the convicts with naked hands might overpower the soldiers, for though the soldiers were alert fellows with much presence of mind, they were few in number.

The impression produced by these people was peculiar. They were all strong and sturdy, mainly of the peasant class. They were by no means downcast, grieved, or troubled. Forty of them were manacled, and even those men seemed in no way affected. One could not think while looking at these convicts that they were an oppressed and punished people. I was very anxious to talk with some of them, but it was not permitted to go inside the line of soldiers.

After a rest of an hour or so command was given to "raise camp," and five minutes later fires had been stamped out, kettles packed, and the long-bodied wagons were again moving forward over the dusty road.

I then went to visit Andrei Mihailovitch at his summer place. When about a mile and a half from his house I met him riding over to Usturdi in a little one-horse trap. He turned back, however, and drove forward rapidly, so as to reach home and be ready to welcome me. I wished greatly to photograph the "Ongons" or gods supposed to protect his house and property. I was doubtful about getting his consent, but he gave it with many pleasant words. I first photographed those that guard the home and are always hanging high up in one corner of the house. Then I went out to photograph the Ongons that guard the property. They were in a box having a door made of four small panes of window glass; this box was fastened to the top of a corner post of the carriage shed. With much difficulty it was unscrewed, and brought down and placed where I could photograph the gods which it contained. Andrei Mihailovitch could not carry these gods into a house nor could he take them out of the box, for that would bring misfortune to the family.

Inside the large box were two small boxes of home manufacture. In these were crude pictures of the gods, tiny men and women in outline, also the skin of a ground squirrel, and one or two other dried skins of very small animals. When these were photographed Andrei Mihailovitch invited me to visit his winter home, saying that on the way we would pass his field Ongons.

We drove over level pastures to the hill eastward, climbed rather slowly to the top and, after we had passed a gate, descended gradually to the brow of the hill, or rather to a point of the slope, whence there is a fine view of the country beyond: several villages, a narrow, winding river, and, somewhat to the left, the winter residence of my host. On the brow of the hill is a collection of twenty-five or thirty pillars, or hewn posts, with four flat sides. Across the top of each post a small board is so fastened that it projects on the east side like half a roof. Under this roof, in a square aperture in the post, is a small box with handle and sliding cover. The aperture also has a sliding cover which protects and secures the box inside.

Andrei Mihailovitch took the box out of his own post, opened it and showed me the gods which were on pieces of silk or cloth. Fastened on a narrow strip of blue silk were several little metal images. On two small pieces of cloth were tiny painted figures. I photographed the pillars, and then tied the images around a pillar and photographed them as best I could. After I had finished, Andrei Mihailovitch took the pieces of cloth from the pillar, folded them carefully, put them back in the box, and, placing the box on the ground near a small pile of dry juniper, which our driver had collected for him, lighted the herb. When it was burning well he put his foot on it three separate times to make it smoke and quench it. In the box, purified by the smoke, Andrei Mihailovitch placed a little bag of tobacco, which he had taken from it, then he closed the box, put it back in the pillar, and covered the aperture. Everything was done with the greatest care and reverence.

Each Buriat, as soon as he marries and has a home, must set up in the field one of these posts or pillars and place images of his gods in it. The Shaman assists him. When a man dies the box containing his Ongons is removed from the pillar, carried to the forest and hung high up on a tree, and there it remains till it rots away. The person carrying the Ongon from the pillar to the forest must not look back; should he do so it would bring great misfortune to the family of the dead man.

Andrei Mihailovitch's winter house is built on the Russian plan with large brick stoves in the partitions between the rooms. In the yard, however, are two or three eight-cornered Mongol houses where I think the family lives during winter unless some "governor" happens along.

Toward evening I started for Usturdi. The road was through a hilly or rolling country. We passed several rye fields, but with one or two exceptions the grain was very poor. After crossing an elevated ridge we came down into an opening in a forest of small timber—just such a weird opening as Sienkiewicz describes in *The Deluge*—and later on we reached another and larger opening, a remarkably lonely looking place in the dusk of approaching night, and there we came upon a Russian. He was uncouth, sturdy, and somehow uncanny. His horse was feeding near a cart, and the man himself was occupied in smoking, and in stirring something which he was boiling in a kettle over a small fire. He did not notice us or answer my greeting.

It was late in the evening when we reached Usturdi.

A few days passed now, during which I made no effort to get story-tellers but spent my time in studying the language. On the 2d of August the Horse Sacrifice was to be made and I needed to bring my work into order and prepare for this remarkable ceremony.

The Buriat country is one of two places in Asia where the Horse Sacrifice may still be seen. This ceremonial has existed among the Mongols from time immemorial and is a wonderfully interesting survival of a primitive religion.

Andrei Mihailovitch had finished his mourning now and he came over to be present at the great festival. With all his politeness I felt sure that he was not anxious that I should see the death of the horses,—on the contrary, that he was determined I should not see it.

He said to me the evening preceding the sacrifice and then again the following morning: "I will leave about nine o'clock;

that is very early. If you start an hour later you will have plenty time." The evening before, however, I had made sure that horses would be waiting at the post station near by, and within ten minutes after the departure of my host I was driving rapidly across the country.

When we had gone a mile or so my driver wished to get a drink of milk at a house by the wayside. He was terribly thirsty, he said. He was as dilatory as might be in getting the milk, then drank a whole gallon, I should think. After that we drove on very slowly. I urged and urged, but still he would not hurry the horses.

Later, when more than halfway to the Hill of Sacrifice he was again about to stop before a house. I would not permit a halt this time, and commanded him to hasten forward. When at last we reached the Hill I found that seven out of nine horses had been sacrificed already. Two fine, white mares remained. I had come very near losing the ceremony. The two, however, were among the best animals, and as every detail was observed in their case, there was a chance to see the sacrifice. The death of the two was sufficiently painful.

Beyond the Caspian [8]:

DOUGLAS CARRUTHERS

[*Many of the authors dubbed "authorities" by the writers of dust-jacket blurbs have little claim to the title. Douglas Carruthers is an exception. He was a traveler; collector of natural-history museum specimens; surveyor, geographer; and writer of no mean ability and charm. In addition, he had an eye for beauty and the vocabulary to communicate what he felt. His active field career began in 1904 and was stopped by World War I. Thereafter, he produced a series of books the last of which was* Beyond the Caspian, *from which we quote.*]

This is . . . the last resort of the tiger on the Upper Oxus; its range coinciding almost exactly with the area frequented by the deer.

[8] From *Beyond the Caspian,* by Douglas Carruthers.

Geography, climate and vegetation, I remarked, are often a clue to a discovery of biological interest. In Central Asia there is one particular land feature of outstanding character, namely, the Pamir, a phenomenon more fully developed here than anywhere else in the world. . . .

A Pamir is notoriously difficult to describe concisely. A series of high, wide, sheltered depressions in a surrounding world of shale and snow—covers it fairly well in a few words. . . . It is easy to see . . . that such a phenomenon should have an interesting fauna. In the case of the Great Pamirs, it is principally the giant mountain-sheep, named after Marco Polo, who first reported their existence in 1274. But there are other Pamirs [which] . . . might also furnish study for the naturalist. The nearest approach to the prototype, in size and construction, and at no great distance from it, is the Ak Sai.

This Pamir lies to the east of the Farghana, where the Tian Shan mountain system is linked to the true Pamir massif, by the connecting ridge of the Alai. Although lying wholly within the Russian frontier, the Ak Sai actually drains to China, for it is situated around the headwaters of the Ak Sai source of the Taushkan branch of the Tarim River, which ultimately ends in Lop Nor. Adjoining the Ak Sai, but separated from it by the self-contained basin of Chatir Kul (corresponding to the Kara Kul basin on the Great Pamirs) is another, but smaller, Pamir, the Arpa. The two together cover an area about as large as Wales. They were famous grazings in Timur's day, and still are. The more I examined this particular region, the more I realised its possibilities, for the Tian Shan was a distinctive faunistic and floristic zone, and in no way connected with those lands beyond the Caspian wherein I had so far traveled and worked.

The way to the Ak Sai and Arpa Pamirs led up through that great cul-de-sac of Central Asia, the Farghana, which entices the traveler hopefully eastwards, only to bar his further passage by a formidable mountain wall. There is no easy exit from the Farghana. Perhaps this accounts for its peculiar atmosphere, which I found to contrast strangely with other parts of Central Asia. If I wished to feel the pulse of Asia, I should go to the Farghana and sit in the bazaars of Khokand, being certain that if anything of importance happened in Khiva or Kumul, Kabul or Kuldja, I should know of it sooner here than I should else-where. Although the Farghana might be called the Kashmir of Central Asia, in so far as climate, scenery, fruit and flowers are concerned, there is a very marked difference in their respective inhabitants. The men of the Farghana are men of action, and have thrown up such comets as Baber and Yakub Beg. Under any but Russian rule, the green flag of fanaticism would have been unfurled more often. The Khokandis are of a particularly explosive temperament, and are certainly more full of guts and energy than the dwellers in more southerly oases. As fiery as the horses, for which they were famous, they have more than once provided the spark that set alight a local rising or some more serious conflagration.

That indefinable line of demarcation between what have been called northern and southern temperaments, which runs across southern Europe, the Black Sea and the Caucasus, seems to extend across Central Asia on about this latitude. The Far-ghana I should place on the borderline. To the north are hardier and more virile races than to the south.

The Farghana is chiefly famous for Baber's brilliant, if some-what ephemeral, little kingdom. And you have only to read his *Memoirs* to understand what a delectable region it is. Even to Baber, who loved life and all the good things of life, and en-joyed to the full everything that life had to give, the Farghana seemed the last word in excellence. Whether it was food, hunt-ing, or horses, those of the Farghana were, to him, the best. Its pheasants were the fattest, its waters the purest, its melons sur-passed the finest Bukharan, its horses were "celestials" and the envy of all Asia. He extols its climate; I do not think he exag-gerated. For the climate of the Farghana, being ameliorated by the surrounding protective mountain-walls, is more mellow than that of any other part of the Duab of Turkistan. It does not suffer from those extremes of temperature for which the region is remarkable. It is unusual for the Syr to freeze up here, although it freezes at a *lower* altitude. Hence the wealth of fruit of all sorts: the wild varieties, such as strawberries and raspber-ries, grow in such profusion that there is unlimited jam for all who care to go and pick, while even the tender Pistachio pro-duces nuts. Such was the Farghana in Baber's day and so it is now, for of all Middle Asia it is the least changed, tucked away between the ranges, and cut off on all sides but one from the outside world. . . .

On entering the Farghana valley from the west we are immediately upon historic ground. It was here, in the narrow entrance gap, that Alexander the Great founded the farthest of his cities—a veritable outpost of Greek civilisation in the barbarous wilderness. The position was well chosen, on the southern bank of the river Syr, with the main trans-continental trade-route between East and West, the northernmost Silk Route —the most northerly indeed of any established way across Asia— passing close by. The Syr in those days marked the uttermost limit of settled life and government in this direction, for beyond it was Nomad's Land, where nothing was established, and nothing remained fixed. It was the frontier of Iran and Turan; many centuries were to elapse before the Turanian flood flowed southwards to the Hindu Kush. All that vastness of Asia north of the Syr—"eternal motherland of vigorous migrants"—had been for all time the home of those innumerable, fluid, roaming peoples, against whom not even the Greeks could make any headway, and into which void the Persian Empire at its zenith never expanded one yard.

This bottle-neck leading to the Farghana is about twenty miles wide, and through it flows the Syr Darya, the third of our great rivers "beyond the Caspian.". . .

Cross-sections, especially from unusual angles, are always instructive. With the eye of a vulture soaring high over the Syr, I let my imagination take a short cut direct to India. Below me the black frowning flanks of the Alai stood like the guardian of the South; and close under it I could just discern the track that the old caravans used when passing from Kashgar to Sogdiana. Beyond the Alai lay a broad, flat, transverse valley, like a green trough, dotted with innumerable Kirghiz encampments, and along it ran the second great arterial trade route between East and West. Beyond, again, rose the Trans-Alai range, greater than its northern namesake, and the impressive pile of Peter the Great range, amongst whose summits were the highest peaks in the Russian Empire. Further to the south, Pamir succeeded Pamir, in giant corrugations, to where a thin silver streak denoted the upper Oxus. Here again a narrow track indicated the third "way-through" this mountain world, the corridor by which passed all the learning and the art that India gave to China. Beyond this rose the stormy Hindu Kush, guardian of the North; and beyond again a labyrinth of lesser ranges dropping to the Indus and the plains of Hindustan.

Turning north, the outlook was very different. The encirclement of the Farghana was completed by mountains, it is true, but they were less impressive and less famous than those to the south. There seemed to be no romance about them. They were not inhabited by mountaineers of ancient lineage, there were no sedentary cultivators tied to the soil by virtue of acquisition and reclamation. There were few ancient sites or time-worn ways. In other words, it was not "Central Asia," although it might be called a neutral zone between it and Siberia. And beyond the northern ring of mountains?—vast horizon-bounded plains as far as eye could see and imagination carry one. First desert, then steppe, then downland, then cornland merging into the cold northern forests and tundras that border the Arctic Seas. The Syr is, indeed, the dividing line between two fundamentally different spheres; as Baber remarked, it is "the extreme boundary of the habitable world."

Back in Andijan I found the busiest horse-bazaar that I had yet seen, which is not to be wondered at since this is rail-head. And what a rail-head! To see another train one would have to go up to the Turkestan-Siberian Railway, south to Peshawar or east to Pekin. I bought four horses of an excellent type, and hoped to be gone quick from the flies, and the heat, and filth of my caravanserai. This was, I suppose, the best the place could offer, and for aught I know had been honoured by all the great travelers who had passed this way, from Chang Kien onwards. Perhaps it used to be under better management, but at the time of my visit, its sanitation was nil, and its lack of privacy revolting. There was no reason to *look* "how wide also the East is from the West." I can live "native" in the wilds and enjoy it, but to attempt the same on the edge of civilisation is disastrous. The one redeeming feature was the fruit, which not only ripened earlier here than elsewhere, but was of a quality which well merited Baber's many allusions to its variety and excellence. I used to breakfast off green-tea, native bread, and little white figs, which were hawked round already skinned and iced. Apricots, peaches, pomegranates and melons followed during the day.

The inhabitants of this ancient capital of the Farghana, like those of most key-towns on trunk trade routes, were crafty, money-grabbing, pleasure-seeking and shockingly immoral. I was glad to leave for Osh, where the air was cleaner, the horses better and even cheaper. Here I completed my caravan and rode for Uskent—the last town in the eastern Farghana. The inhabitants of Osh must be possessed of a certain aesthetic sense, for they have deliberately utilised the natural beauties of the locality in their town-planning. Their eating-houses and tea-shops were built out on little piers overhanging the river, which flowed through the town. Here they could sit and enjoy the natural beauties of waterfalls and gushing torrents, and benefit by the cooler air which accompanied them. The "picturesque" was in marked evidence at every turn in the bazaars, and on every stretch of the river.

Between Osh and Uskent is lovely country, rather like the Canadian foothills of the Rocky Mountains. The altitude was about 4,000 ft. and crops could be grown without irrigation. So it was not altogether surprising to come suddenly upon colonies of Russian peasants, who had emigrated to this distant corner of their Empire, and settled down permanently and apparently successfully. The rolling hills were one wide wheat-field, and typically-Russian villages nestled in the hollows, looking homely and prosperous. But the fact of them being here at all gave one much food for thought. They were an isolated community, living cheek by jowl with the indigenous native population, a population consisting of mixed races of purely Asiatic origin, and of a different religion.

Below them on the plain was, perhaps not a seething, but a very numerous society of Moslem cultivators, who had been there always. Above them in the mountains, and on the plateaux, was another and possibly more incompatible element, the nomadic or semi-nomadic Kara Kirghiz, a race much more likely to resent the presence of incoming Russian emigrants, and one, owing to their Turkish-Mongol origin, more likely to be aggressive. Yet, all seemed to go well. There was no race-hatred and no religious antagonism between the two. The Russians did not look upon the "natives" as such; they fraternised in a way I have never seen East and West do before. I racked my brains for an equivalent within the British Empire, but could not recall one. The fact remained that if this was a true example of how Russia deals with Asia, her future there is assured. Indeed, it appeared to me that the Russians had inherited that quality which certain ancient Asiatic invaders of the West had possessed in full measure, namely—"the necessary gift for all people destined to political predominance—tolerant assimilation."

My forty rouble (£4) ponies pleased me, and as I rode along, enjoying their paces, after donkey transport, I recalled that the Farghana had always been famous for its horses, and that their excellence had been responsible for one of the greatest horse-raids in history. The possession of good horses was as vital to the early Empires of Asia, as the ownership, or control, of oilfields is to-day for the well-being of progressive States; while for war-making they were as essential as tanks are now. The simple fact that the Huns possessed more and better horses than the Chinese forced the latter to build the Great Wall, which, far from being a "folly," was one of the most stupendous and effective defensive works ever conceived and carried out by Man. Not having sufficient horses to compete in open warfare, the Chinese completely double-crossed their arch-enemies by rendering their own territory secure against aggression. But on the other hand they could not take the offensive without many more horses of an improved type. And so it happened that the Farghana, far away as it was, appeared in the Chinese Annals about two thousand years ago. Having first tried diplomacy and failed, the Chinese had to resort to force, and sent a military expedition to "acquire" what they needed. Thus, about 100 B.C., Farghana horses were driven off in large numbers to augment, and improve, the Chinese Imperial stud.

Here I cut all ties with so-called civilisation—that is to say, with an existence in which one is entirely dependent on somebody else for everything. From now onwards I was absolutely dependent upon myself. I had four good ponies, two rotten servants, no guide, and my own wits. As I faced the main Farghana range I confess my spirits sank. The Russian 40 verst map, a marvel of production, covering a colossal area, is on too small a scale to travel by in mountainous country. It showed a pass, aptly called Suok—the cold—at the head of the Kara Kuldja valley, up which I was riding, which appeared to lead direct to the Ak Sai Pamir. But passes, in this part of the world, are not always as they appear on the map.

Cultivation extended beyond Uskent for a day's journey, above this there was a zone of rank vegetation such as I had not seen before in Turkestan. The ponies ploughed their way through high grass and golden sorrel, which reached to their bellies. There were tangles of roses, and sweeps of senecios; starwort grew by the acre, hollyhock, pyrethrum, columbine, flea-bane, asphodel, and poppies spangled the hill-sides, and all were smothered in a flutter of bright butterflies. There was not much tree growth, but in certain localities the valley bottom was choked with poplar, plane and giant walnuts. There were some birch, oak and apple.

This solved some bird problems for me. For instance, those Scarlet Finches (*Carpodacus erythrinus roseatus* Blyth), which I had noticed passing through the Samarkand valley at the end of April, obviously going farther north to breed—this was their breeding zone and they were here in numbers. So were many other birds, the majority of which were new to me, but they were all in such a dilapidated state of moult that I did not bother to collect them.

At about 8,000 ft. vegetation ceased in the face of the terrific and appalling disintegration which was going on all around. The hillsides were denuded of all growth, there being no holding ground for even a blade of grass. There must have been an everlasting movement of material in order to produce this state of affairs, snow-slide in spring, mud-avalanche and land-slip later, and slither of rock and shale going on all the time. The result was a scene as forbidding as it was dangerous. It was black, jagged, craggy, slippery, and cold.

Such a place one would hardly expect to be inhabited, but, as a matter of fact, nearly every side-valley had an "alp" in its upper reaches, and there, far away up under the snow-fields, were bright green meadows which were dotted with the white felt tents of the Kirghiz. If any of these were within reasonable distance of my evening camp I would send a man up there to procure sour-milk, junket or cheese.

On the fourth day I began to doubt the wisdom of going on, progress was so slow and so hard on the ponies. But, at this juncture, a party of Kirghiz came on the scene, ten of them, riding their little hill-ponies, and each one carrying a leathern bottle of *kumiz* as their sole ration for the journey over the range to Kashgar. They passed me at a shuffle, which exactly describes the action of their ponies as they traversed the shale-slopes at an easy speed. They hailed me, pointed upwards towards the pass, crying the equivalent of "Excelsior," and were soon out of sight. This was encouraging, so we proceeded till nightfall, when we lay down amongst the rocks, and the ponies had no feed.

Next morning, as we were loading up, who should appear but our friends the ten Kirghiz, riding their little ponies, and each one still carrying his bottle of *kumiz*. They came scurrying down the valley, as sure-footed as yaks, and seemed in no way disconcerted at their failure to make the pass. They told me that it was closed, and that I had better follow them along to the next one, the Sur-Tash, which was sure to be open. They passed on down the valley at what appeared to me to be break-neck speed. I was only too glad of a reasonable excuse to follow them, for I certainly could not have hoped to succeed where they had failed. The truth was that the way up the Kara Kuldja to the pass at its head is entirely at the mercy of the elements, and in the hands of Nature. . . .

I was in no hurry to follow my Kirghiz friends as I knew I could not keep up with them. So, retreating down the valley, I found a convenient summer encampment in a lateral valley, and spent two days there resting my ponies and recuperating myself on the native diet of fermented milk of mares. I agree with Marco Polo that it is "a right good drink," but the local brew must have been an exceptionally strong one; I found it pleasantly intoxicating, but my servants, drinking deeper, became incapable of rendering any service, until they had slept off the ill-effects. Around my tent was spread a perfect little garden of wild flowers—ranunculus, pansies, omphaloides, gentians, forget-me-nots, purple and yellow fumitory, orange erigeron, alpine poppies, and many other varieties I could not name. There were many birds, too, new to me, but the Dippers were White-bellied, the same as those on the high Hissar streams, and the Whistling Thrush I found to range thus far northwards. It was a pretty spot—a wide green grassy flat, flower-strewn, and watered by innumerable little rills fresh from the snows. There were the clusters of snug felt tents, domed like bee-skeps, and droves of horses, flocks of sheep, and herds of cows grazing over the hillsides. The inhabitants were hospitable by custom, but avaricious by nature. They kept open-house, the evening meals being veritable Belshazzar feasts, but they would quibble over threepence for a purchase. The women, of course, were the worst; a bargain might be completed with the man, but should the wife disapprove, the deal was off! I always found this with the Kirghiz, one never knew exactly where one was with them. No reliance could be placed upon them. Shifty, cunning, self-seeking in everyday life, one met a more generous and more likeable nature only when it came to companionship in travel, hardship or hunting.

The same strong type still endures: as of yore, "it is the women who do the buying and selling, and whatever is necessary to provide for the husband and household, for the men all lead the life of gentlemen, troubling themselves about nothing but hunting and hawking."

The approach to the Sur Tash pass was clearly marked out for me by the devastation caused by some thousands of sheep which had been driven over it recently from the plateau beyond. They had eaten off every living thing on a wide front. The shepherds who drove them were as primitive as their flocks, being clothed from head to foot in sheep-skins. . . .

The actual crossing of the pass was comparatively easy. Snow still lay (August) in the valley bottom, and we kept to it for preference, for the rock walls on either side looked most uninviting. The passage of the sheep had made a good hard track over the mile-long snowdrift which led up to the final climb, and though this last pull was stiff, the reward was great. For, from the crest of the pass, I got one of those views that only a country as vast as Central Asia can supply. Below and behind us was the Farghana, spread out like an old, mellowed Bukharan rug. The snowy crest of the Alai shimmered mysteriously high above the haze of the plain—cloud-like—baseless. To the south were regions of colour, as mountain succeeded mountain to infinity. But before us on the other side of the pass was something entirely new. No steep descent led down to the inevitable valley that usually greets the climber to the summit of a great divide. There was practically no descent at all. The rocks and the shale and the snow-fields ran down at an easy gradient to beautiful grassy slopes. The slopes spread themselves out into broader sweeps of undulating downland. A free country, easy-going, unhampered. I had reached the famous plateau pastures, which are a governing factor in the economic life of Central Asia.

Here scenery was designed on a colossal scale. The Pamir before me was the Arpa. I overlooked the whole of it, with the Arpa river winding like a silver thread through the midst. Beyond it, over a far distant horizon, I knew, but could not see, that the Arpa merged into the Chatir Kul basin, and that again into the Ak Sai—my destination. A boundless and inspiring landscape—High Tartary indeed.

Skirting the snow-fields that lay along the northern slopes of the Farghana range, we kept to the highest grass just under the shale and found the going good. Occasionally snouts of snow extended across our track, which showed that our altitude was about 10,000 ft. A few days ago I was sweltering in the heat, and living on semi-tropical fruit; now I rode through drifting misty icy wind, and rain, with the marmot's whistle for my morning call, and hot tea the only antidote to shivers. It was austere and exacting, and the first evening proved it, for the one essential of life at high altitude—fuel to cook on—was lacking. Timberless countries and desert areas usually produce something in the way of a scrub or a root which will serve the purpose and boil a kettle, but these plateaux did not; and unless they have been habitually used as grazing ground, even dung is denied one. But such famous pastures as the Arpa can supply this commodity in variety, and it is not long before one becomes an expert in deciding the respective merits of the droppings of horse, cow, sheep and camel. Cow and sheep were the best, if dry and of a certain age; even when damp they were better than the others, and this being the wet season they were always my choice. The only thing that defeated us was a fresh fall of snow; then we had to go without cooked food and hot drinks—a sore trial at this height, in a land far beyond the reach of my native whisky.

There were no nomad encampments along my route but I

passed great flocks of sheep that were being driven down to market on the plains below, and occasionally parties of Kirghiz, wayfarers like myself—men in company, on pleasure or business bent. Many carried falcons and I noted that these were always carried right-handed—not left, as in Europe—and yet the art originated in these parts.

On a landscape of emerald green, blue-black, and white—alpine meadows, shale screes, and glistening snow-fields—I came upon a Kirghiz encampment, and at the door of the first *yurt* stood a figure who hailed me from afar as if I was his long-lost brother. A little hill pony, sleek and plump, grazed on the succulent grasses, and the familiar *kumiz* bottle hung, empty, on the side of the tent, for its owner now dined daily, like a prince, on mutton and rice. It turned out that he was one of the party who had attempted the Suok Pass as a short-cut home.

At his invitation I pitched my tent nearby, and for the next few days I enjoyed Tartar hospitality, fed as they fed, on proper food instead of camp-fare, and hunted with them in the evenings. They were too lazy to hunt during the day, or perhaps they knew that the daytime was not the best time to pursue the shepherd's worst enemy—the wolf.

At these high encampments, surrounded as they were by a wild turmoil of hills, the flocks were at the mercy of the wolf-packs which infested them. Only constant hunting and harrying kept them at bay, and in spite of this it was quite common to find large packs of wolves lying within sight of the flocks around the tents. We hunted them with horse and hound, and they gave us as exciting a run as anyone could wish for, in fact it was far too exciting at first until one had become accustomed to one's mount—which refused nothing—and to keeping up the pace when the angle of the slopes was about 45°. The "meet" was fixed for the highest *yurt,* the one farthest up the valley, beyond which was the most likely ground to draw. The "field" consisted of six or eight of us mounted on their incomparable little hill-ponies, without which one could not ride a yard in such country. The pack was composed of three or four dogs of the long-haired greyhound type, something like the so-called Afghan greyhound, there being many varieties of that particular breed up here. The ponies breasted the steep shale slopes as if they were on the flat, slopes so steep that they crumbled away beneath each step, but short shuffling paces of the ponies seemed to counteract the slip. Once we reached the top we rode over great rounded humps, on which the snow lay in broad drifts. It was strange ground to draw for wolves, and to me it seemed unlikely; the Kirghiz, however, knew what they were about. They knew full well that the wolves followed the sheep, and that this particular desolation just below perpetual snow-line became their summer quarters, when the flocks were driven up to the highest pastures. We had not gone far before we rode right onto a pack (I believe *route* is the correct word) lying asleep on the shale, resting before their nightly raid on the sheep below. . . .

Now the fun began. We played their own game on them, using the wolf's tactics of running down the quarry with the object of singling out a victim. As the hounds ran in the wolves moved off over appalling ground, and made for a stronghold of rock and crag, where no horse could live. But the Kirghiz rode hard to cut them off from their objective. This manoeuvre turned the wolves towards the lower slopes, where the going was hell, but not suicidal. The slopes were so steeply tilted that the whole surface slid away as we crossed them, yet the ponies never made a mistake and seldom reduced their pace. Gaining confidence, I accustomed myself to the art of lying back with my head on my pony's tail.

After a "ski" down shelving rock and scree, slanting at a ridiculous angle, the dogs turned a single wolf out of the pack and quickly brought it to bay. Then the riders came up, and one man, throwing himself off his pony, slipped in behind the wolf and slit his throat.

It was tough hunting in cruel country, and it was evidently considered to be more of a duty than a pastime, an arduous and often risky business carried out largely in self-protection. The evenings, especially if we had been lured far afield by some pack more elusive than usual, were bitterly cold at this high altitude, so that the felted tents were all the more appreciated when we returned to them, while the lavish dishes of steaming hot mutton and rice were to be remembered by us for many a long week when reduced to very Spartan diet.

The predatory Wild dogs are also a menace to the flocks, but they are mostly confined to the forested zone at a lower altitude, and do not come up to these high barren plateaux (although they have been recorded from the forested zone on the eastern wall of the Pamirs). They, like the wolves, hunt in packs, but for some reason they pay more attention, and are more deadly, to wild game than to domestic animals. They seem to fear man and his belongings far more than do the wolves, although they are daring and savage enough when in pursuit of their prey. These Cuon (probably *Cuon javanicus jason* Pocock) hunting-dogs are wolf-like in appearance and tawny in colour: the Russians call them the Red Wolf to distinguish them from the Grey, although there is no generic relationship between them.

I wondered why the Kirghiz never used their trained eagles in the chase, since the wolf is one of their favourite quarries, but was told that they dislike using their hunting-eagles at this season. Eagles have great powers of fasting, in consequence they are difficult to get into . . . keen flying condition, at any time, and more especially during the summer months, when the birds, being dull, often abscond. It is preferable to reserve them for the winter's sport, when they fly better. But another reason may be that, since their use is largely utilitarian, as a means of procuring good fur, their owners forego these risky summer flights when pelts are in poor condition.

The Golden Eagle must be fairly common in these parts, judging by the numbers one sees in captivity. Hawking with eagles . . . is a favourite pastime of the sedentary people and the nomads alike. It is somewhat select in that it is only the yeoman farmers, Begs, Khans, and such-like, who can afford them. For although an eagle may be said to be worth a horse or two, a good one seldom comes on the market, for he is priceless. They are taken from the nest, of course, not caught on passage, but occasionally adult birds may be captured, for they can be easily ridden down when gorged on carrion. These will sometimes submit to training. In early stages they are wrapped up in a sheep-skin, in the same way as the Dutchmen use a sock—the lower portion of a worsted stocking, either of which making an ideal straight-jacket for the purpose. They are probably no more difficult to train and handle than a Goshawk, a bird of somewhat similar temperament and inclined to the same faults—sulkiness, for example. But they vary individually in character, some being easy to handle, others impossible to train at all.

Eagles are entered to fur only, which they clutch and hold.

They "bolt" or fly straight from the fist at the quarry. They cannot be "cast" as falcons are, nor thrown as short-winged hawks usually are, and always should be. When let fly, they do not mount aloft in order to stoop onto the quarry, therefore the actual flight is a somewhat dull show, neither impressive to watch, nor exciting to follow, apart from the actual "kill"; the eagle just flaps along, and without apparent effort easily over-takes its victim. There is no thrill, no swift thrust up into the sky, and no sudden stoop earthwards. Having seen one flight you have seen the lot, there being little variation except in the nature of the quarry.

Herein lies the excitement of the chase, for the quarry con-sists mostly of foxes, gazelle, wolves, and, in earlier days, the Saiga antelope. It is said that a good eagle can kill a wolf unaided, but I have never seen it happen. Some authorities, Levchine for instance, declare that if a wolf is too strong, and goes off with the eagle still hanging on to it, the eagle is able to hold it with one foot and anchor itself with the other, until the wolf exhausts itself in the struggle! Believe it or not, but one must remember that *smaller* birds of prey, such as Peregrines and Sakers, are habitually flown at gazelle in other countries. These Tian Shan wolves may be a trifle smaller than the Si-berian or Tundra wolf, but the difference would scarcely be discernible to any but an expert eye.

.   .   .   .

But to return to High Tartary and the Black, or Wild Moun-tain Kirghiz. They were a healthy-looking lot—and who would not be, living up here in this rarefied atmosphere, on a diet of sour milk? For those who were fit enough to survive, it was as near everlasting-life as could be. I benefited from it even during my short sojourn, and came to know the ecstasy of assured immortality. One felt very near to Nature, and very near to Heaven, lifted up as one was so high above the world below, surrounded by boundless horizons and bountiful skies. . . .

When the wolves were not troubling us, I attempted to find the big wild sheep in company with these Kirghiz, but soon gave it up as a . . . waste of time and energy. "Solo" should be the motto of the hunter of wild sheep; indeed, the first essential towards success in this, the most exacting of all hill-stalking, is to be *alone*. To depend on a native hunter for eyes, ears and brain is a deplorable acknowledgment of inefficiency. Those who cannot rely on their own had better go away and try something easier. The extra labour and self-imposed difficulties, resulting from an ignorance of local conditions and lack of acquaintance with the game, are very soon refunded in the form of an intense enjoyment in solitude, and an exhilarating sense of independence. I confess that I have never got any real satisfaction from hunting, unless I have found, stalked, killed, and carried home the trophy I had set my heart upon, *unaided*. More than that, I require virgin country, and if possible a "new" beast, to satisfy me. This may sound like snobbery or bravado, but it is not. It is a legitimate indulgence in the exultation derived from self-reliance, which is a form of intoxication that agrees with some, but is poison to others. It corresponds to the mania of the mountaineer who prefers to find his own way up a difficult and dangerous peak, disdaining professional guides. There is in many men a special satisfaction in reliance on their own resources, and this compensates for the greater risk incurred. It is, I assure you, a grand tonic.

So I forsook my comfortable quarters in the shepherd's encampment, and went out into a region where maps were useless and guides would have been a curse. I wandered southwards into very high, very bleak country, until I was somewhere in the void that exists at the sources of the Tarz tributary of the Kara Kuldja, and the Suok sources of the Kashgar river, and was probably more often in Chinese territory than in Russian. Judging by the number of days I spent there, and by the amount of ground I covered on my hunting-pony and on foot, there must be an enormous area which is too high for domestic flocks, but not too high for wild sheep. This implies that there is a large expanse of shale, with a little grass, which, although not good enough to tempt the Kirghiz shepherds, is sufficient for wild-game during this short period (perhaps two months at the most), when they are pushed to the uttermost limits of their rightful domain. For the other eight or ten months the wild sheep have the whole place to themselves.

.   .   .   .

After many fruitless days of hard hunting, during which period I saw only small flocks of ewes, I eventually reached the sanctum of the old gentlemen. It was as remote and secluded a retreat as any I had ever encountered, and I am sure I could not find my way back to it again. There did not appear to be a main ridge or watershed to the range, and there were no landmarks; it was a confused jumble of very high, very worn mountains, and the streamlets flowed north, south and west in the course of a day's hunt. It was this featureless wilderness of shale and snow that the old rams had taken as their own for this brief period of the year. And they had it to themselves—except for me. Even at this early date in August I was hampered by snowfalls, and on two occasions had to retreat to lower ground. But late one afternoon I spied two old rams before they saw or scented me, and one of them paid the penalty.

It was a short stalk and a long shot, success depending on negotiating a loose scree noiselessly. When that was safely accomplished there was no further possibility of a nearer approach, and I lay at a distance of 250 yards from the prize I had come so far to win. . . .

There was a rare grassy strip between the sterile shale slides half in sun and half in shadow, and on it fed those two wondrous beasts. They were vast: their heads seem to weigh them down—such was the length and the girth of their twisted, gnarled horns. I lay there—it may have been an hour—hypnotised by the primeval scene, vainly hoping that they might feed towards me, but they only fed away in the opposite direction, and the distance widened. They were never at rest, but always on the *qui vive*, looking round and sniffing the breeze; yet they might have been a hundred miles from any danger. Then the shadows lengthened, and I knew it was to be now or never. But before the climax was reached, the anticlimax set in, and I had the same revulsion of feeling that I have had on previous similar occasions. I had succeeded in my quest, what more? Must I break the silence that was gold? Must I kill? What was the treasure compared with the hunt? Why not go away and cry quits? Yet they were fair game; they were old—far past their prime. Next winter, or the winter after, they would be caught in some snowdrift, and suffer a horrible death from wolves. But I would kill in a second; and instead of a nameless grave, and their great horns lying to rot by wind and weather, they would live for ever; their magnificence would be the wonder and awe of multitudes in some far western city. They were fair game indeed, for when I looked along my sights I realised that the betting would be about 100 to 1 on a miss. Sheep on shale, at that range, are never conspicuous, but when there is the shimmer of sun rising off it they are hardly discernible.

However, a single shot left me in possession of a trophy which now gazes down on you and me from its pedestal in the Natural History Museum at South Kensington.

During these days spent in the chase, I had obtained some stupendous views of the surrounding regions, views not allowed to the ordinary traveler who is relegated by circumstances to the orthodox routes, which perforce follow the easiest lines through difficult country. Even as in England it is the shooting man and the hunting man who gets the best of the scenery, and thereby develops an "eye for country." My diary records—"I got some of the biggest views I have ever set eyes on. I was in the midst of a vast creation of mountains; as far as eye could reach they extended north, east, and south—ranges of rock and shale, ranges of shale and snow; beyond were open plateaux and then more ranges. I could see Chatir Kul, a turquoise dot on the tawny steppe. I could see the Ak Sai plateau, and beyond that again the ranges that border it on north and east. I could see where the mountains began to drop towards the deserts of Chinese Turkestan, and I could see where they rose as eaves to the Roof of the World."

This was a lot to say of innermost Asia, where Nature is built on such a colossal scale, and where everything is immoderate and abnormal. The effect on one is an abiding sense of helpless inferiority and insignificance; indeed I know of no better corrective to any tendency towards self-importance!

Marmots, like the Kirghiz, preferred this locality to others. They were all of the Short-tailed Brown species, which, by the way, are not nearly so vociferous as their Red cousins. But still the air was full of their whistling, and this, together with the animated shoreline with its Grey Lag Geese, Ruddy Sheldrake, and many Waders, contrasted strongly with the silent, birdless plateaux I had just vacated. A few days in the neighbourhood might have been well spent, but my food supply was all but finished and I had to prepare for eventualities. My great stand-by, on this sort of journey, was one of my own concoction, namely, all sorts of dried fruits and nuts—apricots, raisins, plums, walnuts, and almonds—mixed and pounded into a solid lump. The resulting mess was compact, indestructible, and a very sustaining diet. But even this supply was now finished. The local Kirghiz were not helpful, so I rode south to the Turugart pass, leading to Kashgar, where there was said to be a temporary trading-post, and I hoped to buy flour—at a price. At the entrance to the pass, which is but a col leading off the plateau down to the plain (the plateau being over 11,000 ft. and the pass under 13,000 ft.), I found a group of *yurts*. One of them was the biggest I had ever set eyes upon, and in it sat an old Tartar with his bales of trade goods stacked around him. He looked like some giant spider lying in wait for victims to enter his web. He caught me. In spite of an hour's haggling, he extorted the utmost, knowing full well that I was starving, and was not going to leave without my flour.

With full saddle-bags I returned to the bleakness of the naked Chatir Kul, and then headed east to the Ak Sai plateau. Although I now had a small reserve of food for myself and my men, feeding the ponies was still a problem. The upper end of the Ak Sai was destitute of fodder and almost waterless. No doubt at the right season there was good grazing, but in August it was a stony barren waste, so I hurried on to the border-ranges on the south-eastern side where there was some nourishment to be found. This was my ultimate goal, for I decided that neither time, money, nor animals would last out for a journey further east. In a way, the handicap was a blessing; for however delightful the forested valleys of the Tian Shan, around its culminating peaks of Khan Tengri may be, they are better known than these wilder and less attractive ranges, and so less useful for my purpose.

The ranges of Kok Kia and Kok Shal do not appear much in literature—they are side-tracked, and therefore a refuge for all wild-life. In fact, I would place this region high in my (private) list of unknown hunting-grounds, the sort of place I should like to be able to go to every August, in preference to Scotland! It would take a lifetime of Augusts to know it well, and I should be able to hunt a different area every autumn for the best years

of my life. At about thirty-five years of age I would have to
go slow, and at forty to give it up altogether, for I defy anyone
over that age to do any good on that particular ground. It was
cruel going for man and beast.

There is another factor which renders this retreat so favourable for the same purpose. Although harried on the north by
nomadic tribes with a taste for hunting, they are not so molested
from the south, where there is a wide zone of less inhabited
country. On this, the Chinese flank of the watershed, parallel
ridges and outliers, actually higher than the frontier range,
protect it. Also this region, being outside the rain-belt, is not so
frequented by nomads, nor is it likely to be developed, as
Russian territory may be; for even if enthusiasts succeed in
"growing strawberries on the Pamirs," it is unlikely to be
attempted here.

I found the Kirghiz in occupation of all the lower valleys of
the Kok Kia, but they were an ill-mannered lot, and none too
pleasant to deal with. They were independent to the point of
insolence, and I put this down to their living on a frontier,
which gave them a freedom of movement denied to others. They
could snap their fingers at Moscow and Pekin in turn, and run
with the hare or hunt with the hounds just as they pleased.
Younghusband had come up against this same tribe, on the
Chinese side in 1887, and noted their churlish truculent nature;
in fact on his transcontinental journey covering some three
thousand miles, and involving contact with a variety of race and
religion, they were the one black spot in human nature which
he encountered. These were the tribes who took advantage of
the first World War to make trouble in the rear. When all the
Russian men had been called-up to fight, these rascals descended
from their plateaux onto the pleasant and peaceful colonies
in Semirechia, and wreaked their vengeance on the remaining,
unprotected, population of old men, women and children. They
destroyed, and robbed and killed to their hearts' content, and
finally carried off into slavery any women they pleased. For
years afterwards Russian fathers were seeking their abducted
daughters amongst the nomad encampments on the Chinese side
of the mountain frontier.

I was glad to see the last of them, and to gain freedom
from the human element in the vast and delightful solitudes of

the Kok Kia. This was a country after my own heart. There was no fear of running into anyone. Once only, in three weeks, did I meet strangers, and on that occasion it was a band of Kirghiz who had to ask me the way!

When I had got clear of the last Kirghiz encampment, and had moved on a couple of days' journey into the Kok Kia, I found game. First of all ewes, and then rams, of the true *Ovis ammon humei* type, with some remarkably big ibex on the crags above the open sheep-country. These ibex were not of the same calibre as the giants of the central Tian Shan, but they were very big for a region where the feed was not super-abundant. I witnessed one old fellow through my glass scratching his backside with the tip of one horn, and he seemed to exert no effort whatsoever in order to reach his posterior.

.   .   .   .

My second winter in the heart of Asia was spent largely in another valley, eight hundred miles east of Samarkand, namely the Ili. This locality is even more remote from the ameliorating influence of the sea, and consequently has a far more severe climate than that of the Zarafshan.

The Ili valley, although of no special economic or strategic value, is definitely a landmark in Middle Asia. From the early days when it was a favourite camping ground of Mongol chieftains, down to the nineteenth century when advancing Russia came up against a static China, the locality has been well to the fore in the history of the Central Asian borderlands. But since the valley lies at right angles to all natural lines of communication, and itself leads to nowhere, its ownership is not a matter of vital importance either to Russia or China. But had the Muzart Pass, at its head, been an easy one instead of a very bad one, the frontier might have been adjusted to the advantage of the Russians. As it is they share it between them, Russia retaining the fairway across the plains and the lower rich agricultural lands, and China its less productive but far more attractive upper half.

The Ili valley is divided into three very distinct zones; the lowest portion is desert-bound and of little account, its upper reaches are mountain-locked, inaccessible and unproductive for the most part, while its middle course is well-favoured and of great potential value. To the Mongols, when they first emerged from Mongolia, it must have appeared a land of promise sheltered, watered and pastured on an extravagant scale. So the Chagatai heir of Jenghis Khan settled on the best of it and made it his permanent encampment.

I made it mine for the worst of one winter.

At the end of November there was a series of snowstorms, accompanied by a sudden ominous drop in temperature. By the first week in December the Ili river was frozen stiff, and the whole land was frost-bound. Snow would occur every ten or twelve days, not the big slow-falling flakes of the English scene, but a steady, continuous, relentless fall of minute particles of frozen snow, which lay, or drifted . . . in sheltered valley or stormy steppe. The immense landscape of endless plain and gigantic ranges lay under a glistening white mantle, unbroken, save where black lines of dead vegetation denoted the river courses, or dark blue shadows on the mountains showed where precipices and ravine allowed no snow to lie. Always a land of immensity, it is seen at its best in mid-winter, when no dust-haze hides, and all its matchless grandeur is revealed. The intervening periods between the snowfalls were brilliant and sunny, but the temperature dropped to zero and then far below it. So long as the air was still the fifty degrees or so of frost were not felt, but if the wind blew, man could scarcely face the elements. Across the landscape moved occasional natives, Kalmuk and Kirghiz, wrapped in great sheep-skin coats, and wearing fox-skin headgear; or Chinamen in quilted jackets and quaint but most serviceable ear-caps. For the most part the inhabitants had gone into winter quarters, hibernating like the marmots, and would not be much in evidence until the following spring. Groaning ox-waggons gave place to silent sledges; the camel-caravan disappeared from the scene; tumult died in the bazaars of Kuldja, trade centre of the Ili valley.

Bird-life, as might be expected, was scarce at this dead-end of the year. Had it not been for certain hot springs in the vicinity of the town my larder would not have been so well supplied with duck, and, but for a letter from Lord Rothschild requesting a series of skins of the local pheasants, I would never have seen the upper tributaries of the Ili river. And until the traveler has seen the Tekkes, the Kunges or the Kash he does not know

the Central Asian borderlands, nor the intrinsic beauty of the
Celestial Mountains. For it must be remembered that the southern flanks of the Tian Shan bear little resemblance to its
northern face. The one belongs to the desiccated heart of Asia,
the other pertains to the temperate southern borderlands of
Siberia, and gathers its loveliness from the moister climate.

On the Eaves of the World [9]:

REGINALD FARRER

[*Reginald Farrer (1880–1920) was British and in 1914 made a
journey of exploration, in the interests of horticulture and
forestry, from south to north along the Kansu-Tibet border.
Unlike most plant collectors who gather dried specimens of
plants to file away in museums for reference purposes, Farrer
was interested in plants that might be usefully cultivated in
Britain. He traveled with William Purdom, also a plant collector, and three Chinese youths.*]

It is not good that one man should be alone too long amid
the huge and splendid oppression of Alps unknown; I would
not willingly have faced the prospect for myself, realising too
well the weight of lonely awe that sometimes descends upon
one even in the compact and well-trodden fastnesses of the
European ranges. And the heart of Asia is a strange and
haunted land, playing very strange tunes on nervous systems bred for so many thousand years in the different at-
mospheres of the West. China, sooner or later, bends the
solitary European inexorably but placidly to her mysterious
will; and, for effective resistance, those who venture far and
long into her uttermost territories should be two or three. But
with a companion and a companion so ideal, who had himself
borne the test (and as an untried novice, too, in his time) of
three years' solitude all across Northern China and down to the
fringes of Tibet, there could no longer be cloud or hesitation
over the delight of the plan. . . .

[9] From *On the Eaves of the World,* by Reginald Farrer.

The Roof of the World is indeed a suitable and sonorous title, but how few people can make to themselves any notion of what it really means? The Roof of the World is a huge and hideous lifeless waste, some seventeen thousand feet above sea-level, an undulating abomination of desolation pitted with grim little salt lakes over which for ever wails the merciless wind which makes all life impossible. This is Tibet. The Tibet of popular imagination is that deep and fertile valley-trench that lies in a curve immediately behind the sweep of the Himalayas. Here, thickly crowded, is the life of the country, here are the famous Abbeys, and here the Supreme Holiness of Lhasa and Tashi-lumpo have their seats. The eastern fringe of that vast high tableland, however, is very much more vague.

Here you have rolling downs, incapable of supporting more life than the nomad caravans passing through, and the roving herds of brigands that prey on the strings of pilgrims hurrying along the sacred roads to Lhasa from Sining or Batang. The country is still a desolation, still the wind-swept barren roof of the world. But now, as you move eastward still, the scene changes, and the eaves of the roof present a quite different aspect. The great rivers of Central Asia are here born, in the golden wilderness of Eastern Tibet, and wear their way down into China between huge mountain ranges that all bear south-wards in parallel walls towards the plains of the Flowery Land. It is a country almost incomprehensible in the vastness of its scale and the complexity of its systems. But it is no longer a No-Man's Land. All along the courses of the rivers are scattered frequent and powerful Abbeys, and the country is divided into many petty principalities nestling amid the mountain chains where the spirits of the air hold their mysterious sway. They are the only powers that do. For perfect lawlessness is the privilege throughout that impregnable wilderness of Alps that composes the whole eastern fringe of Tibet, from where the Mekong and the Salwen in the south make their double rush downwards into Burma, to where the Yellow River in the far north swings on its wild sweep northward from Lanchow into the barren sands of the Ordos.

Look at the official maps. You will find a huge stretch of country gaily and gallantly labelled Szechwan, and attributed to the Chinese Empire. In point of fact, all the western half of that tract is pure Tibet, where the writ of China so little runs current that no Chinaman's life is safe for an hour off the recognised tracks, and the official pilgrim road by Tatsienlu and Litang and Batang to Nagchukka and Lhasa. This country is occupied by countless small independent sovereignties, nominally in the obedience of China, but only so long as that obedience is never exacted; and divided among fragments of old or aboriginal races, now almost indecipherable. And, where there are not these barbarous guerilla chieftainships, there are big Abbeys no less barbarous and of hardly less guerilla habits. Where the sway of China fails, it is useless to look to the authority of the Dalai Lama up among the eastern ranges of Tibet. The Supreme Pontiff's effective authority lies, if anywhere, only in the valley-trench of Lhasa itself; though acknowledged as spiritual overlord throughout the domains of Tibetan Lamaism, his practical hold over the Abbeys of North and East Tibet is of the most shadowy, and the warmest personal recommendation from His Holiness would be of as little value to the traveler as would a letter from Dr. Clifford or the Bishop of Zanzibar. In point of fact, all up the Tibetan Marches, Princes and Abbots join forces in complete independence, snapping their fingers as complacently at Lhasa on the one hand as at Peking on the other.

Thus, from Tatsienlu northwards to Nan-Ping and on to Labrang there is no safety of travel, and hardly any possibility of travel. Certain tracks can indeed often be traversed (as, for instance, the roads down from Sungpan), but for the real exploration of that serried mass of mountains we must wait for altered circumstances in the Chinese Empire. The Chinese, indeed, already have nearly all they want for themselves. They possess a nominal suzerainty over Lhasa and the Tibetan Marches; the two big roads are kept open to Lhasa, and the Chinese are able, gradually and with their usual slow and patient pervasiveness, to infiltrate themselves, their families and farms, into any fertile oasis or promising nook for cultivation up among the fastnesses of the ranges. True, they are often stamped out in a sudden massacre by the aboriginal tribes, who reward their presence and their contempt with an enthusiastic hatred. But they always by degrees return, often after a bout of impartial shooting and burning by some Chinese regiment or other. The situation is one of intense mutual animosity, enlivened by occasional outbursts of bloodshed. Yet, on the whole, it must be considered satisfactory by all parties concerned. . . .

Even nowadays it would take a powerful Empire many seasons of exceedingly difficult and expensive warfare to bring the Tibetan March under any real control. It is not to be wondered at that the Chinese Empire, as unable as unambitious for such wholesale conquest, is inclined to rest content with having, on the whole, all it needs, at the price of occasional assertions of power here and there. The Chinese have no wish to dominate a country so indomitable and profitless. Let them have safe caravan way along certain roads, and a certain amount of safety in settling along their course where crops can be raised or profits accumulated, and they are perfectly satisfied to leave the vast and terrible wilderness of the mountains to the Tibetans and their flocks and herds. They have the name of sovereignty, in fact, but its reality rests on the tacit assumption that it is never to be put in action, and that the two races shall keep rigidly apart, each transacting its own business in its own way on an understanding of mutual forbearance. In fact, it may fairly be said, even in provinces so generally Chinese as Kansu, that where the mountains begin there Chinese interest at once ceases, and the country is no longer China but Tibet.

It will be seen then how hopeless of thorough exploration are the Tibetan Marches at present. Neither from Peking nor from Lhasa does any authority there hold good, and it would be too much to expect China to go to the expense of subduing the Marches into complete tameness for the convenience of rare globetrotters, seeing that her citizens already have as much food out of the country as they want for the present, trusting as they do for conquest less in the irruptions of the rifle than in their own power of steady, peaceful, and undaunted percolation wherever their needs beckon them. It is true that, during the later years of the Grand Dowager, a genuine and thorough attempt was made by the Manchu Governor, Jao-erh-Fung, to reduce the Tibetan March effectually under Chinese sway, real as well as nominal. His methods were drastic and successful. He dealt faithfully with the Princes, and if within a stated space the big Abbeys did not definitely acknowledge their allegiance to the Dalai Lama (and thus to the Emperor of China, his overlord), he would batter down the walls with his guns, and hew off the holy heads by hundreds.

So that in the short space of his rule there was a terrified peace all up the Marches. But the Grand Dowager died, and not even the tremendous prestige of her name could long avert the overdue doom of the Manchurian line. Jao-erh-Fung, then seated in Cheng-tu, was one of the first victims of reviving China. His troops entertained him to a sumptuous banquet, at the end of which they informed him that, with infinite regret, they now proposed to remove his head. The transaction was immediately accomplished in the garden, with the most perfect dignity and urbanity on the part of all concerned; after which the decollated head was photographed on a dish, and the result sent round throughout the Empire as a postcard, to inculcate on the rest of China the proper way of dealing with Manchu officials. The lesson was efficacious, but among its results was the complete relapse of the March into all its pristine lawlessness. And now, in the vacillations, feebleness, penury, and internal troubles of the various Governments that have since vainly tried to occupy the Dragon Throne and fill the place of that awe-inspiring old woman whose memory is still the most living force of order up the border of Tibet, the Marches have once again been left to their own sweet will, and are more than ever difficult for the traveler.

These difficulties are manifold. In the first place, it may fairly be claimed that they are most especially daunting for the collector of plants and seeds. The traveler on tour goes his way quickly and once for all through a district, and never stays and rarely returns; therefore with proper provision and escort he may hope to pass rapidly and securely through the most dangerous districts and the most ill-disposed peoples—so long, at least, as he refrains from affronting religious prejudices, and preserves that firm yet genial civility which is so absolutely indispensable in dealing with Tibetans. Far otherwise is it with the botanist. In the first place, it is necessary for him to explore the heights of the great mountains, and this alone is of itself enough to bring the whole country out against him like a hive of furious bees. For does not everybody know that up in the gaunt crags the Powers of the Air have their seat, and that if annoyed by rash or unauthorised visitors they will assuredly manifest their wrath most terribly on guilty and innocent alike, in the form of stone-falls that wreck villages, and hailstorms that destroy the crops and the whole year's hope of subsistence for the bone-poor villagers?

Therefore a very evil eye is cast from the first upon any stranger proposing to explore the high places—whither nobody in their senses, of course, would ever venture, so that his purpose must plainly be nefarious (as indeed is shown by the transparent thinness of his pretences). For whoever heard of anybody going up into the cold, uncomfortable mountains after anything so profitless as silly weeds that you can neither eat nor weave? The fraud is quite insolent in its barefacedness. This is pre-eminently the view insisted on by the monks, who have reasons of their own for intensifying all the scruples of their parishioners as to invasion of the mountains. For Tibet is probably the richest gold-bearing land in the world, and all its riches are the monopoly of the Church. Now gold is known to be especially a child of the high Alps, and nobody who knows the romantic tales current in our own European ranges about its movements and development, and how it *"wachsens"* [springs up] about over the glaciers and its chosen places of deposit, emitting a ghostly glare as it goes, will wonder at the Tibetan monks and peasants having their own kindred superstitions on the matter.

Seeing strangers, accordingly, and strangers bent on going off for days and weeks into the uninhabitable recesses of the topmost crags, the monks know better than to believe they are after anything less lucrative than gold. And where foreigners come seeking gold, are they not soon invariably followed by mission-aries and swords and guns, and all the bloodshed and disturb-ance which is so beautiful a feature in the spread of what is called civilisation by the civilisers? Therefore on all counts the Church sets its very sternest face against errant foreigners in the hills, and calls out every weapon in the ecclesiastical ar-moury. And this is fatal to the botanist. . . .

Nor do the Chinese authorities entertain any tenderness for such wild-cat ventures. The Chinese hates traveling even on the smoothest of beaten tracks, and calls it "eating bitterness." How much less, then, is he capable of understanding the curious pas-sion that sends an Englishman lairing under rocks on cold wet mountains all among the snow, in order that he may either kill something inedible or collect something unprofitable? . . .

A hot summer and a coldish winter prevail in South Kansu; the rainfall is well distributed, and the loess downs do not find it difficult to produce their crops. But the conditions become much more extreme when at last you meet the high ranges descending from Tibet. Here you suddenly come upon the conditions of the desert in combination with those of the Alps. Deep in their beds flow the big rivers, the Blackwater, the Whitewater, the Hwang Hor, the Mekong, the Salwen, the Yangdze; their zone is of a torrid droughtiness impossible to imagine. Waterless, perpetually parched and thirsty for the Alps above take all the rain they bring to birth), those barren slopes bear only a typically desert flora, thorny hedgehogs of plants, dry dust-coloured growths of the burning sand and loess. And then from this you ascend straight and immediately to the heights; and within four hours or so of leaving the river-levels are luxuriating in cool alpine conditions and mountain-forests and lawns of flowers as alpine as the flower-fields of the Mont Cenis or the Rolle Pass. In fact, I can best paint to you the violent diversity of the two climates here by saying that the ascent of a high peak above the Blackwater Valley is as if you could climb straight up from the burning rocks of Aden to the clear lake that mirrors Mont Lamet.

It was the beginning of the beginning; and in a rapture of anticipation after all those many weeks of loess and culture I wound my way solemnly along the down, and deep into the wide dry river-plain at its feet, where little hamlets crouched amid the vivid green of willow and poplar. I could hardly notice my golden Ground Daphne here recurring in rather poorer mats over the naked face of the fell. My satisfaction continued, too, when the plain was reached, for, instead of turning away from the mountains, as is too often the perverse way of paths, we headed straight towards them, and they remained beautifully visible ahead of us to our stage at Yao Village, where we found a most delightful little clean whitewashed room, brand-new, with delicate fresh woodwork, and dried lotus-blooms in a pot, and two stiff and stately armchairs, and a long red-lacquered table set between them. It was a cheerful evening for us in such unwonted luxury, with the mountains now heaving into sight, and with the morrow due to bring us to Kiai-jô, the end of this the third section of the journey.

Under a stormy sky the rugged, earthy hills were livid in rosy blue as we advanced, and soon we turned aside out of their sight into a deep and hideously savage ravine by which alone it seems that Kiai-jô is possible of approach from the north. But before we got into the defile we found our way down the river valley blocked with a practically unbroken stream of people. Some holy festival was evidently in process at some shrine away behind us up the road. Ladies of quality had donned their finest silks, and were being convoyed along on ponies by their bands of retainers; the common folk trudged afoot; strings of donkeys laden with coffin-planks yet further impeded our way; and every now and then a little divinity would come along at a run, borne in a small gay palanquin of his own with silken curtains, and a gong being beaten behind to warn the world that he was on his way, no doubt, to pay his visit to the superior deity who was evidently that day being at home to heaven and earth. Austere or bland the images looked out impassively, and the Go-go was in a continual course of giggles.

For the robust good sense of the Go-go's [their Chinese servant's] simplicity found nothing in all his travels a more inexhaustible fund of amusement than the various manifestations of piety he met with, whether it might be small gods taking a day off, or the wine-veiled litanies of Abbot Squinteyes, or the vociferous caperings of a Chinese exorcism, or missionaries chanting dismal psalms in the basement, accompanied by the meat-woman and the cook, to an obbligato of the baby's yells upstairs. At all and sundry the Go-go would convulsively explode; and, indeed, towards the end of his travels developed such trust in laughter as a panacea that he became unable to answer the simplest and soberest question without wriggling spurts of merriment.

.   .   .   .

Into Tibet

At Wen Hsien the anticipated difficulties began immediately to gather round our path. For here we were well within reach of the reputation of Chagola, now not more than four days' distant to the west; and that reputation proved to be of the very worst. The Mandarin was in a high state of alarm when he heard that we wanted to proceed there, and every step consistent with courtesy was taken to dissuade us. . . . We did not, indeed, as yet set eyes on the great man in person. He proposed to call in state, sedan-chair, flounced umbrella of scarlet silk, and all, and kept us hanging about through the morning trying to prepare suitable pomp for his reception. Finally, we sat down to snatch a morsel, and were in the middle when, lo! in the words of the classic, "I hear far off the trumpets of the King," and there was the procession advancing down the street. . . .

So the days passed, and at length, O miracle! on the second of May the mules and everything were as ready for the start as we. Our parting from the old landlord was a parting from a friend. . . . Cakes and eggs in elegant parcels were the parting present he brought in to us at dinner the night before we left, and in the morning it only remained to bid farewell to the Mandarin. . . .

The scene was short and sweet; I was glad to bring it soon to an end, pleading the imminence of our start. Not till we got outside the main hall would the Mandarin let me go; then we turned face to face for the profound final bow of leave-taking, and on to the white horse I mounted with what majesty I might, from the saddle swept an elegant salute, and without any misadventure came riding out down the stone stairs from court to court with such an air as made me think of Alexander on Bucephalus proceeding in triumph down the palace precincts of Persepolis.

The air was alive and pregnant of marvels after the rain, the fields were filled with happy people agog with their first chance of successful cultivation in these long lean years. Busily they came and went and ploughed and sowed. I rode along in high contentment, and here at last made acquaintance with the titanic uncouthness of the yak, great patient hairy buffalo that he is, as you see him tamed to the plough. The beck becomes perceptibly more alpine as you advance, and in a bend I alighted after a most beautiful little briar, of delicate tiny foliage and set all over with a dense profusion of tiny pearl-pink dog-roses. Encouraged by this, I next made a foray up into a steep oak-wood that descended on the right. The shade was delicious in the young heat of the day, but otherwise its slithering steeps of compost yielded nothing new. After this the journey steadily improves; the sere strips of attempted culture diminish, and finally fade away altogether; and up the lateral glens and over the lesser hills more and more frequently peer forested tall points clothed thickly in solemn and enormous firs, that tower amid a fleecy haze of umber and soft violet from the deciduous trees as yet in bud, while lower down the Oaks and Celtis are in the first flush of their emerald loveliness, and lower yet the Golden Rose is in a blaze of loveliness unparalleled before, and Dipelta in arching hillocks of shell-pink, amid a crowded lesser fry of snowy Fringe-trees, flesh-pale Ribes, and orange Jew's Mallow, all in a riot of luxuriant colour, with rare Lilies thrusting up their stems occasionally in the jungle, and the virginal magnificence of *Pæonia Moutan* here and there refulgent in the more open places.

Pay here, then, your last respects to this memorable marvel; for never again (with me) will you set eyes on it wild in China. To make up, here greet, for the first and only time in my company, the little Ruthenian Iris, perhaps the farthest runagate of its race. For assuredly it is a far cry from Ruthenia to the North-Eastern Marches of Tibet; yet here are the small sapphire blossoms of the Iris, straying across a level healthy place of turf and scanty scrub above the beck, where gipsies have their camp, and making one think, although so different, of the little violet flags of the Ground Iris as you see them straying through the short aromatic scrub about St. Raphael. And yet more fresh company do you meet on this last day of traveling towards Tibet.

For suddenly overhead, in the painted gateways of the road, you look up and salute the lords Buddhas and Bodhisattvas smiling down benignantly in glory, and know that now you are indeed in the precincts of the sacred and mysterious land, which no doubt, if not so difficult and remote, would prove no more sacred and mysterious than any other. But here they sit, the Holy Ones; and between them, in the central space of the roof-beam, is a vane like a turbine, painted with emblems, and perpetually revolving the words of aspiration to every breath of the wind. Left behind is the dry and sensible materialism of

China, and here you enter the grip of the most tremendous mysticism, and the most materially organised, of any that still holds the fettered imagination of man. Salute, then, as you pass under their gateway and into their territory, these strange legendary shapes, these indefinitely multiplied mysterious forces, whose very presence here, and whose almost every function in the creed they have coagulated, is an insult to the memory of the Wholly Perfect One, and to the Truth that they have darkened through the ages with a multitude of counsels. Yet it is a moment of note, this, of entering upon a land where truth is apprehended at all, though no longer naked indeed, but disguised with load upon load of multifarious trappings.

We are now actually so far in Tibet as to be on the Prince of Jo-ni's property. His main sovereignty and his capital lie about twelve days' journey to the north, but he, like many other of these petty sovereigns of the March, possesses various outlying territories, far from his central jurisdiction, and where, in fact, his authority goes no farther than the acceptance of an irregular tax, having occasionally paid which, the local prelates and peasants of these No-Man's Lands proceed to do precisely as they please, feeling quite secure that the Prince of Jo-ni will certainly not put himself to the trouble and expense of sending troops down all that distance to reduce a few wretched hamlets, whose inhabitants would long since have gotten themselves safe into the mountains before the soldiers came anywhere near the scene. Hence the evil temper of such places as Chago, confident in their remoteness, and with even their own acknowledged overlord so far away. Not until these isolated little plague-spots of unowned and unruled independence are finally merged in China, together with all the half-independent feudal sovereignties to which in theory they belong, will there be any sure guarantee for peace and prosperity up the Kansu March of Tibet.

Let these political speculations about these remote people introduce us to our first Tibetan inn at Second Look, a dim-yarded, storied place, not, in fact, purely Tibetan, but wholly different from the Chinese style. The population was inquisitive, but not friendly; they refused to sell us anything, and their picturesque bedizened women were coy to all attempts at conversation. In the big lower room, smoky and dark, there was a noble open hearth, at which, for the first time since leaving England, I was able to enjoy the luxury of warming my feet at a fire, while in and out of the shadows ran gruntling and routing a tiny pet black pig, who was ultimately captured and put to bed in his basket like any puppy or kitten. Round the hearth gathered the staff, Rembrandtesque in the effects of the firelight, busily engaged in chat about Chago and other perils of the way. It seems hard to realise that here we are now actually at the very foot of this elusive mountain that we have so long been chivying through the untracked wilds of Western China. To-morrow we dare the perils of the pass and the Abbey. The population talks of nothing else. Even here, just over the other side of the mountain wall, but in a country more tinctured with China, the place has an almost fabulously evil reputation; you would fancy that no Chinese could manage to pass through it without being burned alive in a bonfire of brushwood. It is quite certain, anyhow, that nobody does pass through it, except on the most urgent necessity, and then in bands of as many as can be got together. The tale was all of Chago and local broils; at Wen Hsien we had said farewell for weeks to the outer world behind us, and now for a long time all the happenings in China and elsewhere were to be a complete blank.

EPILOGUE

TRAVEL, they say, broadens the mind; but can we say that just reading about travel automatically does the same thing? When a traveler is on his journey he is always in the present tense although a traveler who is also a scholar, like Sir Aurel Stein, may enrich his experience of the present by drawing on his knowledge of the past. But once the traveler has written down whatever it is he has to tell us, it is for the reader part of the past—it happened before the reader opened the book, whether it happened only last year or a thousand years ago.

For the man who is reading an account of a journey, there are always problems of adjustment. The story may be about a country in which he has traveled himself, and about people and conditions with which he is more or less familiar. Of course the reader, all the time he is reading, is unavoidably comparing what the author has to say with his own knowledge and ideas; but there are complications. Was he in the country before the author or after him, and was it a long or a short time before or after? And did both of them know the language of the country, or one of them know it (and if so, did he know it well, or just so-so), and the other not know it? And again—and this is a very important point—did one of them just happen to go through the country, while the other one knew about it from research and reading, as well as from what he could see with his own eyes?

Obviously, in the case of a book like this one, almost all of the readers are living a long time, usually a very long time, after almost all of the authors. This difference of time interposes a kind of viewing-lens between our eyes and the descriptions we are reading. Nothing whatever can eliminate entirely the danger that we will slightly or grossly misunderstand the past simply because we are people of the second half of the twentieth century, with the assumptions and preconceptions appropriate to our times—just as the authors whom we read had the preconceptions and assumptions appropriate to the times in which they lived.

Nobody can guarantee that he can psychoanalyze, so to speak, both what he himself thinks he knows, but in fact doesn't know, and the corresponding misconceptions in the minds of men long ago. On this kind of problem Vilhjalmur Stefansson wrote a little classic of deadpan humor and deep philosophical insight, *The Standardization of Error*. Professional historians can trip over such difficulties, like anybody else. More than one historian has written about the Great Silk Road that led from the Chinese Empire to the Roman Empire as though it came into being because the Chinese were producing more silk than they could sell on the domestic market and so had to mount an export drive to sell the stuff abroad. This kind of misinterpretation arises from taking accepted, unquestioned modern notions of economics and "reading them back" into times when people had different notions. The truth is that the Chinese, considering themselves civilized, did not consider that any imports from the barbarians around them were necessary. The civilized products of China should therefore be kept within the country as far as possible, to improve the general well-being so that people would be contented and have no reason for rebellion. If, however, the barbarians were troublesome about *demanding* trade, and might disturb the frontiers if not granted access to trade, then trade could be granted to them—but as a diplomatic convenience, not an economic necessity.

This was known even at the Roman end of the Silk Road, in a general sort of way. In the first century A.D. Pliny wrote of the Chinese that they, "though ready to engage in trade, wait for it to come to them instead of seeking it." Later, this knowledge was forgotten and had to be rediscovered. Indeed, it is one of the great lessons of the history of knowledge that even knowledge which has a practical value is frequently forgotten and has to be discovered all over again. Moreover it is one of the characteristics of professional scholarship, with its tendency to quote from "the established authorities" instead of doing its own thinking, that rediscovery is often slowed down because, in each generation of scholars, the more conservative representatives of the profession resist having their "established authorities" proved wrong.

We are left with a rather challenging suggestion—that in reading old accounts of travel not only can we learn things that we never knew before, not only can we be amused by learning what people once thought that they knew, but that we now know to be untrue or only partly true; but we can also keep our minds alert for the occasional shock and stimulus of finding that something that we always thought we knew turns out to be wrong, or to need some new thinking.

BIBLIOGRAPHY

An Account of Tibet: The Travels of Ippolito Desideri of Pistoia, S. J. (1712–1727). Edited by Filippo De Filippi. London: George Routledge and Sons (Broadway Travelers Series), 1932.

Akbar and the Jesuits. By Father P. Du Jarric. London: George Routledge and Sons (Broadway Travelers Series).

Beyond the Caspian. By Douglas Carruthers. London: Edinburgh, Oliver and Boyd, 1949.

Buddhist Records of the Western World. Translated from the Chinese of Hsüan Tsang (A.D. 629) by Samuel Beal. 2 vols. London: Trübner & Co., 1884.

Cathay and the Way Thither. Translated and edited by Colonel Sir Henry Yule. Revised by Henri Cordier. 4 vols. London: Hakluyt Society, 1915.

The Heart of a Continent. By Francis E. Younghusband. London: John Murray, 1896.

History of the Two Tartar Conquerors of China. By P. J. D'Orleans, S. J. London: Hakluyt Society, 1854.

The Japan Expedition. By J. Willett Spalding. New York: Redfield, 1855; London: Sampson Lowe, 1856.

A Journey in Southern Siberia. By Jeremiah Curtin. Boston: Little, Brown & Co., 1909.

The Land of the Lamas. By William W. Rockhill. New York: Century, 1891.

The Mongol Mission. Edited by Christopher Dawson. New York: Sheed and Ward, 1955.

On the Eaves of the World. By Reginald Farrer. London: Edward Arnold and Co., 1917.

Records of the Grand Historian of China. Translated from the *Shih Chi* of Ssŭ-ma Ch'ien by Burton Watson. 2 vols. New York and London: Columbia University Press, 1961.

Sand Buried Ruins of Khotan. By Sir Mark Aurel Stein. London: T. Fisher Unwin, 1903.

Travels in Tartary, Thibet and China, 1844–1846. By Huc and Gabet. Translated by William Hazlitt. 2 vols. London: George Routledge and Sons (Broadway Travelers Series), 1928.

The Travels of an Alchemist. By Li Chih-Ch'ang. Translated and with an introduction by Arthur Waley. London: George Routledge and Sons (Broadway Travelers Series), 1931.

The Travels of Fa-Hsien (391–414 A.D.) or Record of the Buddhist Kingdoms. Translated by H. A. Giles. Cambridge: Cambridge University Press, 1923.

The Travels of Marco Polo. Translated by L. F. Benedetto. London: George Routledge and Sons (Broadway Travelers Series).

The Voyage of François Pyrard. Translated and edited by Albert Gray. 2 vols. London: Hakluyt Society, 1887.

A Voyage to Cochinchina, 1792–1793. By Sir John Barrow. London: T. Cadell and W. Davies, 1806.

INDEX

NOTE: Page references in *italics* are to excerpts from authors' works